ORGAN
REGISTRATION

Inscribed to the
American Guild of Organists

ORGAN REGISTRATION

A COMPREHENSIVE TREATISE

ON THE DISTINCTIVE QUALITY OF TONE OF ORGAN STOPS

THE ACOUSTICAL AND MUSICAL EFFECT OF COMBINING
INDIVIDUAL STOPS, AND THE SELECTION OF STOPS AND
COMBINATIONS FOR THE VARIOUS PHRASES OF ORGAN
COMPOSITIONS; TOGETHER WITH SUGGESTED REGISTRA-
TION FOR ONE HUNDRED ORGAN COMPOSITIONS, HYMNS,
AND ANTHEMS INTENDED TO BE PLAYED ON SPECIFIC
ORGANS

BY

EVERETT E. TRUETTE

MUS. BAC., A. G. O.

A Founder of the American Guild of Organists and Dean
of the New England Chapter; Organist and Choirmaster
of the Eliot Congregational Church, Newton, Mass.

BOSTON

C. W. THOMPSON AND CO.

1919

Republished 1972
Scholarly Press, Inc., 22929 Industrial Drive East
St. Clair Shores, Michigan 48080

Library of Congress Cataloging in Publication Data

Truette, Everett Ellsworth, 1861-1933.
  Organ registration.

  "The acoustical and musical effect of combining
individual stops, and the selection of stops and
combinations for the various phrases of organ compositions; together with suggested registration for
one hundred organ compositions, hymns, and anthems
intended to be played on specific organs."
  1. Organ--Registration. I. Title.
MT189.T89 1972   786.7   78-181284
ISBN 0-403-01707-6

PREFACE

In planning a work of this character, which requires the expression of a great deal of personal opinion, it is evident, at the outset, that the author renders himself a target for considerable criticism, from those organists who happen to entertain different opinions on any branch of the subject. I am not unmindful of the fact that the success of the work would perhaps be assured, if it were possible to pronounce opinions with which every organist would agree. From the nature of the subject itself, and from a great diversity of personal tastes, any one can see that such a course is absolutely impossible.

I have attacked the subject of Registration from many angles, have treated it from many points of view, and have recorded my personal conclusions. In recording these personal conclusions, I wish, at the outset, to have it understood, that, while I am firm in my personal convictions, I do not put them forward *ex cathedrá*, with the idea that they are to be accepted without a question. As I have just stated, these conclusions can only be considered as an expression of my personal taste, and I am fully conscious that some organists will differ with me. As one English author wrote: " Where the standpoint of criticism is almost wholly subjective, great diversities of judgment are inevitable."

I trust that my readers will readily see the impossibility of treating the subject impersonally, or of presenting all the personal opinions of others who happen to disagree with me on any branch of the subject. I bow my head to the different opinions of other organists who disagree with me, and hope that the young organist will fully consider the various opinions, in forming his personal taste and individuality in registration.

It will be observed that many statements are repeated several times in the course of the book. This is unavoidable, as these statements have an important bearing on the subject-matter which occurs in various parts of the book. Furthermore, frequent repetitions of some of the important statements will ensure a permanency in the mind of the young organist which, otherwise, might not prevail.

For the sake of clearness, I have treated the names of all organ stops as proper names, beginning them with capital letters. I am aware that this is not customary, but it seems to me that the importance of the names of the stops, and the method of referring to them so frequently, justifies this plan.

In the technical description of the pipes of various stops, free use has been made of " A Comprehensive Dictionary of Organ Stops," by James Ingall Wedgwood, F. A. S.; F. R. Hist. S. (England), an excellent work which ought to be in every organist's library.

If, after perusing the following chapters, the young organist finds that a keen interest in the subject of registration has been kindled within his mind, my efforts will not have been in vain.

Boston, January, 1919.

CONTENTS

PART ONE

ORGAN REGISTRATION

PART ONE

CHAPTER I

DEFINITION AND DESCRIPTION OF REGISTRATION — REGISTRATION AND ORCHESTRATION COMPARED

ORGAN REGISTRATION is the art of selecting and combining the various stops of an organ, in such a manner that a satisfactory effect is produced when a composition is played on the organ with the selected stops and combinations. The word " registration," when used in connection with organ music, is derived from the word " register " — a term used to denote any stop of an organ, whether it be a " speaking stop " or a " mechanical stop." Registration bears the same relation to organ music that orchestration bears to orchestral music. The selection and combination of the orchestral instruments are generally spoken of as " orchestral coloring "; the selection and combination of the stops of an organ are likewise classed as " organ coloring "; and there is considerable truth in the similes. The stops of an organ are to an organist what the palette is to the painter, though it may be carrying the analogy too far to compare the tone of the individual stops to various specific colors.

A knowledge of registration requires a familiarity with all the properties, both tonal and mechanical, of each stop in the organ. It requires a familiarity with the acoustical effect which the tone of each stop exerts on the tone of each other stop, when the stops are combined. It also requires a due consideration of the general character of the composition and of its individual sections, a proper regard for the relative power and character of the phrases, and a keen appreciation of the value and effect of the various tone-colors when selected for these phrases. The importance of an exact knowledge cannot be over-estimated. In addition, the young organist who seeks a knowledge of registration must develop a personal taste and imagination, with regard to the tone of the various stops of the organ, so that he can make good use of the knowledge already mentioned. Just as a painter may have a thorough knowledge of every color on his palette, and yet be a poor colorist, so may an organist be familiar with the tone of the organ stops in general, and yet be lacking in any individual taste for registration. Such taste must be ordinate to be of much value.

The young organist should aim to be eclectic in his taste for registration, and should develop some skill as a " colorist " — one who treats the various tone-colors of the organ somewhat as a painter treats his colors in paint. He will then produce a great variety of shades and contrasts of tone-color in registrating various organ compositions. Otherwise, he will have neither taste nor liking for the individual tone-colors of the various stops and combinations, and his interpretations of organ music, while technically perfect, will be like etchings printed in black or sepia — all of one color. Worse still, his registration will most likely be of the "hit or miss" character which is kaleidoscopic rather than artistic. It is obvious that contrasts of tone-color prevent monotony, and yet, too frequent changes of the registration tend to produce a restless effect, and leave only a vague impression of the registration.

Inasmuch as the registration of a composition depends, to a great extent, on personal taste, and there is always a wide diversity in all matters of taste, it will at once be seen how impractical it would be to attempt to promulgate any absolute rules for the guidance of the young organist. A certain combination of stops may be considered pleasing by one organist, and objectionable by another organist. It even seems possible to find an admirer for almost any conceivable combination of stops, though the majority of the listeners will condemn certain combinations. I once heard an organist improvise for fifteen minutes, using the Vox Humana, *without the Tremolo*, combined with a Four-Rank Mixture. I once heard another organist play that beautiful, quiet and peaceful *Andante Religioso* movement of Mendelssohn's Fourth Sonata *entirely on the Full Organ*. A third organist, in giving a recital, played the first four pages of the Toccata in G of Dubois *on the Vox Humana*.

In the following chapters, I have attempted to describe the recognized properties, and the character of the tone, of certain stops; the acoustical effect of certain combinations of stops; the various methods of manipulating the stops and of obtaining the combinations; the effect which certain combinations of stops produce in musical phrases of a certain character; and lastly, I have suggested certain possible plans of registration for various compositions.

Many details of a purely technical nature, which seem to me to exert considerable influence in various phases of the subject, may appear to some organists as extraneous matter which could well have been omitted. These chapters or sections can easily be passed over, if so desired, until a time when they happen to become of value for reference.

While registration for the organ is, to a certain extent, similar to orchestration for the orchestra, there are many details which are entirely unlike in the two subjects. Quite a number of organ effects are impossible in the orchestra, and hundreds of orchestral effects cannot be reproduced or even suggested in the organ. In the first place, we must bear in mind that one performer at the organ cannot produce the infinite variety of changing tone-colors and changing dynamics that sixty or more men in an orchestra can produce. In the second place, while the tone of a few organ stops is a fair imitation of the tone of their orchestral prototypes, the tone of many of the stops gives only a slight suggestion of the tone of the instruments bearing the same names. Then again, it is the perfection of a voicer's art to produce a perfectly even quality and *timbre* of tone from all the pipes of an organ stop, from the lowest tone to the highest; and, after the pipes have been voiced, the performer cannot vary that tone, except to make it louder or softer by opening or closing the swell-box, if the pipes happen to be in a swell-box. On the other hand, the tone of an orchestral instrument can be varied in *timbre* to a marked degree, besides being made louder or softer. Observe the difference in *timbre* between the lower octave and the upper octave of the tone of an orchestral Clarinet, or of a Violin. What a changing variety of tone can be produced in a French Horn by " stopping " the bell! Organ stops retain exactly the same tone-color when the swell is open and the tones are as loud as possible, as when the swell is closed and the tones are softened. With many orchestral instruments the player can produce an entirely different tone-quality by increasing the wind-pressure. This is especially noticeable with a Trombone, Alto Horn and Trumpet (or Cornet), the tones of which assume a very different color when the player forces the wind-pressure.

It is a good plan to copy, as far as is possible, the combinations and effects of the orchestra; but we must recognize the limitations in that direction in the organ, and confine ourselves to the most successful imitations. There are numberless beautiful combinations and effects in an organ, which are purely organ-like, that cannot be reproduced or imitated on any other instrument or combination of instruments; and the performer who confines himself to those effects, together with such of the orchestral effects as can be successfully reproduced, will make the instrument sound like a good organ and not like a poor orchestra.

Many young organists who rarely play on any organ, except the one in the church in which they are regularly engaged, are apt to fall into the habit of selecting the stops unconsciously from their location, without a thought of the name of the stops or of their tone-quality. Consequently, when they have occasion to play on some other organ, they are at a loss to know which stops to use, not having any definite idea of the names or tone-quality of the individual stops. Their only idea of the registration of a composition, developed solely by experimenting with the stop-knobs of the one organ, is, for example, that the first, third and fifth stops on the left-hand side, and the fourth and sixth stops on the right-hand side, produce an agreeable combination. If the stop-knobs bore no inscription at all, it would not matter. This plan may pass for the one organ, but its narrow limits preclude the possibility of acquiring any idea of registration *per se*, and the player experiences great difficulty in attempting to play on any other organ.

In pictorial art, there is much beauty in steel engravings, etchings, and photographs, whether printed in blue, sepia or platinum tints, but the oil-painting overshadows them all, not only in the beauty and variety of coloring, but in faithfully reproducing all the colors of the subject.

With organ music, similar conditions prevail. A few compositions are like steel engravings. They are satisfactory if played correctly in notes, rhythm, and relative power of the various phrases, even if tonally monochromatic, so to speak. Most organ compositions, however, lose a large part of their charm if rendered in this manner; and the young organist should develop a habit of giving much thought to the possible coloring in the registration of organ compositions.

One of the principal characteristics of the organ, which differentiates it from all other musical instruments, is the great number of widely varying tone-colors which can be reproduced by the organist who is familiar with all the tonal elements of the instrument. If he has some familiarity with the acoustical characteristics and influence of each of the stops, he can greatly increase the variety of his combinations and produce effects and tone-colors in various organs of which he otherwise would be unconscious.

CHAPTER II

CLASSIFICATIONS OF ORGAN STOPS

EVERY one who intends to acquire a knowledge of organ registration must have, at the outset, a clear understanding of the significance of the various terms used in stop nomenclature, as well as the several classifications of the stops. It is unfortunate that there is so much ambiguity and such a lack of system in the various terms which are found in stop nomenclature, but, as yet, no system of naming the stops has been devised which is consistent, comprehensive, and practical.

The word " stop " primarily signifies a complete set of pipes, one for each key (a few special stops have two or more pipes for each key), all of which produce the same tone-color. Each set of pipes is controlled by a mechanism which begins at the console with a " draw-stop knob," " tablet," or " stop-key," by means of which the organist is enabled to connect that set of pipes with the keyboard, or to disconnect it at pleasure. Until within the last quarter of a century, the stops were controlled only by " draw-stop knobs," which were called " stops " for short. More recently, " tilting tablets " and " stop-keys " have been substituted for this purpose in some organs.

In the evolution of the organ, when Couplers and Tremolos were added, they were controlled by draw-stop knobs, similar to those of the speaking stops, and thus became classed as " stops " (now called " mechanical stops ").

By the following table, it will be seen that we have several classifications of the stops of an organ. Whether the stops are controlled by draw-stop knobs, tablets, or stop-keys, is immaterial in these classifications.

For convenience, we first divide all the stops of an organ into two classes; viz., Speaking Stops and Mechanical Stops. The significance of the term " Speaking Stops " is self-evident. The Mechanical Stops are all the stops which, by themselves, produce no tone, and include the Couplers and Tremolos. The size of an organ is indicated by the number of distinct speaking stops which it contains.

The Speaking Stops are divided into Flue Stops, Reed Stops, and Percussion Stops, according to the manner in which the tone is produced. The tone of the Flue Stops is produced by the wind being impinged against the thin upper lip of the pipe (like a flue), which causes the air within the pipe to vibrate. Examples: — Diapason, Flute, Gamba, Salicional, Bourdon, Melodia, etc. The tone of the Reed Stops is produced by means of a reed, the tongue of which is caused to vibrate by the wind, the tone being modified and perfected by a pipe which is connected with the reed. Examples: — Oboe, Cornopean, Trum-

13

CLASSIFICATIONS OF ORGAN STOPS

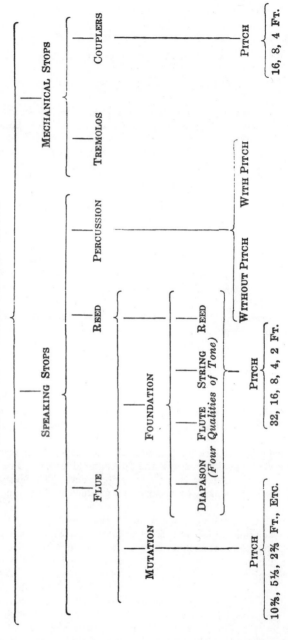

pet, Tuba, Clarinet, Trombone, Ophicleide, Clarion, Vox Humana, and Physharmonica. The tone of the Percussion Stops is produced by the stroke of some kind of a hammer (wood, metal, or felt), upon various forms of metal, glass, wood, or membranes. The Percussion Stops which have thus far been introduced in our church, concert, and house organs, have a definite pitch for each note of their compass; e. g., Chimes, Carillons, Harp, Celesta, and other modifications of the Carillons. All these stops, except the Chimes, generally have a qualifying pipe attached, which modifies and beautifies the tone. These stops are more specifically treated in Chapter IV. In the modern theatre organs, there are being introduced various kinds of " Traps " which are controlled by drawstops or pedals. While these Traps, at first thought, do not seem to belong within the realm of organ stops, as they have little or no definite pitch, their growing popularity in theatre organs indicates that they must be mentioned. The principal Traps of the present day are: — Bass Drum, Snare Drum, Tam-Tam, Gong, Triangle, Cymbals, Sleigh Bells, and Swiss Bells.

The speaking stops, exclusive of the percussion stops, are also divided into Foundation Stops and Mutation Stops. In this classification the term " Foundation Stops " includes all stops (except the percussion stops) which sound the note which is played or one of its octaves. The Mutation Stops are the stops which sound one or more notes other than the note played, or one of its octaves. Outside of the classification of stops, the term " Foundation Stops " has a less broad significance. The reeds, at least most of them, and the 2 ft. stops are generally excluded, when " Foundation Stops " are indicated in the registration; although all speaking stops (except the percussion stops) of 32, 16, 8, 4, and 2 ft. pitch (explained more fully later in this chapter), and all reed stops, come under the head of Foundation Stops in this classification. In the registration of a composition, " Gt. Foundation Stops 8 and 4 ft." does not include the Gt. Trumpet. Likewise, " Sw. Foundation Stops 8 and 4 ft." may include a soft-toned Oboe, but does not include the Cornopean or the Vox Humana.

As stated above, the Mutation Stops are the stops which sound one or more notes other than the note played or one of its octaves. Such stops are also called " Mixtures." The Pedal Quint 10⅔ ft. sounds a fifth above the Ped. Bourdon 16 ft. The Manual Quint 5⅓ ft. sounds a fifth above the manual pitch of an 8 ft. stop. The Twelfth 2⅔ ft., often called " Octave Quint," sounds a twelfth above an 8 ft. stop. There are other mutation stops called " Compound Mutation Stops," or " Compound Mixtures," which have two or more pipes for each key. The Sw. Dolce Cornet III ranks has three pipes for each key (indicated by " III ranks "), usually sounding the 12th, 15th, and 19th above the note played; e. g., if we draw the Sw. Dolce Cornet III rks., and hold

down on the Sw. the key corresponding to this note 𝄢 the following tones are produced: — 🎵 The Gt. Mixture IV rks. has four

pipes for each key; and if we hold down the same key on the Gt., with

this stop drawn, the following tones will be produced: — 🎵

The various methods of allotting the intervals in the different ranks of these stops, and "breaking back," as the upper octaves are reached, need not be explained here; these features more properly belonging to the study of organ construction. The object of the mutation stops is to add fullness and brilliancy to the louder combinations and to the Full Organ, by adding overtones or harmonics which are not sufficiently prominent in the separate stops. The mutation stops also serve to counterbalance the effect of the loud reeds in the Full Organ. An organ which contains loud reeds and no mutation stops generally produces an effect with the Full Organ akin to a brass band. Obviously, there must be a proper balance between the Diapasons, reeds, and mutation stops, to build up a satisfactory volume of tone with the Full Organ.

The most important classification of organ stops refers to the *quality* of tone which is produced by the individual stops. Although we consider only the tone of the various stops in this classification, it will materially assist the young organist, if a brief explanation is given of the various influences which cause the different qualities of tone. It would require too much space to enlarge upon the minute details in the construction of the pipes which produce the various qualities of tone. Suffice it to say that, in general, the shape of the pipe, the scale (ratio of the diameter to the length), the size and shape of the mouth of the pipe, the quantity of wind admitted to the pipe, the pressure of the wind, and the character of the "nicking" (fine nicks or grooves between the languid and the lower lip of the pipe), are some of the details of construction which influence the quality of tone. The material, — wood or metal, — and the varieties of the latter, also influence the quality of tone to a certain extent. The pipes of such stops as the Bourdon, Gedeckt (St. Diapason), Melodia, and most of the Flutes, are made of wood. The pipes of the other stops, except the 16 and 32 ft. stops, are generally made of metal; for example, the Op. Diapason, Gamba, Dulciana, all the string-tone and most of the reed-tone stops. The large pipes of the 16 and 32 ft. stops frequently are made of wood. The difference of material has some influence on the quality of tone of the pipes, but the choice of material of many of the stops is regulated largely by economy and convenience. The pipes of most of the stops are open at the upper end and are called "open pipes." The pipes of a few stops are closed at the upper end, either by means of a cap over the end of the pipe or by a plug forced into the end of the pipe, and are called "stopped pipes." The tone of the "stopped pipes" is somewhat hollow and sounds an octave lower than the tone of an open pipe of the same length. Examples: — Bourdon, Gedeckt, Rohr Floete and Doppel Floete. The acoustical effect of stopped pipes is explained more fully in Chapter III. The pipes of some of the stops are "harmonic"; e. g., the Flauto Traverso and Harmonic Flute. The pipes of these stops produce a tone an octave higher than they would produce without the conditions which cause them to be harmonic. The causes of the harmonic tones are various. Some pipes are overblown, causing them to sound the octave. Some pipes are of double length, with a small hole in the side of the middle of the pipe, which causes the pipe to sound the octave. The pipes of the Quintadena are stopped and overblown, causing the pipes to sound both the fundamental tone and, quite prominently, the twelfth above.

According to the quality of tone, we divide the speaking stops, exclusive of the percussion stops, into four classes; viz., Diapason-Tone, Flute-Tone, String-Tone, and Reed-Tone.

The Diapason-Tone may be described as a full, rich and sonorous tone, which is represented by the Open Diapason. This tone-quality is peculiar to the organ alone. It cannot be imitated or even approximated in the orchestra. In organ stops, there are several modifications of this tone-quality, but they all belong distinctly to the Diapason class. Besides the various stops which contain the word Diapason in their names, as, Open Diapason, Bell Diapason, Geigen Diapason (or Geigen Principal), Violin (or String) Diapason, we have the Octave (also called Principal), Twelfth, Fifteenth, Æoline, and Dulciana. The last named stop, as invented by Snetzler, might well be called "Echo Diapason," as its tone is very soft and yet is of the Diapason-quality. Although the tone of the Dulciana, being soft and quiet, is naturally not sonorous like the Open Diapason, it is of the same tone-color and sounds like the tone of an Open Diapason when heard at a great distance. In many organs, the stop which is labeled "Dulciana," is really a soft Viola, or a soft Salicional, having a distinct string-tone quality. The string-tone quality undoubtedly gives more character to the stop, but the peculiar, mellow and quiet tone-quality of a real Dulciana is more valuable for soft accompaniments to the soft solo combinations. In most organs, the Twelfth and Fifteenth have a somewhat soft Diapason-tone quality, but in small organs these stops are frequently voiced with a Flute-tone quality, as they would sound harsh and strident in such organs if voiced with the usual Diapason-tone quality. Much confusion arises in the mind of the young organist from the stop named "Stopped Diapason." Quite naturally, he supposes that this stop is one of the Diapason-tone stops. This supposition, however, is incorrect, as the stop is a Flute-tone stop. The word "diapason" has various usages, among which is its reference to the "normal pitch" or "the standard pitch" as "the diapason." From this usage, the term "Open Diapason" may be said to signify the normal, or standard, *open* pipe, and the term "Stopped Diapason" to signify the normal *stopped* pipe. The confusion, to which reference is made above, is avoided by adopting the German name of this stop, Gedeckt (formerly Gedackt), which in this country is steadily superseding the name Stopped Diapason. In French organs, this stop is named "Bourdon 8 ft.," but in this country we have so long associated the name Bourdon with the 16 ft. stop of that name, that it would only substitute one confusion for another were we to adopt the French name of the stop. Whether the stop is named Stopped Diapason, Gedeckt, or Bourdon, it is classed among the Flute-tone stops.

The Flute-Tone stops are both numerous and varied. The tone-quality may be described as bright and cloying, with few overtones. The tone of some of these stops, e. g., the original Flauto Traverso, the Concert Flute and Hohl Floete (frequently called "Hohl Flute"), is somewhat suggestive of the tone of the orchestral Flute, but most of the Flute-Tone stops of the organ have an individual tone-quality of their own, which cannot be imitated by any orchestral instrument. Obviously, all the stops whose name contains the word "Flute" belong to this class of stops. Other stops of the same class are the Gedeckt (Stopped Diapason), Bourdon, Clarabella, Melodia, Bifra, Night Horn, Philomela, and the various Tibias.

A variety of Flute-tone stops whose pipes are "stopped," such as the Gedeckt, Rohr Floete, Doppel Floete, and Bourdon, is classed by some theorists as a fifth quality of tone, under the name of "Gedeckt-Tone." As these stops are only modifications of the Flute-Tone stops, and as other modifications of the various tone-qualities are just as pronounced, it does not seem necessary or advisable to increase the number of tone-classifications by adding "Gedeckt-Tone."

The Flute-Tone stops are more numerous in many organs than the stops of the other tone-qualities, principally on account of the many varieties of this quality of tone which are possible. However, the combined Flute-Tone stops of an organ should always be less prominent in volume than the combined Diapason-Tone stops.

The String-Tone stops have a thin, keen, and somewhat pungent quality of tone, slightly resembling, in a few cases, the tone of the stringed instruments of the orchestra. While the resemblance is very slight, and no player of a stringed instrument would deign to recognize the resemblance, the influence of these stops in organ combinations is not unlike the influence of the stringed instruments of the orchestra. The pipes of the string-tone stops, except those of the 16 ft. pitch, are very slender scale, metal pipes, with mouths cut low. The principal string-tone stops are, the Gamba (Viola da Gamba), Salicional, Viol d'Orchestre, Voix Céleste, Violone, Cello, Violin or Violina, Fugara, Gambette, and Salicet. The tone of the stop named Violin (or Violina), which is usually of 4 ft. pitch, does not have the slightest resemblance to the tone of the instrument of that name. As a single stop it is of little value, but in combinations it is of inestimable value. The tone of the Voix Céleste, if the stop consists of two ranks of keen string-tone pipes, more nearly approaches the tone of a stringed instrument than does the tone of any other string-tone stop. However, we frequently find, especially in small organs, a stop called "Voix Céleste," which has two ranks of Æoline pipes. Such stops, which undoubtedly have a beautiful quality of tone and are useful in soft passages, are devoid of the vitality which is characteristic of the genuine Voix Céleste.

The Reed-Tone stops are those stops whose tone is initially produced by the vibrations of the tongue of a reed; a pipe serving to modify the tone and to assist in tuning. Examples: — Oboe, Trumpet, Cornopean, Clarinet, Fagotto, Tuba, Trombone, Ophicleide, Clarion, Vox Humana, and Physharmonica. In some organs a reed-tone stop of considerable power, called "Horn" is located in the Swell organ, in place of a Cornopean. The word "Horn," however, does not necessarily indicate that the stop is a reed-tone stop, as the Night Horn and French Horn are Flute-tone stops. The pipes of nearly all the reed-tone stops are inverted, conical, metal pipes. It is impossible to give a description of the tone of the reed-tone stops collectively, as there are so many varieties of tone in these stops. The tone of the individual reed-tone stops is described specifically in Chapter IV.

Some theorists name two distinct classes of reed-tone stops, under the heads, "Trumpet-Tone" and "Clarinet-Tone," the latter classification including the Oboe and Vox Humana, as well as the Clarinet. This sub-division of the reed-tone stops, like the sub-division of the Flute-tone stops previously mentioned, seems of questionable value, in the study of the classifications of organ stops, and tends to befog the mind of the young organist on the subject. The difference in tone-quality of many of the other reed-tone stops might as well be taken as a basis for further sub-divisions, and we would have nearly as many different classes as we have reed-tone stops. The classification, "Reed-Tone Stops" is at once comprehensive, including all the stops whose tone is initially produced by the vibrations of the tongue of a reed. While there is a great variety of reed-tone stops, it seems futile to attempt to classify the varieties, as the stops which are included in the sub-divisions differ nearly as much as those of one sub-division differ from those of another sub-division.

All the speaking stops, as well as the couplers, are further classified according to their pitch, which is indicated by 32, 16, 8, 4, 2 ft., etc. The term "8 feet" or an "eight-foot stop" has a two-fold significance. Fundamentally, the term signifies that the pipe of the lowest note (C) of any 8 ft. "open" stop is eight feet long. A variation of a few inches, one way or the other, is frequently necessary, according to the scale of the stop, but this fact has no influence on the use of the term "8 feet." The lowest pipe of a 16 ft. Open Diapason is approximately sixteen feet long, and the lowest pipe of the Octave 4 ft. is approximately four feet long. The other terms (32 and 2 ft.) have a similar significance. The more important, and at the same time an arbitrary significance of "8 ft." refers to the *pitch* of the stop. Every stop which is labeled "8 ft." or "8" has the same pitch as the piano. Every stop which is labeled "16 ft." or "16" sounds an octave lower than the piano, and every stop which is labeled "4 ft." or "4" sounds an octave higher than the piano. Likewise, a 32 ft. stop sounds two octaves lower than the piano, and a 2 ft. stop sounds two octaves higher than the piano.

The stops Gedeckt (St. Diapason), Rohr Floete, and Doppel Floete, are generally 8 ft. stops. They sound the same pitch as the piano, but as the pipes are "stopped," they are only half as long as the corresponding pipes of an "open" stop. Hence, the lowest pipe of these stops is only four feet long, notwithstanding the term " 8 ft.," which arbitrarily refers to the pitch of the stop.

The pipes of some of the " harmonic " stops, as the Flauto Traverso, are of double length, with a hole in the middle of one side of the pipe, which causes the pipe to sound the (harmonic) octave. A Flauto Traverso 4 ft., while sounding the octave above the unison pitch (8 ft.), theoretically should have its lowest pipe eight feet long, instead of four feet; but the pipes of harmonic stops are rarely made harmonic *in the lowest octave*, as the tone of such pipes is not satisfactory; therefore, the lowest pipe is four feet long. Incidentally, I would state that not all harmonic stops have pipes of double length, the harmonic tones being produced in some stops principally by " overblowing."

In the mutation stops, we find 10⅔, 5⅓, 2⅔ ft., etc., as previously explained. The pitch of the Compound Mutation stops, such as the Dolce Cornet, III Rks., Mixture, IV Rks., etc., cannot be designated, as the different ranks of each stop obviously are not of the same pitch.

The young organist should not be misled by such names as Quintaton or Quintadena. These stops are not mutation stops, which might be supposed from their names. The former is generally a 16 ft. stop and the latter is always an 8 ft. stop. The pipes of each stop are so made and voiced that the twelfth (second overtone) is quite prominently developed, though the fundamental tone is 16 ft. or 8 ft. pitch.

The Unison Couplers, between two manuals, or between a manual and the pedal, are " 8 ft. Couplers," though the " 8 ft." is generally omitted on the stop-knobs. The " 16 ft. Couplers," which are also called " Sub-Couplers " or " Sub-Octave Couplers," couple the octave below between two manuals or on the same manual. The " 4 ft. Couplers," which are also called " Super-Couplers " or " Super-Octave Couplers," couple the octave above, between a manual and the pedal, on the same manual, or on the pedal itself.

A few stops have a peculiar tone-quality, which makes it difficult, if not impossible, to classify them. Among these is the Gemshorn, which has a soft and somewhat reedy tone-quality, though it is a flue stop. The tone of this stop may be called a hybrid — a cross between Diapason tone and string tone. The Quintadena is another stop with a hybrid quality of tone — a cross between the Flute tone and the string tone. Another stop which cannot be classified is the Diaphone, as invented by the late Mr. Robt. Hope-Jones. This stop has a very powerful tone, produced by the vibrations of a vibrator, somewhat similar to a Tremolo, which is located within a chamber at the base of a pipe. This stop is neither a flue stop nor a reed stop. Several forms of this stop, with varying tone-qualities, have been experimented with, but, as yet, they have not become popular. In England, one occasionally meets with a stop called " Corno Flute " — a soft-toned reed stop — and a " Clarinet Flute " — a Flute-tone stop with a somewhat reedy quality of tone.

There are a number of stops whose names are fanciful; consequently, any attempt to classify them is confusing to the young organist; e. g., the " Salicional Oboe," which is sometimes substituted for the real Oboe in small organs. The pipes of this stop are not reed pipes, and the tone has practically no characteristic Oboe quality. The tone is a very strong and keen string tone, and is produced by very slender pipes, sometimes of metal and occasionally of wood. Other stops with fanciful names are the " Phoneuma," " Erzahler," and " Nitsua."

Some stops are called " Solo Stops," as they are especially suitable for solo purposes. In modern organs nearly all the stops, except the mutation stops, can be used in one way or another for solo purposes: hence, a special classification is needless.

CHAPTER III

A FEW FUNDAMENTAL PRINCIPLES OF THE ACOUSTICS OF ORGAN PIPES AND THEIR INFLUENCE ON THE TONE OF VARIOUS STOPS AND COMBINATIONS

IN combining organ stops, certain fundamental principles of the acoustics of organ pipes exert much influence on the resultant tone of the combination. In order to more clearly explain the fundamental reasons for certain resultant tone-qualities, in various combinations of stops, it is necessary to carefully consider these underlying acoustical principles.

It is well known that all musical tones are composed of a fundamental tone and a series of overtones (also called " harmonics " or " upper partials "). It is also well known that the completeness or incompleteness of the series of overtones, and the prominence or weakness of certain individual overtones, are the scientific influences which cause the difference in tone-quality between two musical sounds of the same pitch. The presence or absence of certain individual overtones, and the prominence or weakness of certain other overtones, are the acoustical factors which produce the difference in tone-quality between two instruments or between two organ stops.

The series of overtones is as follows: —

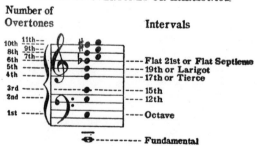

SERIES OF OVERTONES OR HARMONICS

Higher overtones are present in some musical tones but for our purpose it is not necessary to consider those above the 6th overtone.

When the air is caused to vibrate with 435 vibrations per second, a musical tone corresponding to A' (International Pitch) is produced. If there are no overtones or sub-vibrations, a hollow, colorless and characterless tone is the result. When this note is sounded on the violin, oboe, piano, or on a Diapason stop in the organ, the number of vibrations per second is exactly the same in each case, but the character of the overtones is entirely different with the tone of these different instruments. The acoustical difference in the tone-quality of all the stops of the organ is only this difference in the overtones.

A practical and *visible* demonstration of the presence of these overtones is both interesting and instructive. If the fundamental note (C), of the above series of overtones, is sounded on the piano, *without lifting the dampers* (by means of the damper pedal), the overtones which make up the tone-quality of the piano tone are present, though not separately distinguishable by the average ear. If these overtones (without the fundamental tone) are produced, each with its proper relative power, we have the fundamental tone (C) as a resultant. (This point I will prove and illustrate further on.) This acoustical principle is made use of by organ builders, in making up a " 32 ft. Resultant Bass " in the Ped. organ without using any pipes of 32 ft. length, which is fully explained on page 39. If the same note (C) is sounded on the piano, *with all the dampers lifted from the strings* (by means of the damper pedal), the strings of each note which corresponds to the notes of the overtones will vibrate sympathetically, corroborating the overtones and adding volume to the resultant tone. This is the function of the damper pedal. If the key of this fundamental note (C) is forcibly struck a dozen times in quick succession (with the damper pedal held down), the strings of all the notes which correspond to the notes of the harmonic series will vibrate vigorously in sympathy. If the strings of the fundamental note (C) are then silenced by pressing the finger on them, the fundamental tone (C) will continue to be audible, though somewhat softer; conclusively showing that the vibrations of all the overtones combined produce the fundamental tone, even if the strings of that fundamental note are at rest.

To *visibly* illustrate these points, cut out a piece of soft tissue paper, about three-quarters of an inch long and an eighth of an inch wide.

Fold it to the following shape   ⟋‾‾‾⟍   .   Place this piece of paper on top of the strings (of a grand piano) of the note c, which corresponds to the first overtone of the harmonic series under consideration. Hold down the damper pedal in order to lift the dampers from all the strings. Gently strike the key (C) which corresponds to the fundamental note of the series. It will be observed that the piece of tissue paper dances on the strings, although the note (c) has not been sounded by its own hammer. This shows that the strings are vibrated sympathetically. If the fundamental note is sounded loud enough, the piece of paper will dance off the strings entirely. After all the strings have been silenced, by releasing the damper pedal, replace the piece of paper on the same strings and hold down the damper pedal as before. Strike the key D or BB, either side of the fundamental note (C). The piece of paper will not move at all, as the strings under it are not affected, this note (c) not being in the harmonic series of the notes sounded (D or BB). The above experiment can be tried with each note of the harmonic series, up to the 6th overtone (c, g, c', e', g', b-flat'), always sounding the same fundamental note. With each of these overtones, the paper will dance less vigorously than with the next lower overtone, and after the sixth overtone the paper will not move noticeably. The experiment can be carried still further, by placing pieces of tissue paper on the strings of all the six overtones at the same time, and observing the relative vigor of the dancing pieces of paper, as the fundamental note is sounded vigorously.

To render the acoustical effect of overtones of varying power more comprehensible to the eye than is possible by lengthy verbal descriptions, well known mathematicians, physicists, and such acousticians as Rameau, Helmholtz, Tyndal, Ball, and Radau were in the habit of applying geometrical curves to graphically illustrate the difference in the soundwaves caused by the various overtones. For the purpose of comparison, these curves are of much value, in illustrating the effect of the first three or four overtones on the fundamental tone. It is impractical to carry the illustration beyond these first overtones. There are several systems of applying these geometrical curves, the simplest being founded on the vibrations of a tuning fork, which have been recorded on a piece of paper or on a plate of glass that has been coated with lamp black.

Fig. 1

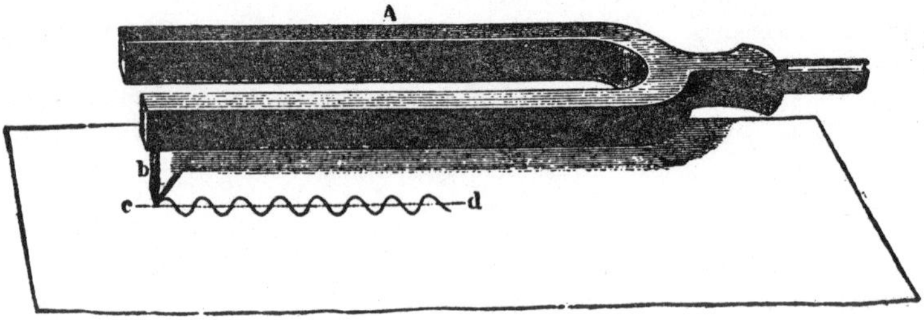

The tuning fork is provided with a drawing point (b), fastened at right angles on one prong of the tuning fork in such a manner that it will mark on a piece of paper, or on a plate of glass which has been coated with lamp black, if the fork is gently drawn across the paper or the glass.

If the tuning fork is quiescent, when it is drawn across the paper or glass, it will mark a straight line, corresponding to the dotted line between c and d, in the accompanying illustration (Fig. 1). If, however, the tuning fork has been agitated sufficiently to produce a tone, just before being drawn across the paper, the vibrations of the tuning fork will cause the marking point to follow the undulating line, as shown in the illustration. The width of the undulations indicates the power of the vibrations and, consequently, the power of the musical tone.

Fig. 2

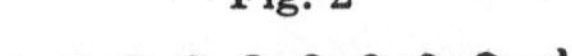

c ‑∿∿∿∿∿∿∿‑ d

This undulating line (Fig. 2) shows the simple vibrations of the fundamental tone of the tuning fork; and, as there are practically no overtones in the tone of a tuning fork, the undulating line is taken as a basis for the following illustrations.

If a small section of this undulating line, representing two vibrations, to and fro, is enlarged about ten diameters, the result will be the curve indicated in Fig. 3, representing two vibrations (enlarged) of the fundamental tone of the tuning fork.

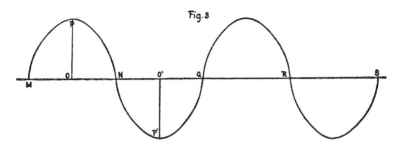

Fig. 3

The line M-Q (also Q-S) represents the period of time occupied by one vibration, and may serve to represent the pitch. If this line were longer it would indicate a lower pitch; or if the line were shorter it would indicate a higher pitch. The line O-P represents half the amplitude of the vibration, and O'-P', the other half. The greater the amplitude, the louder the tone. ("The power of a musical tone varies in proportion to the square of the amplitude.") Therefore, 2 O-P represents the power of the tone.

Starting from this basis, I have indicated in Fig. 4 the vibration of a mild first overtone (the octave).

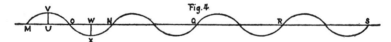

Fig. 4

The lines M-Q and Q-S, as in the previous figure, represent the period of time of one fundamental vibration. M-N and N-Q represent the two vibrations of the first overtone (octave) which occur in the period of time of the single vibration of the fundamental tone. The lines U-V and W-X represent the halves of the amplitude. By comparison with the lines O-P and O'-P', the lines U-V and W-X show that the power of this overtone is only about one-sixteenth of the power of the fundamental tone.

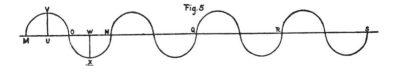

Fig. 5

In Fig. 5, I have indicated the vibrations of a strong first overtone. The only difference between the curves of this figure and those of the

preceding figure is that the lines U-V and W-X, which represent the
halves of the amplitude, as in the other figures, are twice as long as the
corresponding lines in Fig. 4, thus showing that the power of this overtone is four times greater than the power of the overtone shown in
Fig. 4.

In Fig. 6, I have indicated the vibrations of a mild second overtone
(the twelfth). As in all these figures, the line M-Q represents the period
of time of the one fundamental vibration. The curves M-K, K-L, and
L-Q represent the three vibrations of the second overtone, which occur
in the period of time of the single vibration of the fundamental tone.

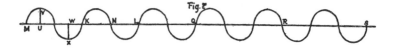

In Fig. 7, I have indicated the vibrations of a stronger second overtone. The reference letters are the same as in the previous figures and
indicate the same points.

To apply these principles to organ pipes, let us first consider an open
Flute pipe, like the Hohl Floete. The tone of such a pipe is made up of
the fundamental tone and a few mild overtones, including the first overtone (octave). The tone of the orchestral Flute contains, besides the
fundamental tone, its sharpened octave (first overtone) and sometimes
the twelfth (second overtone). The intonation of these two overtones
is well defined, but the other overtones are very indistinct, if present at
all. The sharpened first overtone is sometimes quite disagreeable to
sensitive ears, and there is a very old saying that "the worst thing in
the world after a Flute solo is a duet for two Flutes." In most of the
Flute stops of the organ this disagreeable element is absent and these
stops are of much value as solo stops, as well as in combinations.

If we consider the curve in Fig. 3 as representing the vibrations of the
fundamental tone, and the curve in Fig. 4 as representing the vibrations
of a mild first overtone (octave), by combining these two curves we
produce a combination curve which may be said to represent the combination of the fundamental tone and the first overtone. Such a curve may
be used to represent the vibrations of the tone of an open Flute like the
Hohl Floete. (Fig. 8.)

The dotted line, which is similar to the curve in Fig. 3, represents the
vibration of the fundamental tone. The solid line is the combinational
curve. This combinational curve is obtained geometrically as follows: —
The line U-V represents the half of the amplitude of the vibrations of
the first overtone, which exerts its influence at this point (half way
between M and O) and forces out the curve. The line W-X represents

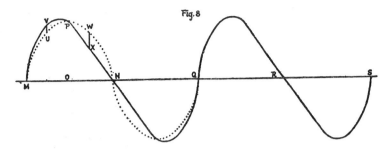

Fig. 8

the other half of the amplitude of the vibrations of the first overtone and exerts its influence at this point by drawing in the curve.

In musical tone the fundamental sound and the overtones intermix. Likewise, these curves can be geometrically combined, and, to a certain extent, may be used to represent, to the eye, the compound vibrations of the fundamental tone and a few overtones. The combined curve is principally determined by the curve of the fundamental sound, but the curves of the overtones cause its contour to shrink and swell at certain points, by their influence. Curves of this species can be used to characterize the *timbre* and quality of the tone of organ stops. They change form according to the relative intensity of the overtones, but the number of the great arcs (M-Q) or periods is always the same, and, for this reason, the pitch of the mixed sound is that of the fundamental sound. Such curves, obviously, are not accurate. They are only approximate, but they are sufficient to enable the organist to get a visible idea of the influence of the overtones in the vibrations produced by organ pipes. Furthermore, from these curves the organist can get a general idea of the acoustics of various organ stops, as well as the influence which certain stops exert in stop combinations.

The tone of a medium-scaled Open Diapason pipe is fuller and richer than that of an open Flute. It has more and stronger overtones, the first overtone being more prominent. In Fig. 9, I have indicated the curve which is produced by combining the curve of the fundamental tone (Fig. 3) with the curve of a strong first overtone (Fig. 5).

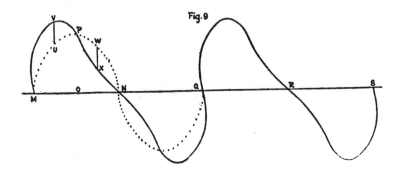

Fig. 9

This curve, more or less influenced by other overtones, we can consider as the curve of a medium-scaled Open Diapason.

In Fig. 10, I have indicated an exact comparison of the curves of the fundamental tone of a tuning fork (fine dotted line), the Hohl Floete (solid line), and the medium-scaled Open Diapason (broken line).

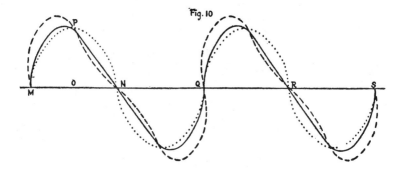

Fig. 10

To show the influence of the higher overtones in these curves, it would be necessary to still further enlarge the curve of the fundamental tone, twenty or more diameters. This is, of course, impractical, and withal unnecessary, in a work of this character. It seems to me that the organist can get a very good idea of the influence of the overtones from these illustrations of the first and second overtones.

The string-tone stops, like the Salicional, Gamba, and Viol d'Orchestre, are much richer in overtones than either the Flutes or the Diapasons. In Fig. 11, I have indicated a combination curve of the fundamental tone and somewhat strong first and second overtones.

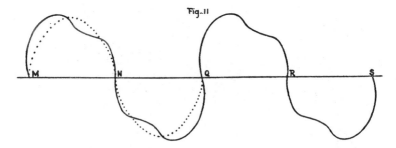

Fig. 11

The resultant curve shows the influence of additional overtones and may be used to represent the vibrations of the tone of a Salicional pipe.

In Fig. 12, I have indicated the resultant curve of the combination of the fundamental tone with very strong first and second overtones, to indicate the curve of the Viol d'Orchestre. This stop is rich in the higher overtones but they cannot be considered in these illustrations.

As all stopped pipes, like the Gedeckt (Stopped Diapason), contain only the even-numbered (2, 4, 6, etc.) overtones, the vibration curve of

this stop is produced by combining the curve of the fundamental tone
and the curve of the second overtone. In Fig. 13, the curve which is the

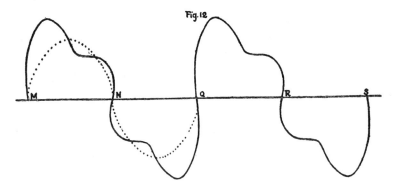

Fig. 12

result of such a combination is indicated. As in all the illustrations,
the dotted line indicates the curve of the fundamental vibration of the
tuning fork. In this resultant curve, the absence of the influence of the
first overtone is pronounced.

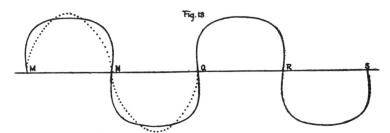

Fig. 13

The tone-color of the Gedeckt is considerably varied in different organs. If the pipes have been voiced so that the twelfth (second overtone) is prominent, the tone of the stop is full and liquid. On the other
hand, if the twelfth has been suppressed the tone is bright and crisp.

The stop known as Quintaton (or Quintaten) is a Gedeckt with the
twelfth very prominent. In Fig. 14, the curve of such a pipe is shown.

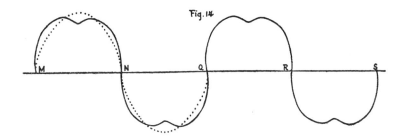

Fig. 14

The Quintadena is a species of a Quintaton, though the tone is of a hybrid quality, between Flute-tone and Diapason-tone. The pipes are made of metal, large-scale, stopped and overblown, so that the twelfth (octave quint) is very prominent and distinctly audible. This is easily proved by placing a pencil over the mouth of a small Quintadena pipe, so as to shut off about a third of the wind-way, when the octave quint alone will be audible, the fundamental tone being silenced by the process. In Fig. 15, I have indicated the curve of a Quintadena, showing the effect of the prominent second and fourth overtones (twelfth and seventeenth).

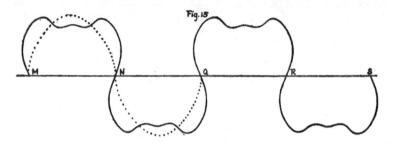

The Gemshorn, a slender-scaled, tapering, metal pipe, has a delicate tone (a cross between string-tone and Flute-tone), in which the fourth, fifth, and sixth overtones (17th, 19th, and flat 21st) are quite prominent.

The Rohr Floete (Chimney Flute) of the original type has a half-stopped pipe, the stopper having a hole through it with a small tube (chimney) over this hole. The pipe, being practically a stopped pipe, sounds the octave below its speaking length, and is devoid of the odd-numbered overtones. As the pipe is only partially stopped, a series of "inharmonic overtones," i. e., overtones which do not belong to the regular series, is produced. These "inharmonic overtones" give to the stop its peculiar tone character, and at times prevent its combining well with a few other stops. The modern Rohr Floete is rarely made with the projecting tubes. It is more frequently made like a Gedeckt, with a hole through the handle of the stopper, and is frequently substituted for the Gedeckt.

To give the young organist a further idea of the influence of overtones in stop combinations, I call attention to Fig. 16, which, to a certain limited extent, illustrates, *by means of notes*, the difference in the

Fig. 16

| Gedeckt | Melodia | Salicional | Oboe | Flute d'Amour | Flauto Traverso | Violina |
| A | B | C | D | E | F | G |

tone-color of one pipe of seven different stops (four eight-foot stops and three four-foot stops). In this figure, the whole notes represent the fundamental tone of each pipe. The overtones are represented by the black notes, the larger notes indicating the more powerful overtones. The numerals indicate the number of each overtone.

At A, the tone of a pipe of a Gedeckt (Stopped Diapason) is indicated. As the pipe is a stopped pipe, only the even-numbered overtones are present. The twelfth (second overtone) is quite prominent and the fourth and sixth overtones are very soft, oftentimes entirely absent. This stop blends well with almost every stop. In combination with other 8 ft. stops, it thickens the resultant tone, without materially increasing any of the overtones except the twelfth (second overtone). When it is combined with a 4 ft. stop of softer intonation, the 4 ft. stop supplies the missing links in the harmonic series (as will be shown further on) with a somewhat different tone-color, and oftentimes a charming combination is the result.

At B, the tone of a Melodia pipe is indicated. As the pipe is an open pipe, all the notes of the harmonic series are possible, but generally only a few overtones above the first (octave) are prominent enough to exert any influence. The octave is quite prominent.

At C, the tone of a Salicional pipe is indicated. Such slender-scaled pipes produce many overtones, as indicated, though the individual stops vary a great deal according to the taste of the voicer.

At D, the tone of an Oboe pipe is indicated. The tone of the reed stops, except the Clarinet, is rich in overtones. Nearly all the overtones are present and many of the upper overtones are prominent. The tone of the Clarinet, if it is at all imitative of the orchestral instrument, generally possesses only the even-numbered overtones.

At E, we see the similarity of the tone of a Flute d'Amour to the tone of a Gedeckt (A). The pipes of this stop are generally like those of a Gedeckt, except that they are a trifle smaller in scale, and are an octave higher.

At F, the tone of a Flauto Traverso 4 ft. is indicated. The pipes of this stop are harmonic and sound the first overtone (octave) instead of the fundamental tone; therefore in the illustration, it is necessary to mark the first overtone " F," as it is the fundamental sound of the pipe. Consequently, the overtones begin with No. 2. The overtones of this stop vary in the different makes of the stop, several of them being practically absent in some makes. The marked difference between the Flute d'Amour 4 ft. and the Flauto Traverso 4 ft. should be carefully noticed.

At G, the tone of a Violina 4 ft. is indicated. The string-tone stops have prominent overtones, but with this little stop it is better to have the higher overtones suppressed, as the stop is more useful if it has a tone which is not assertive.

In Fig. 17, four varieties of a combination of 8 and 4 ft. Flute-tone are indicated, for comparison. The numerals at the left indicate the number of the overtones of the stop of lower pitch. Those at the right indicate the number of the overtones of the stop of higher pitch. (Note: In Figures 17, 18, and 19, all the tones indicated in each measure are presumed to sound simultaneously.)

At H, a Gedeckt with 4 ft. Coupler is indicated. The delicacy of this

combination is apparent from the few overtones, the two fundamentals (F) and two twelfths (2) being the principal part of the com-

Fig. 17

bination. No note of the harmonic series is doubled. A Bourdon 16 ft.
and a Gedeckt 8 ft., played an octave higher, produces nearly the same
result, though a Bourdon is generally, and always should be, softer than
a Gedeckt. A Gedeckt and a Flute d'Amour 4 ft. produce nearly the
same effect, but these two stops are rarely found on the same manual.

At I, the combination of a Gedeckt and a Flauto Traverso 4 ft. is indicated. The difference between H and I is very pronounced. If the
Flauto Traverso happens to be of about the same power as the Gedeckt,
the combination is quite unsatisfactory. If the Flauto Traverso is softer
than the Gedeckt, the upper partials (overtones) of this stop are not
so objectionable in the combination. It will be observed that the overtones of the Gedeckt are doubled, and the missing overtones are supplied
by those of the Flauto Traverso. Another difference in these two combinations is the fact that the Flauto Traverso is a harmonic stop and
the overtones are an octave lower than those of the Gedeckt pipe of the
same pitch.

At J, the combination of a Melodia and a Flute d'Amour 4 ft. indicates
the delicate effect which the Flute d'Amour adds to the Melodia. This
combination is extremely useful in the Ch. for accompanimental purposes. A comparison of this combination with that at H shows the
doubling of two notes of the harmonic series, and the presence of all the
notes of the series in the lower octaves.

The combination of a Melodia and a Flauto Traverso 4 ft. at K,
shows how much more assertive a Flauto Traverso is than a Flute
d'Amour. In the combination of a Melodia and a Flauto Traverso 4 ft.
all the overtones are strengthened at the expense of the fundamental
tone.

In Fig. 18 a comparison is indicated, between the combination of an
Oboe with a Gedeckt and the combination of an Oboe with a Flauto
Traverso 4 ft.

At L, the combination of an Oboe with a Gedeckt is indicated. The
Gedeckt strengthens the fundamental tone of the Oboe without adding
a corresponding amount of overtone power, and tends to overshadow a
little of the distinctive quality of the Oboe, as this quality is due largely
to the pronounced overtones. In old organs the Oboe is generally coarse
and uncertain in intonation. With such Oboes, the addition of a Gedeckt
is necessary to cover up the deficiencies of the Oboe.

At M, the combination of an Oboe with a Flauto Traverso 4 ft. is indicated. A Flauto Traverso 4 ft. produces an entirely different effect,

Fig. 18

when combined with an Oboe, from the effect produced by the combination of a Gedeckt with an Oboe. If the Flauto Traverso is somewhat softer than the Oboe, it adds much to the distinctive character of the Oboe. It will be observed that the first overtone is much strengthened by the fundamental of the Flute, and several other overtones are more or less strengthened. All this happens without "fattening" the fundamental tone of the combination. This preserves the principal characteristic of the Oboe.

At Q (Fig. 19), the combination of a Gedeckt 8 ft. with a Violina 4 ft. is indicated. This combination gives all the overtones up to the sixth,

Fig. 19

with an octave doubling of the upper four of these six overtones. There being no unison doubling of any overtone, the combination is delicate and very useful for soft effects. With many modern organ builders, the Violina is underrated, and the stop is omitted in quite a number of modern organs. The only explanation given is: "The stop is useless and the Salicional with a 4 ft. Coupler answers just as well." To show how entirely different is the combination of the Gedeckt and Salicional with a 4 ft. Coupler, which is the suggested substitute for a Gedeckt and Violina 4 ft., I have indicated at N the overtones of the Gedeckt with a 4 ft. Coupler; at O, the overtones of a Salicional with a 4 ft. Coupler; and at P, the combination of the two stops with a 4 ft. Coupler. A comparison of Q and P cannot fail to convince any one that the two combinations are decidedly unlike. A Gedeckt and Violina 4 ft. is a delicate and flexible combination. The other combination is strong, full, and somewhat rich, but is devoid of any delicacy, and in passages where a Gedeckt and a Violina are desired, the other combination is unsatisfactory. In a few organs a Bourdon 16 ft. and a Salicional 8 ft., playing an octave higher, is a possible substitute, but generally the tone of the Salicional is too strong and stringy for the desired effect.

For convenience, in all these illustrations (to keep the notes within
the staff as far as possible), I have used a low note for the fundamental.
The best *audible* effect can be obtained by playing a note two octaves
higher, and for a comparison of the combinations it is better to hold

this chord:

I wish to repeat what I have before stated; viz., Accuracy is obviously
impossible, in illustrations of the above character. They are intended
only to be approximate and suggestive, and, if accepted just as they are
intended, the young organist cannot fail to obtain from them a good idea
of the influence of the overtones, not only in the individual stops, but also
in combinations of stops. He will also realize that a certain amount of
knowledge of the fundamental principles of the acoustics of organ pipes
will aid him materially in selecting his combinations, and save him the
trouble of " trying " many combinations which, at the outset, he ought
to know will not produce the desired tone-color.

In the preceding illustrations, I have attempted to describe certain influences of the overtones on the tone-quality of individual stops, and on
the resultant tone of a few combinations of stops. There remains another phase of the influence of overtones on the resultant tone of combinations of stops which ought to be well understood: viz., " Interference."

When two musical tones are nearly of the same pitch (only a few
vibrations per second apart), beats or pulsations are produced which in
most cases are unpleasant to the ear. The pipes are said to be " out of
tune with each other." Frequently, two pipes which are exactly of the
same pitch (both having been tuned to a third pipe) produce similar
discordant beats or pulsations, if they are located near each other and
sounded at the same time. This acoustical effect is known as " Interference." The vibrations of one pipe " quarrel " with the vibrations of
the other pipe. Organ builders call this phenomenon " Sympathy," but
it seems to me that the acoustical term " Interference " better describes
the phenomenon.

It is possible for the tone of one pipe to " interfere " with the tone
of another pipe in such a manner that the resultant tone is unsatisfactory. In such cases the vibrations of the fundamentals or of the overtones (or both) do not synchronize. On account of the possibility of
" interference," organ builders rarely place the pipes of two stops which
are exactly alike in one department of an organ. They locate the pipes
of certain stops, the tones of which are inclined to " interfere," as far
apart as is feasible.

In some cases the tone of a pipe of one stop partially nullifies the tone
of a pipe of another stop. Some acousticians claim that the tones of
two Gedeckt pipes which are *exactly alike* in scale, construction, and
pitch, will nullify each other and leave only a blowing sound, if the
pipes are placed near and facing each other, and sounded simultaneously.

" Interference " or " sympathy " is sometimes annoying to the organist when he is playing on a strong-toned Gamba; e. g., in playing low F and A in harmony an objectionable discord is occasionally heard. The organist at first imagines that one of the pipes is out of tune; but, on trying each pipe separately, it is found that each pipe is in good tune. The second overtone of the low F pipe is middle c'. The fourth overtone of the A pipe is c♯², an octave above c'. As the overtones of strong string-tone pipes are very pronounced, especially with the pipes of the lowest octave, the overtones c' and c♯² " interfere " and cause a noticeable discord. This " interference " does not always exist, and, singularly, it is more noticeable in major thirds than in minor thirds, especially in the two lowest octaves. Occasionally this " interference " can be overcome by causing the pipes to face in opposite directions.

In many English organs, the Gamba is placed in the Ch. instead of in the Gt. This is partly due to the " interference " which sometimes exists between the tone of a strong-toned Gamba and the tone of the full Diapason. In American organs a large-scale Flute — either a Gross Flute or a Doppel Floete — is usually placed in the Gt., in addition to the Gamba and Diapasons, and serves as a " mixer " between the Gamba and the Diapason. The three stops combined rarely show any interference.

If the nature of the " interference " is such that a combination of stops sounds unsatisfactory throughout the entire compass, it is generally necessary for the organist to select a substitute combination; but if the " interference " is objectionable only in the lowest octave, the organist can resort to one of several " dodges " to avoid the disagreeable effect. If the combined tenor and bass parts of certain phrases produce this disagreeable effect of " interference," one or both of these voices can be played on a Melodia for a few counts, giving the effect of two horns. It is often possible to play a few of the bass notes 8 va. on a soft Ped. Bourdon. If the stop is not loud, the difference in tone-color is not objectionable.

A composer or conductor of orchestral music rarely gives a thought to many of the technical details which are found in theoretical works on orchestration; and yet he unconsciously shows the influence of a knowledge of those details in his routine work with or for the orchestra. So it is with organ registration. The highly experienced organist may rarely think of the technical details of registration, such as the acoustics of organ pipes, and yet unconsciously exhibit a thorough knowledge of those details by the good taste, skill, and judgment which he exhibits in selecting the combinations which he uses in his public performances of organ compositions.

CHAPTER IV

DESCRIPTION OF THE STOPS MOST COMMONLY USED IN REGISTRATION INDICATIONS

A. DIAPASON-TONE STOPS   D. REED STOPS
B. FLUTE-TONE STOPS   E. PERCUSSION STOPS
C. STRING-TONE STOPS   F. THE TREMOLO

FOR the purpose of assisting the young organist to obtain a clear understanding of the nature of the various speaking stops, and the basic causes of the many tonal effects which are described later in this work, this chapter is devoted to a description of the stops which are most frequently mentioned in registration.

The incongruities of stop nomenclature are numerous, but, as yet, no one, not even the severest purist, has been able to outline any system which would improve the condition. In looking over the names of the speaking stops of a dozen English or American organs, one finds English (and American), German, French, Italian, and even "Dog Latin" terms, used singly and collectively without rhyme or reason. Worse yet, words of two different languages are unnecessarily coupled together in the names of some stops.

The origin of many stop-names is obscure and the real significance of many others is past finding out. While a few names are legitimate and their meaning is self-evident, many stops have been named by their inventors much as some parents name their children; purely from fancy, without a thought of the possible incongruity. However, it is not my purpose to quarrel with the inevitable, in this branch of the subject, nor to attempt to offer substitutes for such names as Voix Céleste, Vox Humana, Vox Angelica, Vox Aetheria, Erzahler, and other names which seem to have little significance relative to the real tone of the stops; but I do not see any reason for retaining such stop-names as: —

"Doppel Flute" for Doppel Floete
"Spitz Flute" for Spitz Floete
"Wald Flute" for Wald Floete
"Rohr Flute" for Rohr Floete
"Vox Céleste" for Voix Céleste or Vox Celestis.

A. DIAPASON-TONE STOPS

Open Diapason or Diapason. To begin with the stops which have Diapason tone, we naturally consider first the Open Diapason, or "Diapason," as it is now generally called. The 8 ft. Diapason is the primary foundation stop of the Great organ. Different varieties of this stop serve as the foundation stops of the other manuals. In large organs, two, three, and even four Diapasons, of varying character, are placed in the Gt. organ. The Diapason 8 ft., or " **First Diapason**," as it is called in organs which have two or more Diapasons in the Gt., has large-scale, heavy, cylindrical, metal pipes; open at the upper end and copiously winded. As this stop is the "back-bone" of the organ, its tone must be heavy, rich and sonorous. These are the recognized characteristics of the Diapason, and fittingly describe the tone-quality of the stop.

Violin Diapason. There are several varieties of the Diapason. The principal one is the Violin Diapason (also called " **String Diapason** "). The pipes of this stop are smaller in scale than those of the First Diapason. The tone is modified, with a tendency toward the string quality, though it possesses a round and rich tone of somewhat less sonority than the tone of the First Diapason. Diapasons of this character are found in the Gt. (named " **Second Diapason** " when there are two Diapasons in the Gt., or " **Third Diapason** " when there are three Diapasons in the Gt.), in the Sw. (named " Violin Diapason "), and in the Ch. (named " **Geigen Diapason** " or " **Geigen Principal** ").

The 8 ft. Diapason on any manual supplies the body and foundation for the louder combinations. It is also frequently combined with the louder reed stops when they are used in harmony. When used alone, or combined with one or two Flute-tone stops, the Diapason produces a rare tone-quality which is distinctly associated with the organ.

Stentorphone 8 ft. In large four-manual organs, an extremely heavy and powerful Diapason tone is produced by a Stentorphone in the Solo organ. This is the most powerful flue stop. The pipes are very large-scale, open, metal pipes, voiced on a heavy wind. Occasionally, we find, instead of a Stentorphone, a Diapason 8 ft., voiced on a heavy wind, in the Solo organ.

16 ft. Diapason in the Gt. This stop, which sounds an octave lower than the First Diapason, also has metal pipes, but they are of a smaller scale than those of the First Diapason. The object of this stop is to give great depth to the heavy combinations and to the Full Organ, it being the principal 16 ft. manual stop. The large metal pipes which are placed on the front of many organs are selected from this stop.

16 ft. Diapason in the Ped. This stop, except in large organs which have two stops of this name in that department, has quadrangular, open, wood pipes of very large scale. The tone is deep and powerful, being the foundation of the Pedal organ. In large organs, there are frequently two 16 ft. Diapasons in the Ped. The second one has pipes of heavy metal, and gives a firmer tone, though of less depth, than the wood Diapason. The Ped. Diapason 16 ft. is generally used with all loud combinations of the Gt., which include the 8 and 4 ft. stops to the Octave. It is also used, occasionally, without any coupler, for short, staccato notes in softer passages. It should generally be assisted by a Bourdon 16 ft., as this stop materially improves the definiteness of pitch. In large organs, we find a **32 ft. Diapason** in the Ped. This stop is of the greatest value in large Ped. organs and in the Full Organ.

Octave 4 ft. in the Gt.   The Octave (called "**Principal**" in old organs) may be called a small-scale 4 ft. Diapason.   The tone is of Diapason-quality, an octave higher than the tone of the Diapason 8 ft.; but, as
the pipes are considerably smaller in scale than those of the Diapason,
the tone is less powerful or rich.   The object of this stop is to give
sufficient prominence to the first overtone, which is the octave above
the fundamental, and to supply the brilliancy which would be lacking
without such a stop.   In addition, it is sometimes serviceable, in small
organs, as a soft Diapason, by playing an octave lower on this stop
alone.   Very large Swell organs frequently contain an Octave (or
Principal) 4 ft., its object being the same as in the Gt.

Twelfth and Fifteenth.   In large organs, the Twelfth and Fifteenth
are generally voiced with Diapason-quality of tone, though much softer
than the tone of either the Diapason or the Octave.   In small organs,
the Twelfth and Fifteenth are, occasionally, voiced with a soft Flute-
tone quality.   In such organs the Diapason-quality for these stops
would sound harsh, as there are generally but a few stops of 8 and
4 ft. pitch to balance the Twelfth and Fifteenth.   In some organs
the Twelfth is named "**Octave Quint,**" and the Fifteenth is named
"**Super Octave.**"   The object of these stops is to add brilliancy to the
loudest combinations and to the Full Organ.

Dulciana 8 ft.   The other stops which have the Diapason-quality of
tone are the Dulciana, Unda Maris, and Æoline.   These stops are so
soft in tone that, to the young organists, they seem to lack all the
characteristics of Diapason-tone quality.   To test the quality of tone of
the Dulciana, the organist should sound a chord on the Diapason.   After
waiting about ten seconds, the organist should sound the same chord on
the Dulciana.   While waiting, the organist should imagine that the
tone of the Diapason which he has just heard is becoming more and
more distant and, consequently, much softer.   When he sounds the
same chord on the Dulciana, he will observe that the tone-color is the
same as that of the Diapason, only much softer.   In some organs the
stop which is labeled "Dulciana" is not a real Dulciana but is a soft
Viola or Salicional, with a distinct string-tone quality.   The Dulciana,
as invented by Snetzler, had no string-tone quality.   The pipes of the
Dulciana are open, metal pipes, of slender scale and sparsely winded.
The tone is soft and quiet.

Keraulophon 8 ft.   In this country, many old organs contain a Keraulophon for the softest stop in the Ch., Gt. or Sw.   This stop is a large-scale
Dulciana, with a hole or slot in the pipes near the upper end which
imparts to the tone a slight "horny" quality.   In the Ch. or Gt. the use
of the stop is principally for the accompaniment of the solo combinations
of the Sw.   In the Sw. the stop must generally be used for both the Salicional and Æoline; though, occasionally, one finds a Gamba (Salicional)
in addition to the Keraulophon.

Unda Maris 8 ft.   The Unda Maris, as generally made in this country,
consists of two sets of Dulciana or Æoline pipes, one set being tuned a
little sharp, so that the two sets together produce an undulating tone
of a pleasing character.   In England and Germany this stop generally

consists of two ranks of Flute-tone pipes, tuned slightly apart in pitch.

Dulciana 16 ft. A 16 ft. Dulciana is frequently found in the Ch. and in the Ped. This stop is really a sub-octave extension of the 8 ft. Dulciana, with the same characteristics. It is very useful in either department.

Aeoline 8 ft. The Æoline is an extremely soft stop — the softest stop in the organ. The pipes are somewhat like those of the Dulciana, but are slenderer and more sparsely winded.

The Dulciana, Unda Maris and Æoline, all of 8 ft. pitch, are used for very soft passages, in full harmony, or as accompaniment for soft solo combinations. They are occasionally combined with 4 ft. stops, with which they are barely audible, for the purpose of supplying a soft sub-octave tone. They practically produce no effect when combined with the other 8 ft. stops, but they are frequently drawn with the 8 ft. stops, which later are put off, leaving these soft stops to sound alone.

Mixture or Mutation Stops. The terms " Mixture Stops " and " Mutation Stops " are generally used interchangeably. A Mixture Stop, as stated elsewhere, is one which has two or more pipes for each key, at least one of which sounds a note other than the note played or one of its octaves; e. g., a **Dolce Cornet III Rks.**, in the Sw. This stop has three pipes to each key, and if the lowest note of the Sw. is played, with this stop drawn, the following notes are sounded: — g, c′, g′ (12th, 15th, and 19th). In one of the upper octaves, the allotment of the pitch of the different ranks is changed to the 8th, 12th, and 15th. All Mixture Stops, by definition, come under the head of Mutation Stops, but there are other Mutation Stops which have only one pipe for each key; e. g., the Quint and Twelfth.

Pedal Quint, 10⅔ ft. This stop sounds a fifth above the Bourdon 16 ft. and in modern organs is generally derived from this stop by augmentation.

Quint 5⅓ ft. The manual Quint sounds a fifth above the 8 ft. stops on the manual.

Twelfth 2⅔ ft. The Twelfth, also called " **Octave Quint,**" sounds a twelfth above the 8 ft. stops on the manual.

Resultant Bass 32 ft. A Pedal Mixture Stop of two ranks. It consists of a 16 ft. rank and a Quint rank of 10⅔ ft. When these two ranks are sounded simultaneously they produce an approximate 32 ft. tone.

The question, whether or not organs shall contain any Mutation stops, is today a much mooted question. Until quite recently, nearly every organ of any size contained Mutation stops, but a few of the most modern organs have no Mutation stops. Until within the last quarter-century, the science of acoustics was little understood by pipe makers and voicers. The subject of overtones was rarely considered, and modern distinctive tone-qualities were unknown. If an organ contained only Foundation stops it lacked brilliancy and dash. To supply this lack of brilliancy, the Mutation stops were added, in increasing numbers, which easily overcame the deficiency. As these Mutation stops consisted of small pipes, they required but a little metal, and little room in the organ for their accommodation. It was a simple matter to obtain increased power by an inordinate multiplication of these Mutation stops. This tendency culminated in the organ which was erected in the Benedictine Abbey at Weingarten, in 1759. This organ contained 95 ranks of mutation-tone, two stops of which comprised respectively twenty-one and twenty pipes to each key. The reaction which followed gradually reduced the number of Mutation stops in the organs, besides reducing the power of the individual ranks. Today, the most satisfactory Mutation stops are voiced much softer than formerly, and the effect produced by them is most satisfactory.

Modern pipe voicers have become so proficient, and are so well versed on the subject of overtones in organ pipes, that many most beautiful and distinctive tone-colors, which are primarily due to the treatment of the overtones, have been produced. Those who consider the modern organ a close competitor of the orchestra are, therefore, claiming that the additional tones of the Mutation stops are, today, no more necessary in an organ than in the orchestra. However, the Full Organ without any Mutation stops, even in a modern organ, lacks brilliancy and vitality. To cover up this lack of brilliancy, the Sw. to Gt. 4 ft., and Gt. to Gt. 4 ft. couplers are requisitioned. The effect produced by these couplers in the Full Organ is frequently unsatisfactory. Nothing in a modern organ tends to produce so much unevenness of tone, in the Full Organ passages, as the 4 ft. couplers, when they are used primarily to give brilliancy and power. The upper one or two notes of every chord receive the full re-enforcement of the 4 ft. couplers, while the other notes of the chords gain little or nothing. If the 16 ft. couplers are also used, only the lower one or two notes of the chords are thereby re-enforced. It is obvious how unbalanced the chords are rendered, by the addition of the tone of many pipes to the upper and lower two notes of the chords, without a similar re-enforcement of the middle three or four notes of the chords. If one plays single notes or melodies, there is, of course, no unevenness of tone in the passage; but in chords and in four or five-voiced polyphonic phrases, the unevenness of the tone of the various voices is very objectionable.

There is another objectionable feature in the substitution of the 4 ft. couplers for the Mutation stops. The upper tones, which are supplied by the Mutation stops, are only about one-quarter as loud as the tones which are added by the 4 ft. couplers, and the effect produced by the Mutation stops is sufficiently brilliant, better proportioned, and less harsh.

As previously stated, the Mutation stops vary in different organs, both in their power and tone-quality. They are, generally, of soft Diapason-quality; but, occasionally, one or two ranks are voiced with Flute-quality. Their use in registration is almost entirely with Full Swell and F or Full Great. Somewhat rarely, one can use the Dolce Cornet of the Sw. combined with a Gedeckt and Tremolo, for soft solo passages in the upper two octaves only. A stop named " Solo Mixture," which produces a similar effect in nearly the entire compass of the stop, is somewhat rarely inserted in the Sw.

B. FLUTE-TONE STOPS

Melodia. Of the Flute-tone stops the Melodia is a representative stop. A Hohl Floete or a Concert Flute is sometimes substituted for a Melodia, the tone-quality being much like that of the Melodia. The pipes of the Melodia are slender-scaled, quadrangular, open, wood pipes, with inverted mouths (the upper lip beveled on the inside instead of on the outside). The tone is quite mellow, though hollow, with good blending quality. In some small two-manual organs, this stop is frequently the only Flute-tone stop in the Gt., and, as such, it is frequently voiced too loud and lacks real beauty of tone. In three-manual organs, the Melodia (Concert Flute or Hohl Floete) is the foundation Flute stop of the Ch. On this manual the Melodia shines with its best merits. It is useful alone or with other stops in harmony; is a good accompaniment stop, and also is useful as a solo stop. In the latter capacity, it should not be used too long as the tone palls on the ear if used very long. Occasionally, we find in the Ch. a **Wald Floete 4 ft.** with pipes and tone similar to those of the Melodia.

Gedeckt or St. Diapason 8 ft. The Gedeckt (St. Diapason) is one of the most useful stops in the whole list of organ stops. In this country, one rarely finds an organ, large or small, which does not contain at least one form of this stop. It is found, under varying names, in 16, 8, and 4 ft. pitch, and in one form or another is found in the Sw., Gt., Ch., Ech., or Ped.

On account of the large number of stops which are closely related to the Gedeckt, both in the construction of the pipes and in the tone-quality, some theorists segregate these stops into a fifth quality of tone which they call " Gedeckt-Tone." While it is convenient to group these stops into one group, it does not seem necessary to establish a fifth quality of tone (" Gedeckt-Tone "), as this tone, after all, is only a variety of Flute-tone.

Fundamentally, the Gedeckt, which is also called " St. Diapason," has quadrangular, wood pipes, stopped at the upper end. (See Chapter IV for the acoustical characteristics of these stops.) In England, the pipes of the Gedeckt are frequently made of metal. The scale of the different stops of the Gedeckt group varies considerably, according to the part of the organ in which the stops are located. The tone-quality of all the stops of the Gedeckt group is pure and limpid Flute-tone, which blends well with the tone of other stops. The various stops of the Gedeckt group are as follows (1-11) :

(1) **Sw. or Ch. Gedeckt (St. Diapason).** The pipes are of medium scale and the tone is of medium power. The tone-quality of this stop is a liquid Flute-tone, somewhat hollow, of most pleasing character. The stop is one of the most useful of the soft stops, as it combines well with every other stop on its manual, and may be used alone, in harmony, or as a solo stop.

(2) **Lieblich Gedeckt.** This stop has all the characteristics of the preceding stop, but the pipes are smaller and the tone is more delicate.

(3) **Ped. Bourdon 16 ft.** This stop is the most universal Ped. stop. It is a large-scale Gedeckt of 16 ft. pitch. In some old organs this stop is called "**Double St. Diapason.**" The tone-quality of the upper notes is a clear Flute-quality, but in the descending scale this quality disappears, and in the lower notes the tone is dull and thick, due partly to the prominence of the second overtone.

(4) **Sw. or Ch. Bourdon 16 ft.** The pipes of this stop are of smaller scale than those of either the Gedeckt 8 ft. or the Ped. Bourdon. The tone is softer than that of either stop but it possesses the same liquid Flute-quality. The stop is most useful in combinations, and supplies the sub-octave foundation for the Full Sw. or Ch. Occasionally, the stop is called "**Lieblich Bourdon 16 ft.,**" when it is generally softer in tone than the regular manual Bourdon.

(5) **Gt. Bourdon 16 ft.** Larger scale and generally more powerful in tone than the Sw. or Ch. Bourdon. This stop is substituted for the Gt. Diapason 16 ft. in small organs, and, in large organs, it is often found in addition to the Diapason 16 ft. Its principal use is in supplying the sub-octave foundation for the F and FF combinations of the Gt.

(6) **Ped. Gedeckt 8 ft.** This stop is generally an extension of the Ped. Bourdon, by the addition of 12 pipes to the upper octave. It is a most useful stop as a soft 8 ft. Ped. stop. When combined with the Bourdon 16 ft., it adds definiteness of pitch and makes the Ped. tones somewhat stronger.

(7) **Echo Lieblich Bourdon 16 ft.** Smaller scale and softer tone than the Sw. Bourdon.

(8) **Ped. Lieblich Bourdon 16 ft.** Either the Sw. or the Echo Bourdon borrowed in the Ped. Somewhat rarely it is an independent stop.

(9) **Ch. Flute d'Amour 4 ft.** A small-scale Gedeckt of 4 ft. pitch. This stop is, perhaps, the most beautiful and most useful of the soft 4 ft. Flutes. Like the Gedeckt 8 ft., it combines well with all the other stops.

(10) **Rohr Floete 8 ft.** Occasionally, this stop is found in place of a Gedeckt or St. Diapason. In modern organs, the pipes are made quite similar to those of the Gedeckt, but they generally have a small hole bored through the "stopper." This hole modifies the tone somewhat by giving greater prominence to the second and fourth overtones. (See Chapter IV.) A **Rohr Floete 4 ft.** is, occasionally, found in the Sw. in place of a Flauto Traverso, or in the Ch. in place of a Flute d'Amour.

(11) **Gt. Doppel Floete 8 ft.** The pipes of this stop are somewhat like those of a large Gedeckt; but they are of double width and have a mouth on each side of the pipe, whence the name. The tone is a distinct Flute-tone, very full and of considerable volume, due to the two mouths and copious winding. In the Gt. organ, this stop is always useful: first, as a solo stop of considerable beauty; second, in combination with the Gamba or with the Harmonic Flute 4 ft.; third, in adding volume to the Diapason; and fourth, in helping to weld together the tones of the Gamba and Diapason.

Clarabella 8 ft. A full-toned, open, wood Flute, which is very popular in England and some years ago was popular here. At that time, it was, frequently, the only 8 ft. Flute stop in the Gt. or Ch. of many organs. Of late years, it has been superseded by the Doppel Floete or the Gross Flute.

Gross Flute (or Gross Floete) 8 ft., Gt. or So. This is a powerful 8 ft. Flute-tone stop which is common in this country. The pipes are large-scale, open, wood pipes, copiously winded, similar to a large-scale Clarabella. The tone is heavy and of much carrying power; more powerful but less refined than that of the Doppel Floete. It adds considerable volume when combined with a Diapason; blends well with a Gamba; and acts somewhat as a "pacifier" when combined with a Diapason and a Gamba, as it seems to prevent the "quarreling" (interference, q. v.), which is sometimes noticeable when a Gamba and a Diapason are combined without any other stop.

Tibias. A group of stops, known as the "Tibia Family," deserve special mention, on account of their great value in welding together the other tone-colors of the organ. The pipes are of extra large scale, are generally sounded by a heavy wind, and the tone of the different stops of the family is full, clear, and very powerful. The principal stops of this family are: The Tibia Major, Tibia Minor, Tibia Plena, Tibia Clausa, of 16 and 8 ft. pitch, and the Tibia Dura of 4 ft. pitch. Obviously, such large-scale and powerful stops are suitable only for large organs.

The **Tibia Major 16 ft.** and **Tibia Minor 8 ft.** are the German stops of the Tibia family. The Tibia Minor has also been made in England. The Tibia Clausa 8 ft., Tibia Dura 4 ft., and Tibia Plena 8 ft. were invented by the late Mr. Robert Hope-Jones. The **Tibia Clausa** is a very large-scale Gedeckt, with a powerful, clear Flute-tone. The **Tibia Dura** has open, wood pipes of peculiar shape. The tone is bright and powerful. The **Tibia Plena** is the most powerful of the Tibias. Its pipes are large-scale, open, wood pipes.

Philomela. This is a powerful Flute-tone stop of the Tibia class. The pipes are large-scale, open, wood pipes, frequently with double mouths. The tone is a powerful and bright Flute-tone.

Spitz Floete 8 ft. This is a species of the Flute-tone stops which is found frequently in the Sw. or Ch. as a second Flute-tone stop: i. e., in addition to the Gedeckt or Melodia. It has a bright Flute-tone tending towards a string-tone. The pipes are open metal pipes with conical-shaped tops.

Flauto Traverso. The Flauto Traverso is a Harmonic Flute (see Chapter III) and is frequently found as an 8 ft. stop, but more frequently as a 4 ft. stop in the Sw. or Ch. The pipes are made nearly like those of the Melodia, except that they are of double length and have a small hole near the middle, which causes the pipes to sound the first overtone (octave). Originally, the tone of this stop possessed a slight "lip tone," intended to imitate the tone of an orchestral flute; but this characteristic in an organ stop is unsatisfactory, and has been discarded. In this country, the 4 ft. Flauto Traverso is frequently found in the Sw., and is a most useful stop, in both large and small organs. Its tone combines

well with the tone of many other stops, and it can be used in many ways.
As a solo stop in the Ch., it is, perhaps, less useful than a Flute d'Amour.
The latter stop, having stopped pipes and not being harmonic, has a more
limpid Flute-tone.   Occasionally, the Flauto Traverso, when used as a
solo stop and played staccato, has a disagreeable tendency to " hoot."

Harmonic Flute 4 ft., Gt.   This stop is quite different from the Flauto
Traverso, though frequently substituted for it.   The pipes are open,
metal pipes of double length, with a small hole near the middle which
causes the pipes to sound the first overtone (octave) instead of the
fundamental tone.   The tone is a bright Flute-tone; occasionally somewhat cloying, and less delicate than the tone of the Flauto Traverso.
It combines well with the tone of the other stops of the Gt., and brightens
various combinations.   In large organs, we frequently find 8 ft. Harmonic Flutes of this character.

Flute 8 ft., Ped., also called **Pedal Flute** or **Bass Flute.**   A powerful
8 ft. Flute-tone, much in contrast to the Ped. Gedeckt, which has a soft
Flute-tone.   The pipes are large-scale, open, wood pipes.   In many organs,
this stop is derived from the Ped. Diapason (wood) 16 ft. by the addition of 12 pipes to supply the necessary upper octave.   This plan of
augmentation or extension is convenient, and, generally, satisfactory in
Ped. stops.   Theoretically, to extend a Diapason and call the extension
a " Flute " seems an anomaly.   If a 16 ft. metal Diapason were extended,
the extension could not be called a " Flute," as both the pipes and tone-
quality would be distinctly Diapason.   On the other hand, the 16 ft.
wood Diapason is practically a large-scale, open Flute of 16 ft. pitch.
Its tone is very heavy and is the foundation of the Ped. organ.   Hence,
from the power and weight of tone, it may well be called " Pedal Diapason."   However, when the stop is extended, the tone-quality of the
upper pipes is so recognizable as that of a powerful, open Flute that it
must, necessarily, be called " Flute."   In many organs this extension of
the 16 ft. wood Diapason is called " Octave 8 ft.," but the anomaly is
only transferred, for the Octave is always considered Diapason-tone,
and this extension of the 16 ft. wood Diapason does not produce a
Diapason-tone.

Flautino 2 ft.   The tone of this stop is delicate and of Flute-quality.
It sounds two octaves above the fundamental pitch of the manual.   The
pipes are small, slender, open pipes.   The stop has two functions; first,
it supplies brilliancy to the larger combinations of the manual, by
strengthening the third overtone (fifteenth) ; second, when it is properly
voiced, it assists in producing many delicate and useful combinations of
8 and 2 ft., 16 and 2 ft., or 16, 8, 4, and 2 ft. pitch.

Piccolo 2 ft.   A distinct Flute-tone stop, somewhat fuller and louder
than the Flautino, sounding two octaves above the fundamental pitch
of the manual.   The pipes are open, metal pipes, frequently of double
length, thus being harmonic.   If not too shrill, the stop is useful in
various combinations in the Ch., besides adding brilliancy to the Full Ch.

Flute Céleste 8 ft., II Rks.   A Flute Céleste consists of two sets of
Flute pipes, tuned slightly apart in pitch, which produce an undulating
tone of Flute-quality.   In old Continental organs, such a stop was

called " Unda Maris." The principle of the stop is similar to that of the
Voix Céleste, but numerous difficulties arise in the voicing of a Flute
Céleste, and only a small proportion of the stops named " Flute Céleste "
can be considered a success. It is extremely difficult to produce an even
and pleasing undulation of Flute-tone. If the two ranks are of 8 ft.
pitch, and the scale of each rank is nearly the same, the tone is liable
to " wobble " and sound distressingly out of tune, on account of " interference " (q. v.) or " sympathy." The most pleasing Flute Céleste that
the author ever heard was made by E. F. Walcker and Son, of Germany,
and was named " Bifra." It consisted of one rank of stopped, wood
Flute pipes of 8 ft. pitch, and a rank of open, metal Flute pipes of 4 ft.
pitch, tuned slightly sharp, so as to produce a slow wave. A slow
Tremolo was attached to the stop. The tone of a good Flute Céleste is
very pleasing, and the stop is useful, mostly by itself, in contrast to other
tone-qualities.

C. String-Tone Stops

The String-tone stops of the organ exert an influence on the tone of
combinations quite similar, though in a smaller degree, to the influence
of the tone of the stringed instruments of the orchestra. These stops
add not only color, but vitality, to the tone of organ combinations; and
many beautiful effects are produced by their aid which cannot even be
suggested by any other stops. While the tone-quality of these stops
possesses a few of the characteristics of the tone of the stringed instruments, it must be remembered that the vibrations of a column of air
within a pipe cannot successfully be made to imitate the tone produced
by the vibrations of the strings of the Viol family. The friction of the
bow on the strings causes a " bite " in the tone which probably never
can be imitated in the tone of organ pipes.

Gamba 8 ft. The full name of this stop is **Viola da Gamba** (or **Viol
de Gambe**), from the name of the stringed instrument which the stop
is intended to imitate. This instrument is a Viol which is held between
the legs, whence the name. From an etymological view-point, the name
" Gamba " (which means " leg ") for an organ stop is most inappropriate. However, the necessity for abbreviated names on the draw-stops
and long usage have established this name for the stop.

There are many modifications of the Gamba, in most of which the
imitation of the orchestral instrument is remote. The early Gambas
had pipes of slenderer scale than those of the Diapason, with mouths
cut low. The tone-quality, from a modern view-point, was only *slightly*
stringy. These stops, in American organs, were most always placed in
the Gt. They were of much utility, though frequently slow of speech.
The more modern Gambas consist of open, cylindrical, metal pipes (frequently made of pure tin), of very slender scale (frequently the pipes
have less than half the diameter of the Diapason pipes), with mouths
cut low and narrow. A wooden roller or a bridge is generally placed
across the mouth of the pipes to increase the string-tone quality. If
the stop is placed in the Gt., the tone is keen and pungent, though some-

what full. If the stop is placed in the Co. organ, the wind-pressure is generally greater and the tone-quality is more stringy though of a forced quality. The higher overtones are well developed, at the expense of the ground-tone.

In the Gt. organ, the stop is used for solo purposes, in the tenor range; is combined with a Doppel Floete (or a Gross Flute) for a piano Gt. combination; or is combined with a Harmonic Flute 4 ft., for a special combination of a cutting character. When added to the combination of a Doppel Floete (or Gross Flute) and Diapason, the Gamba adds firmness. It rarely combines well with a Diapason alone, a firm Flute-tone being necessary to weld together the tones of a Diapason and a Gamba. Occasionally, a stop named " Gamba " which is practically a Salicional is found in the Sw.

Salicional 8 ft., Sw. or Ch. A Salicional is a small-scale Gamba which is usually placed in the Sw., though it is, occasionally, found in the Ch. The character of the tone varies in different organs. In large modern organs, in which the Sw. contains both a Salicional and a Viol d'Orchestre, the Salicional is generally of the old style; i. e., a small-scale, old-fashioned Gamba, having a somewhat stringy but not pungent tone. Salicionals of this character are also found in many old organs, which have only this one string-tone stop in the Sw.

In many small, modern organs, the Salicional is more like a soft Viol d'Orchestre, and has a keen, pungent string-tone. The tone of such Salicionals in these small organs, frequently, is too prominent in the soft combinations, because it cuts through the tone of the other stops to an objectionable degree. The object of a keen, pungent tone in a Salicional is, generally, to give the desirable string-quality to the Voix Céleste, of which it is a part. An old-fashioned Salicional, especially in the Sw. which also contains a Viol d'Orchestre, is very useful, as it gives the only satisfactory graduation of tone between the Æoline and the Gedeckt. Useful combinations with such a Salicional are: Salicional and Gedeckt, Salicional and Flute 4 ft., and Salicional and Violina 4 ft., unless the Flute 4 ft. and Violina are voiced too loud. A Viol d'Orchestre, if present, supplies all that an old-fashioned Salicional lacks. It will be noticed that, in organs which contain only one 8 ft. string-tone stop in the Sw., the organist must often compromise somewhat in selecting his combinations. If there are two such stops, e. g., Viol d'Orchestre and Salicional, all the various shadings of tone-color which require these stops are available.

A Salicional, whether of an old-fashioned or a modern type, is a useful stop in the Sw. It may be used alone for soft harmony or accompaniment to soft solo stops of the Ch., and is useful in the combinations mentioned above. Occasionally, it is useful to even the tones of the scale of a poor Oboe, or to re-enforce the tone of a good Oboe.

In very old organs that have only four or five stops in the Sw., we occasionally find a **Viola 8 ft.** which is a cross between a Dulciana and a Salicional, both in power and tone-quality. In a few modern organs we find a Viola 8 ft. which has a strong string-tone quality.

Viol d'Orchestre 8 ft., Sw. The modern Viol d'Orchestre is the keenest and most pungent of the string-tone stops, though it is less powerful than a Gamba. It was invented about 1885 by Messrs. Michell and Thyne of England. The pipes are open, cylindrical, metal pipes (often of pure tin), extremely slender scale (the lowest pipe has about one-third of the diameter of a Gamba pipe), with a mouth cut low and partially covered with a roller.

As previously stated, the tone of the Viol d'Orchestre is a keen, pungent, and animated string-tone. It *combines* well with the various Flute-tone and reed-tone stops, but rarely *blends* with any tone-quality. It generally retains its own individuality in all combinations. To be more specific, a Viol d'Orchestre combined with a 4 ft. Flute gives a pleasing combination, but the tone of each stop remains distinctly discernible. On the other hand, if an old-fashioned Salicional and a 4 ft. Flute are combined, the tones of the two stops *blend* so well that they are hardly distinguishable in the resultant tone.

The Viol d'Orchestre is a good solo stop, if one avoids the two upper octaves. It may be used alone, for sustained harmony, but generally requires a combination with other stops for short chords or arpeggios. It may be used to strengthen the tone of the reeds, as it does not destroy any of their characteristics; and it may be used to add firmness to the stronger combinations of its manual.

Voix Céleste (Ger. **Vox Celestis**) **8 ft., Sw., Ch., or Ech.** In stop nomenclature, the word " Céleste " is used to indicate a set, or " rank " of pipes which is tuned slightly sharp (or flat). This difference of pitch produces an undulating effect, when this rank of pipes is combined with another rank of about the same character, which is tuned to the normal pitch. In modern organs this rank of pipes is connected with a companion rank of about the same power and tone-color, and both ranks are brought on at once by means of one draw-stop. The Voix Céleste varies in different organs. Generally, it consists of two ranks of string-tone pipes (Viol d'Orchestre or Salicional). Occasionally, we find a stop named " Voix Céleste " which consists of two ranks of Æoline pipes. A Voix Céleste of the latter character is very soft and of limited combinational utility, as it has practically no influence on any other stop, on account of its extreme softness. It seems to me advisable to name such a stop " Unda Maris " (q. v.), reserving the name " Voix Céleste " for the string-tone stop of undulating character, and " Viol Céleste " for the delicate, undulating stop of the Viol family. The primary effect of the undulations is somewhat similar to the effect of a number of violins playing in unison. There is generally a slight difference in pitch between the instruments, which adds " nerve " or " vitality " to the ensemble. Likewise, the difference in pitch between the two ranks of a Voix Céleste gives " nerve " and " vitality " to the tone of the stop. The tone of a good string-tone Voix Céleste is the nearest approach to the tone of a violin or cello of any stop in the organ.

A whole chapter could be devoted to the numerous uses of a good Voix Céleste, but it would be repeating various statements which will be found in other parts of the book; therefore, it is only necessary to state here the general uses of this stop. It is an excellent solo stop, is ef-

fective in harmony, and exerts much influence on the tone of combinations. It adds vitality to the tone of the reeds, when they are used as
solo stops, and increases the firmness and assertiveness of several mixed
combinations. The real influence of the Voix Céleste, in the various
combinations mentioned above, varies according to the keenness and
power of the individual Voix Céleste.

Incidentally, it should be noted that, in large organs, we sometimes
find a Céleste which is tuned flat instead of sharp. This rank of pipes
is, generally, intended to be used *in addition* to the two ranks of a Voix
Céleste, for the purpose of increasing the undulating effect.

Viol or Muted Viol 8 ft. This stop may be called a very delicate
Viol d'Orchestre, as it produces a keen string-tone, but of delicate and
subdued character. The pipes are generally of slenderer scale than
those of the Viol d'Orchestre, and taper towards the upper ends. When
well voiced, it is a most beautiful soft, string-tone stop, which may be
used alone or combined with other equally soft stops. A **Viol Céleste**
consists of two ranks of Viol pipes, one rank tuned slightly sharp. In
reality this stop is a soft Voix Céleste.

Viol d'Amour 8 ft., Ch. or Gt. Theoretically, this stop is a very soft
string-tone stop, even softer than an old-fashioned Salicional, but in
this country, it is generally voiced like a very soft Violin Diapason, and
is placed in the Ch. or Gt., as an accompaniment stop, somewhat
stronger than a Dulciana. Its tone possesses more character and volume
than the tone of a Dulciana, but it is not assertive like the tone of the
regular string-tone stops. The pipes are small-scale, cylindrical, metal
pipes, with somewhat delicate intonation. This stop is extremely useful
for the accompaniments of solo combinations of the Sw., when a Dulciana is too soft and indefinite.

Fugara 4 ft., Ch. or Sw. In this country this stop is generally a soft
Octave Salicional, and is used for combinational purposes. In several
organs it is the 4 ft. string-tone stop of the Ch., and as such, is quite
useful in brightening several combinations of that manual. It may also
be used as an 8 ft. stop, by playing an octave lower, thus serving as a
mild-toned Salicional. This stop is sometimes named "**Salicet 4 ft.**"
or "**Gambette 4 ft.**"

Violina (or Violin) 4 ft., Sw. This stop, like the previous one, is
rarely found outside of this country; and even in this country, it is now-
a-days less common in new organs than formerly. It seems to me that
the neglect of this little stop is unfortunate. If it is voiced about
one-third as loud as an old-fashioned Salicional, with little or no cutting
string-tone quality, it has a combinational value which cannot be ap-
proached by any present-day substitute. If it is voiced with a somewhat
keen string-tone quality, its tone is frequently objectionable, as it cuts
through the tone of the other stops in the combination to a disagreeable
degree. Perhaps the name of the stop is the cause of its unpopularity;
for the tone of such a stop, as is described above, has no suggestion of
the tone of a violin. Combined with a Salicional, Gedeckt, or Bourdon
16 ft., the Violina gives several useful, delicate combinations, which are
serviceable for the soft accompaniment of solo stops or of voices. The

pipes are generally medium scale, metal pipes, frequently tapering towards the upper ends.

Violone 16 ft., Ped. This stop, the most common 16 ft. string-tone stop in the Ped., has slender-scale, wood pipes, considerably smaller than those of the Diapason. The tone is somewhat stringy, and occasionally suggests the tone of a contra bass. In large organs we also find a **Contra Gamba 16 ft.**, which generally has metal pipes and a pronounced string-tone. The Violone is useful as the logical Ped. stop for the manual string-tone stops. A Contra Gamba is generally too strong for such a purpose. When a Violone is added to a Bourdon 16 ft., it gives firmness and additional power to the Ped. tones. A Contra Gamba 16 ft. has the same effect when it is added to a Diapason 16 ft.

Cello 8 ft., Ped. This stop is the only 8 ft. Ped. stop in many old organs; but in modern organs it is more commonly one of three such stops — Flute (or Octave), Gedeckt, and Cello. In old organs the pipes are generally medium-scale, metal pipes. In modern organs the stop is generally an extension of a Violone; and as such, the pipes are wood pipes, except those of the upper octave, which frequently are metal pipes. The tone of a Cello is slightly stringy; oftentimes hard rather than stringy. This stop is rarely satisfactory for " Cello effects," these being better obtained from a manual Voix Céleste. A Cello is useful to strengthen the 8 ft. octave of the Ped. combinations, and gives firmness to all the loud combinations. In a few organs we find a Cello on one of the manuals, which closely resembles a Viol d'Orchestre. Occasionally the stop has the full name — " **Violoncello 8 ft.**"

D.   REED-TONE STOPS

Oboe 8 ft. Among the reed-tone stops, the most common is the Oboe 8 ft., in the Swell organ. In very old organs, this stop is frequently called " **Hautbois** " or " **Hautboy.**" In many small organs in this country, the Oboe is the only reed-tone stop in the organ; and it is included in nearly every well-balanced organ of any size. Undoubtedly, this is due to the great utility of the stop, both as a solo stop and as a combinational stop. In a few organs which have no reed-tone stop in the Gt., we occasionally find a Cornopean (q. v.) in the Swell organ, instead of an Oboe. This stop is substituted for the purpose of providing a stronger reed-tone for the Full Organ, in the absence of a Trumpet in the Great organ; the one stop (Cornopean) being intended to answer for both Oboe and Trumpet. From the point of economy, pure and simple, there seems to be but little criticism of this substitution, but from a tonal point of view, the substitution is questionable. A Cornopean, if voiced loud enough to answer for a Gt. Trumpet, is not a good substitute for an Oboe, as it is much too loud. On the other hand, if the Cornopean is voiced soft and smooth enough to be a fairly good substitute for an Oboe, it is of little value as a substitute for a Gt. Trumpet.

The pipes of an Oboe are slender-scale, inverted conical, metal pipes. Technically, the pipes are known as " beating reeds," in contradistinction to " free reeds," and have slender tongues beating on closed shallots.

The tone of a modern Oboe stop is a quiet, smooth, but firm, reed-tone, which is absolutely free from rattle, unless the pipes are " out of voice." It is devoid of the plaintive quality which is characteristic of the orchestral instrument. In old organs, and in a few very small modern organs, the Oboe terminates at tenor C. The octave below is omitted, for the sake of economy, or is supplied by another stop, called " **Bassoon** " or " **Bassoon Bass**," which has only twelve pipes of the lowest octave. In a few organs, not of modern construction, the above two stops are combined into one stop called " **Oboe and Bassoon**." In modern organs, the word " Bassoon " is dropped, and the stop, which runs through the entire compass, is always called " Oboe." A few organs contain an additional complete stop called " **Bassoon 8 ft.**," but the tone of this stop is quite different from that of an Oboe. This stop should not be confounded with the Contra Bassoon 16 ft. or Contra Fagotto 16 ft. (q. v.). Incidentally, it should be noted that the upper twelve pipes of an Oboe, and also of all 8 ft. reed-tone stops, are flue pipes, as reed pipes are rarely carried above the pitch c^3.

A modern Oboe is an excellent solo stop, when used either alone, or in combination with such stops as a Gedeckt, Rohr Floete, Bourdon, Flute 4 ft., Salicional, Viol d'Orchestre, or Voix Céleste. It combines well with most of the stops on its manual. It is also effective when used in harmony, either close or open position, and is a useful stop for strengthening the combinations of medium power, either in organ music or in accompanying voices.

Salicional Oboe, or String Oboe 8 ft., Sw. A keen, hard, and forced *string-tone* stop, which is sometimes substituted for an Oboe, in small organs. The pipes are very slender-scale, metal, *flue* pipes, like those of a Viol d'Orchestre; or very slender-scale, wood pipes, with a roll across the mouth of the pipes. The name of this stop is unfortunate, and somewhat of a paradox. Reed-tone stops require the attention of a tuner more frequently than the other stops. Small organs, which are located beyond the services of a tuner, may well have the reed-tone stops omitted; and a keen string-tone stop, like a Viol d'Orchestre, may well be substituted for an Oboe; but why call such a stop any kind of an Oboe? The tone of the stop would be no less attractive under a more appropriate name.

If an organ contains a " Salicional Oboe," it must be substituted for the Oboe, in the registration, as far as is possible. Occasionally, it will have to be omitted, as the combination will be more satisfactory without the stop. Personal taste, and the exigencies of the individual organ, must be the sole guide.

Orchestral Oboe 8 ft. A slender-scale Oboe, the tone of which somewhat resembles the plaintive tone of the orchestral instrument. The pipes are made and voiced differently by different pipe-makers; but in all Orchestral Oboes the overtones are more pronounced than in the ordinary Oboe. For this reason, the stop is less satisfactory in harmony than a regular Oboe. As a solo stop, alone or in combination with other stops, the Orchestral Oboe is valuable. Its tone-quality is fascinating and haunting.

Trumpet 8 ft., Gt. A powerful reed-tone stop, found in the Gt. of most organs. The pipes are inverted conical, metal pipes; larger in scale than those of an Oboe. The tongues of the reeds are thicker, and generally have a greater curvature than those of an Oboe; which gives more " clang " to the tone, indicating the presence of many of the higher overtones.

The tone of a Trumpet is powerful, rich, thick, and vibrant. If supported by a proper amount of foundation tone, and surrounded by sufficient mixture-work of not too assertive character, the Trumpet gives dignity and power to the Full Organ. It can rarely be used alone, as a solo stop, though some special solo effects, of short duration, are obtained by combining a Trumpet with one or two Diapasons and heavy Flutes. In all small combinations the tone of the Trumpet is conspicuous, as it does not blend with the tone of the other stops. A good Trumpet, combined with a Diapason and a Tibia or Gross Flute, can be played in harmony (mostly below c^2), for the purpose of producing an effect somewhat like the tone of the brass instruments of the orchestra when played *forte*.

Tuba or Tuba Mirabilis 8 ft., So. or Gt. A Tuba Mirabilis is an extremely powerful reed-tone stop — the most powerful stop in a modern organ. The pipes are large scale, inverted conical pipes, generally made of extra heavy metal. The tongues of the reeds are thick and the wind-pressure is extreme, occasionally being as high as 30 inches, whereas the wind-pressure of many Trumpets is only 4 or 6 inches, and sometimes even less. A 16 ft. extension of the Tuba is, frequently, called " **Ophecleide 16 ft.**," and the 32 ft. extension of the same stop in the Ped. is called " **Bombarde 32 ft.**"

The tone of a Tuba Mirabilis is most powerful and assertive, frequently harsh, being intended to stand out above the tone of the Full Organ. Sometimes the stop is called " **Tuba Magna,**" or " **Tuba Major.**" A **Tuba Minor,** frequently called " **Tuba,**" when the organ contains also a Tuba Mirabilis, is smaller and much less powerful than a Tuba Mirabilis. This stop is substituted for a Trumpet in the Gt., in some modern organs. The tone of the Tuba Minor is smooth and full, and possesses some blending property, though it is, frequently, less brilliant than the tone of a Trumpet, owing to the absence of many of the higher overtones.

Cornopean 8 ft., Sw. A Cornopean is practically the Trumpet of the Sw. organ; and as such, it is frequently made like a small-scale Trumpet. The best stops of this name, however, have a smoother and more refined tone than a Trumpet, and possess more blending property. Like a Trumpet, the pipes of a Cornopean are of inverted conical shape. They are of larger scale than the pipes of an Oboe, but smaller than those of a Trumpet. The tongues of the reeds are fairly thick, with more curvature than those of an Oboe.

The tone of a Cornopean is strong, full and resonant. This stop is valuable in the Sw. organ, and has many uses. It gives firmness and body to the tone of the Full Sw., and renders that tone influential when the Sw. is coupled to the Gt. If a Full Sw. is coupled to a F Gt. combination, opening and closing the swell produces more of an effect when there is a good Cornopean in the Sw. than when it is absent. Unlike a Gt. Trumpet, a Cornopean is a good solo stop, especially if it is combined with a few other stops. In a few cases, a Cornopean, combined with an Oboe, Flute 4 ft., Voix Céleste, and Vox Humana, suggests the tone of the lower register of the G string of a Violin, if this combination is used as a solo combination in that register. A Cornopean is also useful as the chorus reed of the Sw., and many effects in harmony are obtainable with this stop. Occasionally, it is necessary to substitute a Cornopean for an Oboe (or to add it to the Oboe) for a solo passage, when the only combination in the Gt. or Ch. which is available for a moving accompaniment is too loud for the Oboe.

Contra Fagotto 16 ft., or **Contra Bassoon 16 ft.**, **Sw.** While the name of this stop signifies a **Double Bassoon,** the stop is rarely voiced to imitate the tone of that instrument. In this country, a Contra Fagotto is very common as the 16 ft. reed-tone stop of the Sw. organ. It generally consists of slender-scale, inverted conical, metal pipes, with narrow reed tongues. The scale of both pipes and tongues is slenderer than those of an Oboe. The tone is generally soft, nasal, and somewhat piquant. It combines well with the 8 ft. Flutes, is a good solo stop, and forms an excellent 16 ft. foundation for the reed combinations. In large organs a **Double Trumpet 16 ft.** is frequently substituted for a Contra Fagotto, or is added to that stop in the Sw. organ. This stop is much like a 16 ft. Cornopean. It has more power and body than a Contra Fagotto, but it is less satisfactory as a solo stop. A large-scale Double Trumpet is found in the Gt. in some organs.

Clarinet 8 ft., Ch. Unlike the other reed-tone stops already described, a Clarinet has *cylindrical,* metal pipes, of about one-half the length of the pipes of the other 8 ft. reed stops. As the tongues of the reeds are much larger than those of the other reed stops, the unison pitch is obtained, notwithstanding the short pipes. The pipes generally flare at the upper ends, or are surmounted by a sliding bell which modifies the tone and assists in the tuning. By means of the above-mentioned details, a smooth, hollow reed-tone, of great beauty, is obtained. Cylindrical pipes for reed stops have a tendency to strengthen the even-numbered overtones, at the expense of the odd-numbered overtones; and, like stopped flue pipes, they produce a peculiar, hollow tone which is characteristic. The tone somewhat resembles the tone of the orchestral Clarinet. The treble of the stop is far superior, being smooth, even, and less shrill; but the bass of the stop possesses none of the richness of that portion of the tone of the orchestral instrument.

The stop is an excellent solo stop, used alone or combined with other stops. A modern Clarinet is effective in close harmony, in the middle octaves, but many of the older stops have a coarse and rattling tone which prevents such use. Full Ch. and Full Organ rarely includes the Clarinet, as its tone is not necessary or beneficial in such combinations.

Trombone 16 ft., Ped. In the Ped. organ, a 16 ft. reed-tone stop is, frequently, named " Trombone "; principally because the functions of the stop are similar to those of the Bass Trombone of the orchestra, rather than on account of any similarity of tone. The pipes, wood or metal, are inverted conical shape. The tongues of the reeds are heavy, and are often re-enforced by a weight attached to the lower end.

Contra Trombone 32 ft., Ped. Sometimes an independent stop, but frequently a 32 ft. extension of the 16 ft. Trombone. The principal function of these two stops is to give weight, body, and depth, to the Ped. notes, in Full Organ passages. Occasionally, the stop is used in melodic phrases, in the Ped. part, when F combinations are employed on the manuals.

Posaune 16 ft., Ped. Generally a heavy Trombone.

Tromba (or Trombe) 8 ft., Gt. or Ped. As a manual stop, a Tromba is a species of Trumpet. As a Ped. stop, a Tromba is generally an augmentation of a 16 ft. Trombone, by the addition of the necessary twelve upper pipes. The lower 30 (or 32) pipes serve as a Trombone 16 ft., and the upper 30 (or 32) pipes serve as a Tromba 8 ft. The middle 18 (or 20) pipes are thus used in both stops. The function of this stop is to supply the 8 ft. pitch of a similar character to the 16 ft. pitch of the Trombone, principally in Full Organ passages.

Clarion 4 ft., Gt. or Sw. This stop bears the same relation to an 8 ft. Trumpet that an Octave bears to an 8 ft. Diapason. It is, in reality, an Octave Trumpet, only it is of small scale and less powerful. In the Sw. this stop can be considered as an Octave Cornopean. The principal functions of the Clarion are to add brilliancy to the Full Sw. or Gt., and to supply the 4 ft. tones in the heavy reed combinations. Occasionally, the stop can be used with a 4 ft. Flute, playing an octave lower than the music is written, for a Trumpet combination, which is somewhat softer than the 8 ft. Trumpet.

Vox Humana 8 ft., Sw. or Ech. From a historical point of view, the Vox Humana received its name in several attempts (years ago) to imitate the tone of the human voice. Very little success resulted from these attempts. In a very few instances, the stop, combined with a Gedeckt which was, generally, slightly out of tune, and much influenced by various echoes and cross echoes of the barren auditoriums, produced an effect somewhat suggestive of a girlish soprano voice. Continued experimenting has developed a stop which possesses much beauty and usefulness, notwithstanding its failure as an imitation of the human voice.

It seems to me that the Vox Humana is a much-maligned stop, due largely to its unfortunate and inappropriate name. One English writer has written: " Instead of resembling the human voice, its tone is anything from Punch's squeak to the bleating of a nanny-goat." The stop has been variously dubbed " the gas pipe," and " Nux Vomica with a gargle." I suspect that the stop would escape much of the criticism, and would be judged on its merit as a distinctive tone-color, if it were called by some less inappropriate name. If organ stops were numbered like the stops in French reed organs, and this stop were " Number 36," no one would expect an imitation of the human voice, and hence, would not be disappointed. One would then accept the tone of the stop just as it sounds.

The tone of the best Vox Humanas, without resembling the tone of a human voice in the slightest degree, has a strikingly beautiful quality of tone. Aside from its own beauty as an individual tone-quality, its " timbre-creating " power is of much value in stop combinations, but it must be used with moderation. When a Vox Humana is combined with reed-tone or string-tone stops, it may be called a good *tone-color intensifier*, if I may be allowed to use the term, in the absence of any other satisfactory term. The tone of an Oboe, as a solo stop, is frequently improved and rendered more animated by the addition of a Vox Humana. The tone of a Voix Céleste, if it is a real string-tone Voix Céleste, is intensified, and frequently seems to have more vitality, if a soft Vox Humana is combined with it. A combination, consisting of a Cornopean, Oboe, Salicional, and Flute 4 ft., as a solo combination, frequently gains warmth and emotion by the addition of a Vox Humana. These illustrations are but a few of the many instances when this stop may be used to improve other tone-colors. A Vox Humana sounds well alone, as a solo stop or in harmony. It combines well with a Gedeckt, Rohr Floete, or a 4 ft. Flute.

The pipes are large-scale, cylindrical, metal pipes, of varying lengths. The stop is always an 8 ft. stop in pitch, but the lowest pipe is never 8 ft., or even 4 ft., in length. The length varies with different pipe-makers, from about 2 ft. down to even 10 inches. The pitch of each pipe is, therefore, controlled entirely by the reed, and each pipe-maker has his own method of shaping the tongues. In this country, the tops of the pipes are, generally, covered with a metal cap, which almost closes the upper ends of the pipes; only a narrow crack at one edge being left open. This cap regulates the tone to a large degree. The tone is thin and nasal, but of much character. The Tremolo is always used with the stop; in fact, most modern Vox Humanas are connected directly with a Tremolo, which is thus drawn with the one draw-stop. In this country, a very few Vox Humanas have two pipes to each note. The value of the additional pipe is yet to be proved.

Musette 8 ft. This stop was originally an imitation of the bagpipe and the tone was produced by " free reeds " (q. v.). In recent years, it has consisted of slender " beating reeds " and very small-scale pipes. The construction of the pipes varies with individual pipe-makers. Sometimes the pipes have metal caps and are pierced with a small hole about one-third from the top. The tone is a smooth reed-tone of piquant quality.

Free Reeds. A variety of reed-tone pipes, whose tone is produced by *free reeds* (similar to the reeds of a cabinet organ), instead of by *beating reeds*, was somewhat popular at one time. Now-a-days, they are somewhat rarely employed, as more satisfactory tone-colors can be produced and kept in order by the use of beating reeds. There still exist some good specimens of " free reed " stops in old organs: e. g., **Cor Anglaise, Cremorne, Clarinet, Euphone,** and **Physharmonica.** The last-named stop is the only one of the list which is still made with " free reeds."

A few stops have such a hybrid quality of tone that they cannot be positively classed with any one of the five qualities of tone: e. g., Quintadena, Gemshorn, Erzahler and Nitsua.

A **Quintadena 8 ft., Sw. or Ch.**, may be called an outgrowth of a **Quintaton (or Quintaten)**, which is a narrow Gedeckt, made and voiced so as to sound the twelfth (second overtone) quite prominently with the ground tone. In this country, the Quintadena has been greatly developed, and is now a distinctive stop, quite unlike the original Quintaton.

The pipes of a Quintadena are large-scale, metal pipes, with low, narrow mouths and beards. They are stopped at the top with sliding metal caps, and are so voiced that they sound the twelfth almost as loud as the fundamental tone. In the classification of stops a Quintadena must necessarily be called " a hybrid." The stopped pipes produce only the even-numbered overtones, like a Gedeckt, but their large scale and the shape of the mouths prevent any similarity to the Gedeckt tone-quality. In this country two kinds of Quintadenas are in use. A rather loud stop, voiced for solo use only, is frequently placed in the Ch., and a much softer one for both solo and harmony use is found in the Sw. The principal difference in the two stops is in their volume and power.

In the Sw. a Quintadena is a useful stop both by itself and in combination. It frequently can be substituted for a Salicional, for a variety of tone-color, and can be combined with a Gedeckt or Flute 4 ft. (much the same as a Vox Humana), both for harmony and soft solo uses. It may be added to other combinations as a " timbre-creator." The louder stop in the Ch. is a beautiful solo stop.

Gemshorn 8 ft., Ch. or Gt. This stop is also a hybrid. Some people class it as a Flute-tone stop, while others are undecided whether to call it a string-tone or a Diapason-tone stop. The pipes are slender and taper from the mouth to the top of the pipe, being about one-third of the diameter at the top. This shape causes the prominence of the fourth and fifth overtones, to which is attributed the peculiar tone-quality.

The tone is soft, slightly reedy in character, but of a clear and beautiful quality. Being somewhat louder, and possessing more character, than the tone of a Dulciana, a Gemshorn is very useful for soft accompaniments, in passages which require more definiteness in the accompaniment than can be obtained with a Dulciana. The stop is useful by itself, for its own tone-color; is a good soft solo stop; and adds character when it is combined with other soft stops, such as Melodia and Gemshorn, or Flute 4 ft. and Gemshorn. Occasionally we find a 4 ft. Gemshorn in the Sw. or Ch., in place of a Violina, or Fugara.

Erzahler 8 ft. A modern stop, invented by Mr. Ernest M. Skinner, of a pronounced quality of tone, which is of a hybrid character. The pipes are conical shaped, even more so than Gemshorn pipes, and produce a tone which exerts considerable influence of a varied character in small combinations. This influence is largely due to the great prominence of the first overtone (octave).

The **Kleiner Erzahler** has two ranks (4 and 2 ft.) and is voiced much softer than the 8 ft. variety.

Nitsua 8 ft. A stop somewhat like a Gemshorn which is found in the Austin organs.

E. The Percussion Stops and Their Use

Outside of the various " Traps " which are found in theatre organs
and need not be considered here, the most common Percussion stops are
the Chimes and Carillons, the latter also called " Celesta " and " Harp."

Chimes, or " Cathedral Chimes " as they are occasionally named,
consist of 20 (sometimes more) tubular bells, hung on a frame, and
sounded by the stroke of electro-pneumatic hammers which are generally
covered with felt. The most usual compass of a set of Chimes is from
A to e^2 (20 notes).

The tone of Chimes consists of a series of prominent overtones or
harmonics in which the fundamental tone is either absent or so faint
that it cannot be discerned. The fourth overtone of the natural harmonic series is so overpowering in the tone of a chime that it determines
the pitch of the chime. To illustrate, the organist should sound one of
the chimes several times — C for example — to accustom the ears to
the confusion of overtones and to definitely locate the pitch of the chime
in the ear. Then he should play the triad of C (C, E, G) on a soft stop,
while continuing to sound the chime. It will be observed that the tone
of the chime does not accord with the tones of the triad. One will, at
first, declare that the chime is " out of tune." If the organist should
sound the chime again and play the triad of A-flat (A-flat, C and E-flat),
it will be found that the tone of the chime is perfectly consonant with
this triad. While the recognized pitch of the chime is C, its harmonic
series of overtones is A-flat, E-flat, A-flat, C, etc. The fourth overtone
(C) is so prominent that it determines the pitch of the chime, but the
series of overtones exerts so much influence on the tone of the chime
that the chime sounds more or less " out of tune " with any other series
of overtones, such as the triad of C (C, E, G) or the triad of F
(F, A, C).

As a further illustration, the organist should play the first four
measures of the hymn-tune " Bethany " (" Nearer, my God, to Thee ")
on the Chimes.

Without the harmony of the hymn-tune, the melody sounds pleasing
when played on the Chimes; but if the organist plays the harmony on a
soft stop at the same time that he plays the chimes, he will observe that
the chimes marked 2, 3, 4, 7, 8, and 10 sound dissonant to the harmony
— " out of tune " — while the chimes marked 1, 5, 6, and 9 are perfectly
in accord with the harmony. The fourth overtone of the natural harmonic series, to which reference is made, is in the " third " of a triad;
and only those notes of the melody which are the third of their respective

triads will be perfectly in accord with the harmony. According to the overtones of the chimes, the melody should be harmonized thus to have each chime sound perfectly in tune:

If these triads are played with the chimes, it will be found that each chime sounds " in tune "; but even the harmonic progressions of the most ultra-modern composers have *not yet* prepared our ears for such progressions of harmony.

By exercising a little care, the organist can produce many beautiful effects with the Chimes, but if he ignores the scientific principle of the overtones in the chimes he will produce effects which will distress every musical ear.

Notice how Meyerbeer treated one bell in the fourth act of " The Huguenots," where the bell is sounded for the massacre of the Hugue-nots. A stroke of the bell sounding tenor F is accompanied by the B-natural below, played on the bassoons and clarinets. This B-natural is the same as C-flat, which is the sixth overtone of the series of which F is the fourth overtone (low D-flat being the fundamental tone). The B-natural is a diminished fifth below the F of the bell, and is in perfect accord with the bell. The effect is very impressive. If the composer had written a note of the triad of F (C or A) for the wind instruments the effect would have been intolerable.

There are numerous themes or melodies in which a chime can be sounded with some of the notes of the melody and produce a pleasing effect, provided the chimes are not sounded with the intervening notes of the melody. If the organist accompanies the melody which is being played on the chimes with the harmony played on a soft stop, especially if the harmony is played *below* the pitch of the Chimes, his musical ear frequently will be shocked. It is sometimes possible to accompany the melody which is played on the Chimes with the harmony, if the latter is played on a soft stop or combination *two or three octaves higher* than the octave of the Chimes. Such hymn-tunes as " Eventide " (" Abide with me ") and " Lux Benigna " (" Lead, Kindly Light ") are suitable for such treatment. If the harmony is played in the upper octaves of the Swell with the Vox Humana and Gedeckt, or with the Voix Céleste and Flute 4 ft., the difference between the harmonic series of the Chimes and the chords is less pronounced and the Tremolo assists in destroying the apparent dissonance between the harmonics of the two tone-colors.

Various composers of organ music have introduced the Chimes in the registration of certain sections of their compositions with very pleas-ing effect: viz.,

Evening Chimes	Wheeldon
Echo Bells	Brewer
Evening Bells and Cradle Song	Macfarlane
Chanson du Soir	Frysinger
In Moonlight	Kinder
Sunset (Pastoral Suite)	Demarest
Sunset and Evening Bells	Federlein
Meditation (from Suite in G-minor)	Truette
Vesper Hymn	Truette

Carillons. The organ stop called "Carillons," like its prototype in the orchestra, from time to time has varied considerably in form. Four or five distinct forms have been used with different degrees of success, and, in like manner, the name of the stop has varied. Besides "Carillons" the stop has been called "Glockenspiel," "Gongs," "Chimes," "Stahlspiel," "Clochettes," and in the present day, "Harp" and "Celesta."

One form of this stop was a set of small bells which were struck by some form of a pneumatic hammer.

An ancient form of the stop which is now obsolete, was a set of gongs, over which was situated a set of metal bars. The resonant gongs were made of brass and were tuned by being filled with plaster of Paris, until the required pitch was obtained. This form of Carillons was much affected by the temperature of the building and rarely remained in tune.

A third form of Carillons is a set of tubular bells; but in this country, this form of the stop is called "Chimes" (q. v.).

A fourth form of the stop, which is now also obsolete, was a mixture stop or combination of flue pipes, of different pitch, but always tuned to a high pitch, such as the 12th, 17th and 22nd. The stop was generally used with some kind of a 4 ft. Flute, such as a Night Horn, to give definiteness to the pitch; and a Tremolo was added to produce a wave-like effect. These stops were rarely in tune, as the pipes were so small that slight changes of temperature put them out of tune.

Different organists with different organs have produced bell effects with special combinations of stops peculiar to the individual organ. On one organ, a Bourdon 16 ft., Flautino 2 ft., and Vox Humana produce a good bell imitation. On another organ a soft Gedeckt in the Gt., coupled with a Harmonic Flute of 8 ft. pitch and a Tremolo in the Solo organ, with which is combined a soft Céleste in the Sw., produces a fairly good bell effect.

A fifth form of Carillons, variously called "Carillons," "Harp," or "Celesta," which is most successful and popular now-a-days, is a set of bars, made either of steel or glass, which are struck by pneumatic hammers. These bars are placed either in a horizontal position on a frame, or are suspended in a vertical position from a frame. Underneath each bar is placed a short section of wood pipe with its lower end closed. This pipe acts as a resonator; adds breadth and roundness to the tone, which would, otherwise, be of thin metallic quality; and prevents the pitch being easily affected by changes of temperature. Felt hammers, somewhat like those of the pianoforte, are so arranged that, by means of a collapsible pneumatic bellows, they are caused to strike the bars and rebound to their normal position. Generally some form of a damper is connected with the action to prevent the bar vibrating after the key is released. The tone thus produced is of a peculiar bell quality, and when heard at some distance is very pleasing.

Carillons.

In organ music the Carillons ("Celesta" or "Harp") can be used with considerable success in several different manners. Short arpeggioed chords, as at A, of eight or ten notes, produce a good harp effect. Sometimes this effect is heightened if a soft Gedeckt or 4 ft. Flute is added.

Carillons and Gedeckt.

A good variation of this effect, which sounds like two distinct manuals, is to use the Gedeckt with the Carillons, and sustain the chord which has been played in a quick arpeggio manner as at B.

Carillons.

Another good effect is produced by playing two or three notes together in thirds or chords, as shown in a short excerpt from a Capriccio of Faulkes at C. These should be played staccato and if alternated with a Flute stop the effect is improved.

A passage in the Berceuse of the same composer (D) can be played with good effect on the Carillons while the melody is played with the other hand on the Vox Humana.

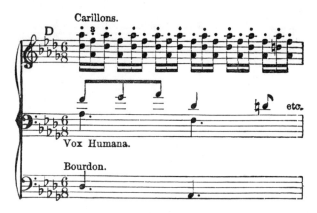

Slow melodies in single notes and rapid scale passages frequently do not sound well when played on the Carillons. With the former the pitch is too wavering and uncertain. With the latter the fact that the steel bars vibrate beyond the length of the notes, even if dampers are provided, makes such passages discordant. With chords and arpeggios this condition acts advantageously and adds to the good effect of the chords and arpeggios. The Carillons combine well with flutes of eight and four-foot pitch and sound well in contrast to strings and soft reeds, but when combined with strings and reeds in the same chords or arpeggios they are less satisfactory.

F. TREMOLO (TREMULANT)

The **Tremolo** is a mechanical appliance which is attached to the wind-chest of each of the manuals except that of the Gt. organ, by means of which a rapid and regular disturbing of the wind supply causes an undulation of the tone of such pipes as are on the wind-chest with which the Tremolo is attached.

The effect of a Tremolo on the tone of the pipes is somewhat similar to the effect of the shake of the left hand, with which players of the violin and violoncello produce a vibrato. With the tone of some stops and combinations, a Tremolo adds nerve and vitality. With the tone of other stops and combinations, the effect of a Tremolo may be called a " mixer " of tone-colors and overtones.

A good illustration of the " mixing " property of a Tremolo is the familiar practice of an artist painter. He paints two contiguous lines of different colors; e. g., green and yellow. Before the paint is dry, the painter, with a soft brush, makes a short and gentle wavy motion across the two colors, in such a manner that the line of demarcation is entirely obliterated, and a rainbow effect, or a complete blending of the colors, is the result. The outside edges of the two colors preserve their original color, but elsewhere the separate colors cannot be distinguished.

A somewhat similar effect on the resultant tone-color of a combination of stops is often produced by the Tremolo. For a practical illustration, draw the Sw. Bourdon 16 ft., and the Flautino 2 ft. Hold a chord with the R. H. anywhere in the two upper octaves of the manual. The effect will generally be unpleasant. The individual tones of the two stops stand out too prominently. The tone of the Flautino is the third overtone of the Bourdon and does not blend at all with the fundamental tone of the Bourdon. If a Tremolo is added, an entirely different effect is produced as the tones of the two stops are thereby " mixed " and blend well. The same effect will be noticed with a Vox Humana without a Tremolo. The prominent overtones which are characteristic of this stop do not blend at all until a Tremolo is added.

Notwithstanding this valuable " mixing " property of a Tremolo, quite a number of organists condemn the stop altogether, and pronounce it " a cheap and tawdry abomination." These same organists recognize and admire the vitality which a solo violinist or cellist imparts to sustained melodies with the aid of the vibrato or tremolo. The fact that there is no similar effect possible with the wood-wind instruments of the orchestra, cannot properly justify the stigmatizing of the effect of a Tremolo as an illegitimate effect. It is distinctly an organ effect and can be used with great advantage; though it is, of course, possible to weary the ears with an excess. The Tremolo is much misunderstood, both in its use and in its abuse.

CHAPTER V

COUPLERS AND OCTAVE COUPLERS

COUPLERS are mechanical contrivances by means of which the various departments of an organ can be connected and played as one department: e. g., by means of the Sw. to Gt. Coupler, the Sw. organ is "coupled" to the Gt. organ, and can be played from the Gt. manual, with or without the stops of the Gt. sounding. There are eight kinds of Couplers; viz.: —

Manual to Manual	Unison	e. g.	Sw. to Gt.	8 ft.
Manual to Manual	Sub	"	Sw. to Gt.	16 ft.
Manual to Manual	Super	"	Sw. to Gt.	4 ft.
Manual on Itself	Sub	"	Sw. to Sw.	16 ft.
Manual on Itself	Super	"	Sw. to Sw.	4 ft.
Manual to Pedal	Unison	"	Gt. to Ped.	8 ft.
Manual to Pedal	Super	"	Sw. to Ped.	4 ft.
Pedal to Pedal	Super	"	Ped. to Ped.	4 ft.

The Manual to Manual Couplers connect one manual with another manual, so that the first-named manual can be played from and with the second-named manual. The Manual to Pedal Couplers connect a manual with the Pedal. The Manual and Pedal on Itself Couplers cause each key to sound its octave. (Note: Care should be taken to use correct names for the couplers. In these couplers the first department of the name of the coupler is coupled to the second department of that name: i. e., Sw. to Gt. means that the Sw. is coupled to the Gt., not the reverse. The term "Ped. to Gt.," which is frequently found in printed music, is a misnomer. The Ped. cannot be played from the Gt. The correct name is Gt. to Ped.)

These couplers are grouped into three classes: viz., Unison (8 ft.), Sub (16 ft.), and Super (4 ft.) Couplers. The Unison Couplers couple the same notes between the manuals or between the manual and Pedal. The Sub Couplers couple the octave below, and the Super Couplers couple the octave above. In modern organs the individual Sub and Super Couplers are more frequently named, "16 ft." and "4 ft." Couplers, although collectively they are called "Sub" and "Super" Couplers.

The term "Super-Octave Coupler" in old organs caused some confusion, on account of the presence of a stop named "Super-Octave," which sounded two octaves above the unison pitch. In modern organs this stop is generally named "Fifteenth," the significance of the name being obvious and the confusion avoided.

In many modern organs the couplers do not act *through* one another: i. e., a Gt. to Ped. Coupler does not include the Sw. when the Sw. to Gt. is on. A Sw. to Gt. does not include the Sw. to Sw. 16 or 4 ft., if these couplers are on. In a few modern organs, some of the couplers are specially designed to act through one another. There are advantages and disadvantages with both kinds of couplers. In a few organs, in which the couplers do not act through one another, a special coupler, "Gt. to Sw.," is provided. This enables the organist to use Full Gt., Full Sw., and Sw. to Sw. 16 and 4 ft. Couplers, together, playing on the Sw. In other organs, Sw. to Gt. 16 and 4 ft. Couplers are provided (in addition to the Sw. to Sw. 16 and 4 ft. Couplers), which obviates the necessity of the Gt. to Sw. Coupler.

The Unison Manual Couplers (also called "8 ft. Couplers"), Sw. to Gt., Ch. to Gt., and Sw. to Ch., as well as the additional couplers for the Solo and Echo, when the organ contains these manuals, have two uses: first, for the purpose of combining the stops of two manuals into one tonal combination; and second, for the purpose of re-enforcing the tone of one manual by the addition of several stops of another manual.

The Sw. to Gt. Coupler is probably the most used, and likewise the most abused, coupler in the organ. Many organists draw this coupler when they sit down at the organ, and do not push it off until they close the organ. While it is a most useful adjunct in playing, it is frequently unnecessary and sometimes objectionable to have it on. In small organs the tone of the Gt. organ, except when only the soft stops are being used, is frequently thin, unless the 8 and 4 ft. stops of the Sw. are coupled. Furthermore, many of the louder combinations of the Gt. are enriched by the addition of several stops of the Sw. Obviously, Full Gt. is improved by the addition of Full Sw. On the other hand, if a Flute solo is played on either an 8 or 4 ft. Flute stop on the Gt., the Sw. to Gt. Coupler, if on, mars the effect. Again, contrast is frequently destroyed, when the player is alternating between somewhat soft combinations on the Sw. and on the Gt., if the manuals are coupled; e. g., if the player is alternating between the Gt., with 8 and 4 ft. Flutes, and the Sw., with Oboe, Salicional and Flute 4 ft., the sharp contrast between these two combinations is missed, if the Sw. stops are heard when playing on the Flutes. These two combinations coupled together produce a very pleasing effect, but the contrast between the separate combinations is sacrificed if the Sw. to Gt. Coupler is on.

Occasionally, an organist plays a solo on the Gt., with the accompaniment on the Sw., without the Sw. to Gt. A short F passage for the Gt. Diapason follows, which in turn is followed by a repetition of the first passage for solo and accompaniment. To add the Sw. to Gt., when drawing the Gt. Diapason, is unnecessary and frequently awkward. Many similar passages are simplified, without any loss of effect, by omitting the Sw. to Gt. Coupler.

The Ch. to Gt. Coupler, except in large organs, is somewhat limited in usefulness. A few solo combinations, such as the 8 ft. Flute of the Gt. combined with the 8 and 4 ft. Flutes of the Ch.; the Gamba of the Gt. combined with the 4 ft. Flute of the Ch.; and the 8 ft. Flute of the Gt. combined with the Clarinet of the Ch., are useful. The MF combinations of the Gt. are sometimes enriched by coupling the Flutes of the Ch. to the Gt. In larger organs a much greater variety of similar combinations is possible.

The Sw. to Ch. Coupler is likewise limited in usefulness. A few distinct combinations of the stops of the two manuals are possible, especially in large organs. All the 8 and 4 ft. stops of each manual, with the Sw. to Ch. Coupler, or Full Sw. and Full Ch. coupled together, produce good accompaniment combinations for the louder solos of the Gt.

In old organs which have mechanical action, the manual couplers generally make the key action so stiff, that rapid execution in Toccatas and like compositions is extremely difficult, if not impossible. In playing such compositions, it is advisable, and oftentimes imperative, to omit the Sw. to Gt. Coupler, until the last chords of the composition. It is preferable to sacrifice a little of the volume of tone, rather than to seriously mar the execution of the composition.

Manual to Pedal Couplers. The primary uses of the Manual to Pedal Couplers are: first, to re-enforce the tone of the pedal stops; second, to enable the performer to play with the Pedal, the bass notes of the manuals which cannot conveniently be played with the left hand; and third, to produce solo effects on the Pedal keyboard. When both hands are playing harmony on one manual, and the pedal-part is a melodic bass part of that harmony, the manual should generally be coupled to the Pedal. If the pedal-part is an independent pedal-part, instead of a melodic bass, or if the pedal notes are staccato bass notes, it is frequently more effective to omit the Manual to Pedal Coupler, except in loud passages when the coupler is necessary. If there is no soft 8 ft. stop in the Pedal organ, and the 16 ft. stop proves too indefinite in pitch and power, an 8 ft. Flute on one of the manuals can be coupled to the Pedal, to supply the additional tone which is lacking in the Pedal organ.

If various short phrases are played alternately on two different manuals, and the changes are too sudden to permit changing of the Manual to Pedal Couplers, it is frequently advisable to compromise, by coupling one of the manuals to the Pedal, letting that coupler suffice for all the phrases. When this is necessary, the organist should select that coupler which does not prove objectionable with either manual; e. g., if the phrases alternate rapidly between the Sw. (with 8 and 4 ft. stops and Oboe) and the Ch. (with Melodia and Flute 4 ft.), the Sw. to Ped. does not answer for both manuals, as the Oboe stands out too prominently in the pedal notes when the phrase is played on the Ch. On the other hand, the Ch. to Ped. is less objectionable when playing on the Sw. On some organs, however, even this compromise is impossible, as the Flute 4 ft. in the Ch. stands out too prominently when one is playing on the Sw.

It is perhaps needless to state that the Manual to Pedal Couplers should always be used in very loud passages, when the pedal part is the real bass of the passage.

OCTAVE COUPLERS

In considering Octave Couplers, it seems advisable to consider first the old-style octave couplers, as their effects and uses are not only much limited, but are radically different from those of the modern octave couplers. The oldest octave coupler is the " Sw. to Gt. 8-Va.," which connects the octave above of the Sw. to the Gt. This coupler was placed in nearly every small two-manual organ which was built thirty or forty years ago, as well as in a few three-manual organs of that period. As the action of these old organs in nearly every case was mechanical, these octave couplers moved the keys of the Sw. organ and made the action of the Gt. very stiff.

The prime object of this octave coupler was to increase the power of the organ, without a corresponding increase of the cost, which would have been necessary if additional stops had been provided. Unfortunately, this " increased power " was frequently shrill and objectionable. However, in some of these old organs which are still in existence, a few fairly agreeable combinations can be obtained, with the aid of the Sw. to Gt. 8-Va. Coupler. If the softest stop in the Sw. is drawn, with the Sw. to Gt. and Sw. to Gt. 8-Va. Couplers, quite an agreeable combinational tone is produced by playing on the Gt. manual (without any stops of the Gt. organ drawn). Naturally, the character of this combination is much varied by the character of the softest stop in the Sw. In many of these old organs, the softest stop is variously called, " Gamba," " Salicional," or " Viola," but it possesses only a fraction of the real tone-quality of these stops, as we know them now-a-days. If the softest stop happens to be a Keraulophon, Dulciana, or Æoline, the tone of the combination is much more delicate and agreeable. Occasionally, a St. Diapason in the Sw. can be used to advantage with these two couplers; and quite rarely, a Flute 4 ft., if one plays an octave lower.

Sometimes an agreeable combination on the Gt. is produced by drawing a Dulciana (or Keraulophon) on the Gt., the softest stop that is on the Sw., and the Sw. to Gt. 8-Va. Coupler (without the Sw. to Gt. Unison Coupler). A good Flute-tone combination is obtained by drawing the 8 ft. Flute (Melodia, Clarabella, or Hohl Floete) on the Gt., the St. Diapason on the Sw., and the Sw. to Gt. 8-Va. Coupler. Occasionally, a solo combination on the Gt., corresponding to the Melodia and Piccolo of a modern Ch. organ, can be produced by drawing the 8 ft. Flute on the Gt., the Flute 4 ft. on the Sw., and the Sw. to Gt. 8-Va. Coupler. The accompaniment of such a solo combination, if the organ is a two-manual organ, must be played on the Sw. an octave lower than it is printed. Adding the Sw. to Gt. Unison Coupler sometimes gives an agreeable variation of this combination.

As I have reiterated many times, the agreeable effect of each of these combinations is much influenced by the relative power of the stops named, in the individual organ. On some old organs every one of these combinations is pleasing; but on some other old organs, many, if not all, of these combinations are objectionable. In many of these old organs the key action, being mechanical, is so stiff that it is almost impossible to use both the Sw. to Gt. and the Sw. to Gt. 8-Va. Couplers in rapid music.

While all the combinations mentioned above, which include the Sw. to Gt. 8-Va. Coupler, are intended specially for old organs, many of them

can be used with even greater effect on modern organs. The presence of
the Sw. to Sw. 16 and 4 ft. Couplers in modern organs (especially treated
later) does away with the necessity of resorting to the roundabout
method of obtaining some of the desired combinations, which is necessary
in the old organs.

The next octave coupler which came into use was the Ch. to Gt. Sub-
Octave Coupler, which was introduced primarily to add 16 ft. tone to
the Gt. organ, without providing a separate 16 ft. stop. This coupler
was rarely included except in organs which had pneumatic action;
hence, it did not stiffen the key action of the Gt. when it was drawn. The
use of this coupler in modern organs will be considered later.

Since the introduction of the two octave couplers, previously mentioned, there has been a steady and rapid improvement in organ action,
which has been accompanied by a corresponding improvement and increase of octave couplers. In a modern four-manual, electric organ,
which contains an Echo organ, it is possible to have over twenty octave
couplers, as follows: —

List of Octave Couplers in a Modern Four-Manual Organ

Sw. to Sw.	16 ft.	
Sw. to Sw.	4 ft.	
Ch. to Ch.	16 ft.	Somewhat rare.
Ch. to Ch.	4 ft.	
So. to So.	16 ft.	
So. to So.	4 ft.	
Ech. to Ech.	16 ft.	
Ech. to Ech.	4 ft.	
Gt. to Gt.	16 ft.	Rare and questionable.
Gt. to Gt.	4 ft.	Somewhat rare.
Sw. to Gt.	16 ft.	
Sw. to Gt.	4 ft.	
Ch. to Gt.	16 ft.	
Ch. to Gt.	4 ft.	Somewhat rare.
So. to Gt.	16 ft.	
So. to Gt.	4 ft.	
Sw. to Ch.	16 ft.	Somewhat rare.
Sw. to Ch.	4 ft.	
Gt. to Ped.	4 ft.	Somewhat rare.
Sw. to Ped.	4 ft.	
Ch. to Ped.	4 ft.	Somewhat rare.
So. to Ped.	4 ft.	
Ped. to Ped.	4 ft.	

In modern organs, the pipes of the Sw. are generally extended an
octave above the compass of the manual, 73 pipes in all, so that the
4 ft. Coupler may have the same effect in the upper octave of the manual as in the other octaves. Otherwise, the octaves would cease at c^3
and the notes above this note would sound much weaker than those
below. In a few organs, the pipes of some or all of the other manuals
are also extended. The only disadvantage of this extension of the compass is, that the pipes of the extended octave are so tiny that they are
much affected by the slightest change of temperature and are generally
more or less out of tune.

In modern organs, there are three distinct uses of the octave couplers (16 and 4 ft.) : First, they are used in various ways to strengthen the tone of the louder combinations; such as increasing the power of Full Sw., by adding the 4 ft., 16 ft., or both, couplers. Second, they are used to produce a variety of distinct tonal effects; such as a Flute-tone stop with a 4 ft. coupler, a string-tone stop with a 16 ft. coupler, or a combination of the two colors with one or both couplers. Lastly, they are very valuable for the purpose of modifying the tone of solo combinations; such as adding a 16 ft. Coupler to a reed or string-tone solo stop, or to a combination of such stops.

The first use of the octave couplers just mentioned, — to increase the power of a manual or of the whole organ — is fraught with danger. Frequently the Full Organ of a small organ, which, otherwise, has an agreeable though somewhat subdued tone, is rendered almost intolerable by the addition and frequent use of an octave coupler. If this organ has but a few stops in the Gt., and the 4 ft. Flute of the Sw. is a loud one, the Sw. to Gt. 4 ft. Coupler renders the Full Organ harsh and shrill. If this 4 ft. Flute is omitted when the octave coupler is on, the effect is much less offensive, but there is an inborn tendency, among young organists, to draw all the stops in sight, when playing FF, even if one particular stop spoils the effect of the whole organ. In larger organs, the above mentioned 4 ft. Flute is generally less obtrusive, and besides, there are more and heavier stops in the Gt. to absorb and balance the tone of this Flute in octaves.

In a large Swell organ, the addition of the 4 ft. Coupler adds both brilliancy and power. As such a Swell organ always has between six and ten 8 ft. stops, and one or two 16 ft. stops, the effect of the octaves on the 4 ft. stops is counterbalanced by the addition of the octaves of the 16 and 8 ft. stops. If this Swell organ has 73 pipes for each stop, the upper octave of the manual is provided with the additional octaves, when the 4 ft. Coupler is on. Otherwise, the upper octave of the manual should be used sparingly, when the 4 ft. Coupler is on, as the octaves of the coupler end with c^3 and the notes above c^3 are proportionately weak.

Using the 4 ft. Coupler on the Ch., for the purpose of increasing the power of that manual, also requires special thought. If the Piccolo (2 ft.) of the Ch. is on, with the 4 ft. Coupler, the effect is generally very objectionable. The best method to add power to the Ch., by means of the Ch. to Ch. 4 ft. Coupler, is to use only the 16 and 8 ft. stops, when the 4 ft. Coupler is on. If the 4 ft. Flute is not very loud, it can be included, if the music does not run too high.

The 16 ft. couplers, when used for the purpose of increasing the power of a manual, also require more thought than is frequently given to them. The Sw. to Sw. 16 ft. Coupler frequently causes the Full Sw. to sound gruff and objectionable. This is generally due to the Sw. Bourdon 16 ft., which becomes a 32 ft. manual stop, if the Sw. to Sw. 16 ft. Coupler is on. When this Bourdon is somewhat loud, the effect of the Sw. to Sw. 16 ft. Coupler is improved if the Bourdon is omitted. A 16 ft. reed-tone stop (Contra Fagotto) frequently produces a similar ob-

jectionable effect, and is better omitted if the Sw. to Sw. 16 ft. Coupler
is on.   The Ch. to Gt. 16 ft. Coupler is useful in adding 16 ft. tone to
the Gt. organ, but the 16 ft. stop of the Ch. frequently should be
omitted, as it produces a 32 ft. manual effect, which is not often desired.

In very large organs, the objectionable features of the octave couplers
are much minimized; and furthermore, using both the 16 ft. and 4 ft.
couplers together frequently overcomes the objectionable feature of either
coupler when used singly.

The Second Use of the Octave Couplers

In a moderate-sized Swell organ there are at least two distinct combinations of 8 and 4 ft. Flute-tone.   Practically every Swell organ contains an 8 ft. Flute stop (Gedeckt, St. Diapason, or Rohr Floete) and a
4 ft. Flute (Flauto Traverso, Harmonic Flute, Rohr Floete, or Wald
Floete).   These two stops together produce a combination of 8 and 4 ft.
Flute-tone.   Likewise, nearly every moderate-sized Swell organ contains
either a 16 ft. Bourdon or a 16 ft. Lieblich Gedeckt.   This 16 ft. stop
combined with the 8 ft. Flute-tone stop, if one plays an octave higher,
produces another combination of 8 and 4 ft. Flute-tone, but of a somewhat different character from the first-mentioned combination.   In this
Swell organ the number of 8 and 4 ft. Flute-tone combinations is increased from two to five, by means of the 16 and 4 ft. couplers.   The exact difference in tone-color between some of these combinations may be
slight, but the discerning organist has the chance to choose the individual combination which, in both color and power, best produces the
effect desired.   The five combinations are: —

1.   Gedeckt 8 ft. and Flauto Traverso 4 ft.
2.   Bourdon 16 ft. and Gedeckt 8 ft. (playing an octave higher).
3.   Gedeckt 8 ft. and 4 ft. Coupler.
4.   Bourdon 16 ft. and 4 ft. Coupler (playing an octave higher).
5.   Flauto Traverso 4 ft. and 16 ft. Coupler.

The real difference between Nos. 2 and 3 is as follows: in No. 2
(playing an octave higher) the 8 ft. tone from the Bourdon is generally
softer than the 4 ft. tone from the Gedeckt; while in No. 3 the 4 ft. tone
from the 4 ft. Coupler is of exactly the same power as the 8 ft. tone of
the Gedeckt.   The difference between Nos. 3 and 4 is very slight, but
No. 4 has a trifle more delicate tone, as the Bourdon is softer than the
Gedeckt.

The above illustration with three Flute-tone stops can be partially
duplicated with two string-tone stops.   It will be readily observed how
the finer shades of tone-color can be produced by a discriminating use
of the stops and octave couplers.

With a combination of two Flute-tone stops of 8 and 4 ft. pitch and
two string-tone stops of 8 and 4 ft. pitch, the variety of effects can be
increased, with the aid of the octave couplers, from 15 to 60.   In the
following table is indicated the number of combinations (60) which are
possible with these four stops combined with the 16 and 4 ft. couplers.

The term "combination" is somewhat ambiguous, in referring to single stops, but it has long been customary to use the term in this manner, as there is no other word which designates the use of the various stops singly and collectively. The fifteen combinations numbered 1, 5, 9, 13, 17, 21, 25, 29, 33, 37, 41, 45, 49, 53, and 57 are possible without the aid of the couplers.

LIST OF 60 POSSIBLE COMBINATIONS WITH FOUR STOPS AND THE OCTAVE COUPLERS

1.	Salicional			
2.	"	with 16	ft.	
3.	"	" 4	"	
4.	"	" 16 & 4	"	
5.	Gedeckt			
6.	"	" 16	"	(upper three octaves only)
7.	"	" 4	"	
8.	"	" 16 & 4	"	(upper three octaves only)
9.	Flute 4 ft.			
10.	"	" 16	"	
11.	"	" 4	"	(lower three octaves only)
12.	"	" 16 & 4	"	
13.	Violina			
14.	"	" 16	"	
15.	"	" 4	"	(lower three octaves only)
16.	"	" 16 & 4	"	
17.	Gedeckt and Salicional			
18.	" " "	" 16	"	(upper three octaves only)
19.	" " "	" 4	"	
20.	" " "	" 16 & 4	"	
21.	Gedeckt and Flute 4 ft.			
22.	" " "	" 16	"	
23.	" " "	" 4	"	
24.	" " "	" 16 & 4	"	
25.	Gedeckt and Violina			
26.	" " "	" 16	"	
27.	" " "	" 4	"	
28.	" " "	" 16 & 4	"	
29.	Salicional and Flute 4 ft.			
30.	" " " "	" 16	"	
31.	" " " "	" 4	"	
32.	" " " "	" 16 & 4	"	
33.	Salicional and Violina			
34.	" " "	" 16	"	
35.	" " "	" 4	"	
36.	" " "	" 16 & 4	"	
37.	Flute 4 ft. and Violina			(lower four octaves only)
38.	" " " "	" 16	"	
39.	" " " "	" 4	"	(lower four octaves only)
40.	" " " "	" 16 & 4	"	(lower four octaves only)
41.	Ged. Sal. and Violina			
42.	" " " "	" 16	"	
43.	" " " "	" 4	"	
44.	" " " "	" 16 & 4	"	
45.	Ged. Sal. and Flute			
46.	" " " "	" 16	"	
47.	" " " "	" 4	"	
48.	" " " "	" 16 & 4	"	
49.	Ged. Flute and Violina			
50.	" " " "	" 16	"	

51.	Ged. Flute and Violina with	4	ft.
52.	" " " "	" 16 & 4 "
53.	Sal. Flute and Violina
54.	" " " "	" 16	"
55.	" " " "	" 4	"
56.	" " " "	" 16 & 4 "
57.	Ged. Sal. Flute and Violina
58.	" " " " " "	16	"
59.	" " " " " "	4	"
60.	" " " " " "	16 & 4 "

It will be observed that a few combinations (Nos. 6, 8, 11, 15, 18, 37, 39, and 40) are unsatisfactory in part of their compass. The exact extent to which these combinations can be used varies with different organs.

While there is a certain amount of similarity in the tone of some of these combinations, a close analysis shows a difference of either tone-color or power, which indicates the great variety of shading that is possible in organ combinations: e. g., A Gedeckt 8 ft. with a 4 ft. Coupler (No. 7) and a Flauto Traverso 4 ft. with a 16 ft. Coupler (No. 10) both produce a combination of 8 and 4 ft. Flute-tone. The exact color of these combinations, however, is somewhat different, as a Gedeckt has stopped pipes and a Flauto Traverso has open pipes of double length (harmonic). A Salicional 8 ft. with a 4 ft. Coupler (No. 3) and a Violina 4 ft. with a 16 ft. Coupler (No. 14) both produce a combination of 8 and 4 ft. string-tone, but the tone of a Violina is much softer and more delicate than the tone of a Salicional; hence there is quite a difference in the tone of the two combinations.

Several of the combinations included in the above list are seldom used, but many of the combinations are used frequently.

The octave couplers are used with the Diapason-tone stops to gain power and volume rather than to produce a variety of tone-color, as the Diapason-tone stops, except the Dulciana, Unda Maris, and Æoline, are characterized by their power and volume. Many beautiful effects of a delicate character are produced by the Dulciana, Unda Maris, and Æoline, combined with the octave couplers; but when these couplers are used with the full Diapasons, the general effect is increased volume and power.

Quite a number of combinations, principally of Flute-tone, of different pitch, selected from the 16, 8, 4, 2, and 1 ft. octaves, are possible with the aid of the 16 and 4 ft. couplers. These combinations are better suited for sustained chords than for repeated chords, and are more effective in the upper half of the manual than in the lower half. Arpeggios and a few solo passages sound well on many of the combinations. Obviously, no passages of a polyphonic character should be attempted on any of these combinations.

A LIST OF COMBINATIONS OF 16, 8, 4, 2, AND 1 FT. PITCH, MOSTLY OF FLUTE-TONE, WHICH ARE POSSIBLE AND EFFECTIVE ON MANY SWELL ORGANS, WITH THE AID OF THE 16 AND 4 FT. COUPLERS

Bourdon 16 ft. and Gedeckt 8 ft.	with 4 ft. Coupler
Bourdon 16 ft. and Flauto Traverso 4 ft.	
Bourdon 16 ft. and Flauto Traverso 4 ft.	with 4 ft. Coupler
Bourdon 16 ft. and Violina 4 ft.	
Bourdon 16 ft. and Violina 4 ft.	with 4 ft. Coupler
Bourdon 16 ft. and Flautino 2 ft.	
Bourdon 16 ft. and Flautino 2 ft.	with 4 ft. Coupler
Bourdon 16 ft., Gedeckt 8 ft., and Flute 4 ft.	
Bourdon 16 ft., Gedeckt 8 ft., and Flute 4 ft.	with 4 ft. Coupler
Bourdon 16 ft., Gedeckt 8 ft., and Violina 4 ft.	
Bourdon 16 ft., Gedeckt 8 ft., and Violina 4 ft.	with 4 ft. Coupler
Bourdon 16 ft., Gedeckt 8 ft., and Flautino 2 ft.	
Bourdon 16 ft., Gedeckt 8 ft., and Flautino 2 ft.	with 4 ft. Coupler
Gedeckt 8 ft., Flute 4 ft., and Flautino 2 ft.	
Gedeckt 8 ft., Flute 4 ft., and Flautino 2 ft.	with 4 ft. Coupler
Gedeckt 8 ft., Flute 4 ft., and Flautino 2 ft.	with 16 and 4 ft. Couplers
Violina 4 ft. and Flautino 2 ft. (lower octaves)	
Violina 4 ft. and Flautino 2 ft.	with 16 ft. Coupler
Violina 4 ft., Flautino 2 ft., and Æoline 8 ft.	with 16 and 4 ft. Couplers
Violina 4 ft. and Æoline 8 ft.	with 16 and 4 ft. Couplers
Flautino 2 ft. and Æoline 8 ft.	with 16 and 4 ft. Couplers

As with all the combinations of stops which are mentioned in this work, the effect of these combinations is materially influenced by the relative power of the individual stops. In some Swell organs the 2 ft. stop is a Fifteenth (Diapason-tone) instead of a Flautino (Flute-tone). On such organs it is doubtful if those combinations of the above list which include the 2 ft. stop will be found desirable. If the Bourdon is louder than the Gedeckt many of the combinations which include the Bourdon are undesirable. In a well-regulated Swell organ, the Bourdon is several scales smaller than the Gedeckt, the Flauto Traverso 4 ft. is softer than the Gedeckt, and the Flautino is softer than either of these stops.

Nearly every one of these combinations is improved by the addition of a Tremolo. Without a Tremolo the different octaves of the combinations are too distinctly audible; but with a Tremolo, which acts as a "tone-color mixer," the several octaves are so blended together that one hears only the composite tone-color. This composite tone-color is quite different from the effect of the several octaves, which are so distinctly audible when a Tremolo is omitted.

In three of the above combinations, an Æoline is included. Although this stop is so soft that its addition to most combinations has practically no effect, in these particular combinations it adds a pleasing effect, by supplying a very soft ground-tone of 16 and 8 ft. pitch, with the aid of the 16 ft. Coupler.

In quite a number of organs, the Sw. organ contains a Rohr Floete 8 ft. instead of a Gedeckt or St. Diapason; and in some other organs, there is a Rohr Floete 4 ft. instead of a Flauto Traverso 4 ft. Some of the combinations of the above list are effective with the substitution of these stops, but frequently this substitution renders the combinations objectionable. If these Rohr Floetes are full-fledged Rohr Floetes, with inharmonic overtones more or less pronounced, many of the specified combinations, in which these stops are substituted, will not be pleasing; but if the Rohr Floetes are only slightly modified Gedeckts, though labeled "Rohr Floete," the combinations will be acceptable.

THIRD USE OF THE OCTAVE COUPLERS

The octave couplers can be used with much effect to modify the tone of solo combinations of reed-tone, string-tone, or of combinations of both reed and string-tone. This use of the octave couplers is especially popular with many organists, some of whom rarely use these couplers in any other manner. A solo combination of reed-tone or string-tone is much strengthened by the addition of the 16 ft. Coupler, provided the solo does not run into the two lower octaves of the manual. Besides being strengthened, the tone of the combination sounds more dignified with this coupler added. On the other hand, the addition of the 4 ft. Coupler adds power and brilliancy, but reduces the dignity of the combination. Almost any combination of 8 ft. reed-tone or string-tone with a 4 ft. Flute-tone stop sounds well with a 16 ft. Coupler added. If, instead of combining a 4 ft. Flute-tone stop with the reed-tone or string-tone combination, one uses an 8 ft. Flute-tone stop, the effect (with the addition of the 16 ft. Coupler) is not quite so pleasing, as the sub-octave of the 8 ft. Flute-tone somewhat unbalances the desired predominance of the reed-tone or string-tone. This is best illustrated on a staff as below:—

At A, the whole note represents the 8 ft. string-tone and the black note represents the 4 ft. Flute-tone. As this Flute-tone is generally softer than the 8 ft. string-tone, the black note is smaller than the whole note. At B we see the result of the addition of the 16 ft. Coupler. At C, the whole note also represents the 8 ft. string-tone and the black note represents the 8 ft. Flute-tone. As the 8 ft. Flute-tone is nearly as loud as the 8 ft. string-tone, both notes are of the same size. At D, is indicated the result of the addition of a 16 ft. Coupler. A comparison of B and D shows to the eye the difference in the audible effect of these two combinations.

A PARTIAL LIST OF EFFECTIVE SOLO COMBINATIONS, WITH THE AID OF THE 16 FT. COUPLER

Oboe	with 16 ft. Coupler
Cornopean	with 16 ft. Coupler
Voix Céleste	with 16 ft. Coupler

Salicional or Viol d'Orchestre	with 16 ft. Coupler
Vox Humana	with 16 ft. Coupler
Oboe and Gedeckt	with 16 ft. Coupler
Cornopean and Gedeckt	with 16 ft. Coupler
Salicional or Viol d'Orchestre and Gedeckt	with 16 ft. Coupler
Voix Céleste and Gedeckt	with 16 ft. Coupler
Vox Humana and Gedeckt	with 16 ft. Coupler
Oboe and Flute 4 ft.	with 16 ft. Coupler
Cornopean and Flute 4 ft.	with 16 ft. Coupler
Salicional or Viol d'Orchestre and Flute 4 ft.	with 16 ft. Coupler
Voix Céleste and Flute 4 ft.	with 16 ft. Coupler
Vox Humana and Flute 4 ft.	with 16 ft. Coupler
Oboe, Gedeckt, and Flute 4 ft.	with 16 ft. Coupler
Cornopean, Gedeckt, and Flute 4 ft.	with 16 ft. Coupler
Salicional or Viol d'Orchestre, Gedeckt, and Flute 4 ft.	with 16 ft. Coupler
Voix Céleste, Gedeckt, and Flute 4 ft.	with 16 ft. Coupler
Vox Humana, Gedeckt and Flute 4 ft.	with 16 ft. Coupler
Oboe, Vox Humana, and Flute 4 ft.	with 16 ft. Coupler
Oboe, Sal. or Viol d'Orchestre, and Flute 4 ft.	with 16 ft. Coupler
Oboe, Voix Céleste, and Flute 4 ft.	with 16 ft. Coupler
Oboe, Gedeckt, Vox Humana, and Flute 4 ft.	with 16 ft. Coupler
Oboe, Gedeckt, Sal. or Viol d'Orchestre, and Flute 4 ft.	with 16 ft. Coupler
Oboe, Gedeckt, Voix Céleste, and Flute 4 ft.	with 16 ft. Coupler
Vox Humana, Sal. or Viol d'Orchestre, and Flute 4 ft.	with 16 ft. Coupler
Vox Humana, Gedeckt, Sal. or Viol d'Orchestre, and Flute 4 ft.	with 16 ft. Coupler
Vox Humana and Voix Céleste	with 16 ft. Coupler
Vox Humana, Voix Céleste, and Gedeckt	with 16 ft. Coupler
Vox Humana, Voix Céleste, and Flute 4 ft.	with 16 ft. Coupler
Vox Humana, Gedeckt, Voix Céleste, and Flute 4 ft.	with 16 ft. Coupler
Cornopean and Oboe	with 16 ft. Coupler
Cornopean and Viol d'Orchestre	with 16 ft. Coupler
Cornopean and Voix Céleste	with 16 ft. Coupler
Cornopean and Vox Humana	with 16 ft. Coupler
Cornopean, Oboe, and Gedeckt	with 16 ft. Coupler
Cornopean, Oboe, and Viol d'Orchestre	with 16 ft. Coupler
Cornopean, Oboe, and Voix Céleste	with 16 ft. Coupler
Cornopean, Oboe, and Vox Humana	with 16 ft. Coupler
Cornopean, Oboe and Flute 4 ft.	with 16 ft. Coupler
Cornopean, Viol d'Orchestre, and Flute 4 ft.	with 16 ft. Coupler
Cornopean, Voix Céleste, and Flute 4 ft.	with 16 ft. Coupler
Cornopean, Vox Humana, and Flute 4 ft.	with 16 ft. Coupler
Cornopean, Gedeckt, and Viol d'Orchestre	with 16 ft. Coupler
Cornopean, Gedeckt, and Voix Céleste	with 16 ft. Coupler
Cornopean, Gedeckt, and Vox Humana	with 16 ft. Coupler
Cornopean, Voix Céleste and Vox Humana	with 16 ft. Coupler
Cornopean, Oboe, Gedeckt, and Viol d'Orchestre	with 16 ft. Coupler
Cornopean, Oboe, Gedeckt, and Voix Céleste	with 16 ft. Coupler
Cornopean, Oboe, Gedeckt, and Vox Humana	with 16 ft. Coupler
Cornopean, Oboe, Gedeckt, and Flute 4 ft.	with 16 ft. Coupler
Cornopean, Oboe, Viol d'Orchestre, and Flute 4 ft.	with 16 ft. Coupler
Cornopean, Oboe, Voix Céleste, and Flute 4 ft.	with 16 ft. Coupler
Cornopean, Oboe, Vox Humana, and Flute 4 ft.	with 16 ft. Coupler
Cor., Oboe, Gedeckt, Viol d'Orchestre and Flute 4 ft.	with 16 ft. Coupler
Cor., Oboe, Gedeckt, Voix Celeste and Flute 4 ft.	with 16 ft. Coupler

Cor., Oboe, Gedeckt, Voix Céleste, Vox Humana, and Flute 4 ft.	with 16 ft. Coupler
Clarinet	with 16 ft. Coupler
Clarinet and Melodia (or Concert Flute)	with 16 ft. Coupler
Clarinet and Flute 4 ft.	with 16 ft. Coupler
Clarinet, Melodia and Flute 4 ft.	with 16 ft. Coupler
Cor., Oboe, Gedeckt, Vox Humana, and Flute 4 ft.	with 16 ft. Coupler

(Note: The above combinations are generally unsatisfactory below middle C, and sound better above f^1 than below.)

It will seem, at first glance over the above list, that the difference between many of the combinations is hardly distinguishable. On some organs, this is true: e. g., if the Cornopean is very loud and out of proportion with the balance of the stops in the Sw., a majority of the combinations, which contain this stop, will sound so nearly alike that one can hardly distinguish them. If, however, this stop has a tone proportionate to that of the other stops in that manual, it will be easy to distinguish between all the combinations: e. g., between the Cornopean alone, and the Cornopean combined with an Oboe; between the Cornopean, Gedeckt, and Vox Humana, and the Cornopean, Voix Céleste and Flute 4 ft., etc.

There are but a few organs on which every one of the above list of combinations sounds satisfactory. A certain group of combinations is especially attractive on one organ, and an entirely different group of combinations is especially effective on another organ. Although the list is long, it is by no means complete, as no attempt has been made to have the list exhaustive.

With many of the combinations indicated in the above list, a 4 ft. Coupler can be substituted for the 16 ft. Coupler. This substitution, however, does not change the tone-quality of the combination, but renders it an octave higher: e. g., an Oboe and Flute 4 ft., with a 4 ft. Coupler, produces the same resultant tone as an Oboe and Flute 4 ft., with 16 ft. Coupler, *if one plays an octave higher on the latter combination.* Obviously, if one plays in the same octave, with the 4 ft. Coupler, the *effect* is different from the combination with the 16 ft. Coupler, though the real tone-color remains the same.

In most of the combinations of the above list, the 4 ft. Coupler can be *added* to the 16 ft. Coupler, rendering the tone louder and more brilliant. With those combinations which contain a Flute 4 ft., it is doubtful if the addition of the 4 ft. Coupler is desirable, as the effect is generally unpleasant.

A further variation of these solo combinations can be produced by substituting a Bourdon 16 ft. for the 16 ft. Coupler. The 4 ft. Coupler can be used in addition to the Bourdon, with those combinations which do not contain a Flute 4 ft.

The 16 and 4 ft. couplers, between two manuals, have their own distinct usages. Besides being used, in a general way, to add power and volume to a manual, by coupling the octaves of another manual, these couplers are convenient for special effects. When the organist desires a combination of two tone-colors, of different pitch, each of a certain power, which cannot be obtained on one manual, he frequently can obtain the desired combination from two manuals, with the aid of the 16 or 4 ft. couplers between those manuals; e. g., draw Doppel Floete 8 ft. on the Gt., Oboe on the Sw., with Sw. to Gt. 4 ft. Coupler. If one plays on the Gt. an octave lower than the music is printed, this combination produces a solo effect which is entirely different from any combination which can be obtained on the Sw. Again, draw Gt. Doppel Floete, Ch. Clarinet, and Ch. to Gt. 16 ft. Coupler. A solo played on the Gt. gives a combination of Clarinet 16 ft. and Doppel Floete 8 ft., which is entirely different from Clarinet and Hohl Floete or Concert Flute of the Ch. Lastly, draw Gt. Doppel Floete, Sw. Flauto Traverso 4 ft., and Sw. to Gt. 4 ft. Coupler. An obligato played on the Gt., with this combination, gives 8 and 2 ft. Flute-tone. The 2 ft. tone can be made louder or softer as desired, by opening and closing the swell. Many other combinations, of a similar, special character, can be obtained by the aid of the 16 and 4 ft. couplers between two manuals.

In modern organs, a mechanical stop, frequently called a " Coupler," is named " Unison Off." This mechanism first appeared in this country as " Great Organ Separation," and was generally a piston that cut out all the stops of the Gt. organ, when this piston was " off." Now-a-days, a separate stop, piston, or tablet, for " Unison Off " is provided for each manual, in many large organs. This mechanism, while not, strictly speaking, a coupler, is used only in connection with the Couplers. Its object is to silence the unison pitch of the manual, leaving in operation only such couplers (16 and 4 ft.) as are drawn. By its aid, the organist can arrange special combinations of 16 and 4 ft. pitch, or 8 and 2 ft. pitch; e. g., if a Gedeckt is drawn, with 16 and 4 ft. Couplers, three Gedeckt pipes (16, 8, and 4 ft. pitch) sound with each key. If the " Unison Off " is in operation, the unison pitch is silenced, and only the 16 and 4 ft. pitch of the couplers sound with each key. If a Flauto Traverso 4 ft. is drawn, with 16 and 4 ft. Couplers, and the " Unison Off " is in operation, a combination of Flauto Traverso 8 and 2 ft. is the result, as the 4 ft. pitch is silenced. Any 8 ft. stop can be used alone, as a 4 ft. stop, by drawing the 4 ft. Coupler and " Unison Off "; and any 4 ft. stop can be used alone, as an 8 ft. stop, by drawing the 16 ft. Coupler and " Unison Off."

It will thus be seen that a great variety of combinations can be produced with the aid of the 16 and 4 ft. couplers; but the organist must use discretion in making up the combinations, as many unpleasant effects will be produced if he combines stops and couplers at random. The 16 ft. couplers should rarely be used when the combination contains a 16 ft. stop and the harmony runs low. The 4 ft. couplers frequently produce harsh effects when 4 ft. stops are included in the combination; especially if reed or string-tone stops are included, and the music runs high. Furthermore, the effect of all the combinations depends as much on the character of the music which is played on the combinations, as upon the combinations themselves. I reiterate over and over again that the relative power of the individual stops in each organ has much to do with the effect of all combinations of stops and couplers.

CHAPTER VI

COMBINATION MOVEMENTS

COMBINATION Movements (thumb pistons, pedals or pedal studs) are mechanical appliances which are placed in organs for two purposes: First, for changing various groups of stops, collectively, without the necessity of removing the hands from the keys for the purpose of manipulating the draw-stops. Second, for changing large groups of stops with one motion of either hand or a foot, irrespective of whether or not the hands are removed from the keys. Various kinds of combination movements are found in existing organs, though several kinds are practically obsolete, being found only in very old organs.

LIST OF COMBINATION MOVEMENTS

COMBINATION PEDALS

1. Fixed combinations, movable, single-acting.
2. Fixed combinations, movable, double-acting.
3. Fixed combinations, non-movable, locking down.
4. Adjustable combinations, non-movable, locking down.
5. Adjustable combinations, non-movable, mutually-releasing.
6. Adjustable combinations, movable (double-acting).

COMBINATION PISTONS

(Thumb Pistons)

7. Fixed combinations, non-movable, non-releasing.
8. Fixed combinations, non-movable, mutually-releasing.
9. Adjustable combinations, non-movable, mutually-releasing.
10. Adjustable combinations, movable (double-acting).

PEDAL PISTONS OR STUDS

11. Pedal duplicate of No. 8.
12. Pedal duplicate of No. 9.
13. Pedal duplicate of No. 10.

" Adjustable " combination movements are those which can be " set " or " adjusted " at the pleasure of the organist, either at the console or within the organ case.

" Fixed " combination movements are those which cannot be changed or " adjusted " by the organist.

" Single-acting " pedals move the draw-stops in only one direction, either all out or all in.

" Double-acting " pedals or pistons give the specific combination of stops by drawing the necessary stops and pushing in such other stops as happen to be " out."

" Movable " combination pedals or pistons move the draw-stops and in modern organs are necessarily " double-acting." Recently, " Movable Combinations " have been termed " Absolute Combinations."

76

" Non-movable " (also called " Immovable " and " Dead ") combination pedals or pistons have no effect on the draw-stops. Recently, " Non-movable Combinations " have been termed " Dual Combinations."

Combination Pedals which " lock down " serve to continue their specific combinations until the pedal is released. They have no effect on the draw-stops and are not affected by other pedals or pistons.

" Mutually-Releasing " pistons or pedals release each other, the one pushed last remaining " on." In some organs the thumb piston remains " in " until released by another piston or by the " Zero Piston." In other organs the thumb piston springs back to its normal position when the thumb is removed from the piston, although the combination remains " on " until released. (Special " Combination Indicators " are generally provided in organs which have the last-named style of combination movements.) A separate piston called " Release " or " Zero Piston " releases any combination which is " on " in that department (Gt., Sw., Ch., etc.), and another piston called " Double Release " or " Double Zero " releases all the combinations in all the departments at once.

Two other kinds of " Releases " are found in various organs. A thumb piston labeled " Pedal Release," in combination with the systems numbered 7 and 8 in the above table, puts off the *loud* pedal stops that are brought on by any piston, without affecting the manual stops that are brought on by the piston. A " Combination Pedal Release " is a mechanical pedal which releases all combination pedals that are locked down.

The old-style combination pedals (Nos. 1 and 2) are found only in very old organs that have mechanical stop-action. Old organs that have " tracker-pneumatic " action (in contradistinction to " tubular-pneumatic " or " electro-pneumatic " action) generally contain combination pedals of the style numbered 3 in the above table.

The earliest combination piston (No. 7) had a " fixed " combination and the piston remained " in " until released by a small auxiliary piston which was located beside the combination piston. This style of combination piston is likewise found only in very old organs.

Modern combination movements (pistons or pedals) may be classed as either " fixed " or " adjustable," and " movable " or " non-movable."

The " adjustable " combination movements (pistons or pedals) are universally preferred to the " fixed " combination movements. There is, however, a wide diversity of opinion among organists on the relative merits of the " movable " and " non-movable " combination movements.

There are various methods of *adjusting* the combinations on the pistons, according to the particular builder of the organ. If the combination pistons are of the non-movable type, the combinations are frequently adjusted by means of thumb-keys in a " recorder-frame," which is located at a convenient point inside the organ, or located in two draws underneath the draw-stop jambs at either side of the console. If the combination pistons are of the movable type, the adjusting is generally effected at the console by means of an " adjuster piston " (or stop). The desired combination is first drawn, and, while holding *in* the piston on which the combination is to be adjusted, the adjuster piston is pressed in. This locks the combination on the particular piston which is held in. In some organs this process is reversed: i. e., after the desired combination has been drawn, the adjuster piston is pushed in and the combination piston is pushed *last*, which locks the combination on that piston. Another method of adjusting the combination is to hold in the piston while drawing the stops of the combination. In this method, the combination is automatically locked on the piston which is held in.

Pedal studs, which are frequently duplicates of some of the thumb pistons, possess a certain amount of convenience, though, from their character and position, many awkward and unintentional situations are sometimes caused. Their use requires the greatest caution, and special care must be exercised to avoid accidentally touching them with a foot at inopportune moments.

The Sforzando (Sfz) is a combination pedal which brings on Full Organ with all couplers (with or without the Tuba according to taste). It has no effect on the draw-stops and is therefore classed as " nonmovable." In some organs it locks down. In other organs it is " reversible."

Several other pedals and pistons, whose function is akin to that of the combination movements, are frequently classed with the combination movements, although they control only individual stops instead of combinations. A reversible pedal (or piston) which puts on or off the Gt. to Ped. Coupler (generally named " Gt. to Ped. reversible ") is frequently classed with the combination movements. Similar reversible pedals (or pistons) which operate the Sw. to Ped., Sw. to Gt., and So. to Gt. Couplers, or a Tremolo, are sometimes provided.

The primary object of combination movements is to facilitate the changing of several stops at moments when the demand upon the hands in the performance of the music is such that insufficient time is available to change the stops, one by one, by means of the draw-stops. Combination movements, therefore, enable the organist to quickly make changes of stops that would, otherwise, be impossible or that would cause awkward breaks in the flow of the music.

The various uses of these combination movements are multitudinous, according to the size of the organ and the style of the composition which is being performed. Different organists use the various combination movements in quite a different manner. With modern organs, some organists obtain nearly all their stop changes by means of the combination movements, while other organists manipulate the draw-stops in conjunction with the combination movements and thus obtain a larger number of varied combinations.

In old organs that have only the stereotyped " P. and F. Gt." combination movements, the use of the combination movements is naturally limited, although by combining hand-manipulation of the stops with the combination movements the utility of the combination movements is frequently increased. In such organs, the F. Gt. combination pedal generally brings on all the stops of the Gt., although the Trumpet is frequently omitted, being out of tune or out of commission entirely. As an example, let us suppose that the organist is playing on the Sw. (the combination of stops is immaterial), and has only the Dulciana drawn on the Gt. A few measures later he desires Gt. to Oct. If the F. Gt. combination pedal does not bring on the Ped. Op. Diapason, the organist, while playing on the Sw., can put on Full Gt. by means of the F. Gt. combination pedal, and, at the instant that he changes to the Gt. manual, he can put off the few undesired stops by the right hand. If the F. Gt. combination pedal brings on the Ped. Op. Diapason, the organist must make the two movements, suggested above, at the instant that he changes to the Gt. manual.

In many of these old organs the P. Gt. combination pedal is " single-acting," being available only to *reduce* from a larger combination to the P. combination. On such organs, if the organist wishes to add the Melodia (or Hohl Floete) to the Dulciana (or Keraulophon), which is already on, he can put down the F. Gt. pedal, and immediately afterward the P. Gt. pedal, thus obtaining the Melodia and Dulciana. Obviously, this method is of no value, except when there is insufficient time to draw the Melodia by hand.

In modern organs, in which the combination movements are thumb pistons with fixed combinations of the movable type, the combination pistons can be used, not only to give their specific combinations, but to assist in obtaining other combinations which are somewhat like the specific combinations. By putting on or off one or two stops, an instant after the specific combination is brought on by the piston, the desired combination can frequently be obtained: e. g., if a combination piston of the movable type brings on the Cornopean, Oboe, Violin Diapason, Gedeckt, Salicional and Flute 4 ft., and the organist does not wish the Cornopean or Violin Diapason in the combination, he can put off those stops by hand immediately after pushing the piston which brings on the whole combination. Again, if he wishes the Bourdon and the Flautino in addition to all the stops which are brought on by the piston, he can draw those two stops by hand immediately after bringing on the whole combination by the piston.

If the combination pistons are of the non-movable type, one can also use them to assist in obtaining combinations which are more or less unlike the specific combinations of the pistons. While one cannot put off any stop which is on by means of a piston of the non-movable type, one can add one or two stops to the combination of a piston which brings on a smaller combination, and thereby obtain the desired combination; e. g., consider the same two illustrations of the preceding paragraph. One cannot put off the Cornopean or Violin Diapason if it is brought on by a piston of the non-movable type, but the next smaller combination is frequently the 8 and 4 ft. stops without the Oboe or the Violin Diapason, and one can add the Oboe immediately after the smaller combination has been brought on. The Bourdon and Flautino can be drawn by addition to the combination, the same as with the piston of the movable type.

If the combination movements are " adjustable " instead of " fixed," it is unnecessary to make use of the plan suggested in the two preceding paragraphs. The desired combinations can be adjusted on the pistons if the organist so desires.

The adjustable feature of modern combination movements is a great adjunct, though its use by different organists is of a widely varying character.   When giving an organ recital on a modern organ which contains numerous adjustable combination pistons, some organists adjust all the principal combinations of each composition just before playing the composition.   Other organists adjust most of the combination pistons to general combinations just before beginning the program, and readjust only a few pistons during the program for certain radically different combinations as occasion requires.   The latter method has the advantage that the organist can associate certain combinations with certain pistons, and thus avoid the necessity of charging the mind with numerous changes of combinations on these pistons, at the beginning of each composition.

It is not necessary, nor is it advisable, to adjust beforehand every combination of stops which is to be required in playing a certain composition.   Oftentimes, it requires less effort (physical and mental) to make certain changes of stops by means of the draw-stops at the required moment, than to adjust the combination on a piston beforehand, remember the number of the piston, and to operate the piston at the required moment.   Undoubtedly, there are certain changes of stops which cannot satisfactorily be made by means of the draw-stops.   Without question, these changes should be adjusted on the pistons as required.

Each organist uses certain combinations of stops as a basis in planning his registration; although this basis may differ a great deal with different organists.   Certain general combinations are used many times by every organist in the course of a recital.   If these combinations are adjusted on some of the pistons at the outset, and the other pistons are reserved for the special combinations which are required only occasionally, the necessity for adjusting a large number of pistons before playing each composition is absent.   In this manner the long delays between the compositions of a program, which the audience is sometimes compelled to endure, may be avoided.

Many modern organs contain from twenty to forty, or even more combination movements.   (Pistons, pedals and pedal studs are frequently found in the same organ.)   When the young organist has occasion to play an organ of this character, he should study the combinations as he finds them.   If necessary he should write down upon a piece of paper the combination of stops which is on each combination movement.   Familiarity with the tone-color of each stop, as explained in the previous chapters, will enable him to determine the stops which are included in the combinations.   With care and a little experience, he can soon get a bird's-eye view (so to speak) of all the combination movements, so that he can proceed intelligently with the selection of combinations for the compositions which he is to play.

Further suggestions for the use of the combination movements may be found in the chapters devoted to the registration of individual compositions on specific organs.

CHAPTER VII

THE GRAND CRESCENDO

A GRAND Crescendo is a mechanical appliance, operated by means of a shoe similar to, and located beside, the balanced swell pedals, which brings on some of the couplers and nearly all the speaking stops (one at a time), from the softest to the loudest, thus producing a crescendo from the softest stop to the Full Organ. The reverse process releases the stops (one at a time) and produces a diminuendo. In modern tubular and electric organs, the mechanism of the Grand Crescendo is extremely simple. The crescendo can be made as slowly as desired or instantly; it can be halted or reversed at any point; in fact, the control of the crescendo is absolute.

The selection of the progressive order of the stops in the Grand Crescendo is of vital importance. Theoretically, there is but one entirely satisfactory order for the Grand Crescendo in each organ, though the order is different in different organs. In planning the order of the stops for a Grand Crescendo, one should keep in mind the object, nature, and use of the appliance. The primary object of the Grand Crescendo is to bring on the stops *progressively*, one at a time, *from the softest to the loudest*. Many of the best crescendos in organ music are made in an entirely different manner from the progressive order of a Grand Crescendo. This, however, has no influence on the specific order of stops which should be selected for the Grand Crescendo.

In most three-manual organs, it is possible to draw the stops one at a time (while holding a single chord), in such a progressive order that the crescendo is even and gradual, from the softest stop to the Full Organ. Naturally, the swell pedals must be operated judiciously in connection with such a crescendo, to avoid the sudden increase of power when some louder stops are first added. If the progressive order of the stops for the Grand Crescendo is planned in this manner, and the swell pedals, which cannot be controlled by the Grand Crescendo, are operated judiciously by the organist in the middle of the crescendo, an even and gradual crescendo will be produced by the Grand Crescendo.

The position of the couplers in the order of the stops is of no less importance than the position of the speaking stops. In some Grand Crescendos, all the unison couplers are brought on in a bunch at the first move of the Crescendo shoe. If one uses the Crescendo only when playing on the Gt., this plan is unobjectionable; but the presence of the Gt. to Ped. Coupler at the outset proves to be an annoyance if one is playing on the Sw. or Ch., while using the Grand Crescendo.

To illustrate the various points mentioned above, I give the progressive order of the stops in a Grand Crescendo, as arranged in a certain three-manual organ which I have in mind. The relative power and intensity of such stops as the Salicional, Cornopean, and all the 4 ft. stops, varies in different organs, and frequently causes a change of the position of these stops in the Crescendo.

PROGRESSIVE ORDER OF THE STOPS FOR A GRAND CRESCENDO IN A THREE-
MANUAL ORGAN WITH 36 SPEAKING STOPS
(Sw. and Ch. swells closed at the outset)

> Sw. to Gt., Ch. to Gt., and Sw. to Ped.
> Sw. Æoline and Bourdon Bass
> Ch. Dulciana
> Sw. Salicional
> Ped. Bourdon
> Sw. Gedeckt (St. Diapason)
> Sw. Violina 4 ft.
> Sw. Flute 4 ft.
> Ch. Melodia
> Sw. Diapason
> Ped. Gedeckt 8 ft.
> Sw. Oboe
>> Open the Sw. swell one half
> Ch. Flute d'Amour
>> Open the Ch. swell one half
> Sw. Viol d'Orchestre
>> Open the Sw. swell wide
> Gt. Doppel Floete
> Gt. Gamba (old style)
> A—Ch. Diapason
> Gt. Flute Har. 4 ft.
> Sw. Cornopean
> Ped. Violone
> Sw. Bourdon Treb. and Flautino
> B—Sw. Dolce Cornet
>> Open Ch. swell wide
> Ped. Cello
> Gt. Diapason
> Gt. to Ped.
> Ped. Diapason (16 ft.)
> Gt. Octave
> C—Gt. 16 ft. Diapason
> Ped. Flute 8 ft.
> Ch. Piccolo
> Gt. 12th and 15th
> Gt. Mixture
> Gt. Trumpet

Note: The following stops are purposely omitted from the Grand Crescendo: Vox Humana, Voix Céleste, Clarinet, and Tremolos; Sw. to Ch., Ch. to Ped., and all Sub and Super Couplers.

Note: Obviously, this order cannot be followed in every organ with the same specification, although it is satisfactory in this particular organ.

A Grand Crescendo is useful, in its entirety, to gradually increase the volume of tone from any particular combination to the Full Organ. In the reverse order, it is useful to gradually reduce the volume of tone from Full Organ to whatever combination has been previously prepared.

This particular Grand Crescendo can be used as far as the point indicated by " A " while playing on the Sw. or Ch. without the intrusion of any objectionable stop. It can be used on the Sw. as far as the point indicated by " B " (Full Sw.) without the intrusion of the Gt. to Ped. Coupler. It can be used as far as the point indicated by " C " for the combination, Gt. to Octave, Full Sw., Couplers and appropriate Ped. Obviously, it can be used in any position while playing on the Gt., as a partial crescendo or as a crescendo to the Full Organ.

The above Grand Crescendo is useful for various purposes besides producing a crescendo. If one wishes to add the Sw. to Gt. or the Sw. to Ped., while playing, a slight movement of the Grand Crescendo brings on these stops without adding any other stop. If one is playing on the Sw. with Salicional (or Voix Céleste or Oboe) and Flute 4 ft., and desires to add the Gedeckt without removing the hands, a slight movement of the Grand Crescendo adds that stop. If one is playing on the Sw. Gedeckt and Flute 4 ft. and wishes to add the Salicional, it can be added by a slight movement of the Grand Crescendo. If one is playing the accompaniment to a solo combination, on the Ch. Dulciana, and wishes the Melodia for a few measures, the Grand Crescendo up to that point will add that stop.

If one is about to play a March or other movement which requires F Gt., Full Sw., F Ped., Gt. to Ped. and Sw. to Gt., for the first section; and Oboe, Gedeckt, and Flute 4 ft. in the Sw., Dulciana in the Ch., and Bourdon in the Ped., without any coupler, for the second section; the stops which are required for the second section can be drawn at the outset, and the Grand Crescendo opened to the point indicated by " C " in the above order. The entire change of stops for the second section can then be secured by closing the Grand Crescendo.

In some organs of this size, the 16 and 4 ft. Couplers are included in the Grand Crescendo. If the organ also contains a SFZ pedal, the 16 and 4 ft. Couplers are generally connected with that pedal and omitted from the Grand Crescendo. The Grand Crescendo is thus used a great deal for a Full Organ pedal.

If the Grand Crescendo, at its various stages, does not give the specific combinations which the organist wishes, the Crescendo should be combined with the piston combinations or with the individual stops which can be drawn by hand.

If the Grand Crescendo is so arranged that it brings on Full Sw. and Full Ch., before bringing on any stop in the Gt.; or if it brings on the Gt. to Ped. Coupler at the outset; or if the order of the stops is such that certain stops come on too early to produce a gradual crescendo; the utility of the appliance may be somewhat restricted, but the organist must use his ingenuity to devise a method of avoiding the objectionable features of the individual Grand Crescendo. He can make a liberal use of its good features and will soon discover roundabout methods of obtaining his desired combinations and effects.

CHAPTER VIII

BORROWED STOPS — DUPLEXED AND UNIFIED CHESTS

A " BORROWED Stop " is a second draw-stop, by means of which the individual stop whose name it bears can be played from some other keyboard than the one with which its first draw-stop is primarily connected, without the assistance of a coupler. It is of the nature of a " Special Coupler," which couples one specific stop to some other keyboard, without including any of the other stops of its own department which would be included by a regular coupler.

As an example, the Sw. Bourdon 16 ft. is frequently " borrowed " in the Pedal organ, by means of a second draw-stop labeled, " Ped. Lieb-lich Bourdon 16 ft." This " borrowed " stop enables the organist to use the 30 (or 32) lower pipes of the Sw. Bourdon as a soft Ped. stop (softer than the regular Ped. Bourdon). Unlike the Sw. to Ped. Coupler, which produces the same result, if the Bourdon alone is drawn in the Sw., this " borrowed " stop does not prevent the organist using any or all of the Sw. stops at the same time, in whatever manner he may desire.

In modern organs, various individual stops are frequently " borrowed " on other manuals. Furthermore, all the stops of a manual are sometimes " borrowed " on another manual; i. e., a duplicate set of draw-stops is provided for the second manual, so that any one or all of the stops may be played independently from the second manual. When all, or nearly all, the stops of one manual are " borrowed " on another manual, the manual is said to be " duplexed " or provided with a " duplex chest." Sometimes, such a chest is called a " unified chest," but this term more properly signifies that all the stops on that chest can be played, by means of separate draw-stops, from each of the other manuals, as well as from the Pedal.

Borrowing stops from one department for another department of the organ, *under certain limitations*, is convenient, advantageous, and commendable. It should, however, be used only when necessary, and should be carried out with a keen sense of the value of individual and distinct tone-colors, and their importance on the different manuals. Borrowing the 16 ft. Bourdon of the Sw., to supply a 16 ft. Lieblich Gedeckt in the Ped., is always commendable, and cannot cause any annoying complications; but borrowing the 16 ft. Ped. Bourdon for a 16 ft. Quintaton on the Gt. (in the absence of any other 16 ft. stop on the Gt.) seems to me to be questionable. In the first case, the pipes of the Sw. Bourdon, which are utilized in the Ped. Lieblich Bourdon, are the 30 (or 32) lower pipes, and their use as a Ped. stop does not interfere with any passage work which is played on the Bourdon with other stops in the Sw. In the second case, the pipes of the Ped. Bourdon, which are being played on the Gt. manual, as the borrowed stop called " Quintaton," cause many silent notes in the Ped. phrases, and this is generally very annoying.

" Borrowing " or " Duplexing " is utilized to advantage in small organs, where either insufficient space or insufficient funds make it necessary. In such instances, it is a *convenience* which enables the organist to use separate stops and groups of stops on two manuals at the same time, thus permitting a greater variety in his registration than would be possible without the borrowed stops.

A stop which is " duplexed " for two manuals is not " just as good " as two separate stops, though, by a little compromising, it can occasionally be made to answer for the two stops. " Borrowing " or " Duplexing " never increases the size of an organ, notwithstanding the additional draw-stops, which frequently mislead the unwary. The small boy who changes a dime into two nickels may feel that in the two coins he has more money than in the one coin. The two nickels, oftentimes, are more convenient than a dime (especially in a telephone booth), but they are never " more money." " Borrowed " or " duplexed " stops are similar. They are a convenience but they never make " a larger organ."

In larger organs, some forms of " duplexing " are very convenient. An Echo organ, with a duplex chest, can be used like a small two-manual Echo organ. The Chimes, if borrowed on a second manual or on the Pedal, have their utility much increased. The 16 ft. Dulciana in the Ch., when borrowed, is a useful Ped. stop.

Unfortunately, " duplexing " or " borrowing " is sometimes carried to the extreme. If a Tuba of the Solo organ is borrowed in the Gt. and is called " Trumpet "; is borrowed in the Sw. and is called " Oboe "; is borrowed in the Ch. and is called " Clarinet "; is borrowed in the Ped. and is called " Trombe," — all these separate borrowed stops using the same single set of reed pipes, — it seems to me that such " borrowing " is *ad nauseam.* The stop is the same Tuba in each case and, if borrowed on several manuals, ought not to be called by radically different and improper names.

If a small Swell organ which contains three speaking stops (Gedeckt, Salicional and Flute 4 ft.) and the usual 16 and 4 ft. Couplers is duplexed so as to be played also from the Gt., the following combinations for solo and accompaniment are possible: —

Solo on Gt. Gedeckt	Accompaniment on Sw. Salicional
Solo on Gt. Flute 4 ft.	Accompaniment on Sw. Salicional or Gedeckt
Solo on Gt. Gedeckt and Flute	Accompaniment on Sw. Salicional or Gedeckt
Solo on Gt. Gedeckt and Salicional	Accompaniment on Gt. Gedeckt or Salicional
Solo on Gt. Salicional and Flute	Accompaniment on Sw. Gedeckt or Salicional
Solo on Sw. Gedeckt and 4 ft. Coupler	Accompaniment on Gt. Gedeckt or Salicional
Solo on Sw. Salicional and 4 ft. Coupler	Accompaniment on Gt. Salicional or Gedeckt

Solo on Sw. Flute 4 ft. and 16 ft. Coupler	Accompaniment on Gt. Gedeckt or Salicional
Solo on Sw. Flute with 16 and 4 ft. Couplers	Accompaniment on Gt. Gedeckt or Salicional
Solo on Sw. Ged., Sal. and 4 ft. Coupler	Accompaniment on Gt. Gedeckt or Salicional
Solo on Sw. Ged., Sal. and 16 ft. Coupler	Accompaniment on Gt. Gedeckt or Salicional
Solo on Sw. Ged., Sal. with 16 and 4 ft. Couplers	Accompaniment on Gt. Gedeckt or Salicional
Solo on Sw. Ged., Flute and 4 ft. Coupler	Accompaniment on Gt. Salicional or Gedeckt
Solo on Sw. Ged., Sal. and 4 ft. Coupler	Accompaniment on Gt. Salicional or Gedeckt
Solo on Sw. Sal., Flute and 16 ft. Coupler	Accompaniment on Gt. Salicional or Gedeckt
Solo on Sw. Ged., Sal., Flute and 16 ft. Coupler	Accompaniment on Gt. Salicional or Gedeckt
Solo on Sw. Ged., Sal., Flute and 4 ft. Coupler	Accompaniment on Gt. Salicional or Gedeckt
Solo on Sw. Ged., Sal., and Flute with 16 and 4 ft. Couplers	Accompaniment on Gt. Salicional or Gedeckt

In several of the above combinations one stop is drawn on both manuals. With such combinations the organist must not play passages which include the same notes in both solo and accompaniment.

Note: The practical use of a duplexed Swell organ in registration is more fully illustrated in Chapter XVIII.

CHAPTER IX

ECHO ORGANS AND ANTIPHONAL ORGANS

AN " Echo Organ " is, theoretically, a few stops enclosed in a swell-box, so located in some remote part of the church, or hall, that a distant effect is produced when these stops are played. By common consent, a Swell organ of any number of stops, which is located some distance from the main organ (frequently at the other end of the church), is called an " Echo Organ," for want of a more appropriate term, even if only a few real " echo effects " are possible on such an organ.

In organ music, the occasions when a *bona fide* " echo " is desired are rare, and such an echo is frequently best produced by the Æoline (or softest stop) in the Sw. organ; but many charming effects of distant music, or of music from different locations, can be produced with the aid of the so-called " Echo Organs."

The stops which are most commonly found in real " Echo Organs " are as follows: —

A very soft string-tone stop: e. g., a Muted Viol, with or without a Céleste rank to produce a very soft Viol Céleste.

A soft Dulciana (" Dolce "), with or without a " sharp rank " to produce an Unda Maris.

A soft Lieblich Gedeckt 8 ft., sometimes slightly modified and called " Fern Flute."

A soft 4 ft. Flute d'Amour or Wald Floete.

A Vox Humana, and occasionally Carillons and Chimes.

The larger so-called " Echo Organs " are, frequently, similar to medium-sized Swell organs, and contain, in addition to the above list of stops, a 16 ft. Lieblich Bourdon, Diapason, Oboe, soft Mixture, and various special stops.

Generally, the stops in both kinds of echo organs are voiced with a distinctly different tone-quality from that of similar stops in the main organ: e. g., many organs have a Vox Humana in the Sw. and a second Vox Humana, of a different quality, in the Echo organ.

The principal use of the echo organ is for sections and phrases of compositions, which are suitable for distant effects. The return of a quiet theme or section of a composition is frequently very effective if played on a soft combination in the Echo organ. Repetitions of phrases, if not too loud, are sometimes effective when played antiphonally. *Bona fide* echo effects are sometimes possible. One common use of the Echo organ requires special consideration: viz., using the Echo organ and the main organ at one and the same time. The various ways in which this is possible are as follows: —

A solo on the Sw. or Ch., with accompaniment on the Echo.

A solo on the Echo, with accompaniment on the Sw. or Ch.

Chords or a melody on the Echo, with an obligato on the Sw. or Ch.

Chords or a melody on the Sw. or Ch., with an obligato on the Echo.

The two organs (Sw. and Echo) coupled together.

If the Echo organ is so located that the relation of its tone to that of the Sw. organ has practically the same angle for the audience that it has for the player, the player's ears are a sufficient guide in choosing the registration for the above combinations of the Echo and Swell organs. If, however, the audience sit between the main organ and the Echo organ, i. e., the Echo organ is at the other end of the church from the main organ, the organist must remember that the relative power of the two departments of the organ is materially different in the ears of those who sit near the Echo organ from what it is in his ears. To be more explicit, if the organist plays a solo (R. H.) on the Echo Vox Humana, and an accompaniment (L. H.) on the Sw. Gedeckt, the relative power of the two stops may be satisfactory to the player, but those of the audience who sit at the back of the church (near the Echo organ) cannot hear the accompaniment at all, as the nearness of Vox Humana causes it to sound so much louder than the distant Gedeckt that the latter is practically inaudible to those who are sitting near the Echo organ. If the larger part of the audience is sitting near the Echo organ, the organist must regulate the power of the accompaniment (in the above illustration) so that it sounds much louder to him than the Vox Humana. If the larger part of the audience is sitting near the main organ, he must regulate the power of the accompaniment so that it sounds well-balanced in his own ears. If the audience is evenly distributed between the two departments of the organ, the organist should regulate the relative power of the two stops for the centre of the church, which means that the accompaniment must sound a little too loud to the player.

One especially effective combination of the Echo organ coupled to the Swell organ, both hands being played on the Swell, consists of the Echo Vox Humana coupled to the Sw. Voix Céleste; the two swell pedals being so manipulated that part of the time the tone of the Vox Humana predominates and part of the time the tone of the Voix Céleste predominates. This effect is similarly obtained by coupling the Sw. and Ch. together and was frequently used by Mons. Alex Guilmant in playing his Elevation in A-flat.

Antiphonal Organs: Many of the large Metropolitan churches contain two distinct, good-sized organs, one at either end of the church, with which innumerable antiphonal effects (loud and soft) are possible. Many of these churches originally possessed only a fine old organ in the west gallery. The advent of chancel choirs necessitated chancel organs, with which the old gallery organs have been electrically connected. As the console is generally located near the chancel, the gallery organ is frequently called the " Antiphonal Organ," even if it is considerably larger than the chancel organ. Quite a number of entirely new organs of this character have been built in recent years. Oftentimes, these

" Antiphonal organs " are complete in themselves, and an entire recital can be given on them, played from the console at the chancel.

The selection of the registration for an " Antiphonal organ " is subject to the same influences which obtain in all organs of its size, with the addition that personal taste and judgment must be exercised in selecting on which organ the various sections of the compositions shall be played. In many compositions, the first or main theme can be played on the main organ, and the second theme played on the antiphonal organ. Returning to the main organ for the return of the first theme, the climax can be played on both organs coupled together. If the composition is made up of several short phrases the phrases can be played alternately on the main and the antiphonal organs. Frequently, the best contrast is obtained by playing a whole composition on the antiphonal organ after the preceding composition (or part of the service) has been played on the main organ. Frequently, a Fugue can be rendered effective by playing the " exposition " of the Fugue on the antiphonal organ and playing the entrance of the several voices in the " recapitulation " on the main organ.

CHAPTER X

COMBINING ORGAN STOPS

AFTER the young organist has become familiar with the properties and characteristic tone-color of the individual organ stops, he will be well repaid, if he becomes equally familiar with the theoretical effect which the tone of each stop exerts on the tone of each other stop, in combination.

The question is occasionally asked: "Is it worth while for the student to devote much time and thought to the *theory* of stop combinations, in view of the fact that many combinations sound so differently on different organs?" It seems to me that the organist who is thoroughly familiar with the theory of stop combinations has, at the outset, a larger grasp of the possibilities of any organ, in the way of tonal coloring, than he who relies wholly on a "hit or miss" method of "trying" the stops at random. While theory and practice do not always go hand in hand, a full knowledge of the theory not only explains the tonal effects of the combinations, be they good or bad, but assists the student in his endeavor to overcome the bad effects of some combinations, which, theoretically, ought to be pleasing. Furthermore, a familiarity with the tone of organ stops, and the influence of the various tone-colors in combination, gives the student a larger power of differentiation, in selecting his tonal combinations, and withal enables him to vitalize some combinations which, otherwise, would sound characterless.

When two organ stops are combined, the resultant tone is influenced by one or more of four distinct factors or elements, which contribute to produce the resultant tone: first, by the primary quality of tone of the individual stops (Diapason, Flute, String or Reed); second, by certain specific acoustical principles which vary even in different stops of the same fundamental quality of tone (open and stopped pipes, harmonic stops, and stops which have certain overtones suppressed or overdeveloped); third, by the relative power of the two stops; and fourth, by the relative pitch of the two stops (16, 8, 4, and 2 ft. stops). If we combine a Flute-tone and a string-tone stop, each of which is of 8 ft. pitch, and the two stops have exactly the same power, only the first two of the above mentioned factors exert any influence on the resultant tone of the combination. Furthermore, the second of the four factors, in this particular case, may happen to be very small. In this event, the resultant tone of the combination possesses hardly any pleasing character. Such a combination is sometimes found in old two-manual organs. In such organs, we occasionally find in the Gt. a mediocre Melodia (or Hohl Floete), whose tone is "tubby" rather than beautiful. In the Sw. we may find a Gamba, the tone of which is raspy rather than stringy, and is slow and uncertain in both speech and pitch. These two stops in combination produce a resultant tone which is far from beautiful, being devoid of any attractive character.

On the other hand, let us combine an Oboe and a Flauto Traverso 4 ft., in a modern organ. The two stops have different fundamental tone-qualities (reed and Flute); they are of different power (the Flute generally being about a third softer than the Oboe); the overtones of the two stops are pronounced but are entirely unlike; and the two stops are of different pitch (8 and 4 ft.). All four of the factors, to which reference has been made, are present, and produce a resultant tone which has definite character and is pleasing.

To consider a more extreme example, let us combine a Vox Humana with a soft Bourdon 16 ft., and observe the result. First, we have in this combination reed-tone and Flute-tone; second, the Vox Humana is rich in overtones, while the Bourdon, with its stopped pipes, produces only the even-numbered overtones; third, the Bourdon is softer than the Vox Humana; fourth, the stops are of different pitch. The resultant tone has a most pronounced character and is generally very pleasing (above tenor C).

Thus will it be observed that the character of the resultant tone of combinations of stops is more pronounced and, withal, more attractive, if three or all four of the above named factors are present in the combination.

In combining three or more stops, the same principles hold true; and, with a due regard for the influence of these four factors, we can build up composite tone-color of much character and beauty.

In registration, certain stops are used singly as well as in combination. Although single stops cannot correctly be called " combinations," it is frequently necessary to so class them; for example, if a Gedeckt and a Violina are used for one phrase, and a Salicional alone for the following phrase, reference is made to the contrast " of these two combinations." There seems to be no way of avoiding this seeming inconsistency, and common custom (with long usage) justifies its continuance.

In combining the stops, more particularly the soft stops, the greatest variety of combinations, and I may say many of the most effective combinations, are obtained by combining stops of different pitch. While combinations of two or three stops of the same pitch — e. g., Oboe and Gedeckt; Salicional and Gedeckt; Vox Humana and Salicional — are generally effective and satisfactory, one can obtain more varied and possibly more pleasing combinations of tone-color by combining an 8 ft. stop with a 4 ft. stop, both stops being of the same or different fundamental qualities of tone. Examples: —

8 ft. Flute-tone with 4 ft. string-tone.
8 ft. Flute-tone with 4 ft. Flute-tone.
8 ft. string-tone with 4 ft. Flute-tone.
8 ft. string-tone with 4 ft. string-tone.
8 ft. reed-tone with 16 or 4 ft. Flute-tone.

Occasionally, 8 and 4 ft. Flute-tone stops do not combine well; e. g., we occasionally find, as stated elsewhere, a Rohr Floete of the original type, which is so voiced that the " inharmonic overtones " (see page 30) peculiar to this stop, are quite prominent. Such a stop does not combine well with a Flauto Traverso 4 ft., as the overtones of the two stops " quarrel." If such a Rohr Floete is used with an Octave Coupler, chords in close position sound out of tune. This peculiarity of the Rohr Floete is frequently covered up if an additional 8 ft. stop is used in the combination.

As already stated, one of the important factors which influence the resultant tone of combinations is the relative power of the stops. Different stops of the same fundamental quality of tone, and even of the same specific name, vary in intensity, and the resultant tone of combinations is more or less modified by this difference in intensity.

Let us consider, for a moment, the stops of a well-regulated Swell organ, for an illustration, and let us use the numerals 1 to 18 to indicate the relative power of the several stops. This will give a table somewhat like the following. (The Æoline is frequently so extremely soft that one cannot accurately indicate its power in such a table, but this point is immaterial.)

16 ft. Bourdon	6	4 ft. Flauto Traverso	5
8 ft. Open Diapason	14	4 ft. Violina	3
8 ft. Viol d'Orchestre	10	2 ft. Flautino	3
8 ft. Voix Céleste	12	Dolce Cornet	5
8 ft. Salicional	6	8 ft. Cornopean	18
8 ft. Gedeckt	8	8 ft. Oboe	12
8 ft. Æoline 1, ½, or ¼		8 ft. Vox Humana	8

In this connection, I may say that the relative power of the tone of the different stops in a manual, especially the power of the 4 ft. stops, compared with the power of the 8 ft. stops, is much under-estimated. Some organ builders consider the 4 ft. stops only as factors in supplying the necessary amount of tone in the 4 ft. octave, for the sole purpose of building up the volume of the tone in the loud combinations and in the Full Organ. The importance of the 4 ft. stops, in their combinational use, is much greater than in their use in very loud combinations.

With this table in view, the relative power of the stops in a few two-stop combinations can be indicated as follows: —

Gedeckt	(8)	and	Salicional	(6)
Gedeckt	(8)	"	Flauto Traverso	(5)
Gedeckt	(8)	"	Violina	(3)
Salicional	(6)	"	Flauto Traverso	(5)
Salicional	(6)	"	Violina	(3)
Bourdon	(6)	"	Violina	(3)
Bourdon	(6)	"	Flauto Traverso	(5)
Oboe	(12)	"	Gedeckt	(8)
Oboe	(12)	"	Flauto Traverso	(5)
Vox Humana	(8)	"	Gedeckt	(8)
Vox Humana	(8)	"	Flauto Traverso	(5)

Vox Humana	(8)	and	Bourdon	(6)
Voix Céleste	(12)	"	Gedeckt	(8)
Voix Céleste	(12)	"	Flauto Traverso	(5)

It will be observed that in all these combinations the principal stop is louder than the secondary stop. If the secondary stop is louder than the principal stop, the combination is generally unsatisfactory and should not be used. The author has played Swell organs, of which a comparative table like the above would rank the Flauto Traverso 10, the Bourdon 9, the Violina 9, and the Vox Humana 3. On these organs the following combinations were unsatisfactory and practically intolerable: —

Salicional	(6)	and	Flauto Traverso	(10)
Gedeckt	(8)	"	Violina	(9)
Vox Humana	(3)	"	Gedeckt	(8)
Vox Humana	(3)	"	Flauto Traverso	(10)
Vox Humana	(3)	"	Bourdon	(9)

From the description of the tone of various stops, and the tonal effects which are produced by the addition of certain fundamental tone-colors to the same or other tone-colors (see table on the following page), the student ought to be able to formulate the tonal effect which is produced when several stops are combined. Having observed that the combination of a Gedeckt and a Salicional produces a composite tone of string and Flute quality, without any specially distinctive character; and having observed the characteristics of such stops as the Flauto Traverso 4 ft., the Violina, the Oboe, and the Diapason; the student should know, without trying the combinations, that the addition of a Violina to the above combination adds a little delicate brilliancy; that the addition of a Flauto Traverso 4 ft. adds more pronounced brilliancy, with an improved definiteness of pitch; that the addition of an Oboe gives firmness and a further increase of power and volume.

If the indicated registration calls for an Oboe and a Flute 4 ft. for a solo combination, and this combination, on the organ on which the student is playing, is weak and ineffective, he should remember that the addition of a keen, string-tone Salicional or a Viol d'Orchestre intensifies the tone-color of the solo combination, and makes it more effective. He should remember that the addition of a real Voix Céleste increases the power and vitality of the combination; that the addition of a Gedeckt makes the tone rounder and fuller, but covers up part of the real Oboe quality. He should remember that, if all these added stops are insufficient, he can add, as a last resort, the Diapason, although he should be conscious that the tone of this stop will overshadow the Oboe quality in the solo combination.

If the student, when playing on a certain organ, observes that the Vox Humana and Flute 4 ft., which are indicated in the printed registration, are unsatisfactory, on account of the preponderance of the tone of the Flute, he should understand that an 8 ft. stop must be added. If he wishes to retain the approximate character of the Vox Humana, he should add a Voix Céleste or at least a Salicional. If the only 8 ft. stop that is available is a Gedeckt, he must add that stop, although he knows that it will overshadow the Vox Humana quality.

The following table is intended to indicate, in a general way, as far as mere words can give such an indication, the tonal effect which is produced by adding certain specific qualities of tone to the same and other qualities of tone. For the purpose of illustration, in testing these effects, the student should hold down the following chord for all the combinations.

TABLE OF THE APPROXIMATE EFFECTS OF COMBINING FOUR QUALITIES OF TONE

Adding		to			Approximate tonal effect
Diapason-tone	8 ft.	to	Diapason-tone	8 ft.	Increases the volume
Oct. "	4 "	"	"	"	Adds brilliancy
Super Coupler	4 "	"	"	"	Increases the power (frequently harsh)
Diapason-tone	16 "	"	"	"	Adds heaviness, often gruffness
Sub Coupler	16 "	"	"	"	Generally adds gruffness
Flute-tone	8 "	"	"	"	Enriches the tone
Flute-tone	4 "	"	"	"	Makes the tone more cutting, with more definiteness of pitch
Flute-tone	16 "	"	"	"	Frequently causes gruffness
String-tone	8 "	"	"	"	Variable, frequently undesirable
String-tone	4 "	"	"	"	" "
Soft reed-tone	8 "	"	"	"	Adds firmness
Loud reed-tone	8 "	"	"	"	Overshadows the Diapason-tone
Flute-tone	8 "	"	Flute-tone	8 "	Increases the volume
Flute-tone	4 "	"	"	"	Brightens the tone, with slight increase of volume
Super Coupler	4 "	"	"	"	" " " " " " "
Flute-tone	2 "	"	"	"	Makes the tone more sparkling, sometimes shrill
Flute-tone	16 "	"	"	"	Produces heaviness in lower octaves
Sub Coupler	16 "	"	"	"	" " " " "
Strong string-tone	8 "	"	"	"	Overshadows the Flute-tone
Light string-tone	8 "	"	"	"	Adds firmness
Light string-tone	4 "	"	"	"	Brightens the tone slightly

Stop	ft.		base	8 ft.	Effect
String-tone	8 ft.	to	String-tone	8 ft.	Increases the volume
String-tone	4	"	"	"	Adds brilliancy
Super Coupler	4	"	"	"	Adds power and brilliancy
Sub Coupler	16	"	"	"	Adds heaviness, dignity, and gruffness in lower octaves
Flute-tone	8	"	"	"	Dulls the String-tone but adds volume
Flute-tone	4	"	"	"	Makes the tone more cutting and definite
Flute-tone	16	"	"	"	Adds heaviness, often pleasing
Reed-tone	8	"	"	"	Generally overshadows the String-tone
Reed-tone	8	"	Reed-tone	8	Increases the volume
Super Coupler	4	"	"	"	Increases the power and adds brilliancy
Sub Coupler	16	"	"	"	Adds volume, weight and dignity
Diapason-tone	8	"	"	"	Broadens the tone
Diapason-tone	4	"	"	"	Generally undesirable
Flute-tone	8	"	"	"	Makes the tone rounder
Flute-tone	4	"	"	"	Makes the tone sharper and more definite
Flute-tone	16	"	"	"	Adds weight
String-tone	8	"	"	"	Intensifies the tone-quality
String-tone	4	"	"	"	Makes the tone somewhat piercing

Note: The effect produced by adding a 16 ft. stop to an 8 ft. stop varies materially with the relative power of the two stops. If the 16 ft. stop is only about one-half as loud as the 8 ft. stop the effect is generally added dignity; but if the 16 ft. stop is nearly as loud as the 8 ft. stop its addition causes a gruffness which is not pleasing. If one or two 4 ft. stops are combined with the 8 ft. stop the gruffness caused by the addition of the 16 ft. stop is reduced, and the effect is frequently acceptable.

If the student wishes to obtain a large volume of string tone, suggestive of the combined strings of the orchestra, he must first draw the Gamba of the Gt., the Voix Céleste of the Sw., the Viol d'Amour of the Ch., and the Sw. to Gt. and Ch. to Gt. Couplers. In all probability, he will feel that something is wanting in this combination of string-tone stops, as the tone does not meet his expectation. If there is a Gamba Céleste in the Solo organ, he can couple this stop to the Gt. To further increase the intensity of the combination, he can add a soft Oboe and Flauto Traverso of the Sw. These two stops are not string-tone stops, but the Oboe possesses some of the characteristics of the string-tone stops, and the Flauto Traverso sharpens the combination; hence, these two stops help to intensify the combinational tone. Lastly, the addition of a Vox Humana, as a " timbre creator," will add a little of the vitality which is so noticeable in the combined strings of the orchestra.

In this manner, the student can select and build up the larger combinations from his knowledge of the tonal influences of the individual stops.

In large churches and halls, very soft stops and small combinations of stops are frequently inadequate, as their tone is nearly inaudible in part of the auditorium. Under such conditions it is necessary to enlarge the combinations. A passage of music which, under ordinary circumstances, sounds well as a solo, played on an Oboe and Flauto Traverso, with the accompaniment played on a Dulciana, when played in a large church or hall may require the addition of a Cornopean and possibly a Viol d'Orchestre for the solo, and the addition of a Melodia or other 8 ft. Flute for the accompaniment. Other combinations must likewise be enlarged for such auditoriums.

COMBINATIONS WITH REED-TONE STOPS

Many of the old-style reed-tone stops are so coarse in tone-quality, and so uncertain in speech and pitch, that it is frequently necessary to use an 8 ft. Flute-tone stop with the reed-tone stop. It is unwise to use an old-style Oboe alone, as some of the pipes frequently have the unfortunate habit of not speaking or of " breaking " into one of the overtones — sounding some note other than the one desired. By combining a St. Diapason with such an Oboe, the roughness of the reed-tone is somewhat disguised, and the player is fairly sure of producing a tone of correct pitch with each note that is played.

Most modern reed-tone stops are practically free from these shortcomings, and do not require the assistance of 8 ft. Flute-tone stops. A modern Oboe is such a fine example of the perfection of reed voicing that it can be used alone, as a solo stop or in harmony. However, other stops are frequently combined with the Oboe, each for some specific reason, as follows: —

COMBINATIONS WITH AN OBOE

1. To strengthen the tone, and yet preserve much of the characteristic tone-color of the Oboe, add Salicional, Viol d'Orchestre, or even a Voix Céleste.

2. To broaden the tone and to make it rounder and fuller, somewhat at the expense of the real Oboe quality, add a Gedeckt, or other 8 ft. Flute.

3. To make the tone heavier — more bulky, so to speak — add a Diapason.

4. To make the tone louder (approximately), add a 4 ft. Coupler. This addition sometimes produces a harsh effect.

5. To make the tone more cutting and definite, add a Flauto Traverso, or some other 4 ft. Flute.

6. To make the tone heavier and more dignified, add a 16 ft. Coupler.

Note: Obviously, the tone which is produced by the Oboe pipes is not varied any by the addition of these stops, but the resultant tone of the combinations may be described as above.

Needless to say, further modifications of the tone of an Oboe are produced by adding two or more stops, the effect being a combination of the effects already described; for example: —

1. An Oboe, Voix Céleste, Flute 4 ft. and 16 ft. Coupler, produce a combination of reed-tone and string-tone, dignified by the 16 ft. Coupler, and brightened by the 4 ft. Flute.

2. An Oboe, Gedeckt, and Flute 4 ft. produce a round, full tone, in which the tone of the Oboe is less pronounced.

3. A composite solo combination, having a little of the volume, warmth and flexibility of the tone of a violin, used principally between C and c^2, may frequently be obtained by combining the following stops: — Oboe, Cornopean (if not too coarse and strong), Voix Céleste, Vox Humana, Flute 4 ft., and Tremolo. If the music is mostly above c^2, the 16 ft. Coupler can be added with good effect.

COMBINATIONS WITH A CORNOPEAN

What has already been stated relative to the effect which is produced by combining certain stops with an Oboe, may be repeated for a Cornopean; with the exception that the greater power and volume of the tone of the Cornopean lessen the influence of the specific stops, when they are combined with it, and in a few cases, completely cover up the tone of some of the added stops.

COMBINATIONS WITH A VOX HUMANA

The stops most frequently combined with a Vox Humana are the Gedeckt (St. Diapason), Flauto Traverso or other 4 ft. Flute, Salicional, Voix Céleste, and Bourdon 16 ft. A Vox Humana is frequently added to other combinations, when its own special character is partially overshadowed, being merged in the resultant tone.

1. A Gedeckt, combined with a Vox Humana, covers up some of the distinctive reed-tone quality of the Vox Humana, but produces a fuller tone than the following: —

2. A Flauto Traverso 4 ft., combined with a Vox Humana, preserves the distinctive quality of the Vox Humana, but makes the tone more cutting and pronounced.

3. A Voix Céleste, combined with a Vox Humana, gives a rich combination of reed and string-tone. Obviously, if either stop is much louder than the other, its tone will predominate.

4. A soft Bourdon 16 ft., combined with a Vox Humana, produces a somewhat mysterious effect, which is often pleasing, when used between c^1 and c^3.

5. Other combinations of a more composite character are: —

Vox Humana, Voix Céleste and Flute 4 ft.
Vox Humana, Gedeckt and Flute 4 ft.
Vox Humana, Voix Céleste and Bourdon 16 ft.

A 16 ft. Coupler can be used with all the above combinations, especially for solo purposes, except those combinations which contain a Bourdon 16 ft.

Individual opinions of such combinations as those just mentioned differ. Some writers go so far as to state that a Voix Céleste must never be added to such combinations as those above. With all due deference to those who differ with me, it seems to me that we can look to the orchestra for many examples where the strings are used in similar combinations.

COMBINATIONS WITH A CLARINET

The distinctive tone-quality of a Clarinet is such that only 8 and 4 ft. Flute-tone stops can be combined with it without destroying some of its tone-quality. While string-tone stops are occasionally combined with a Clarinet, the real Clarinet-quality of tone is overshadowed in such combinations, unless the tone of the string-tone stops is quite soft. The most usual combinations are: —

Clarinet and Gedeckt. Fuller than a Clarinet alone.
Clarinet and Melodia (Hohl Floete). Somewhat heavy.
Clarinet and Flute d'Amour (or Flauto Traverso 4 ft.). Sharp and clear.
Clarinet and Soft Doppel Floete. Heavy but effective.
Clarinet Ch., Doppel Floete or Melodia Gt., Ch. to Gt. 16 ft. Coupler.

The last combination is a good solo combination when played on the Gt.

COMBINATIONS WITH A TRUMPET

The tone of a Trumpet is a powerful and thin reed-tone; generally too thin, in proportion to its power, to be used alone. Hence, a Diapason 8 ft. is generally combined with it. A strong-toned 8 ft. Flute is generally beneficial, and the addition of a 4 ft. Harmonic Flute brightens the resultant tone. For greater reed-power, in the absence of a Tuba, the Trumpet is generally re-enforced by all the 8 and 4 ft. stops of the Gt.

COMBINATIONS FOR THE ACCOMPANIMENT OF SOLO COMBINATIONS

In small organs, the number of stops and combinations which are suitable for the accompaniment of solo combinations is limited. The Dulciana of the Ch. or Gt. is frequently the only stop which is available for the purpose of accompanying a solo on the Sw. In larger organs, especially if the Ch. is in a swell-box, one can use the 8 ft. Flute (Melodia, Hohl Floete, or Flauto Traverso). A Flute d'Amour 4 ft. can also be used alone, playing an octave lower. If there is a Viol d'Amour 8 ft. or a Gemshorn 8 ft., either stop is suitable for soft accompaniments. A 4 ft. Fugara or Violina in the Ch. can also be used, if one plays an octave lower. For louder accompaniments on the Ch., more stops must be used, sometimes including the Diapason (Geigen Principal).

For soft accompaniments played on the Sw. more combinations are available. The softest stop, Æoline, Dolce or Dolcissimo, if used alone, is generally too soft for an accompaniment. If the 4 ft. Coupler is used with it, this stop is sometimes sufficient for an accompaniment of the softest solo stop of the Ch. The Salicional alone, unless it has a very pungent string-tone, is available. A Gedeckt alone can be used for a short time only, as the ear tires of its cloying character, when this stop is used alone for a long time. A Gedeckt (or Rohr Floete) and a Salicional, a Gedeckt and a Flute 4 ft. or a Gedeckt and a Violina, are most serviceable combinations for P accompaniments. When more power is required, the Diapason or even the Oboe can be added. One or two of the 8 ft. stops with a 4 ft. Coupler also give a good Mp accompaniment.

In addition to the above combinations, one frequently finds it desirable to use such stops as a Voix Céleste or even a Vox Humana for accompaniments. These stops either alone or in combination give a striking character to the accompaniment which is pleasing and frequently necessary. Short repeated chords do not sound well on such combinations, but accompaniments, which are somewhat melodic in themselves, require definite character in the combination, and sound well on the combinations named.

For loud accompaniments, all the 8 and 4 ft. stops with the Oboe, and even the Full Sw., can be used with good effect. On the Gt., if the accompaniment is sustained in character, a Doppel Floete, or a Gross Floete can be used for a few measures. If more power and body are required, a Gamba or a Harmonic Flute can be added.

For very heavy accompaniments to the solos on the Gt. Full Sw., or Full Ch. (without Clarinet), or even the two combinations with Sw. to Ch. Coupler, are serviceable.

COMBINATIONS OF COMPOSITE TONE

Thus far, only combinations of distinctive tone-color have been treated. For many compositions, and for many passages in other compositions, such combinations are unsatisfactory. Louder, fuller, and larger combinations are necessary. These larger combinations are generally called " Chorus Combinations "; the power and volume being more important than the distinctive tone-color. In fact, many stops of several qualities of tone have a tendency to destroy the distinctive color of most of the individual stops. A few of the more common " Chorus Combinations " are: —

Sw. All the 8 and 4 ft. stops, without reeds.
Sw. All the 8 and 4 ft. stops, with Oboe.
Sw. Full.
Gt. All the 8 ft. stops, without reeds.
Gt. All the 8 and 4 ft. stops, without reeds (with or without a 16 ft. stop).
Ch. Melodia, Diapason and Flute 4 ft.
Ch. All the 8 and 4 ft. stops, without reeds.

APPROPRIATE PEDAL COMBINATIONS

" Appropriate Pedal Combinations " are a problem; partially because few organs have a sufficient number of stops in the Pedal department, but principally because theory and practice, in combining organ stops, cannot always coincide. If one is playing on a Flute-tone combination of 8, or 8 and 4 ft. stops, the Pedal combination, theoretically, ought to be Flute-tone. For this purpose we use a Bourdon, with an 8 ft. Gedeckt, or with a manual to Pedal Coupler. This is generally satisfactory.

If one is playing on an 8 ft., or 8 and 4 ft., Diapason combination, the Pedal combination, theoretically, ought to be 16 and 8 ft. Diapason-tone. The 16 ft. Diapason in the Pedal organ is frequently too loud and ponderous for many manual Diapason combinations, and the Dulciana 16 ft. is too soft. Therefore, we are compelled to use 16 and 8 ft. Flute-tone (Bourdon and Gedeckt), 16 ft. Dulciana, 16 ft. string-tone (Violone) and manual to Ped. Coupler, presuming that all the stops named are in the individual organ.

If one is playing on a string-tone combination, the Ped. 16 ft. string-tone stop (Violone or Double Gamba) is much too heavy, except in those cases when the manual string-tone combination is loud, being reenforced by other stops. For the string-tone combination, we more frequently use (in the Ped.) the Bourdon 16 ft., with or without a Cello or Gedeckt, and a manual to Ped. Coupler. A 16 ft. Dulciana is frequently included.

If one is playing on a reed-tone combination, the " appropriate Ped. combination " is, theoretically, a 16 ft. reed-tone stop (Double Bassoon or Contra Fagotto). Generally, neither of these stops, if used alone, is satisfactory for this purpose. If neither of the stops is in the organ, we are again compelled to use the 16 ft. Flute-tone (Bourdon) with or without a Cello (string-tone) or a Gedeckt (Flute-tone), and a manual to Ped. Coupler.

In selecting " appropriate Ped. combinations " for the combination pistons or combination pedals, it is customary, first, to select a sufficient volume of 16 and 8 ft. tone, principally Flute-tone; second, to add as much " appropriate tone " as possible without making the Ped. combination obtrusive. With such a compromise, the player can add any special Ped. stop which is available for any emergency.

For the softest Ped. passages, one must use the softest 16 ft. Ped. stop which is available. In some organs, the Bourdon of the Sw. is " borrowed " in the Ped. as a " Lieblich Gedeckt." A few organs have a distinct Leiblich Bourdon 16 ft. which is not " borrowed." In some other organs, the 16 ft. Dulciana of the Ch. is " borrowed " in the Ped. In the absence of each of these three stops, one can use the Bourdon Bass of the Sw. (if the stop is divided) with the Sw. to Ped. Coupler, in the passages which do not require other stops in the Sw. As a last resort, one must use the Ped. Bourdon 16 ft. If this is much too loud, it is frequently necessary to play the Ped. notes staccato.

If the Pedal part is melodic, or is a moving bass part of the harmony, an 8 ft. tone must be added to the Bourdon, if possible; either a Ped. Gedeckt 8 ft., or a manual to Ped. Coupler. Likewise, if the Pedal part consists of short detached notes of some rhythmic importance, an 8 ft. tone is necessary, to give definiteness to both the rhythm and the pitch. In the absence of a Ped. Gedeckt, the Ch. to Ped. Coupler with the Melodia in the Ch. sometimes answers as a compromise. In two-manual organs, with the Melodia in the Gt., this compromise is rarely acceptable, as the Melodia is generally too powerful for such a purpose in such organs. A Cello 8 ft. in the Ped. rarely answers for such passages, as the tone of a Cello is somewhat hard and inflexible.

As the manual combinations increase in power, more power is likewise required in the Ped. part. If the organ does not contain a number and variety of Pedal stops, the organist is frequently obliged to resort to numerous compromises. If the organ contains a Violone 16 ft. in the Ped., this stop, with the Bourdon 16 ft. and Gedeckt 8 ft., with or without a manual to Ped. Coupler, answers for the MF Ped. combinations. One can occasionally strengthen the Ped. part by using two manual to Ped. Couplers, with such manual stops as are available; e. g., if one is playing on the Sw., with a fairly loud combination, and the Ped. combination, even with the Sw. to Ped. Coupler, is inadequate, one can add the Ch. to Ped. (or Gt. to Ped. in some two-manual organs), after drawing the Melodia in the Ch. (or Gt.). Furthermore, a 4 ft. Flute can sometimes be included in the Ch. (or Gt.) combination. If one is playing the passage under consideration on the Ch., the Sw. to Ped. Coupler can rarely be used if the Oboe is on, as the tone of the Oboe in the bass octave (by means of the Coupler) is objectionable in the Ped. part.

For special solo passages in the Pedal part, one must generally obtain the desired tone-color by coupling manual stops to the Ped., though occasionally an 8 ft. Flute, Cello, reed-tone stop, or Chimes, is available, and can be used as a distinct Ped. stop. Ped. combinations for specific passages are suggested in the chapters which are devoted to the registration of specific compositions.

Combinations of 16, 8, 4, and 2 ft. Flute-tone are sometimes desirable, particularly in the upper octaves, for certain effects. In the Sw. organ, such combinations are obtained in four distinct ways, the resultant tone varying somewhat in each of the combinations, as follows: —

1. Bourdon 16 ft., Gedeckt (St. Diapason) 8 ft., Flauto Traverso 4 ft., and Flautino 2 ft.

2. Bourdon 16 ft., Gedeckt 8 ft., Flauto Traverso 4 ft., and 4 ft. Coupler.

3. Gedeckt 8 ft., Flauto Traverso 4 ft., Flautino 2 ft., and 16 ft. Coupler.

4. Gedeckt 8 ft., Flauto Traverso 4 ft., with 16 and 4 ft. Couplers.

Combinations of 16, 8 and 4 ft. string-tone can be obtained by using a Voix Céleste (or Salicional), Violina 4 ft. and 16 ft. Coupler; or Voix Céleste with 16 and 4 ft. Couplers.

A few sparkling combinations of Flute-tone, for solo passages, played principally in the upper octaves, can be obtained by using: —

1. Bourdon 16 ft., Flautino 2 ft., 4 ft. Coupler and Tremolo.

2. Gedeckt 8 ft., Flautino 2 ft., 16 ft. Coupler and Tremolo.

3. Bourdon 16 ft., Flute 4 ft., 4 ft. Coupler and Tremolo.

A delicate combination, somewhat suggestive of "divided strings muted," may be obtained by using the Æoline, soft Violina 4 ft., 16 and 4 ft. Couplers and the Tremolo.

In selecting combinations of stops for certain phrases of music, the student must always bear in mind that the tonal effect which is produced by a certain phrase of music, when played on a selected combination of stops, is governed largely by four conditions: 1. The necessary power. 2. The character of the phrase; whether it consists principally of repeated chords, arpeggios, runs, or is polyphonic in character. 3. The rapidity of the consecutive tones. 4. The pitch of the major part of the phrase; i. e., whether the phrase is principally in the two middle octaves, in the two upper octaves, or in the two lower octaves of the manual. A combination of stops which sounds pleasing with repeated chords played in the two middle octaves, may sound the reverse with arpeggios played in the two upper octaves. A combination which sounds pleasing with sustained chords played in the upper octaves, may sound very objectionable with the same sustained chords played in the middle octaves, and may prove intolerable if the phrase is played in the lower octaves. A few combinations are available for all of the above conditions.

It will be noticed that many of the soft combinations, which contain a 16 ft. stop, are generally ineffective in the lower octaves, as the tone of the combination becomes more or less gruff as one approaches tenor C. It will be noticed that combinations containing a 4 ft. Flute frequently sound shrill in the upper octaves. It will also be noticed that combinations which contain a 2 ft. stop (Flautino) sound better in the upper half of the keyboard than in the lower half, and are improved by the addition of a Tremolo, which serves as a "tone-color mixer."

Thomas Elliston, a prominent English writer on organ subjects, has stated: " Stop combinations are in reality problems in acoustics." In addition, one may say that combining organ stops is, to a certain extent, analogous to mixing pigments on the painter's palette. The primary tone-colors of the organ, like the primary pigments on the painter's palette, by themselves, produce great contrasts; but the delicate shading in each case is obtained only by a judicious mixing of the primary colors, either stops or pigments.

CHAPTER XI

INDICATING THE REGISTRATION

WHILE the selection of stops and combinations, for various phases of organ compositions, is a large part of the study of registration, the method of indicating the registration in printed organ music, and of interpreting the indications, is an important branch of the study. In indicating the registration one should keep in mind two important features: first, the desired combinations; and second, the best method of obtaining the specified combinations without disturbing the natural flow of the music.

Many minute indications for the registration may seem superfluous to organists of experience, but I think that all organ instructors will agree that organ students are unable to register a composition by instinct. They must acquire a taste and ability for such registration, and that ability can be acquired only through a careful study of the minute details of registration indications. The fact that organists are frequently unable to follow all the composer's registration indications, on account of the difference in organs, does not seem to me to be any argument against the use of clear and definite indications. The organist certainly can obtain a better idea of the composer's intentions, and also is better able to adapt them to the organ on which he is playing, irrespective of its shortcomings, if the composer has placed definite registration indications in his composition.

As the repertoire of organ music, with which an organist becomes equipped, generally consists of compositions which are published by American, English, French, and German publishers, it is necessary that organists should be familiar with the various terms and expressions which are used in the various countries to indicate the different keyboards.

A COMPARATIVE TABLE OF MANUAL AND PEDAL INDICATIONS

English	Eng.	Ger.	German	French
Great (Gt.)	I	II	Hauptwerk (Hptw.) (H. W.)	Grand Orgue (G. O.) (G.)
			Hauptmanual (Hptm.)(H. M.)	
Swell (Sw.)	II	III	Oberwerk (Oberw.) (Obw.) (O. W.)	Récitif (Récit.)(R.)
			Schwellerwerk	
Choir (Ch.)	III	I	Unterwerk (Unterw.) (U. W.)	Positif (Pos.) (P.)
			Ruckwerk (R. W.)	
			Positiv	
Solo (So.)	IV	IV	Solowerk	Clavier des Bombardes
Echo (Ech.)	V	V	Echowerk	
Pedal (Ped.)			Pedal (Ped.)	Pédale (Péd.)

The English terms which are used to indicate the various keyboards do not require any explanation. The use of Roman numerals for this purpose, which has been adopted by a few English, American, and German composers, is somewhat confusing, on account of the two different plans of allotting the numerals which are in use. If the manuals are numbered according to the natural order of the manuals (first column of numerals in the above table), the plan is easily comprehended, and the numerals indicate the same manuals whether the organ has two, three, or four manuals. If, however, the manuals are numbered from the lowest to the highest, irrespective of which manual is the lowest, considerable confusion is caused; as the numerals for each manual vary according to the number of manuals, and also according to whether the Gt. or the Ch. is the lowest manual. In a two-manual organ, by this plan, the Gt. is numbered " I," and the Sw. " II." In a three-manual organ, if the Ch. is the lowest manual, it is numbered " I," the Gt. " II," and the Sw. " III." If the Gt. is the lowest manual, it is numbered " I," the Sw. " II," and the Ch. " III." There does not seem to be any logical reason for the use of Roman numerals to indicate the manuals in English and American organ music. The abbreviations, Gt., Sw., Ch., etc., require no more space on the printed page than do the Roman numerals. They always indicate the same manuals, whether the organ has two, three, or four manuals, and cannot be misunderstood.

After the specific terms for the indication of the various manuals have been decided, the position of the indications, with regard to the phrases and notes on the printed page, must be considered. The position of the manual indications ought to be so definite and clear that the student cannot possibly misunderstand the composer's intentions. Unfortunately, this is not always the case, and we find many vague indications. Experienced organists can generally interpret the composer's intentions, but the student is frequently confused and misled, if the indications are not definite and clear.

A single manual indication in the first measure of a composition (A, B, or C, in the illustration on the following page), obviously, indicates that both hands are to be played on the manual indicated, until a change of manual is indicated. The exact position of this manual indication (" Sw.") may seem immaterial, but the position at A is preferable. If a voice (or part) enters after the other voices, as at D, the single manual indication holds good just the same, though the addition of the pointers in E makes the indication clearer.

In illustration F, it is perhaps obvious that both hands should be played on the Gt. If, however, the indication " Gt." were inserted at the first note of the L. H. part in both the second and third measures, any doubt in the mind of the student would be avoided. The indications for the two manuals in illustration G require no explanation. The position of " Sw." and " Ch." in the illustration is immaterial.

In some printed compositions, there are no manual indications at the beginning of the composition. Such omission, like the omission of all registration and the omission of all indications for the dynamics, necessi-

tates the exercise of individual taste, and no suggestions in the abstract
can be formulated for such conditions.

After the first measures of a composition, the indications for the
manual changes are of various character, according to the conditions.
Inserting the abbreviation of the name of the manual (Gt., Sw., Ch.,
etc.) at the particular point where the change of manuals is desired, if

that change is for both hands together, is occasionally sufficient, as at
H and I, especially if there is a rest or a definite division between two
phrases at the particular point. Otherwise, it is advisable to insert
brackets or pointers connecting the manual indication with the particular
note on which the change is to occur; as in illustrations J and K.

In illustration L, on page 108, every organist naturally plays
the first two measures with both hands on the Ch. In the third
and fourth measures, students hesitate, and frequently play the R. H.
on the Sw. and the L. H. on the Ch. Obviously, the composer intended
both hands to be played on the Sw. If the manual indication (" Sw.")

were placed between the staves, as in the first measure, the confusion would be avoided.

In illustration M, the composer intended the L. H. melody of the second measure to be played on the Gt. and the R. H. on the Sw.; but students frequently play both hands on the Gt., particularly if the indication " Gt." is located midway between the staves. If the staves are some distance apart and " Gt." is placed near the lower staff, there is less liability of confusion. It seems wiser, however, to avoid the possibility of confusion by placing " Sw." under and over the upper staff at this point, or by inserting a pointer between " Gt." and the voice to be played on that manual.

In illustration N, many students play the second and third measures, with both hands on the Gt., the fourth measure with both hands on the Sw., and the sixth measure with both hands on the Gt. The composer intended the L. H. melody of the second and third measures to be played on the Gt., the R. H. remaining on the Ch. In the fourth measure the composer intended the R. H. melody to be played on the Ch. and the L. H. accompaniment to be played on the Sw. The composer's intention in the fifth measure is to play both hands on the Ch. The sixth measure obviously should be played the same as the second measure. It is a simple matter for a composer to indicate the manuals so that the intention cannot be misunderstood, and, while a few points may be taken for granted, it does not seem wise to leave room for any doubt. Oftentimes, the music-engraver fails to realize the importance of the exact *position* of the indications " Gt.," " Sw.," " Ch.," etc. However, the composer must assume part of the responsibility if he does not place clear and definite indications in his Ms. and insist on their exact reproduction in the proofs. In illustration N, a part of the possible confusion is avoided if " Gt." is placed *below* the L. H. staff in the second and sixth measures; but all possibility of confusion is avoided if " Ch." is also placed above the upper staff in the fourth and six measures.

Having considered the manual indications, we must now turn our attention to the indications for changing the stops. To any one who has examined much English and American organ music, it is apparent that there is an absence of any established system of indicating the stop movements. Different composers use different terms and expressions to indicate the registration; and moreover, individual composers frequently use different terms and expressions to indicate the same stop movement in a single composition.

At the beginning of a composition many composers indicate the specific combinations of stops which are first required on all the manuals and pedal; e. g.: —

Prepare: Gt. to Octave.
           Sw. 8 and 4 ft. with Oboe.
           Ch. Melodia and Dulciana.
           Ped. Diapason, Bourdon, and Gedeckt.
           Sw. to Gt., Sw. and Gt. to Ped.

The word " prepare " is optional and is frequently omitted. These indications for the registration require no explanation. Some composers do not specify the combinations, but indicate only " F " and " P." Some composers indicate the manuals without naming any stops. Other composers, while specifying the combinations which they desire, indicate these combinations only in the measures when they are required. The first plan mentioned above enables the performer to see at a glance just which combinations he can prepare before beginning to play, and frequently enables him to avoid one or two awkward changes during the progress of the composition.

At the beginning of a composition, the music engraver can always allot sufficient space to clearly indicate the registration which the composer desires, but after the first measures there is frequently insufficient space available for the registration indications. To make the indications as brief as possible, composers have resorted to numerous expressions, as will be seen in the following list, each line of which is copied from some piece of printed music:—

SPECIMENS OF REGISTRATION INDICATIONS
(Selected from printed organ music)

{ Add Flute { Flute off	(Draw Sw. to Gt. { Put on Sw. to Gt. (Put in the Sw. to Gt.
{ Open the Gamba { Shut the Gamba (Close the Gamba	⌠ Add the Bourdon | Remove the Bourdon { Put back the Bourdon | Thrust in the Bourdon
{ St. Diapason out { St. Diapason in	
⌠ On Oboe | Off Oboe { In Oboe | Retire the Oboe ⌊ Prepare the Oboe	⌠ Put on the Ch. reeds | Fix Ch. reeds { Put off Ch. reeds ⌊ Take off Ch. reeds
	{ + Salicional { — Salicional

The significance of each one of the above quotations is perfectly clear to any organist, but it is obvious that there is no tangible reason for retaining so many pairs of opposite indications, as each pair of indications has the same significance. The indications "on" and "off"; "out" and "in"; "open" and "shut"; "draw" and "push off," indicate exactly the same operations. Only one pair of such indications is necessary. The plus (+) and minus (—) signs, used to indicate the addition and subtraction of one or more stops, have the merit of clearness and brevity, but, for some reason, they have not become popular with organists.

Organ builders and tuners use the single words "on" and "off" to indicate the position of a stop, and also for imperative directions when the "helper" is requested to "put on" or "put off" a stop. Some composers also use only these words to indicate stop changes; as "Oboe on" (sometimes "on Oboe") and "Oboe off" (sometimes "off Oboe"). The word "add" is oftentimes preferable to the word "on," as it gives a more definite and positive idea of the required registration; e. g., if the indication, "Sw. Oboe and Rohr Floete 4 ft." is followed by "Add Gedeckt," the organist clearly understands that a fuller and somewhat louder combination is to be obtained by adding the Gedeckt. If, however, the organist is obliged to use Oboe and Gedeckt at the outset (instead of Oboe and Rohr Floete), on account of some condition in the individual organ, the expression "Gedeckt on" seems superfluous to him, as the Gedeckt is already on. The expression "Add Gedeckt," in this particular case, is, in reality, just as superfluous as "Gedeckt on," but it conveys the idea that some stop ought to be " added," and nine out of ten organists will add some stop, presumably the Salicional, if the Gedeckt is already on. Unfortunately, the word of opposite meaning, " subtract," requires too much space in the printed page to be used for registration indications. The shortest word that is available for this purpose is " off." There is the same objection to this word that there is to the word " on," but no other word has taken its place, and today, the most popular expressions to indicate "putting on" or " putting off " a stop are " add " and " off "; as " Add Oboe," " Oboe off."

Notwithstanding the lack of system which prevails, it is possible for the composer to partially systemize his registration indications, and thus eliminate a part of the existing confusion. If a specific combination of stops is desired, either at the beginning or in the middle of a composition, it is sufficient to name the stops desired; as, " Sw. Oboe and Rohr Floete 4 ft." This indicates a definite combination which the composer wishes. Obviously, substitutions are frequently necessary on different organs, but this fact has no influence on the meaning of the composer's indication. If, later, the Voix Céleste is to be added to the combination, it is sufficient to indicate, " Add Voix Céleste." If a stop is to be put off, it is sufficient to indicate " Rohr Floete off." If the combination is to be changed entirely, e. g., from " Oboe and Rohr Floete " to " Vox Humana and Bourdon," the change can be indicated in two ways: first, by naming the desired combination, as " Sw. Vox Humana and Bourdon "; or second, by indicating the process of obtaining the new combination, as, " Oboe and Rohr Floete off, add Vox Humana and Bourdon." The first plan has the merit of brevity, though students frequently hesitate with such an indication. The second plan has the merit of definiteness, but it requires more space on the printed page than is sometimes available.

EXPLANATION OF THE MOST COMMON REGISTRATION INDICATIONS

" FF Gt." Full Gt. In modern organs an appropriate Ped. combination is also drawn by the combination piston or pedal which draws Full Gt.

" F Gt." The particular combination piston or pedal which brings on all the 8 and 4 ft. stops of the Gt. (except reeds), with or without a 16 ft. stop. In most modern organs an appropriate Ped. combination is included. In the absence of such a combination piston or pedal, the stops must be drawn by hand.

Note: Many composers make a distinction between " Gt. F " and " F Gt." The former indicates any *forte* combination of stops which the player chooses to use. The latter refers to the particular combination piston or pedal which brings on all the 8 and 4 ft. flue stops (with or without a 16 ft. stop) in the Gt. The same distinction exists between " Sw. F " and " F Sw.")

In very old organs, the usual three combination pedals for the Gt. are labeled " Forte," " Mezzo," and " Piano." In such organs the " Forte " pedal almost always brings on Full Gt. As the combination is distinctly a *fortissimo* combination, including the Mixtures and Trumpet, the name of the pedal seems inappropriate. It certainly causes some confusion; e. g., if the dynamics of the composition call for a *forte* combination in the Gt., one cannot use the " Forte Gt." combination pedal, as its combination is *fortissimo*. The "Piano Gt." pedal is, of course, correctly named. As the word " mezzo " means " half " or " partial " and the " Mezzo Gt." pedal brings on half of the Gt. stops, the name is nominally correct. However, in the dynamics of instrumental music, we use the word " mezzo " only in combination with " *forte* " or " *piano*," which gives us the terms, " *mezzo forte* " and " *mezzo piano*." Now, the " Mezzo Gt." combination pedal does not bring on a " *mezzo forte* " combination. Hence, when the dynamic indication is " MF," one cannot use the " Mezzo Gt." combination pedal. If these three combination pedals are named respectively, " Fortissimo Gt.," " Forte Gt.," and " Piano Gt.," the names of the pedals correspond to the real character of the combinations, FF, F, and P.

" P Gt. " Obviously, " P " indicates a *piano* combination on whichever manual is indicated, but a further meaning of the expression " P Gt." is generally intended. There may be several stops and combinations in the Gt., each of which is " *piano*," but there is generally one stereotyped combination which, by long usage, has received the name " P Gt." and is controlled by a piston or pedal which is called " P Gt." If the piston or pedal is of the " movable " type, it both draws and puts off the stops so as to give the required combination. If the pistons or pedals are " adjustable " the organist generally adjusts one piston or pedal to draw this combination. In two-manual organs, the P Gt. piston or pedal generally brings on Melodia (or Hohl Floete) and Dulciana. In three-manual organs, the P Gt. combination is either Doppel Floete (or Gross Floete) and Gamba, Doppel Floete and Harmonic Flute 4 ft., or Doppel Floete, Gamba, and Harmonic Flute.

" FF Sw." The combination piston or pedal which brings on Full Sw. In modern organs an appropriate Ped. combination is included.

" F Sw." The combination piston or pedal which brings on all the 8 and 4 ft. flue stops (except the Célestes) with the Oboe and an appropriate Ped. combination. The previous remarks concerning the " F Gt." combination pedal in old organs apply equally well to the " F Sw." combination pedal or piston. Much confusion is avoided by naming the three Sw. combination pedals " FF Sw.," " F Sw.," and " P Sw."

" P Sw." The combination piston or pedal which brings on, or reduces to, the stereotyped combination, St. Diapason (or Rohr Floete), Salicional, and frequently one 4 ft. stop (Violina or Flute 4 ft.). This combination varies a great deal in different organs. It sometimes includes the Ped. Bourdon but more frequently is not connected with any of the Ped. stops.

When " P Sw." (or " Sw. P ") is indicated at the beginning of a composition, the choice of the individual stops is left entirely to the taste of the performer. In the middle of a composition, " Sw. P " has the same significance, but the expression " P Sw.," in the middle of a composition, especially if it follows a louder combination on the same manual, generally indicates the particular piston or pedal which gives the above stereotyped *piano* combination. At such points the volume of the tone is of more importance than the specific tone-color. While this distinction between " P Sw." and " Sw. P " is small, it is frequently convenient in indicating registration. With some composers the same distinction is made between " P Gt." and " Gt. P."

" F Ch." Generally all the Ch. stops except the reeds and the Célestes, though the 2 ft. stop is frequently omitted. In old organs the Ch. is rarely large and powerful enough to have three combination pedals which would be designated, " FF," " F," and " P." In large modern organs the Ch. combination pistons are numerous and numbered. This fact, together with the special character of the Ch. stops and combinations, and their usage, prevents the necessity of minute distinctions for the names of the combinations of this manual.

" P Ch." This combination, which is of much utility, varies in different organs. It frequently consists of the Melodia (Hohl Floete or Concert Flute) and Dulciana. In larger organs a 4 ft. Flute is frequently included.

" F Ped." Full Ped. without reeds, except in very large organs where Full Ped. ought to be named " FF Ped."

" P Ped." Bourdon and Gedeckt, or Bourdon alone if there is no Gedeckt in the Ped.

Note: Obviously, the stereotyped combinations mentioned above, in connection with the FF, F, and P combination pedals and pistons, are subject to the variations which individual taste dictates. The student, however, will find the road to artistic registration much smoother if he starts with these stereotyped combinations. He can then vary the combinations as his personal taste matures.

" Sw. Gedeckt and Salicional."

" Gt. Doppel Floete and Gamba."

When a specific combination of stops is indicated, as above, unaccompanied by any qualifying word, such as " add " or " off," only the specified stops are intended to be used. Obviously, when the individual organ does not contain the specified stops, or when, for some reason, the combination is objectionable, other stops must necessarily be substituted, according to the discretion of the player.

" Sw. Gedeckt (St. Diapason) and Salicional."

" Sw. Voix Céleste (Salicional and Flute 4 ft.)."

" Sw. Rohr Floete (Gedeckt) and Oboe."

Stops or combinations of stops whose names are enclosed in parentheses, *in the midst of registration indications*, are intended as substitutes or optional stops or combinations. Occasionally, a stop name enclosed in a parenthesis indicates another name of the same stop; as Gedeckt (St. Diapason). It should be understood that the suggested substitutes are intended only as *possible substitutions*, and are not intended to indicate stops or combinations which are " just as good."

"(Prepare Ch. Melodia and Flute 4 ft.)"

"(F Gt.)"

If the entire phrase of a registration indication is enclosed in a parenthesis, unaccompanied by any other indication, it generally signifies a "preparation" for some future phrase of the music, which can be made at the indicated point, with practically no audible effect on the combination which is being used at the time.   These indications are generally placed in measures which permit the changes to be made (with either hand or foot) with the least interruption in the flow of the music.   Occasionally, these indicated combinations may not be required for several measures, but it is desirable to prepare them when the hand or foot can well be spared for that purpose; especially if they are to be required at an instant when no changing of the stops is possible without an objectionable break in the flow of the music.

"Gedeckt only."

"Gedeckt alone."

Theoretically, the words "alone" and "only" are superfluous, when indicating a single stop; but experience shows that many students fail to reduce the combination to a *single* stop unless the additional word is used.

"Grand Cresc. Full (F Gt.)."

As the Grand Crescendo does not affect the draw-stops, one can prepare "F Gt." independent of the Grand Crescendo, which in this case is open "full."   Hence, when the Grand Crescendo is closed, the F Gt. combination remains on.   It should be noted, in passing, that one of the functions of the Grand Crescendo is to bring on Full Organ when desired, even without attempting a crescendo.   The above plan of combining it with certain combinations of stops to which the player can easily return, in closing the Grand Cresc., is frequently a great convenience.   It may eliminate several stop changes which the flow of the music renders practically impossible without awkward pauses.

"Gt. to Open Diapason." All the 8 ft. stops except the reeds.

"Gt. to Octave." All the 8 and 4 ft. stops except the reeds.   This combination frequently includes the 16 ft. Diapason.

"Sw. to Oboe." The principal 8 and 4 ft. flue stops and the Oboe.

Primarily, the indication "Gt. (or Sw. or Ch.) to" any specific stop, indicates all the stops on that particular manual which would be naturally used in building up a crescendo to, and including, the stop named.

Note: The Vox Humana, all the Célestes, and the Clarinet are not included in any general combination unless specifically named.

"Full Organ."

"Sfz."

There are two kinds of "Full Organ" combinations in large organs.   The Grand Cresc. generally gives all the speaking stops, except the Tuba, the Vox Humana, the Célestes, and the Clarinet, and all the unison couplers.   The Sfz pedal, in addition to the above, includes the 16 and 4 ft. couplers and the Tuba unless it is very loud.   In smaller organs the Sfz pedal is frequently omitted, in which case the Grand Crescendo frequently includes the 16 and 4 ft. couplers.

CHAPTER XII

MANIPULATING THE STOPS

AFTER considering the selection of the stops and combinations for the effective registration of a composition, and the method of indicating the selected registration in the printed copies, it is necessary to consider the method of manipulating the stops — of obtaining the desired combinations at the required instants, without objectionable breaks in the flow of the music.

Stop changes, during the progress of the music, ought to be made quietly, quickly, easily, and without undue exhibition of effort. Otherwise, much of the beauty of the music is unheard or is forgotten, on account of the distraction caused by the mechanical part of the registration. It seems hardly necessary to state that all stop changes ought to be made without any noise of the mechanism of the organ. In modern organs, practically all the mechanism is noiseless, but there still exist many fine old organs whose mechanism requires special care from the player, in order to avoid the distracting blemishes of rattling and pounding mechanism. With such organs, the careful organist does not draw or put off the draw-stops with a rigid, stiff wrist, which generally produces a hard thud. He avoids much of the noise by using as little power as is necessary, and by having the wrist (or ankle) loose, so that its elasticity acts somewhat like a " buffer " when the mechanism " strikes home."

It is just as essential for the organist to manipulate the stops quietly as it is for a pianist to refrain from stamping his feet on the floor when he is playing. Many beautiful passages of organ music have been marred by the noise of the stop manipulations, which, in some instances, sound like the slamming of a door. Old-fashioned combination pedals frequently are noisy, but the noise can generally be minimized by the exercise of a little extra care.

Long pauses in the music, for the sole purpose of changing the stops, at points where such pauses are unnatural, ought to be, and generally can be, avoided. If many changes are necessary at a given point, for the registration of the following measures, the organist should analyze the changes; as he will generally discover that some of the changes can be made earlier, during rests in one hand or the other, which will reduce the number of changes to be made at the given point. When several changes are absolutely necessary at a given point, the organist should *arrange the order* of the changes, so that all changes which are to be made on one side of the manuals, or with one hand, can be made together; thus avoiding the apparent confusion of alternating several times between the two sides of the console, in making the stop changes. It does not enhance the beauty of the music to see the organist, with waving hands, oscillating from one side of the console to the other, while arranging his combinations during a much-prolonged pedal note. Above all, the organist ought never to prolong an incomplete chord, with one hand, while making changes with the other hand. Occasionally, a single note of a chord, either the upper note, the pedal note, or the root of the chord in an inner voice, can be prolonged one or two counts while the changes of stops are made. One should rarely, if ever, prolong the upper note and the pedal note, without any of the intervening notes. Two tones so far apart (frequently five octaves) generally produce an empty effect which is not agreeable.

Changes of stops which are tonally audible as changes, while prolonging a chord or single note, frequently are objectionable. If the changes of stops cannot be made without an objectionable audible effect, it were better to make a distinct break in the music for the purpose of making the changes of stops. There are, however, some exceptions to the above assertion; viz., putting off the stops one by one in such a manner as to produce a gradual diminuendo, while prolonging a chord or note, is frequently acceptable. The reverse process — making a crescendo — is less frequently acceptable. Occasionally, changes of stops, while sustaining a chord or single note, can be made in such a manner that the combinational tone seems to dissolve from one combination to the other, like the dissolving views of a stereopticon; e. g., to change from the combination, Gedeckt, Violina, and Flute 4 ft., to Bourdon, Salicional, and Flute 4 ft., draw the Salicional first, put off the Violina second, and lastly, draw the Bourdon and put off the Gedeckt with one motion. Again, one can sometimes change, from a combination of three or four stops, to another combination of three or four stops, while holding a single note, without an unpleasant effect, in the following manner: to change from Rohr Floete, Salicional, and Violina, to Oboe, Salicional, and Flute 4 ft., while holding a single note; with one motion put off the Rohr Floete and Violina, with a second motion draw the Oboe and Flute 4 ft. This change can be made quickly, without sustaining the single note, but some passages of music require the closest connection between the chords or the notes of the melody, and with such passages this method of changing the stops seems better than any other method. Obviously, these changes should be made with as little pause in the rhythm as possible.

With large modern organs which have many combination pistons or pedals, many stop changes can easily be made without any pause in the music, by pressing one of the pistons located under the manuals, or by pressing a combination pedal with the foot. Such organs frequently have three to eight adjustable pistons, of the movable type, — sometimes called " Full Organ Pistons," — which are connected with all the stops of the organ, so that any conceivable combination of stops on all the manuals and the pedal can be adjusted beforehand, thus enabling the player to change from any possible previous combination to this desired combination with the push of a single piston.

With old organs which are not provided with such combination facilities, the organist is obliged to develop considerable ingenuity and skill, in order to make the necessary changes of stops without awkward pauses in the music.

When playing on a specific combination of stops, if it is necessary to add one or two stops at a certain point, the organist must decide just how the change can best be made. If there is a rest or a natural break in the phrase, for either hand, the change should be made at that point with the hand which is free, unless that hand cannot reach the desired stops. Crossing the arms is frequently necessary in manipulating the stops, but it should be attempted only when the stops can be easily reached by the hand which crosses. At other times, it is frequently necessary to substitute one hand for the other on certain chords or notes, so that the hand on the side where are located the stops which are to be manipulated can be free.

While it is frequently permissible to *ritard* the tempo slightly to facilitate the registration, one ought not to add a count or two in one measure, when such a prolonging of the measure completely destroys the natural rhythm of the phrase. If a certain change of stops is indicated in the printed copy, or it seems desirable to the organist to make the change at a certain point, where there is no rest or natural break in the phrase for either hand, the organist must sacrifice either some of the notes or the intended registration. If he decides to omit some of the notes, he should omit the less important notes or figures in one hand or the other. A long sustained chord or a single note in either hand can frequently be divided for this purpose, if the other hand can supply satisfactory harmony. If the passage consists of a melody in one hand and an accompaniment in the other hand, no positive rule can be laid down regarding which part should be sacrificed. If the melody is a continuous succession of somewhat rapid notes it should not be broken. If the melody contains several sustained notes, and the accompaniment consists of repeated chords or is a flowing accompaniment, it is generally advisable to make a break in the melody for the stop change, dividing it into two phrases, thus preserving the rhythm of the accompaniment.

On organs which have combination pedals or pistons of the movable type, quite a number of the larger changes of stops can best be made by combining a combination piston or pedal with a hand movement of the stops; e. g., if the first combination is Bourdon, St. Diapason, and Fugara, and one wishes to change to Salicional and Flute 4 ft., one can first push a piston or pedal which brings on a stereotyped " P Sw." combination (St. Diapason, Salicional, and Flute 4 ft.), and second, put off the St. Diapason, thus leaving the Salicional and Flute 4 ft. At first glance, this plan seems no better than making the change wholly by hand movement of the stops — putting off two stops and drawing two other stops — as two motions are necessary in both plans. However, experience proves that it is frequently easier to combine the piston with a hand movement of the stops than to make the change wholly by hand movement of the stops.

PART TWO

CHAPTER XIII

REGISTRATION OF HYMN-TUNES

IF the student has attended service in various churches he probably has observed that a few organists " give out " every hymn-tune on the Full Sw., and use F Gt. for every stanza which is sung by the congregation. He probably has also observed that a few other organists use Full Organ every time the words " thunder," " roar " or " loud noise " occur in the hymns, and reduce to a soft combination for such words as " whisper," " silence," " slumber," and " peace." Between these two extremes there is the proverbial " happy medium," wherein the organist avoids the monotony of registering every hymn-tune in exactly the same manner, gives a reasonable amount of variety in the registration, and refrains from the ridiculous. Let us first consider the various methods of announcing or " giving out " the hymn-tune.

Many hymn-tunes which have no distinctive musical character sound equally well when " given out " on almost any combination of stops. No one special combination causes these tunes to sound any more pleasing than another combination; for example, Duke Street (John Hatton), Park Street (F. M. A. Venua) and Rockingham (Edward Miller) sound equally well when announced on any legitimate combination of stops from *piano* to *forte*.

There is, however, as much difference in the musical character of many hymn-tunes as there is difference in the sentiment of the hymns. The melodic and harmonic composition of some hymn-tunes, independent of the sentiment of the hymns which are associated with these tunes, is such that they sound particularly pleasing when announced on a somewhat soft combination of a distinctive tonal character; for example, St. Christopher (F. C. Maker), St. Leonard (Henry Hiles), and Ellers (E. J. Hopkins). These tunes can be effectively announced, on many organs, with the following combinations (without pedal): Voix Céleste and Flute 4 ft., Vox Humana and Gedeckt, Vox Humana and Bourdon 16 ft. (if the Bourdon is not too loud), Salicional and Flute 4 ft., and Oboe and Flute 4 ft.

There are other hymn-tunes which possess so much of the processional character that they sound better when announced on a combination of a March character; for example, Diademata (G. J. Elvey), Webb (G. J. Webb), Greenland (Lausanne Psalter). These tunes sound well when announced on F or Full Sw., on the 8 and 4 ft. stops (F) in the Ch., or on the Gt. to Diapason.

Some hymn-tunes are so closely associated with hymns of loud praise

117

that it seems inappropriate to announce them otherwise than on a loud combination; for example, Mendelssohn (Felix Mendelssohn), Hummel (Charles Zeuner), and Hanover (William Croft).

A few hymn-tunes are so rich in their harmony that they sound particularly pleasing when announced on a rich combination of Diapasons and Flutes (mostly of 16 and 8 ft. pitch); for example, Ewing (Alexander Ewing), Nicea (J. B. Dykes), St. Ann's (William Croft). Combination: Gt. Diapasons 16 and 8 ft., Gross Floete and Har. Flute 4 ft.: Sw. 8 and 4 ft. without Oboe or Voix Céleste: Ch. Diapason, Melodia, and Flute 4 ft.: Ped. 32, 16 and 8 ft.: Sw. to Gt. 16 and 8 ft., Ch. to Gt. 16 and 8 ft., Gt. to Ped.

A few hymn-tunes consist of a melody, which sounds well announced as a solo, and harmony in the three lower voices so arranged that it can be easily played as accompaniment with the L. H. and Ped.; for example, Hamburg (arranged by Lowell Mason), Lyons (J. M. Haydn), Old Hundredth (Geneva Psalter). Combinations: 1. The solo on the Ch. with Clarinet, Melodia and Flute 4 ft., the accompaniment on the Sw. 8 and 4 ft. without Oboe, Ped. Bourdon and Sw. to Ped. 2. The solo on the Sw. with Cornopean, Oboe, Gedeckt, Salicional and Flute 4 ft., the accompaniment on the Ch. Melodia and Flute 4 ft., Ped. Bourdon and Ch. to Ped. 3. The solo on the Gt. with Diapason and Doppel Floete, the accompaniment on the Sw. with 8 and 4 ft. and Oboe (swell open), Ped. Bourdon, Gedeckt and Sw. to Ped.

A few hymn-tunes have a somewhat martial character, due partially to the hymns which are associated with the tunes. These tunes sound well when announced on the Sw. reeds (F); for example, Waltham (J. B. Calkin), to which is sung "Uplift the banner"; Nuremberg (J. H. Ahle), to which is sung "Wake the song of Jubilee"; and Yarmouth (Lowell Mason), to which is sung "Hail to the Lord's anointed." These tunes may be announced on the Sw. with Cornopean, Oboe, Diapason, Gedeckt, Salicional and Flute 4 ft., with Ped. Violone, Bourdon, Gedeckt, and Sw. to Ped.

Still another method of announcing the hymn-tunes is suggested by whatever immediately precedes the hymn; for example, if a hymn (unannounced from the pulpit) follows an organ or choir selection which has ended P or PP, the first two lines of the hymn-tune can be played P, the third line MF, and the last line or lines F. This is especially appropriate in churches where an opening hymn like the Old Hundredth follows the organ prelude. In such cases there are two different courses open to the organist; viz., First, the organist can modulate from the closing key of the prelude to the key of the Old Hundredth, partly on the soft combination with which the prelude ends and partly with a few stops added at various points in the modulation, until the organ is prepared for the combination which is intended to be used for announcing the tune. Second, the organist can modulate wholly on the soft combination with which the prelude ends, draw a few stops, play the first two lines of the tune, add Sw. to Oboe or a similar combination for the third line of the tune, and open the swell or add Full Sw. for the last line or lines of the tune. See examples I, II and III on the following pages.

The use of the pedal in announcing hymns depends largely on the registration which is selected. If a hymn is announced on a soft combination it is generally advisable to omit the pedal. If a hymn is announced

on a loud combination it is advisable to use the pedal. If a hymn is announced as a solo it is, obviously, necessary to use the pedal. At other times personal inclination can be followed regarding the use of the pedal.

In accompanying congregational singing the principal duties **of the** organist are, to play the melody clearly, to give the congregation sufficient support in the harmony, and to mark the rhythm distinctly within

the bounds of good organ playing. Regarding the combination of stops which must be selected to adequately supply the above accompaniment, much depends on the character of the organ and the size of the congregation. Generally, it is necessary to use the Gt. Diapason with the

8 and 4 ft. stops of the Sw. coupled. If the organ is voiced loud and the congregation is small the Diapason frequently can be omitted; but generally, it is the best stop to use as a basis for the accompaniment of congregational singing. If the Diapason is not loud and the congregation is of fair size it frequently is necessary to add the Octave in the Gt. to make the combination more assertive. The Full Sw. coupled to the Gt., without the Octave, is sometimes sufficient. For the Ped. the Bourdon and an 8 ft. stop (either the Gedeckt or the Cello) are absolutely necessary. The Ped. Diapason is usually necessary to give depth and support which assists the congregation in keeping the rhythm steady. Occasionally, the Ped. Diapason is so overpowering that it can be used only with Full Organ. As I have stated above, if the organist uses Sw. 8 and 4 ft. stops coupled to the Gt. to Diapason, with Ped. Bourdon, Gedeckt and Diapason as a basis, he can easily build up the combination to the required volume by adding first the Oboe, then the Full Sw., and lastly the Octave and 16 ft. Diapason. Sometimes the 16 ft. Diapason can be added before the Octave. The position of the swell shades depends on the power of the individual Swell organ. In some organs the swell ought to be wide open, in other organs partially closed.

If the organist wishes to vary the accompaniment while the congregation is singing he must use a great deal of judgment. In the first place, some weak-voiced congregations have a deep-seated and unalterable habit of dragging the hymns. If the organ is a soft-voiced, unassertive instrument, and there is no chorus of strong voices to lead the congregation, nothing, not even the portamento tooting of a cornet, will prevent the congregation dragging. Under such conditions the organist is compelled to accompany every stanza of every hymn with nearly Full Organ. Any variation in power in these accompaniments is disastrous.

If the congregation is supported by a strong chorus and an adequate organ, the organist can, with discretion, vary his accompaniments of the hymns. Then again, some congregations in medium-sized churches are noted for their fine congregational singing. In those churches, whether or not there is a chorus, the organist can vary his accompaniments according to his taste and the character of the various hymns.

In the majority of hymns one of the middle stanzas, according to the sentiment of the stanza, can be selected to be sung somewhat softer than the other stanzas. This stanza can be accompanied by a *piano* Gt. combination with the Full Sw. (partially closed) coupled; or it can be accompanied on the Full Sw. with the 16 and 4 ft. Couplers, the swell partially open, according to the power of the individual Sw.

With a large organ the organist can vary his accompaniments somewhat while playing *forte*. After accompanying one or two stanzas on the F Gt. with the Full Sw. (closed), he can use the Gross Flute and Har. Flute of the Gt., the Philomela of the So. and Full Sw. (open) with So. and Sw. to Gt. Occasionally, the Sw. 16 and 4 ft. Couplers can be added to this combination. On some large organs the 8 and 4 ft. stops of the Ch., with the reeds and flue stops of the Sw. coupled, give sufficient support in the hymns. In some stanzas the organist can play

the melody of the tune on a loud solo combination of either the Gt. or
So., and the harmony on the Full Sw. (open). Another plan is to play
the melody an octave lower with the L. H. on the So. Tuba and Philomela
and the harmony on the Gt. with the R. H.

All these variations depend both on the character of the individual
hymn and the character of the particular organ. Obviously, Eventide
("Abide with me"), Lux Benigna ("Lead, kindly light"), and Geth-
semane ("Rock of ages") should not be accompanied with any of the
last-named variations.

Occasionally, the natural trend of the sentiment of an individual
stanza suggests a gradual crescendo or diminuendo. This suggestion
can be followed by the organist if he uses moderation: but a sudden
crescendo from P to FF or a sudden FF or PP on any one word or
short phrase savors of bad taste.

In Henry Alford's hymn, "Forward be our watchword," which is
generally sung either to Albans (J. M. Haydn) or to the tune Nissi
(Henry Smart), the second stanza is as follows: —

> " Forward, flock of Jesus,
>   Salt of all the earth;
>   Till each yearning purpose
>   Spring to glorious birth:
>   Sick, they ask for healing,
>   Blind, they grope for day;
>   Pour upon the nations
>   Wisdom's loving ray.
>   Forward, out of error,
>   Leave behind the night;
>   Forward through the darkness,
>   Forward into light."

After playing the first stanza *forte* throughout, the second stanza can
be commenced *forte* and continued for four lines. With the fifth line a
gradual diminuendo to MP can be made to the end of the eighth line.
With the ninth line a somewhat more rapid crescendo can be made to the
last line, which should be played *forte*. The harmonic construction of
both of the tunes mentioned is such that this plan of variation fits the
tunes admirably.

From the foregoing remarks, the student will readily observe that it
is neither necessary nor advisable to have the organ sound louder than
the singing of the congregation in all the stanzas. If the congregation
is led by a good chorus it is occasionally impressive to sing one stanza
of a hymn without any organ accompaniment. The entrance of the
organ in the following stanza is frequently effective. However, the
young organist must not experiment in his hymn-playing until he is
sure of the congregation. He must first be convinced that the congregation will respond to his lead before he attempts any departure from the
old custom of playing the tunes *forte* for all the stanzas. Otherwise, he
is liable to cause more or less dissatisfaction with the incumbent of the
organ bench.

CHAPTER XIV

REGISTRATION OF THE ACCOMPANIMENTS OF ANTHEMS

IN considering the registration of anthem accompaniments, one must bear in mind the difference between a mixed chorus, a boy choir, and a quartet choir. If the student hears the same anthem sung by the three kinds of choirs he will observe that the organists of the different choirs generally register the accompaniment somewhat differently. This difference is not so much a difference of personal taste as it is a difference of the proverbial style of accompanying the different choirs.

The majority of the organists of boy choirs use combinations of a general character — "chorus combinations" as they are sometimes called — instead of combinations of a distinctive tone-color. They do not often make sharp contrasts of tone-color in their accompaniments. This statement is no criticism or reflection on their musicianship. It is merely a statement of the long-established style of accompanying boy choirs.

On the other hand, many organists of mixed chorus choirs frequently vary the tonal color of their accompaniments and frequently select sharp contrasts of color. Just as there is a greater difference in the tonal color of the several vocal parts of a mixed chorus than there is in the vocal parts of a boy choir, so does the organist of the mixed chorus frequently select combinations of more widely varying tone-color in the accompaniments.

The organist of the quartet choir, obviously, uses less volume in the louder parts of the accompaniments than either of the other organists. As the nuances are generally more specifically, if not more artistically, observed in a quartet choir, so must the organist accompany the singers with more delicate and appropriate shadings.

Appropriate combinations for the *forte* passages of the accompaniments are treated further on. For the *piano* passages of the accompaniments one can select from a variety of combinations which have distinctive color. If the accompaniment is for a chorus (either mixed or male) the combinations ought to be fuller, though not louder, then if the accompaniment is for a quartet. While distinctive combinations of two or three stops are sufficient and frequently pleasing in the *piano* accompaniments of a quartet, it is often necessary to use four or five stops for the same accompaniment of a chorus; e. g., two Flutes (8 and 4 ft.), Oboe or Voix Céleste and Flute 4 ft., Gedeckt and Violina, and other similar combinations are sufficient for the *piano* accompaniment of a quartet: but it were better to use Gedeckt, Salicional, Flute 4 ft. and Violina; the same stops with a soft Oboe or Violina Diapason; or even Gedeckt, Salicional, Violin Diapason, Flute 4 ft., Violina, and Oboe, with the swell closed, for a chorus.

For the short interludes between the vocal phrases, the organist should select contrasted combinations to obtain variety and avoid monotony.

The use of the pedal in anthem accompaniments is subject to much variation. In a few accompaniments the use of the pedal is suggested in the printed copies, but in most accompaniments the use of the pedal is left to the inclination of the performer.

It is not wise to use the pedal for every bass note of the accompaniment. In full chorus passages the pedal should be used in most of the *forte* phrases. It can well be omitted in many of the *piano* phrases (for variety), and occasionally in a few *forte* phrases where the bass part of the chorus runs in the upper register and is accompanied by the same notes.

Bass notes which are independent of the bass part of the chorus (or quartet) should generally be played by the pedal. Obviously, the pedal must be used when the chords are too extended to be reached by the two hands, and when the accompaniment consists of a solo for one hand and an extended accompaniment for the other hand.

It is generally advisable to omit the pedal, when the notes which could be played by the pedal correspond to the notes of the bass part of the chorus *if the basses are to sing alone or in a duet.*

When low octaves are printed in the piano accompaniment for the left hand, it is advisable to play *the upper* notes of the octaves with the pedal, instead of the lower notes, except in the loudest phrases.

It is better to err on the side of using the pedal too little than to use the pedal all the time. Continuous use of the pedal, especially in quiet music, becomes tiresome, and a rest in the pedal part is oftentimes a relief as well as a source of variety.

There are two distinct species of anthem accompaniments, irrespective of the kind of choir which renders the anthem. The first species consists almost entirely of a duplication of the voice parts. Practically the only phrases which have an independent accompaniment are the short phrases in which one voice part sings alone, the harmony being supplied by the accompaniment. For anthems of this species I will mention:

O How amiable	Barnby
Lift up your heads	Hopkins
O, Saviour of the world	Goss

Practically the only difference in the registration of the accompaniments of these anthems for the three kinds of choirs is in the volume of tone necessary to support the choirs, as there seems to be but little opportunity to use other than " chorus combinations."

In registering the accompaniment of the anthem, " O How amiable," for a mixed chorus or a boy choir, prepare the following: Gt. to Diapason; Sw. all the 8 and 4 ft. stops with Oboe; Ch. all the 8 and 4 ft. stops except the reeds; Ped. Violone (or Small Diapason), Bourdon and Gedeckt; Sw. to Gt., Sw. to Ch., Ch. and Gt. to Ped.

With this preparation as a basis, we must consider the size of the choir. If the chorus is quite large and its tone is sonorous, it is necessary to add the Octave in the Gt. and have the swell open. If the voicing of the organ is weak and the above combinations are insufficient for

the *forte* passages, it is necessary to add the Full Sw., and possibly the
12th and 15th in the Gt., though the last two stops should be omitted if
possible. If the anthem is sung by a quartet choir the Diapason in the
Gt. and the Ped. Violone (or Diapason) must be omitted.

After deciding the volume of tone which is necessary for the accompaniment of the *forte* passages, the organist can formulate the registration for the rest of the anthem. Presuming that the Gt. to Octave with
the Sw. 8 and 4 ft. with Oboe coupled to the Gt. is sufficient for the
first sixteen measures, I suggest the addition of the Full Sw. (only partially open if the Sw. is quite loud) at the *Più mosso.* My reason for
adding the Full Sw. is not so much to increase the power as to change
the color somewhat, and, more particularly, to provide a better accompaniment for the last four measures of the second page. (If the Full Sw.
were drawn at the outset no change can be made at this point.)   In
these four measures there is a *diminuendo* in all the parts except the
tenor part, which is a melodic imitation (*forte*) of the previous four
measures of the soprano part. At this point, by putting off the Gt. to
Ped. and the Octave (if it is on), the R. H. can play on the Sw. (full)
and the L. H. on the Gt. (to Diapason). In the first two measures at
the top of the third page (*Cresc. e rall.*) a good *crescendo* can be made
by opening the swell. The Octave and Gt. to Ped. can be added for the
Tempo 1°. The registration indicated at this point is "Full Organ."
This indication must be interpreted with considerable judgment. Only
with a small organ or with an unusually large chorus can the Full Organ
be used, *when the voice parts do not run above the middle register and
end in the lower register.*

In the middle section of the anthem, in which the tenors and basses
sing in unison (FF), the accompaniment is indicated "Gt. to Prin." If
the tenors and basses are numerous and have strong voices this registration may be satisfactory, but it prevents any variety in the accompaniment. By playing this accompaniment on the Ch. (which was prepared at the outset with the Sw. to Ch. Coupler and the Full Sw. (open),
a sufficient volume and a variety in the accompaniment are generally
obtained. However, if the men's voices are very strong and the Ch. and
Sw. are too weak it is necessary to follow the registration indicated in
the printed copies.

At the return of the first theme on the fifth page (P), play both hands
on the Sw. with 8 and 4 ft. and Oboe. After sixteen measures add Full
Sw. (closed). During the *molto rit. e cres.*, at the bottom of the sixth
page, open the swell and add Gt. to Octave, Gt. to Ped. and Ped.
Diapason, for the Gloria (last page).

For a quartet choir the registration suggested above must, obviously,
be greatly reduced in volume though the general character of it can be
maintained.

For the accompaniment of the anthem, "Lift up your Heads," of
Hopkins, very little variation in the registration from that of the previous
anthem can be made. For the same choir the organ should be prepared
the same. The first page should be played on the Gt. with Ped. A little
variety in the accompaniment can be obtained by omitting the Ped. in

the first five measures of the second page. The entrance of the Ped. at the sixth measure is especially effective, even though it enters in the middle of a vocal sentence. At the end of the upper brace of the third page ("The Lord strong and mighty") the Ped. can be omitted until the same words are repeated in the middle brace, when the Ped. can be used on the upper notes of the L. H. octaves. For the *diminuendo* play both hands on the Sw. (without Ped.) and gradually close the swell. For the words, "The Lord of Hosts," play on the Gt. (with the swell open), omitting the Ped. until the octaves at the top of the last page, when the upper notes of the L. H. octaves should be played with the Ped. No further change of registration is necessary.

For a quartet choir the Gt. Diapason and Octave must be omitted, except in the last section (after the first double bar), where they can sometimes be used.

For the accompaniment of the anthem, "O Saviour of the World," by Goss, when sung by a chorus, prepare the following: Gt. Doppel Floete, Gamba and Flute 4 ft.; Sw. 8 and 4 ft. with a soft Oboe; Ch. Melodia, Dulciana and Flute 4 ft.; Ped. Bourdon and Gedeckt; Sw. to Gt. and Sw. to Ped.

Play the first eight measures on the Sw. Use the swell pedal to produce the Sf effects. At the ninth measure play both hands on the Ch. (possibly with the Sw. to Ch. drawn) for the sake of variety. On two-manual organs this change, obviously, must be omitted. After playing four measures on the Ch. return to the Sw. with the swell open. In the last measure of the upper brace of page 2 play on the Gt. and produce the *crescendo* by adding the Full Sw. and the Gt. Diapason. At the words, "hast redeemed us," reduce to the first combinations. At the last measure of page 2 play both hands on the Sw., reduced to 8 and 4 ft. without Oboe. For the one measure in which the basses sing alone, omit the Ped. For the following phrase, add the Oboe. The tenor imitations can be played on the Gt. At the words, "who by Thy Cross," play both hands on the Gt. and *crescendo* by adding Full Sw. and the Gt. Diapason. When the altos sing alone the word "save," play on the Sw. reduced to 8 and 4 ft. with Oboe. Six measures before the end, put off the Sw. Oboe and Violin Diapason. Omit the Ped. in these two measures, but use it again on the last four measures, when the Sw. should be gradually reduced.

The second species of anthem accompaniments consists of accompaniments which are more or less independent of the voice parts during a part, or even the whole, of the composition. In accompaniments of this description, the organist frequently has many opportunities to exercise his good taste and judgment in selecting registration which is interesting and varied and, at the same time, gives sufficient support to the voices. Obviously, registration which overpowers the voices and effects which are bizarre are most objectionable. The organist who exhibits good taste and refinement in his selection of registration for the accompaniment of anthems adds a great deal to the effect of the anthems when they are sung in church.

For representative anthems of this species I will mention:

O come let us sing unto the Lord	Tours
The woods and every sweet smelling tree	West
The radiant morn hath passed away	Woodward
In heavenly love abiding	Parker
Sing Alleluia forth	Buck

For quartet choirs especially:

Still, still with thee	Foote
O Lamb of God	Brewer
Peace and Light	Chadwick

"O COME LET US SING UNTO THE LORD." TOURS

To accompany a fair-sized chorus in the anthem, "O come let us sing unto the Lord," by Tours, prepare the following: Gt. to Octave; Sw. Full (open) except in large organs; Ch. Melodia and Flute 4 ft.; Ped. Open Diapason, Bourdon and Gedeckt; Sw. to Gt. and Gt. to Ped.

Play the introduction on the Gt. Gradually close the swell in the measure in which the voices begin. After eight measures of the chorus the Ped. can be omitted (ad lib.) during the leads of the several voice parts. It should be used again in the large chords (B-minor) just before the chorus sing, and the swell should be opened on these chords. Gradually close the swell two or three measures later. During the measure in which the chorus is silent, open the swell. Close it again as the voices begin. At the phrase in half-notes which is indicated "Marcato," the accompaniment is indicated "FF." With very large choirs or with small organs it is possible to use Full Gt., but generally the combinations already prepared (with the swell open) are sufficient support for the chorus. For the five marcato chords at the climax (Sfz) the Full Gt., and sometimes the Full Organ, can be used, but only F Gt. must be used after the "lunga" rest. The swell can be opened for the last two chords of this section.

For the interlude (Poco meno mosso) put off the Ped. Open Diapason and Gt. to Ped. Play this interlude on either the Ch. or the Sw. reduced to a Mf combination. The middle section (Andante tranquillo) is very effective sung by a quartet unaccompanied. If the quartet is accompanied a soft unassertive combination (preferably without Ped.) should be used. If it is sung by the whole chorus the accompaniment must be regulated by the capability of the chorus. It is effective sung by the chorus unaccompanied. If the chorus is unable to maintain the pitch it is advisable to play the accompaniment. The combination should be only as loud as is absolutely necessary to keep the chorus up to the pitch. The Gedeckt and Flute 4 ft. blends well with the voices without being assertive, but this combination is not always sufficient in power to enable the chorus to maintain the pitch. In such cases add the Salicional and Violin Diapason with possibly a soft Oboe. Every choir is capable of singing the last three words of this section unaccompanied.

For the next section (Maestoso) use the first combination with the swell open. For the Allegro con Spirito close the swell, and on some organs it is advisable to put off the Octave. For the two measures in which the sopranos sing alone play the accompaniment on the Sw. without Ped. For the unison passage open the swell wide, and on some organs use Full Gt. (only through the unison passage). In the middle brace of the last page the combination can be increased according to the power of the chorus, but in the lower brace the accompaniment is higher in pitch than the voices and the organist must be careful not to cover the voices entirely with the organ.

"THE WOODS AND EVERY SWEET-SMELLING TREE." WEST

In playing the accompaniment of "The woods and every sweet-smelling tree" of West, the organist has an opportunity to select pleasing combinations of contrasted tone-color. As I have stated several times, the tastes of different organists vary, and some organists prefer to use only stereotyped combinations of no distinctive tone-color. They amply support the voices; they observe the nuances indicated. No one can question their musicianship, but their accompaniments are always monochromatic, so to speak.

For this anthem I suggest the following: Prepare Gt. Doppel Floete, Gamba, and Flute 4 ft.; Sw. Voix Céleste and Gedeckt (closed); Ch. Melodia; Ped. Bourdon and Gedeckt; Sw. to Gt. and Sw. to Ped.

Play the first two measures on the Sw. The next two measures are indicated for the Gt. with Ped. These measures are also effective played on the Sw. 8 and 4 ft. stops with the Oboe and Cornopean. At the rest, when the voice part begins, change the Sw. combination to Gedeckt and Flute 4 ft. After four measures use the combination piston or pedal which gives 8 and 4 ft. stops with the Oboe. While the chorus are singing the four measures unaccompanied prepare the Gt. to Octave and add the Ped. Diapason and Gt. to Ped. With the last word of this phrase open the Grand Crescendo full, or, if there is no Grand Crescendo, put on the Full Gt. After two measures (FF) play two measures on the Sw. with the first combination. For the accompaniment of the tenor solo use Gedeckt and Violina if the voice is a light lyric voice. If the voice is more robust this combination perhaps will be insufficient and the Salicional and Flute 4 ft. should be added. After four measures of the solo play the R. H. on the Ch. Melodia for four measures. Return to the Sw. for two measures; back to the Ch. for two measures; and return to the Sw. again for two measures. For the short staccato chords indicated for the Gt. use Doppel Floete, Gamba and Flute 4 ft. For the phrase, "His banner over me was love," use Full Sw. as indicated. During the rest with a hold reduce the Sw. to Voix Céleste and Gedeckt. For the *Tempo 1mo* play both hands on the Ch. For the last two words of the solo reduce the Ch. to Dulciana, play both hands on the Ch. during the word "was" and the R. H. on the Sw. for the word "love." Play the last two measures of this section on the Sw. reduced to some soft stop (Salicional or Gedeckt).

For the final chorus prepare: Sw. 8 and 4 ft. with Oboe, Gt. to Octave, with appropriate Ped. and the Gt. to Ped. Play on the Gt. When the altos and basses sing, "with the mercy," etc., play both hands on the

Sw. (Full and closed) without Ped. Return to the Gt. as indicated. At
the bottom of page 5 play the last two measures (Mf) on the Sw.
without Ped. Return to the Gt. with Ped. at the last count of the third
measure, at the top of the last page. For the FF use as much organ as
the vocal strength of the chorus will permit.

On two-manual organs the registration indicated above, except that
of the interlude on the Ch., can be followed. If the organ is small and
the chorus strong, some of the combinations must be increased. On
large organs which have two or three Diapasons in the Gt. and large
Sw. organs of considerable power, the First Diapason and the open
swell must be used sparingly.

"THE RADIANT MORN HATH PASSED AWAY." WOODWARD

Prepare: Gt. Doppel Floete and Flute 4 ft.: Sw. Gedeckt, Salicional,
Flute 4 ft. and Oboe; Ch. Flutes 8 and 4 ft.: Ped. Bourdon and Gedeckt:
Sw. to Gt. and Sw. to Ped.

Play the introduction on the Sw. without Pedal. If the Oboe is coarse
and loud, omit it. Add the Sw. Violin Diapason and use the Ped.
in the eighth measure. In the 13th measure add the Oboe if it has been
omitted at the beginning; otherwise, open the swell. At the last count
of the 17th measure, play on the Ch. On two-manual organs this phrase
can be played on the Gt. For the interlude put off the Oboe and Violin
Diapason and add the Voix Céleste. If there is no Voix Céleste in the
organ put off only the Oboe. At the 25th measure, play on the Sw. 8
and 4 ft. without Oboe or Voix Céleste. In the next measure, play the
upper notes of the lower staff on the Gt. (L. H.) and put on the Gt. to
Ped. to give emphasis to the Ped. notes. At the last count of the 30th
measure either put on Full Sw. (open) or play on the Gt. with Diapason,
according to personal taste. If one plays the phrase on the Sw., the Gt.
(with Diapason) should be used in the 36th measure. For the two
measures in which the basses sing alone, play both hands on the Sw.
without Ped. Play the following three measures on the Gt. Return to
the Sw. at the second count of the 45th measure and gradually reduce
the Sw. to 8 and 4 ft. without Oboe. After the hold, put off the Sw.
Diapason and close the swell. Gradually crescendo in the following
measure and play on the Gt. (without the Diapason) as indicated. At
the 56th measure add the Diapason. At the 58th measure the accompaniment should be as loud as the power of the chorus will permit. On
many organs Gt. to Octave and Full Sw. (open) are sufficient. In the
61st measure close the swell and put off the Gt. to Ped. At the last
count of this measure play both hands on the Sw. (Full and closed).
This phrase is effective if the L. H. sustains the bass note (B) and
staccato quarter-notes (B's) are played with the Ped. (including the
Diapason). Gradually open the swell and play both hands on the
Gt. (to Diapason) at the last count of the 65th measure. Increase
the organ to Gt. to Octave and Full Sw. (open) at the 70th measure.
On many organs the full chords, during the one measure rest of the
chorus, are sufficiently strong on this combination. If not, more organ

can be used. For the last two braces use as much organ as the vocal power of the chorus will permit. Care must of course be used not to cover up the voices.

It will be noticed that this registration is somewhat softer than that indicated in the printed copies. This is due to the increased volume of most organs now-a-days, compared with the organs of the period when this anthem was first printed. The suggested registration can easily be adapted to a two-manual organ as the Ch. is indicated for only one phrase. If the chorus is small some of the combinations must be reduced. On the contrary, if the organ is voiced rather soft many of the combinations must be increased.

"In Heavenly Love Abiding." Parker

Prepare: Gt. Doppel Floete or Gross Flute: Sw. Voix Céleste, Gedeckt and Violina: Ch. Hohl Floete or Melodia: Ped. Bourdon, Sw. to Gt. and Sw. to Ped.

Play the introduction on the Sw. with Ped. Put off the Voix Céleste for the accompaniment of the solo. If there is no Violina in the organ substitute the Flute 4 ft. At the sixth measure of the third brace, play the L. H. melody on the Ch., as far as the A-sharp in the lower brace. In the fifth measure of the lower brace, increase the combination by adding either a strong Salicional or a soft Violin Diapason. At the seventh measure of the upper brace of the second page, use at least the 8 and 4 ft. stops with Oboe. Gradually open the swell and, in the third measure of the second brace, play the L. H. arpeggios on the Gt. In the fourth measure of the third brace, play both hands on the Full Sw., with the swell more or less open according to the power of the voice and the power of the individual Sw. Gradually close the swell and, in the second measure of the fourth brace, reduce to 8 and 4 ft. without Oboe. For the last phrase of the solo reduce to the first combination. (Gedeckt and Violina or Flute 4 ft.)

For the *Poco animato* use the Sw. 8 and 4 ft. stops with or without the Voix Céleste (according to personal taste). In the first eight measures of the chorus, the tenor part, which is duplicated in the accompaniment, is effective if played on the Gt. Doppel Floete. At the second measure of the middle brace of the third page, add the Oboe. In the lower brace the sustained octave in the R. H. can be played on the Ch. Melodia and Flute 4 ft. with the L. H. on the Sw., or both hands can play on the Sw. The L. H. part should be strong enough to assist the chorus, as (with some choirs) the change of key causes the intonation to be insecure. At the top of the fourth page, with the entrance of the basses, the accompaniment should be heavier, even to the Diapason if necessary. On the last count of the middle brace, increase the power of the combination to Gt. to Octave and Full Sw. At the top of the fifth page, play the R. H. on the Sw. (Full and open) and the L. H. melody on the Gt. to Diapason. On the last count of the third measure, reduce to Doppel Floete or Gross Flute. In the fifth measure play the L. H. on the Sw. (8 and 4 ft. with Oboe). At the last count of the second measure of the second brace, play both hands on the Sw. In the fifth measure put off the Oboe. With the first note of the chorus part, add the Voix Céleste and play the tenor part on the Gt. (On a four-manual organ this tenor part is effective when played on the Solo Philomela.)

In the third measure of the lower brace of the sixth page, add the Sw. Oboe, Gt. Flute 4 ft., and play both hands on the Gt. If there is a Grand Crescendo, open it one-third or more as needed. If there is no Grand Crescendo, add Full Sw. on the fifth measure. At the third measure at the top of the seventh page, use at least Gt. to Diapason and in the last measure add the Octave. At the climax at the top of the last page, the accompaniment should amply support the chorus. Obviously, the number of stops required depends both on the chorus and the organ. With a small organ it may be necessary to use Full Organ. With a large organ it is generally sufficient to use Gt. to Octave and Full Sw. (open).

With a two-manual organ, the two phrases indicated for the Ch. can be played on the Sw. The Sw. to Gt. should be on all the time. If there is no Voix Céleste, use the Violin Diapason as a substitute on account of the necessary assertiveness which should be present in the accompaniment at the points where the Voix Céleste is indicated.

" Sing Alleluia Forth." Buck

Prepare Gt. to Octave: Sw. 8 and 4 ft. with Oboe: Ch. Melodia and Dulciana: Ped. Bourdon, Gedeckt and possibly the Diapason: Sw. to Gt., Gt. and Sw. to Ped.

After playing the introduction on the Gt., put off the Octave and Ped. Diapason (ad lib.) before the chorus begins. With a large chorus or a small organ, these changes may not be necessary. For the accompaniment of the bass solo, add the Cornopean and play on the Sw. (closed), or if there is no Cornopean, open the swell half-way. Put off the Cornopean while the soloist is singing " In hymning." For the following chorus, play on the Gt. as indicated, and on the Sw. for the word " Alleluia." Put off the Oboe during the rests in the R. H. part before the tenor begins the solo. For the soprano solo, play th accompaniment on the Ch. For the bass solo, add the Oboe and Cornopean and play on the Sw. Put off the Cornopean after the word " chant," and put off the Oboe before the word " Alleluia." Play on the Gt. all through the next chorus. Use the Gt. Trumpet and Sw. Oboe as indicated, but put off the Oboe, before playing the G in the accompaniment, unless it is a very soft and smooth Oboe. In the lower brace of page 6, use the 8 and 4 ft. stops in the Sw. After the choir sings the word " lays," add the Oboe. During the rest in the R. H. part, prepare the Gt. Diapason and Trumpet, also add the Ped. Diapason. Generally, it is advisable to put off the Trumpet after the word " Christ." In the middle brace, the composer has indicated " Ch." for one measure. The Ch. combination is frequently insufficient for this phrase and I suggest continuing on the Gt. For the words " endless, endless," etc., use as much organ as

possible without overpowering the choir. Play the first " Amen " on the
Sw. 8 and 4 ft. with Oboe, and the second " Amen " with 8 ft. stops
only.

This anthem is sung by many quartet choirs. The principal difference
in the above registration for a quartet is to use less of the Gt. in the F
and FF passages.

As the following choir selections are more frequently sung by quartet
choirs the suggested registration is for such choirs.

" STILL, STILL WITH THEE." FOOTE

Prepare: Gt. Doppel Floete, Gamba and Flute 4 ft. (on small organs
Melodia and Flute 4 ft.) : Sw. Voix Céleste, Salicional and Flute 4 ft.:
Ped. Bourdon, Sw. to Gt. and Sw. to Ped. If the organ has no Voix Céleste, use only the Salicional and Flute 4 ft., unless the Salicional is very
soft, when it is necessary to add the Gedeckt (St. Diapason). After the
introduction on the Sw. put off the Voix Céleste. Before the word
" fairer " add the Gedeckt and Violina, or a soft Violin Diapason. For
the climax, " dawns the sweet consciousness," add the Oboe, unless it is
coarse and too loud. For the last four words of the solo use the
same combination as at the beginning. The accompaniment of the bass
solo should be somewhat light during the first eight measures. I suggest
Gedeckt and Flute 4 ft. Put off the Flute during the rests in the first
measure of page 3. After the word " born," gradually add the Salicional,
Flute 4 ft., Violin Diapason, and Oboe before the word "breathless ";
after which put them off in the reverse order and use only the Gedeckt
and Flute 4 ft. for the last four measures. With some old organs in
which the intonation of the stops is uncertain and their tone somewhat
weak, it is necessary to use more stops in the Sw. for this accompaniment,
particularly if the bass voice is somewhat large.

For the following quartet passage play on the Gt. with the Sw. 8 and
4 ft. stops coupled. Change to the Sw. (without Ped.) on the last
count of the word " image." For the PP measure use only the Gedeckt
and Salicional or even the Salicional only. The phrase beginning " so
in " is generally sung unaccompanied. If not, use Sw. 8 and 4 ft. without
Violin Diapason. If the organist plays the upper brace of page 4, use
only the Gedeckt (St. Diapason) when the bass sings alone. For the
duet play on the Sw. 8 and 4 ft. with Oboe. Put off the Oboe at the
words " so doth " and the Violin Diapason at the top of page 5. Use
only the Gedeckt (St. Diapason) for the last two measures of the
duet. The *Tranquillo* phrase is generally sung unaccompanied. If
it is necessary to play the accompaniment use as little of the Sw. as
possible — the Salicional only, if the quartet can maintain the pitch. At
the words "beneath thy wings " play on Sw. 8 and 4 ft. without Oboe or
Violin Diapason. Add one or both of these stops in the middle brace.
For the *Animato*, the accompaniment should be quite heavy. Play
on the Gt. with Diapason if possible, though this stop is frequently too
loud for a quartet in this passage. At the first count of the middle
brace of the last page, play both hands on the Sw. without Ped. Gradually

open the swell, and at the FF, play on the Gt. with Ped. The Gt. Diapason generally is necessary here for the proper support of the quartet. For the PP phrase in the lower brace use Salicional and Æoline. Put off the Salicional just before the quartet sings the last four words.

"O LAMB OF GOD." BREWER

Prepare: Gt. Doppel Floete or Gross Flute: Sw. St. Diapason (Gedeckt), Flute 4 ft., Violina and Voix Céleste: Ch. Melodia or Concert Flute with Flute d'Amour or Rohr Floete: Ped. Bourdon, Sw. to Gt. and Sw. to Ped.

Play the introduction on the Sw. and put off the Voix Céleste as the voices begin. At A add the Oboe. The interlude can be played on the Sw. or Ch. If it is played on the Ch. one should return to the Sw. two counts before the voices begin. At the second count of the measure before B put off the Oboe. The staccato notes in the L. H. are frequently ineffective when played on the Sw. They are generally more effective when played on the Gt. (as prepared). At the last count of the fourth measure at the top of page 3, add Full Sw. (closed). Put off the Full Sw. at the last count of the upper brace. Play the interlude, beginning with the R. H. C (before the double bar), on the Ch. The L. H. imitation in the second measure after the double bar is effective when played on the Gt. Omit the A-flat which doubles the Ped. note. Return to the Sw. on the second eighth-note of the *Larghetto*. Add the Oboe at the last count of the fourth measure at the top of page 4. At D play the eighth-notes of the L. H. on the Ch., until the lower brace, when both hands should play on the Sw. One measure before E, put off the Oboe. One count before the *Allargando*, add the Oboe and Voix Céleste and open the swell wide. Put off the Oboe on the second count of the measure before the double bar (page 5). Continue the interlude on this combination (Gedeckt, Violina and Voix Céleste).

As indicated by the composer, sing the six measures of the returned first theme (after *tempo* 1°) unaccompanied. While the choir is singing unaccompanied, prepare the Gt. Mf (Doppel Floete, Gamba and Flute 4 ft.), and the Sw. to Gt.; or, if the organ has only two manuals and has none of the stops named, prepare Gt. Melodia and Flute 4 ft. with Sw. to Gt. Resume the accompaniment at the last count of the upper brace of page 6. At G play on the Gt. (or on the Ch.). Return to the Sw. as indicated. At H, if the Full Sw. (closed) is not too loud, it can be used to prepare for the following crescendo. If the Full Sw. is too loud, use only 8 and 4 ft. with Oboe. At the last count of the middle brace of page 7, add the Gt. to Ped. and play on the Gt. At I (last page), a soft Diapason can be added. If the Diapason is too loud, the Full Sw. coupled to the Gt. will have to suffice. At the climax (FF), the power of the organ and the power of the tone of the quartet must decide how much organ can be used. On some organs Gt. to Octave with Full Sw. is sufficient and is not overpowering. On other organs this combination is much too loud for a quartet and less organ must be used. In either case, the organ must be much reduced just before the choir sings "above." To follow the composer's indications for the last four measures, reduce the Sw. to St. Diapason (Gedeckt) and Flute 4 ft. and the Gt. to Doppel Floete or Melodia. The above registration is indicated for a small three-manual organ. On a larger organ more variety can be secured. On a two-manual organ the passages indicated for the Ch. must be played on the Gt. and the stops selected on the Gt. must conform to the specification of the particular organ.

"PEACE AND LIGHT." CHADWICK

Prepare: Ch. (or Gt.) Melodia and Flute 4 ft.: Sw. Oboe and Flute 4 ft.: Ped. Bourdon, Sw. to Gt. and Sw. to Ped.

Play the introduction on the Sw. without Ped. Put off the Oboe and add the St. Diapason (Gedeckt). Do not use the Ped. until the second brace of the solo. Add the Salicional with the entrance of the Ped. In the last measure of the fourth brace, use Sw. 8 and 4 ft. with Oboe (open). In the last two measures of the solo, use the same combination as for the first measures of the solo. Play the interlude on the Ch. (or Gt.) or Sw. with all the 8 and 4 ft. stops except reeds. The following ensemble section is generally sung unaccompanied. On the lower brace of the last page, while the choir sings the word "light," the independent melody in the L. H. part should be played on a combination which brings out the melody quite prominently. If the two preceding pages have been sung unaccompanied, the chord in the R. H. at this point, obviously, must be omitted. After two measures of this L. H. melody all the harmony must be played leading to the "Amen." A good registration for these five measures is to use the Voix Céleste with the swell partly open at first and gradually close the swell so that the last chord of the accompaniment is very soft as the choir sings the "Amen." If the Voix Céleste is not strong enough to be distinctly heard on the first six notes of the L. H. part, or if there is no Voix Céleste in the organ, the Salicional and Flute 4 ft. with or without the St. Diapason (Gedeckt) frequently answers. Use the Æoline for the last chord. If it is deemed advisable to accompany the quartet in the last two pages one should use a light combination without Ped. Either the St. Diapason (Gedeckt) or Salicional for the first two braces. Add the Flute 4 ft. on the word "joy." Crescendo and use 8 and 4 ft. with Oboe (swell partly open) for the words, "Lead me, O Lord," etc. For the climax at the top of the last page, play on the Gt. with Ped. Return to the Sw. at the word "till." Gradually close the swell and put off the Oboe and Violin Diapason (or other loud stop) on the words "through peace." If the choir cannot sing the middle brace unaccompanied, use the Sw. Diapason alone. Any choir can sing the words "to light" unaccompanied, after which play the accompaniment as suggested above.

From the foregoing suggestions for a few representative anthems, etc., the student can obtain the fundamental principles of registration for such compositions. The voicing of the individual organs has even more influence in selecting combinations for accompaniments than for organ compositions. Various combinations may be perfectly satisfactory in themselves, but are too loud or too soft for certain passages of accompaniment, and, for that reason, must be modified according to circumstances.

In conclusion, it may be stated (1) that, in the registration of the accompaniment of any choir selection, one must first decide whether the accompaniment is purely secondary or is independent and of equal importance to the voice part; (2) that the power and volume of the accompaniment, obviously, depend on the indicated dynamics and the power and volume of the voice parts; (3) that certain phrases of accompaniment must amply support the voices; (4) that certain phrases must only supply a soft undercurrent of harmony (so to speak); (5) that certain phrases are designed to be assertive even to the extent of overpowering the voices for a short time; (6) that the tonal character of the combinations used in the accompaniments is purely a matter of taste.

CHAPTER XV

REGISTRATION OF ORGAN TRIOS

In playing Organ Trios — compositions which consist of three independent melodies for two manuals and the pedal — it is necessary to select contrasted combinations which have sufficient vitality not to become wearisome before the end of the composition. Such compositions are generally so composed that a change of registration in the midst of the composition is frequently quite difficult, if not impossible.

Some of the best examples of Organ Trios are: Six Trio Sonatas of Bach, Four Trios, Op. 39, of Merkel, and Ten Trios, Op. 49, of Rheinberger. For the purpose of illustration let us look at the first Trio Sonata of Bach.

For the first movement (*Allegro Moderato*), prepare: Gt. Doppel Floete (or Gross Flute) and Harmonic Flute 4 ft.: Sw. Cornopean, Oboe, Gedeckt, Salicional and Flute 4 ft.: Ch. Melodia, Flute d'Amour 4 ft. and Fugara: Ped. Bourdon, Gedeckt and Cello. Play the first twenty-one measures with the L. H. on the Gt. and the R. H. on the Sw. These two combinations present a marked contrast in tone-color. Each combination gives precision and definiteness to the various contrapuntal figures. The Ped. combination should not be quite so loud as either manual combination, and yet it should be definite enough in power and pitch to enable the hearer to follow the melodic course of the pedal part. In certain Pedal organs the Cello is too loud for this combination and must be omitted. In certain other organs the Bourdon, Violone and Gedeckt is a good combination for this Trio. Occasionally, it is necessary to use only the Bourdon with the Ch. to Ped. Coupler. If this coupler is used it may be necessary to omit the Fugara in the Ch.

At the twenty-second measure, play the R. H. on the Ch. and two measures later play the L. H. on the Sw. If the swell has been partly open for the preceding section it may be necessary to close it for this section. If the Fugara is somewhat assertive it may be necessary to open the Sw. swell or to omit the Fugara. In the balance of the movement no other change of registration is feasible. As a matter of taste, one can reverse the order of the above registration — begin with the R. H. on the Ch. and the L. H. on the Sw. and change to R. H. Sw. and L. H. Gt. at the twenty-second measure.

For the second movement (*Adagio*) prepare: Gt. Doppel Floete (or Gross Flute): Sw. Oboe, Gedeckt, Voix Céleste and Flute 4 ft.: Ch. Clarinet and Flute 4 ft.: Ped. Bourdon and Gedeckt. Play the first twelve measures R. H. on the Sw., L. H. on the Ch. In repeating this section play the R. H. on the Gt. and the L. H. on the Sw. (partly open). After the repeat, play the L. H. on the Sw., and during the one measure rest prepare the Ch. Melodia and Dulciana, after which play the R. H. on the Ch. Continue to the end in this manner. Another registration for this movement is, to play the R. H. on the Ch. Melodia and the L. H. on the Sw. Voix Céleste and Flute 4 ft. (if the Voix Céleste is too soft add the Oboe). For the repeat put off the Voix Céleste (also the Oboe if it is used) and add the Gedeckt. Play the R. H. on the Sw. and the L. H. on the Ch. After the double bar add the Voix Céleste and play the L. H. on the Sw. and the R. H. on the Ch.

Obviously, the above combinations depend on the relative power of the stops in the individual organs. A very loud Melodia and an exceptionally soft Voix Céleste cannot be used in contrast as indicated above. Likewise, a soft Oboe and an extra loud Doppel Floete (or Gross Flute) necessitate some modification of the combinations. In this movement, if there is no Gedeckt or Cello in the Ped. organ, the Ch. to Ped. must be used to give the necessary eight-foot pitch.

For the last movement (*Allegro*) prepare: Gt. Doppel Floete (or Gross Flute) and Harmonic Flute 4 ft.: Sw. Cornopean, Oboe, and other 8 and 4 ft. stops (generally excepting the Diapason): Ch. Melodia, Flute 4 ft. and Fugara: Ped. Bourdon, Gedeckt and Cello, or Bourdon, Violone and Gedeckt. Play the first section (to the double bar) R. H. on the Ch. and the L. H. on the Gt. Repeat with the L. H. on the Sw. (partly open) and the R. H. on the Gt. After the double bar, play the L. H. on the Ch. and the R. H. on the Sw. If the Ch. is in a swell-box and the Piccolo is not loud and shrill, it can be used instead of the Fugara (with the Ch. swell closed). On many organs, it is difficult to select a Ped. combination which is entirely satisfactory for this movement, on account of the absence of 8 ft. stops. In many compositions one can obtain a fairly suitable effect by using the manual to Ped. Couplers, but in Trios this plan is rarely satisfactory as two manuals are used for the hands and the Ped. combination ought to be of different tonal color for contrast.

Of the Four Trios of Merkel the third one (Canon in F-sharp) is the best-known. This Trio differs from the Bach Trio Sonatas in that the R. H. part consists of two voices. The harmony of these two voices combined with the melody of the L. H. and the Ped. part is naturally much fuller than the harmony of the Trio Sonatas.

Prepare: Gt. Gamba: Sw. Oboe, Gedeckt, Salicional and Flute 4 ft.: Ch. Melodia, and Ped. Bourdon. Play the first eight measures with the R. H. on the Ch. and the L. H. on the Sw. (partly open). At the third count of the first measure of the first ending, play the R. H. on the Sw. One measure later play the L. H. imitation on the Gt. At the third count of the first measure of the second ending, play the R. H. on the Ch. and the L. H. (one measure later) on the Sw. as at first. This registration gives a little variety which is wanting if the whole composition is played without any change of manuals. A different registration (without any change of manuals) is to play the R. H. on the Sw. Vox Humana and Gedeckt, and the L. H. on the Ch. Flute 4 ft. and Dulciana.

CHAPTER XVI

TRANSCRIPTIONS

MANY compositions which were originally composed for the piano, for a string quartet, for the orchestra, or for voices, have been " transcribed " or " arranged " for the organ. These " transcriptions " may be divided into two classes: First, those compositions whose style and character are more or less similar to the style and character of organ music in general, and which, on account of this similarity, do not sound unlike original organ music when they are played on an organ. Illustrations: Largo from " Xerxes," Handel; Andante from String Quartet, Tschaikowski; Larghetto from the Second Symphony, Beethoven; Funeral March from the Pianoforte Sonata of Chopin; Vorspiel to " Parsifal," Wagner; Schiller Festival March, Meyerbeer; War March of Priests from " Athalia," Mendelssohn. Second, those compositions whose style and character are so much unlike the style and character of organ music of today or of any other period, that, while they can be played note for note on an organ, the effect which is produced is so foreign to the recognized style of organ music that many question the expediency of publicly playing such compositions on an organ. Illustrations: Polonaise in A-flat, Chopin; Overture to " Der Freischutz," Weber; The Ride of the Valkyries, Wagner; Scherzo in B-flat minor, Chopin; Sonata Appassionato, Beethoven; Overture to " Poet and Peasant," Suppé. All these compositions have been included in the programs of organ recitals in the last few years.

If the student has a desire to play " transcriptions " of the first class mentioned above, he should obtain the published " Arrangements " of some well-known authority, as the late W. T. Best, and, so far as is possible, adapt the printed registration to the organ on which he is playing. A reasonable amount of capability in registering genuine organ music will enable the student to adapt such " transcriptions " to the individual organ.

In examining the " Arrangements from the Scores of the Great Masters " by W. T. Best, the student cannot fail to observe that the arranger has adopted a very conservative course; that, while he has suggested a reproduction on the organ of many of the tone-colors and effects of the original composition, *so far as those colors and effects seemed to him to be consistent with the real character of organ music,* he has avoided registration which he thought might cause the organ to sound worse than a poor orchestra.

On the other hand, the student who is present at some of the organ recitals of today, will notice that an entirely different course is adopted by a few of the present-day organists. In some of the " transcriptions " of orchestral compositions, the student will hear many surprising effects of which the orchestra itself is entirely innocent, in the attempt of the performer to make the organ sound "orchestral." Many of these effects are ingenious; some are startling; and all of them are attractive to a certain class of listeners.

No one can say, *ex cathdrâ*, that one of the above styles of "transcriptions" is right and the other wrong. It is purely a matter of personal taste, and, as has been stated many times, "individual tastes in registration differ."

CHAPTER XVII

REGISTRATION ON ONE-MANUAL ORGANS

WHILE one-manual organs are rarely constructed now-a-days, many students get their first experience as organist in some small church which has an old-fashioned, one-manual organ. On such instruments, the limitations are numerous, but an organist ought to be so schooled that he can obtain the best possible results from such cramped circumstances.

There are in existence three kinds of one-manual organs, independent of their age, condition, or value: first, those in which most of the stops are divided at middle C; second, those in which only a few stops are divided, the division being at tenor C; third, those which have no stop divided, except the Oboe, which is divided at tenor C into Oboe and Bassoon.

A sample specification of a one-manual organ of the first kind follows: —

FIRST SPECIFICATION OF A ONE-MANUAL ORGAN

MANUAL

{ Open Diapason	Treble	8 ft.
{ Open Diapason	Bass	„ „
{ Melodia	Treble	8 ft.
{ Stopped Bass }	Bass	„ „
Dulciana }	Treble	8 ft.
{ Flute *	Treble	4 ft.
{ Flute	Bass	„ „
{ Oboe	Treble	8 ft.
{ Bassoon	Bass	„ „

PEDAL

Sub-Bass   16 ft.

Tremolo
Manual to Pedal Coupler

In such an organ, all the manual stops, except the Open Diapason, are enclosed in the swell-box. Occasionally, the Open Diapason is also enclosed. The Dulciana always has no Bass of its own, the Stopped Bass answering for the Bass of both the Melodia and the Dulciana.

In playing organ compositions on a one-manual organ, considerable ingenuity must be exercised by the organist to avoid monotony. These old organs are rarely well-balanced in the quality or relative power of the tone of the individual stops, and the organist is really hampered more by this fact than by the absence of a second manual.

* Frequently, the 4 ft. stop is not divided.

140

To assist the student in adapting organ compositions to these organs, I suggest the registration for the following list of easy Preludes and Postludes: —

I

Andante Religioso	Deshayes
Three Short Andantes	Porter
Gothic March	Salomé
Berceuse	Frysinger

II

Communion in A	Deshayes
Allegretto Grazioso	Porter
Two Preludes (B-flat and G)	Merkel
March in B-flat	Silas

III

Finale in E-flat	Faulkes
Meditation in E-flat	Dunham
Andante Grazioso	Rickman

HENRI DESHAYES, ANDANTE RELIGIOSO

Prepare: Melodia Treble, Stopped Bass, Dulciana, Flute Treble and Bass, Sub-Bass, and Manual to Pedal Coupler. At the 21st measure add the Oboe and Bassoon (as indicated). On page 4, second brace, fourth measure, open the swell. In the last measure of the brace, add Open Diapason Treble and Bass (as indicated). At the top of page 5 put off the Open Diapason Treble and Bass, the Flute Treble and Bass, and close the swell. In the third measure of the third brace, add the Flute Treble and Bass. In the sixth measure of the third brace, put off the Flute Treble and Bass. At the second measure of the lower brace, put off the Melodia Treble, leaving the Dulciana and Stopped Bass.

WALTER PORTER, THREE SHORT ANDANTES

Andante in G-minor. — Prepare: Melodia Treble, Stopped Bass, Dulciana, Flute Treble and Bass, Sub-Bass, and Manual to Pedal Coupler. For the repeat of the first eight measures, put off the Flute Treble and Bass. After the double bar add the Flute Treble and Bass. At the last count of the second brace, add the Open Diapason Treble and Bass. At the last count of the first page put off the Open Diapason Treble and Bass. At the last count of the second measure of the second brace, page 2, put off the Flute Treble and Bass. In the next measure put off the Melodia Treble.

Andante in B-flat. — Prepare: All the stops in the organ except the Tremolo. For the repeat put off the Open Diapason Treble and Bass. After the double bar put off the Flute Treble and Bass. At the last count of the fourth measure, second brace of page 3, add the Open Diapason Treble and Bass. At the first count of the fifth measure, lower brace, put off the Open Diapason Treble and Bass.

Andante in G. — Prepare: Melodia Treble, Stopped Bass, Sub-Bass, and Manual to Pedal Coupler. For the second eight measures, which are a repetition of the first eight meaures, add the Flute Treble and Bass. Put these stops off again at the beginning of the third brace. At the last measure of the page, add Flute Treble and Bass, and put off the Stopped Bass. As we require at this point a solo and accompaniment, play the R. H. as printed (Melodia and Flute Treble), and the L. H. an octave lower on the Flute Bass alone. This gives different combinations for the solo and accompaniment. On the last page, after the double bar in the second brace, add the Dulciana and Stopped Bass, and play the music as printed. On the lower brace, at the fourth measure, put off all the manual stops except the Dulciana and Stopped Bass. Play the L. H. part an octave lower and R. H. part an octave higher than printed. For the last three measures play the L. H. part as printed, and the R. H. part an octave higher than printed.

THÉODORE SALOMÉ, GOTHIC MARCH

Prepare: All the stops except the Tremolo. At the last count or the first page, put off the Open Diapason Treble and Bass. On the second page, fourth measure of the second brace, add the Open Diapason Treble and Bass. For the repeat make the same changes. For the Trio use the Melodia and Flute Treble, St. Bass and Flute Bass. At the double bar at the top of the third page, for the solo and accompaniment, use the Melodia and Flute Treble, with only the Flute Bass. Play the L. H. part an octave lower than it is printed. On the fourth page, third measure, shorten the R. H. chord one count, and add the balance of the stops, while playing the L. H. part, so as to have all the stops for the *Tempo Primo*. At the last count of the fourth page, put off the Open Diapason Treble and Bass. Add them again for the FF.

J. FRANK FRYSINGER, BERCEUSE IN A

Prepare: Melodia Treble, Flute Treble and Bass, Sub-Bass. Play the L. H. part an octave lower than it is printed. At the end of the first brace, draw the Tremolo. Play the R. H. solo on the Melodia and Flute, and the accompaniment on the Flute alone an octave lower (equivalent to an 8 ft. stop). The Tremolo will, of course, affect both the solo and the accompaniment, but the effect is agreeable. It can be omitted if desired. On page 3, where the key changes, put off the Flute Treble and Bass and the Tremolo. Add the Stopped Bass. At the top of page 4 play the R. H. part an octave higher, to prevent its interfering with the L. H. part. At the second measure of the lower brace, with only the Flute Treble and Bass, play the music (both hands) an octave lower than printed. For the last page, add the Melodia Treble and the Tremolo. Play the L. H. part an octave lower. Another registration for this last page is, to use only the Flute Treble and Bass and play the L. H. part an octave lower. This melody and accompaniment can also be played on the Melodia Treble and Stopped Bass.

Many of the one-manual organs, especially the older ones, have only an octave and a half of pedals, from CCC to GG. With such a Pedal board, the organist is obliged to transpose some of the Pedal phrases an octave lower, or at least to play a few individual notes an octave lower. In the Andante Religioso of Deshayes, the pedal part of the last two measures of the first brace must be so transposed. These two measures occur three times in the composition. No other transposition is necessary. In the Andante in G of Porter, there is one high B in the Pedal part of the first brace which must be transposed, and the whole of the lower brace of the first page must be played an octave lower. In the Andante in B-flat there is one high B-flat in the second measure to be transposed. In the second brace of page 3, beginning with the second measure, all the Pedal part must be transposed. Two low B-flats cannot be included in the transposition. These must be played as printed. A high B-flat, A-flat, and G must also be transposed. In the Andante in G, the whole of the Pedal part of the second brace must be transposed. At the top of page 5, G-sharp and A must be transposed. At the return of the first theme, after the double bar, play the Pedal part an octave lower, for nine measures and one count. After the G of the tenth measure, play the part as printed. In the Gothic March of Salomé, there are seven high A's in the Pedal part which must be transposed. In the Berceuse of Frysinger, no transposition of the Pedal part is necessary.

A one-manual organ of the second kind has a specification somewhat as follows:—

SECOND SPECIFICATION OF A ONE-MANUAL ORGAN

MANUAL

Open Diapason		8 ft.
⎰ St. Diapason	Treble	8 ft.
⎱ St. Diapason	Bass ⎱	8 ft.
Keraulophon	Treble ⎰	8 ft.
Flute		4 ft.
Hautbois		8 ft.

PEDAL

Sub-Bass	16 ft.

Tremolo
Manual to Pedal Coupler

All the stops, except the Open Diapason and Sub-Bass, are in the swell-box. The Open Diapason and the Flute are not divided. The St. Diapason Treble and the Keraulophon run down to tenor C, the lower octave of both stops being supplied by the St. Diapason Bass. The Hautbois runs down only to tenor C.

Registration of simple organ compositions on such an organ is even more restricted than with the previous organ.

Henri Deshayes, Communion in A

Prepare: St. Diapason Treble and Bass, Keraulophon, Sub-Bass, and Manual to Pedal Coupler. In the last measure of the second brace, add the Flute (as indicated). In the fourth measure of the third brace, add the Hautbois (as indicated). On the lower brace, gradually open the swell, and, in the third measure, add the Open Diapason. On the second page, third brace, second measure, put off the Open Diapason (as indicated). During the fourth and fifth measures of the lower brace, close the swell, put off the Hautbois, and a little later, the Flute. At the last count of the page, put on the Tremolo. At the next to the last measure of the third brace of the last page, put off the St. Diapason Treble and Tremolo, which leaves the Keraulophon and St. Diapason Bass for the ending. If this organ has only an octave and a half of pedals, a few notes of the Ped. part can be easily transposed down an octave.

Walter Porter, Allegretto Grazioso

Prepare: St. Diapason Treble and Bass, Sub-Bass, and Manual to Pedal Coupler. After playing the first brace on this combination, add the Flute. Put off the Flute at the beginning of the third brace, and add it again at the beginning of the fourth brace. At the top of the second page add the Hautbois. On the last page, second brace, play on the Keraulophon and St. Bass. At the third brace, add the St. Diapason Treble. Put it off again for the fourth brace. If the organ has but an octave and a half of pedals, one phrase of two measures, in the Ped. part, which occurs four times, must be transposed down an octave.

Gustav Merkel, Two Preludes (B-Flat and G)

Prelude in B-flat. — Prepare: St. Diapason Treble and Bass, Keraulophon, Sub-Bass, and Manual to Pedal Coupler. At the last count of the first measure of the second brace, add the Flute. At the last count of the first measure of the third brace, put off the Flute. In the first measure of the second page, add the Open Diapason, and gradually open the swell. At the last count of the last measure of the second brace, put off the Open Diapason, and gradually close the swell. At the second count of the sixth measure of the lower brace, put off the St. Diapason Treble. If the organ has only an octave and a half of pedals, the three notes, B-flat, A, and G, of the third and fourth measures of the Ped. part, which also occur at two other places, can be transposed down an octave.

Prelude in G. — Prepare: Open Diapason, St. Diapason Treble and Bass, Keraulophon, Flute, Sub-Bass, and Manual to Pedal Coupler. At the last count of the fourth measure of the lower brace of the first page, open the swell. In the last measure of the first brace of the second page, put off the Open Diapason. Gradually close the swell in the next few measures. On the second count of the fifth measure of the second brace, put off the Flute. On the second count of the third measure of the lower brace, put off the St. Diapason Treble. No transposition of the pedal part is necessary for a restricted pedalboard.

E. SILAS, MARCH IN B-FLAT

Prepare: All the stops in the organ, except the Tremolo, with the swell wide open. At the rest, in the last measure of the first page, put off the Open Diapason. At the beginning of the second brace of the second page, add the Open Diapason. At the rest, in the last measure of this second brace, put off the Open Diapason, and close the swell. At the fourth measure of the upper brace, on the third page, open the swell wide. At the double bar in the third brace, add the Open Diapason. If the organ has only an octave and a half of pedals, a few individual notes in the pedal part, on the first three pages, must be transposed. On the last page, third brace, transpose all the pedal part, beginning with F-sharp.

In the third kind of one-manual organs, no stop is divided, except the Oboe, which has a separate draw-stop (Bassoon) for the lower octave. The specification for such an organ is generally much like the following: —

THIRD SPECIFICATION OF A ONE-MANUAL ORGAN

MANUAL

Open Diapason	8 ft.
St. Diapason	8 ft.
Salicional	8 ft.
Æoline	8 ft.
Flute	4 ft.
{ Bassoon	
{ Oboe	8 ft.

PEDAL

Bourdon	16 ft.

Tremolo
Manual to Pedal Coupler

WILLIAM FAULKES, FINALE IN E-FLAT, OP. 128-6

Prepare: All the stops in the organ, except the Tremolo, with the swell wide open. At the rest in the last measure of the second brace, first page, close the swell. At the last measure of the second brace on the second page, open the swell. At the rest, in the last measure of this page, put off the Open Diapason. On the third page, in the last measure of the second brace, shorten the R. H. chord on the last count, in order to add the Open Diapason with the R. H. At the rest in the last measure of this page, put off the Open Diapason and Salicional, and close the swell. In the second and fourth measures, at the top of the fourth page, omit the note for the thumb of the R. H., as it interferes with the L. H. melody. At the top of the fifth page, add the Salicional. At the top of the sixth page, for the repeat, open the swell. After this repeat, at the first measure of the second brace, add the Open Diapason. At the rest in the first measure of the lower brace, close the swell. At the third measure of the second brace, seventh page, open the swell. Close it again at the second measure of the lower brace. At the first measure of the second brace, on the last page, open the swell wide. If the organ has only an octave and a half of pedals, several upper A-flats in the pedal part, with the following note in each case, should be transposed down an octave.

HENRY M. DUNHAM, MEDITATION IN E-FLAT

Prepare: St. Diapason, Salicional, Æoline, Flute, Bourdon, and Manual to Pedal Coupler. At the last measure of the second brace of the second page, put off the St. Diapason. At the last measure of the third brace, open the swell. Close it again at the last measure of this page. At the return of the theme, in the second measure of the second brace, last page, add the St. Diapason. At the third measure of the lower brace, put off the St. Diapason and Flute on the second count, leaving only the Æoline for the last chord. If the organ has only an octave and a half of pedals, two high A-flats in the pedal part must be transposed.

F. R. RICKMAN, ANDANTE GRAZIOSO

Prepare: St. Diapason, Salicional, Æoline, Bourdon, and Manual to Pedal Coupler. At the last count of the second brace, add the Flute. At the double bar at the top of page 3, put off the St. Diapason. In the last measure of the second brace, add the St. Diapason at the rest in the L. H. part. In the last measure of this page, add the Oboe, and use the swell as indicated. In the third measure of the second brace of the fourth page, put off the Oboe. During the *Rit.* in the second measure of the third brace, put off the Flute, close the swell, and add the Oboe. At the last count of the second measure of the lower brace, add the Flute. In the upper brace of page 5, open the swell. Close the swell in the first measure of the second brace. In the first measure of the third brace, put off the Flute. At the rest in the L. H. part, in the first measure of the lower brace, put off the St. Diapason. In the next measure use the Æoline only. If the organ has only an octave and a half of pedals, one high A in the pedal part must be transposed.

Each of the compositions which are here registered for one-manual organs is, obviously, much more effective when played on two, or three-manual organs. Many compositions cannot be played on a one-manual organ. These compositions have been selected for illustration because it is possible to play them acceptably on a one-manual organ, but the student should not associate them only with one-manual organs.

CHAPTER XVIII

REGISTRATION ON TWO-MANUAL ORGANS

1. SMALL TWO-MANUAL ORGAN WITH 15 SPEAKING STOPS
2. VERY SMALL TWO-MANUAL ORGAN WITH 7 SPEAKING STOPS
3. VERY SMALL TWO-MANUAL ORGAN WITH DUPLEXED SWELL ORGAN
4. LARGE, MODERN TWO-MANUAL ORGAN WITH 22 SPEAKING STOPS

I

SPECIFICATION OF A SMALL TWO-MANUAL ORGAN WITH 15 SPEAKING STOPS

GREAT		DIFFERENT NAMES OR DIFFERENT STOPS COMMONLY SUBSTITUTED
Open Diapason	8 ft.	
Melodia	8 "	Hohl Floete or Clarabella
Dulciana	8 "	Dolce, Dolcissimo or Keraulophon
Flute d'Amour	4 "	Wald Floete or Flauto Traverso
Octave	4 "	Principal

SWELL		
Bourdon	16 ft.	
Violin Diapason	8 "	String Diapason
Salicional	8 "	Viola da Gamba or Viola
St. Diapason	8 "	Gedeckt or Rohr Floete
Æoline	8 "	Dolcissimo or Keraulophon
Flauto Traverso	4 "	Harmonic Flute or Flute Harmonique
Violina	4 "	Gemshorn

COUPLERS	COMBINATION PEDALS
Sw. to Gt.	Forte Gt.
Gt. to Ped.	Piano Gt.
Sw. to Ped.	Gt. to Ped. (reversible)
	Tremolo

Small two-manual organs, with specifications more or less similar to the above specification, which vary in age from one to forty years, are quite numerous. The differences in these organs, outside of the difference in age, are numerous and marked. For this reason, it is necessary, in suggesting registration for such organs, to consider the quality and character of a few of the individual stops. If the stops are voiced and regulated according to a well-balanced scheme, the suggested combinations will be fairly satisfactory. If, however, as is frequently the case, several stops are voiced disproportionately loud, in order to give more volume to the Full Organ, it will be difficult to obtain many of the indicated effects, and the player will be compelled to resort to much compromising in selecting the various combinations. Frequently, in such small organs, the Open Diapason is of medium scale, and the tone is not powerful. To supply some of the volume which is lacking, the Melodia and Dulciana are voiced abnormally loud. In such cases, the Melodia and Dulciana are unsatisfactory for their primary use in rather soft passages, as they are voiced only for the louder effects. Then again, the two four-foot stops in the Sw. are frequently voiced louder than their eight-foot prototypes, thus depriving the player of several useful and effective combinations of 8 and 4 ft. stops.

Seven Compositions for which Registration is Suggested for the Above Small Two-Manual Organ

Uso Seifert	Fantasia in C-minor
William Faulkes	Postlude in A
César Franck	Andantino in G-minor
Edwin H. Lemare	Andantino in D-flat
Arthur Foote	Festival March
Alex. Guilmant	Elevation in A-flat
Georges MacMaster	Grand Chorus in D

Uso Seifert, Fantasia in C-Minor

The registration for this composition is somewhat simple, as no special effects are required. Prepare: Gt. to Octave; Sw. (open) 8 and 4 ft. with Oboe; Ped. Open Diapason and Bourdon; Sw. to Gt., Gt. and Sw. to Ped. The first eight measures should be played on the Gt., as prepared. (On large organs, Full Gt. can be added at the ninth measure, but on a small organ, such a change is inadvisable.) At the hold on the second page, put off the Gt. to Ped. and the Ped. Open Diapason, if it is a loud one. Frequently, this stop is not too loud for the next pedal figure, which should be somewhat prominent. As the leaf is turned, the swell should be closed. It is not advisable to reduce the Sw. here, as a very soft combination would sound out of proportion. At the second measure of the third brace, on page four, add the Full Sw., Gt. to Ped., Ped. Open Diapason, and play on the Gt. At the bottom of page five, use Full Organ.

William Faulkes, Postlude in A

Prepare: Gt. All the stops except the Octave; Sw. All the stops except the Bourdon; Ped. Open Diapason and Bourdon; Sw. to Gt., Gt. and Sw. to Ped. In addition to the printed registration, which should be followed, put off and on the Ped. Open Diapason with the Gt. to Ped. On small organs, it is advisable to use all the stops for the last two pages.

César Franck, Andantino in G-Minor

Prepare: Gt. Flute 4 ft.; Sw. Oboe, St. Diapason, Salicional, and Flute 4 ft.; Ped. Bourdon. With this preparation, the left hand accompaniment, as far as the change of key to major, can be played on the Gt. an octave lower than it is printed. The object is to obtain variety, by using a different registration for the two renderings of the first theme. When the Melodia of the Gt. is soft enough for this accompaniment (somewhat rare), it can be used in place of the Flute 4 ft. If neither of these stops is satisfactory, it will be necessary to use the Dulciana, but, if possible, it is a good plan to reserve the Dulciana for the accompaniment at the return of the theme. At the change of key to major (measure 35), play both hands on the Sw. for 12 measures, using Salicional, Flute 4 ft. and Tremolo. After adding the Gt. to Ped., play the next six measures on the Gt. Melodia. Coupling the Sw. to the Gt. adds vitality to this passage. After these six measures (measure 53), put off the Gt. to Ped., add St. Diapason, and play on the Sw. for four measures. In the next measure (57), there are two quarter-rests in the R. H. part, at which point the L. H. melody should be played on the Gt. Continue with the R. H. on the Sw. for five measures. The sixth measure of this melody, marked "*poco rall*" (measure 62), can be played on the Sw. with good effect, as it leads back to the opening measure of the second theme. The half-note chord of the R. H. can be shortened, so as to put off the St. Diapason. The next six measures should be played with both hands on the Sw. Add the Gt. to Ped. and play four measures with both hands on the Gt. Put off the Gt. to Ped., and play two measures on the Sw., to the double bar. The following return of the first theme (measure 76) can be effectively registered with the solo played on the Sw. Bourdon, Salicional, Flute 4 ft. and Tremolo, unless the Bourdon happens to be a loud one. The accompaniment should, of course, be played on the Gt. Dulciana. If the Sw. Bourdon is too loud for the above combination, and the Salicional lacks sufficient character to make a good solo combination with the Flute 4 ft., the Oboe can be substituted for the Bourdon. This combination is much like the first combination, and hence prevents a variety in the registration, but this is oftentimes unavoidable. After measure 100 (whole measure rest), play the R. H. on the Sw. with Salicional and Flute 4 ft., and the L. H. on the Gt. Melodia (or Flute 4 ft., an octave lower), for four measures, to the second hold. At this point (measure 105), a change of combination is desirable, to avoid monotony. Both hands on the Sw., with St. Diapason, Flute 4 ft., and Tremolo, gives a contrast. At the bar between measures 117 and 118 (*poco rall*), add Salicional (L. H.). In the next measure, ignore the tie in the L. H. part and put off the St. Diapason. At the third count of measure 126 (nine measures before the end), put off the Flute 4 ft. Two measures later, use Æoline only, with the swell open, gradually closing it to the end.

Several variations of the above registration are possible; e. g., one can play the solo (at the beginning) on the Melodia in the Gt., with the accompaniment on the Sw. Salicional, with or without the St. Diapason. The Melodia is frequently without any attractive character, and is thus not always a good solo stop for this style of a solo. The second theme in the major can be played on any attractive combination of 8 and 4 ft. stops on the Sw.: as St. Diapason and Flute 4 ft., or St. Diapason

and Violina. The return of the first theme (measure 76) can be played
on the Oboe with some other stop, especially if the first presentation
of this theme were played on the Melodia. At measure 101, the L. H.
part can be played on the Sw. and the R. H. part on the Gt. Dulciana,
followed by both hands on the Sw. at measure 105.

Edwin H. Lemare, Andantino in D-Flat

The composer's indications for the registration are for a three-manual
organ, and obviously cannot be followed on this small two-manual organ.
I suggest the following: Prepare: Gt. Dulciana; Sw. Oboe and St.
Diapason; Ped. Bourdon. The first page can be played on the Sw. and
Gt. On a two-manual organ, it is rarely possible to play the two
melodies indicated for the R. H., on the second page, on two manuals. In
the first place, it is seldom that the Sw. and Gt. are near enough together,
in a two-manual organ, to enable the player to "thumb" the counter-
melody on the Gt. In the second place, if the manuals are near enough
together, the only possible registration is to use the Gt. Flute 4 ft. for
the thumb melody and also for the L. H. accompaniment (an octave
lower). This registration is rarely satisfactory. On most two-manual
organs, it is necessary to play both of these melodies with the R. H. on
the Sw. The L. H. accompaniment can, of course, be played on the
Dulciana. For the melodies, a combination in contrast to that of the
first page is advisable. I suggest St. Diapason and Flute 4 ft. On
page 3, if we play the R. H. solo on the Gt., as indicated, it is necessary
to add several stops (possibly all but the Bourdon) to the Sw. combination for the accompaniment. Another plan is to add the Melodia on
the Gt. for the solo, and add the Open Diapason and Salicional on the
Sw. for the accompaniment. This plan necessitates a longer pause at
the end of the section, in arranging the combinations for the last section,
but it is unavoidable. At the end of page 3, in order to turn the leaf
and prepare the following combinations, it seems to me advisable to hold
all the notes of the last chord in the L. H. (Sw.), while the Open
Diapason (or Melodia) in the Gt. is put off and the leaf turned. After
this, a short break will enable the player to change the Sw. combination
to Salicional and Flute 4 ft., with Tremolo. No other change of stops is
necessary.

Numerous variations of the above registration are possible: e. g., if
the Gt. Dulciana is too loud, or is practically a soft Viola instead of a
real Dulciana, its string-tone quality may possibly preclude its use
altogether, in the accompaniment of this composition. In such a case, it
is necessary to play the accompaniment on the Sw. and the solo on the
Gt. For the first page, the Melodia can be used for the solo, and the
St. Diapason, Salicional, and possibly the Flute 4 ft., in the Sw. for
the accompaniment. For the second page, add the Violina in the Sw.,
and play both melodies on the Gt. Melodia. For the third page, add the
Oboe and Open Diapason in the Sw. Play the R. H. solo on this combination (with the swell wide open if necessary), and the accompaniment
on the Gt. Melodia. At the end of the page, hold the L. H. chord on the

Gt., as previously suggested, while arranging the Sw. combination and turning the leaf. If one uses only the 4 ft. stops (Flute and Violina) in the Sw., with the Tremolo, the last two pages can be played with both hands on the Sw., the L. H. being played an octave lower than the music is printed. This effect is frequently very good, and occasionally very bad. One must be governed by the individual conditions. Another possible registration for the last two pages, provided the Dulciana is quite "stringy," as mentioned above, is to play the R. H. chords on the Dulciana, and the L. H. accompaniment on any soft combination on the Sw. Sometimes the Æoline with the swell wide open is satisfactory.

ARTHUR FOOTE, FESTIVAL MARCH

Prepare: Gt. Full; Sw. Full (open) without Bourdon; Ped. Open Diapason and Bourdon; Sw. to Gt., Sw. and Gt. to Ped. After the first 16 measures, played on the Gt., put off the Ped. Open Diapason and play on the Sw. The Gt. to Ped. can be put off with the reversible pedal, while playing. On page 3, middle of the second brace, return to the Gt., ritarding a little to allow the addition of the Ped. Open Diapason and Gt. to Ped. At the top of page 4, before playing, put off the Ped. Open Diapason and the Sw. to Gt. While playing the first two measures on the Sw., gradually close the swell, reduce the Gt. to *piano* (with the foot), and put off the Gt. to Ped. In the third measure omit the D-flat of the L. H. (as the Pedal has the same note), in order to put off the Open Diapason and Violina in the Sw. with this hand. Continue R. H. on the Sw., and L. H. on the Gt. No change is advisable on these two pages (except to open and close the swell), until the lower brace of page 5. In the first measure of this brace, change the L. H. D-flat to a quarter-note, in order to add the Sw. to Gt. and Gt. to Ped. While playing the four notes in the Ped., add all the Sw. stops. During the rests in the third measure, add Gt. Open Diapason and open the swell. As the leaf is turned back, add Full Gt. (pedal). The two repeated pages require no further suggestions.

ALEX. GUILMANT, ELEVATION IN A-FLAT

Prepare: Gt. Melodia; Sw. St. Diapason, Violina, and Tremolo; Ped. Bourdon. In the Schmidt edition of this composition (edited by E. E. T.) the combination which is suggested for the first theme is: "Salicional, Violina, and Tremolo." If the Salicional is not too soft, nor the Violina too loud, this combination is delicate and effective. On organs in which this combination is not satisfactory, I suggest St. Diapason and Violina; though there is danger of the Violina being too loud. Occasionally, the Bourdon 16 ft. and Salicional, with the Tremolo, playing an octave higher, is very effective, as these two stops, used an octave higher, are quite similar to St. Diapason and Violina. At the change of key on page 3 (measure 37), I suggest adding the Oboe, irrespective of which combination is used previous to this measure. The L. H. part should be played on the Gt. (on two-manual organs). At the eighth measure after the change of key (measure 45), add the Salicional and Flute 4 ft., if the first combination selected is St. Diapason and Violina; or add St. Diapason and Flute 4 ft., if the first combination selected is Salicional and Violina. At the third double bar (measure 53), where the key returns to D-flat, to prepare a better crescendo and climax, add Sw. to Gt. Four measures later (measure 57), for the climax, play both hands on the Gt. (as indicated in the Schmidt edition), with the swell open. Change back to the Sw. (both hands) on the last count of the second following measure (59). In the next two measures, during the ritarding phrase in the L. H. (on the Sw.), the combination should be gradually changed to the one selected for the return of the first theme. The registration indicated in the Schmidt edition is effective, on three-manual organs which contain a Vox Humana, but, as we are now registering the composition for a small two-manual organ, this combination is not available. Salicional and Flute 4 ft. is effective for this phrase, if the stops are well balanced. To best obtain this combination, from the combination of stops which is already on, put off the Oboe on the F (third count of the L. H. part), in the second measure before the change of key to A-flat. On the G-natural of the next measure, put off the Violina. On the A-natural, put off the St. Diapason. This will leave Salicional and Flute 4 ft. with Tremolo, for the return of the first theme (*tempo primo*). No further change of stops is necessary, except to reduce to the Æoline while holding the last chord.

Several variations of this registration have already been suggested. Occasionally, we find an organ on which no combination of stops, which has already been suggested, sounds well. On such an organ, one should try the first theme on the Sw. with Salicional, alone or combined with the St. Diapason. At the change of key to D-flat (measure 37), if the Oboe is objectionable, add the Open Diapason (Sw.). In the next three braces, it is effective to add the 4 ft. stops (one at a time), even if they are quite loud, as the Open Diapason, together with the other 8 ft. stops which are already on, will balance the excessive power of the 4 ft. stops. At the return of the first theme (measure 61), where the key changes back to A-flat, one can use the same stop or combination as at the beginning; or, for the sake of variety, one can frequently use the two 4 ft. stops (Flute and Violina), without any 8 ft. stop, playing an octave lower. While holding the last chord, the Flute can be put off. It is not always possible to use these stops an octave lower, but occasionally a good effect is thus obtained.

GEORGES MACMASTER, GRAND CHOEUR

Prepare: Full Gt., Full Sw. (open), Full Ped.; Sw. to Gt. and Gt. to Ped. The first two pages and a half should be played on the Gt. On such a small organ, it is inadvisable to attempt to change the registration, in the measures indicated F and FF, as the desired effect all through these pages is massive and heavy. On a larger organ, changes could be made which would be effective. For the middle section on the third page, reduce the Gt. to Melodia and Flute, put off the Sw. Bourdon, Ped. Open Diapason and Sw. to Gt. Play eight measures of the middle section on the Gt., and repeat on the Sw. After the second ending, play on the Gt. At the fourth measure at the top of the fourth page, play on the Sw. On the second brace, beginning at the third measure, play two measures on the Gt. Return to the Sw. in the fifth measure. In the first measure of the third brace, the chords can be played with one hand, as the bass notes are duplicated in the Ped. This enables one to add Full Gt. and Sw. to Gt. In the rest before the return of the first theme, add Ped. Open Diapason, Sw. Bourdon, and Gt. to Ped. No further change is necessary.

II

Specification of a Very Small Two-Manual Organ with 7 Speaking Stops

GREAT		SWELL	
Open Diapason	8 ft.	St. Diapason	8 ft.
Melodia	8 "	Salicional (Keraulophon)	8 "
Dulciana	8 "	Flute	4 "

PEDAL		COUPLERS
Bourdon	16 ft.	Sw. to Gt.
		Gt. to Ped.
Tremolo		Sw. to Ped.
		Sw. to Gt. at Octaves.

All the stops, except the Open Diapason and the Salicional (or Keraulophon), are generally voiced louder than the same stops are voiced in larger organs. The object of this increased power is, to give as much power to the Full Organ as possible. This increased power is, obviously, necessary only for the hymns and postludes. The larger part of the use of the organ is for the preludes, offertories and the accompaniments of anthems, solos, etc. Increasing the power of the stops generally sacrifices the refinement of the tone, and the combinations of stops are therefore much less satisfactory.

Special attention should be called to the Salicional (or Keraulophon) and the " Sw. to Gt. at Octaves." As there is no Æoline or other very soft stop in this organ, the Salicional (or Keraulophon) is generally voiced somewhat softer than usual, as this stop must be used both for a Salicional and for an Æoline. In old organs the pipes of the lower octave of the Salicional and Dulciana were frequently omitted. The pipes of the lower octave of the St. Diapason and Melodia were " grooved in " to the Salicional and Dulciana to supply the deficiency. Frequently, separate draw-stops, labeled " St. Diapason Bass " or " Stopped Bass," controlled this lower octave of these stops, so that they could be drawn at pleasure with either stop. The " Sw. to Gt. at Octaves " is intended to add brilliancy and power to the Full Organ. It generally makes the

Full Organ shrill and should be used with much moderation. A further consideration of this coupler may be found in the chapter on Couplers and Octave Couplers.

The same seven compositions are selected for registration on this small organ, that were selected for the preceding organ, the object being to enable the student to observe the different treatment which is necessary in registering compositions on a smaller organ.

Uso Seifert, Fantasia in G-Minor

Prepare: All the stops, except the Tremolo and Sw. to Gt. at Octaves (swell open). At the middle section, the Gt. to Ped. should be put off, as in the other organ, and added again as one returns to the Gt. The Sw. to Gt. at Octaves can be added after the hold, at the top of the last page.

William Faulkes, Postlude in A

Practically the same registration as that indicated in the previous section, can be used with this organ, with the omission, at the outset, of those stops which are not included in the specification of this organ.

César Franck, Andantino in G-Minor

Prepare: Gt. Melodia; Sw. St. Diapason and Flute; Ped. Bourdon. Play the solo on the Gt. and the accompaniment on the Sw. At the change of key (measure 35), after adding the Tremolo, play both hands on the Sw. At measure 47 add the Gt. to Ped., and play both hands on the Gt. At measure 53 put off the Gt. to Ped., and play both hands on the Sw. At measure 57 play the L. H. melody on the Gt. and the R. H. on the Sw. At measure 62 (*poco rall*) play both hands on the Sw. At measure 69 add the Gt. to Ped., and play both hands on the Gt., for five measures. Put off the Gt. to Ped., and play the next two measures on the Sw. For the return of the first theme, play the solo on the Sw. with all the stops, and the accompaniment on the Gt. Dulciana. Another registration for this phrase is, to play the solo on the Gt. Dulciana with the Sw. to Gt. at Octaves, and the accompaniment on the Sw. Salicional. At measure 101 (after one measure rest in all the parts), play both hands on the St. Diapason alone, for four measures. At measure 105 play both hands on the Gt., with the Gt. Dulciana, Sw. to Gt., Sw. Salicional and Tremolo. At measure 119 play both hands on the Sw. At the last count of measure 126, play both hands on the Gt. Two measures later play both hands on the Sw., to the end.

Edwin H. Lemare, Andantino in D-Flat

Prepare: Gt. Dulciana; Sw. St. Diapason and Flute; Ped. Bourdon. Play the solo on the Sw. and the accompaniment on the Gt. For the second page put off the Flute and add the Tremolo. Play the two hands the same as on the previous page. (The two staves of the R. H. part must be played on one manual in such a small organ.) For the third page put off the Tremolo, add the Melodia and Flute, and play the R. H. on the Gt. and the L. H. on the Sw. For the last two pages play the R. H. on the Sw. with the Salicional (or St. Diapason), Flute and Tremolo, and the L. H. on the Gt. Dulciana.

ARTHUR FOOTE, FESTIVAL MARCH

Prepare: All the stops except the Tremolo and Sw. to Gt. at Octaves (swell open). Play the first sixteen measures on the Gt. Put off the Gt. to Ped. and play on the Sw. At the middle of the second brace of page 3, add the Gt. to Ped., and play on the Gt. At the top of page 4, put off the Gt. Open Diapason, Sw. to Gt. and Gt. to Ped. For two measures play both hands on the Sw., gradually closing the swell. Put off the Flute and play the R. H. on the Sw. and the L. H. on the Gt. At the top of page 5, play both hands on the Sw. After the second ending, play the L. H. on the Gt. as at first. At the rest in the first measure of the lower brace, add the Sw. to Gt. and Gt. to Ped. Play on the Gt. In the next measure add the Op. Diapason. For the repeat of the first two pages open the swell and add all the speaking stops. The Sw. to Gt. at Octaves can be added for the last phrase.

ALEX. GUILMANT, ELEVATION IN A-FLAT

Prepare: Gt. Melodia; Sw. St. Diapason, Salicional and Tremolo; Ped. Bourdon. Play both hands on the Sw. until the key changes to D-flat. At this measure add the Flute and play the L. H. on the Gt., unless the Melodia is too loud. At measure 51 add the Sw. to Gt. At measure 55 play both hands on the Gt. At measure 58, last count, play both hands on the Sw. During the *ritard* of the next two measures, prepare the combination for the return of the first theme, choosing the most satis-factory of the three following combinations: 1. Both hands on the Sw. with Salicional, Flute and Tremolo (unless the Flute covers up the Salicional) : 2. Sw. St. Diapason, Flute and Tremolo: 3. Both hands on the Gt. with the Dulciana, Sw. Salicional and Tremolo and Sw. to Gt. at Octaves.

GEORGES MacMASTER, GRAND CHOEUR IN D

Prepare: All the stops except the Tremolo and Sw. to Gt. at Octaves (swell open). Play two and a half pages on the Gt. For the second section on the third page, put off the Op. Diapason and Sw. to Gt., and play on the Gt. Repeat on the Sw., after putting off the Gt. to Ped. After the second ending play on the Gt. At the fourth measure of page 4, play on the Sw. At the third measure of the second brace, play two measures on the Gt. At the fifth measure return to the Sw. At the return of the first theme, add the Op. Diapason, Gt. to Ped., and play on the Gt. The Sw. to Gt. at Octaves can be added for the last four measures.

III

REGISTRATION FOR A SMALL TWO-MANUAL ORGAN WITH "DUPLEXED" SWELL ORGAN

As stated on page 84, a "duplex" chest is one so constructed that the several stops may be drawn and played, by means of separate draw-stops, cn two separate manuals, without the use of the Couplers.

SPECIFICATION OF A VERY SMALL TWO-MANUAL ORGAN, WITH SEVEN SPEAKING STOPS
(With a "Duplexed" Swell Organ)

GREAT ORGAN

1. Open Diapason   8 ft.
   Salicional   8 "
   St. Diapason   8 "
   Flauto Traverso   4 "

SWELL ORGAN

2. Æoline   8 ft.
3. Salicional   8 "
4. St. Diapason   8 "
5. Flauto Traverso   4 "

PEDAL ORGAN

6. Bourdon   16 ft.
7. Gedeckt   8 "

COUPLERS

Gt. to Ped.
Sw. to Ped.
Sw. to Gt.
Sw. to Sw. 16 ft.
Sw. to Sw. 4 "

COMBINATION PISTONS
(Non-movable)

GREAT ORGAN

1. St. Diapason, Flauto Traverso and Ped. Bourdon
2. Full Gt. and Full Ped.
3. Release
4. General Release

PEDAL MOVEMENTS

Full Organ
Gt. to Ped. (reversible)
Swell Tremolo

SWELL ORGAN

1. St. Diapason and Salicional
2. Full Sw. and Ped. Bourdon
3. Release

Note: It is presumed that this is a modern organ with a somewhat stringy Salicional and a soft Flauto Traverso.

There is but one distinct stop in the Great Organ — Open Diapason. Three stops of the Swell organ are "duplexed" so that they can be played separately from either the Gt. or Sw. manual. In this organ the duplexed stops have the same names on the two manuals. Frequently, they have different names; e. g., the Salicional of the Sw. is sometimes called "Dulciana" in the Gt. The St. Diapason of the Sw. is frequently called "Gedeckt," or even "Melodia," in the Gt. While there may be a slight advantage in associating the separate names with the separate manuals, it tends to destroy one's idea of distinct tone-quality if, for example, a Gedeckt is called Melodia.

In registering compositions for such an organ, the organist must keep in mind the individual stops, and on which manual he wishes to use them. It is obvious that, if one draws the Salicional on both the Gt. and the Sw., without any other stops, the two manuals are like one. Furthermore, if the organist uses the Salicional on the Sw. and the St. Diapason and Salicional on the Gt., he must not play the same notes on the two manuals at the same time, as those notes will be silent on one manual.

FOUR COMPOSITIONS FOR WHICH REGISTRATION IS SUGGESTED FOR THE ABOVE SMALL TWO-MANUAL ORGAN WITH DUPLEXED SWELL ORGAN

Berthold Tours   Allegretto Grazioso
William Faulkes   Grand Choeur in A
S. Tudor Strang   Cantique d'Amour
Johannes Pache   Prayer in A-flat

BERTHOLD TOURS, ALLEGRETTO GRAZIOSO

Prepare: Gt. St. Diapason, Sw. Salicional and Flute 4 ft., Ped. Bourdon, Sw. to Sw. 16 ft. Play the eight measures of introduction on the Gt., the solo on the Sw. and the accompaniment on the Gt. After the three measures rest in the L. H., on the second page, add the Tremolo. For the second theme (quarter-notes in both hands), put off the Sw. to Sw. 16 ft. and play both hands on the Sw. At the eighth measure before the return of the first theme, change the Sw. combination to St. Diapason and Æoline, and play on the Sw. Four measures later, put off the St. Diapason, add Sw. to Sw. 4 ft. and play on the Sw. (swell wide open). Prepare the Gt. Salicional, and play the return of the theme, R. H. on the Gt. and L. H. on the Sw. The Tremolo may be used (ad lib.). Play the last two chords on the Sw. Æoline, with swell closed.

WILLIAM FAULKES, GRAND CHOEUR IN A

Prepare: Gt. St. Diapason; Sw. Salicional, Flute 4 ft. (swell open); Ped. Bourdon and Gedeckt; Sw. to Gt. and Gt. to Ped.; Combination Piston No. 2 on each manual. Play the first two pages on the Gt. As the leaf is turned, put off the pistons (double release) and the Sw. to Gt., and add Sw. to Sw. 4 ft. After turning the leaf, play eight measures on the Gt. The following L. H. melody can be played on the Sw. (open) with the R. H. on the Gt. At the top of page 5, add the Sw. to Gt. and play both hands on the Gt. Play the last two pages on the Full Organ.

S. TUDOR STRANG, CANTIQUE D'AMOUR

Prepare: Gt. Salicional and Flute 4 ft.; Sw. Æoline and Sw. to Sw. 4 ft.; Ped. Bourdon. Play the first four measures on the Sw. (open). Add the Tremolo and play the solo on the Gt. and the accompaniment on the Sw. At the last measure of the third brace of the second page, play both hands on the Gt. In the first measure of the second brace, on page 5, add the St. Diapason in the Gt. (by means of Piston No. 1). Continue both hands on the Gt. for four measures. Put off the St. Diapason (by means of the release) and play four measures more. For the last measure of the page, play both hands on the Gt. with the St. Diapason alone. While holding the last chord with one hand, prepare: Sw. Salicional, Flute 4 ft., Tremolo, and Sw. to Sw. 16 ft. Play the last two pages with the R. H. on the Sw. and the L. H. on the Gt.

JOHANNES PACHE, PRAYER IN A-FLAT

Prepare: Gt. St. Diapason and Flute 4 ft.; Sw. Salicional and Flute 4 ft.; Ped. Bourdon. Play the first page on the Sw. In the second measure of the second page, add the Gt. to Ped. and play both hands on the Gt. In the last measure of this second page, put off the Gt. to Ped. and play both hands on the Sw. At the top of the third page, add Salicional to the Gt., Gt. to Ped., and play both hands on the Gt. At the last measure before the double bar, at the bottom of the page, put off Gt. Salicional and Flute. Play this measure (R. H. only) on the Gt.; during which, put off Gt. to Ped. and prepare: Sw. Flute 4 ft., Sw. to Sw. 16 ft., and Tremolo. Play the return of the first theme on the Sw. At the second measure of the lower brace of the last page, put off the Sw. to Sw. 16 ft. Play both hands on the Sw., an octave lower than printed. Play the last four measures on the Sw. Æoline.

IV

SPECIFICATION OF A MODERN TWO-MANUAL ORGAN
22 Speaking Stops, 9 Adjustable Piston Combinations (movable)

GREAT ORGAN

Diapason	16 ft.
Diapason	8 "
Melodia (or Hohl Floete)	8 "
Dulciana	8 "
Flute d'Amour	4 "
Octave	4 "
Trumpet	8 "

PEDAL ORGAN

Diapason	16 ft.
Bourdon	16 "
Flute	8 "
Gedeckt	8 "

COUPLERS

Sw. to Gt.
Gt. to Ped.
Sw. to Ped.
Sw. to Sw. 16 ft.
Sw. to Sw. 4 "
Sw. to Gt. 16 "
Sw. to Gt. 4 "

SWELL ORGAN

Bourdon (treble and bass)	16 ft.
Diapason	8 "
Salicional	8 "
Voix Céleste	8 "
Gedeckt	8 "
Æoline	8 "
Flauto Traverso	4 "
Violina	4 "
Flautina	2 "
Oboe	8 "
Vox Humana	8 "

COMBINATION PISTONS
(Adjustable)

Four for Sw. and Ped.
Three for Gt. and Ped.
Two for Ped.

PEDAL MOVEMENTS

Sfz, Full Organ with all Couplers
Grand Crescendo (with Unison
    Couplers)
Gt. to Ped. (reversible)
Sw. Tremolo

At the outset, adjust piston combinations as follows: —

Gt. No. 1 Melodia, Dulciana, and Ped. Bourdon.
Gt. No. 2 Diapason, Melodia, Dulciana, Flute, with Ped. Diapason,
           Bourdon and Gedeckt.
Gt. No. 3 Full Gt. with Full Ped.
Sw. No. 1 Salicional, Gedeckt, Æoline, and Ped. Bourdon.
Sw. No. 2 Salicional, Gedeckt, Æoline, Flute and Violina, with Ped.
           Bourdon.
Sw. No. 3 All the 8 and 4 ft. stops with the Oboe, and Ped. Bourdon
           and Gedeckt.
Sw. No. 4 Full Swell with Ped. Bourdon and Gedeckt.
Ped. No. 1 Bourdon and Gedeckt.
Ped. No. 2 Full Ped.

The above combinations are "general combinations" which are used frequently in organ compositions. "Special combinations" should be adjusted on the pistons when needed. Obviously, individual tastes, in manipulating the stops and combinations of an organ, differ to a great extent; but the above combinations seem, to the author, to be convenient for the purpose of playing the following compositions on this particular organ.

TWELVE COMPOSITIONS FOR WHICH REGISTRATION IS SUGGESTED
FOR THE ABOVE TWO-MANUAL ORGAN

Oscar Wagner	Allegro ma non troppo
Frederick Maxson	Grand Chorus
Russell King Miller	Nocturne in F
Théodore Dubois	Fantasia in E
A. Chauvet	Andantino in D-flat
Samuel Rousseau	Elevation in E-flat
Théodore Salomé	Grand Choeur in G
Roland Diggle	At Sunset
Jacques Lemmens	Finale in D
Oscar Wagner	Sonata in E-minor
S. B. Whitney	Processional March
Alfred Hollins	Spring Song

OSCAR WAGNER, * ALLEGRO MA NON TROPPO

Prepare: Sw. 8 and 4 ft. with Oboe (Piston No. 3), (swell open); Gt. to Octave (Piston No. 2 with Octave added); Ped. Diapason, Bourdon, and Gedeckt (Gt. Piston No. 2 gives this combination); Sw. to Gt., Gt. and Sw. to Ped.

Play the first three pages on the Gt. At the top of page 4, at the rest in the first measure, push Gt. Piston No. 1, which reduces both Gt. and Ped. Ritard the second measure, and, at the fourth note (G) of the third measure, play on the Sw. Gradually close the swell. In the second brace, open the swell. During the rests in the R. H. part, in the third measure, push Gt. Piston No. 2, which increases both Gt. and Ped.

* This registration is intended specifically for the organ whose specification is given on page 158.

After the chord in the seventh measure, play on the Gt. On the last page, where FF is indicated, open the Grand Crescendo full. For the last three measures use the Sfz.

FREDERICK MAXSON, * GRAND CHORUS

The composer's indicated registration is for three-manual organs, and can be easily followed on organs of that size. The composition is also easily played on two-manual organs of this size, for which the following registration is suggested:

Prepare: Gt. Melodia, Dulciana and Flute d'Amour; Sw. 8 and 4 ft. stops with Oboe (Piston No. 3), (swell open); Ped. Bourdon and Gedeckt; Grand Crescendo open about three-quarters. The stops which are drawn are for the middle section. The Grand Crescendo gives the *forte* combination for the first section. No couplers are required in the middle section. The Sw. to Gt. and Gt. to Ped. are on, at the outset, by means of the Grand Crescendo.

Play on the Gt. At the top of page 3, open the Grand Crescendo full for the FF. After the last chord of this page, close both the Grand Crescendo and the swell pedal. For the middle section, play both hands on the Gt. (which was prepared at the outset) for sixteen measures. Repeat the phrase with both hands on the Sw. After the double bar, open the swell, play the R. H. on the Gt. and the L. H. on the Sw., for sixteen measures. Close the swell and play the R. H. on the Sw. and the L. H. on the Gt. In the second brace of page 5, after the double bar, open the Grand Crescendo a little more than half (to include the Diapason). For the repeat open the swell. After the second ending, at the bottom of the page, close the Grand Cresc., and play R. H. on the Sw. (which is already open) and the L. H. on the Gt. For the return of the first theme, at the top of page 7, open the Grand Cresc. full. For the Fughetto at the top of page 8, close the Grand Cresc. a little, to put off the Trumpet. In the last measure at the top of the last page, open the Grand Cresc. full. Use the Sfz for the FFF.

RUSSELL KING MILLER, * NOCTURNE IN F

The registration indicated by the composer in the printed copy, can be followed somewhat closely on this organ. I suggest a few possible additions, which will increase the variety without materially disturbing the composer's interpretation.

Prepare: Gt. Dulciana; Sw. Oboe and Gedeckt (St. Diapason); Ped. Bourdon. The composer has indicated a "Soft Flute 8 ft." in the Gt. for the accompaniment. Very few two-manual organs of this size contain such a stop. In three-manual organs which have the Ch. enclosed in a swell-box, the 8 ft. Flute of the Ch. (Melodia, Concert Flute or Gedeckt) with the swell closed is satisfactory for this accompaniment. Otherwise, it is necessary to use the Dulciana (Gt. or Ch.).

In the first two pages the Flute 4 ft. (Sw.) should be added and put off as indicated. At the end of the first section (bottom of page 3), to carry out the composer's indications, push Sw. Piston No. 3, Gt. No. 2, and add Sw. to Gt. and Gt. to Ped. On page 4, last count of the second measure of the second brace, add Full Sw. (Piston No. 4). It is also necessary to push Gt. Piston No. 2 to bring on the Ped. Diapason which is put off by Sw. Piston No. 4. At the bottom of the page, where the printed indication reads, " Add Princ. 4 to Gt.," add the Octave. On page 5 it is necessary, on this organ, to ignore the indication, " Full to 15th." In the second brace, at the indication, " Full Organ," open the Grand Cresc. full. The Sfz is generally objectionable at this point, on account of the 4 ft. couplers which are included. To make a satisfactory diminuendo and return to the first theme (lower brace of page 5), I suggest the following: Close the Grand Cresc. at the first chord of the last measure of the second brace; push Sw. Piston No. 3 at the first chord of the lower brace; push Gt. Piston No. 1 at the beginning of the second measure; put off the Gt. to Ped. (foot) and play on the Sw. in the third measure; push Sw. Piston No. 2 at the beginning of the fourth measure; close the swell gradually, *ritard molto*, and push Sw. Piston No. 1 at the beginning of the last measure. The first half of the last measure can be played with the L. H., in order to prepare Gt. Dulciana, and put off the Sw. to Gt. Prolong the G-sharp (upper note of the last chord) a fraction of a count in order to turn the leaf and add the Vox Humana and Voix Céleste. This combination for the return of the first theme gives a pleasing variety to the registration. If the player prefers he can use Oboe and Gedeckt as at first, which is the composer's indication. No other change of stops is necessary until the last two chords, which can be played on the Gt. Dulciana (as indicated) or on the Sw. Æoline.

It will be noticed that the Ped. stops are taken care of by the pistons. In organs in which such is not the case, the Ped. Op. Diapason should be added at the end of page 3 and put off in the second measure of the lower brace of page 5.

Many variations of the registration of the first two and the last two pages of this composition are possible, according to the taste of the performer. At the outset, there are various solo combinations from which to choose; such as, Oboe, Voix Céleste and Flute 4 ft.; Oboe, Vox Humana and Bourdon; Voix Céleste, Vox Humana, and 16 ft. Coupler; Voix Céleste, Gedeckt and 16 ft. Coupler. A variation of the method of obtaining the indicated effects in the middle section can be obtained by using the Grand Cresc. for the addition of the stops and for the diminuendo: e. g., in the last measure of page 3 open the Grand Cresc. a little more than half, which includes the Op. Diapason of the Gt., the 8 and 4 ft. stops of the Sw., the Ped. Op. Diapason, the Sw. to Gt. and the Gt. to Ped. couplers. At convenient points in the next page the Grand Cresc. can be opened further to include the Full Sw. and the Gt. Octave. The Grand Cresc. Full can be used where " Full Organ " is indicated. The diminuendo at the bottom of page 5 can be obtained in the reverse order, returning to the first combinations for the return of the first theme, without touching any of the stops. This plan is not always possible, and sometimes is unsatisfactory, in which case the player can use the method previously indicated.

THÉODORE DUBOIS, * FANTASIA IN E

Although this composition is named " Fantasia," it is not too brilliant for a church prelude, as it is mostly of a *maestoso* character. The loudest part requires the Diapason and Octave, and most of the composition is registered for soft combinations. With a little imagination, one can hear the words, " Praise the Lord," all through the opening theme, which consists of a dotted quarter-note, an eighth-note, and a half-note.

Prepare: Sw. 8 and 4 ft. with Oboe (Piston No. 3), (open); Gt. to Octave (Piston No. 2 with Octave added); Ped. Diapason, Bourdon, and Gedeckt (brought on by Gt. Piston No. 2); Sw. to Gt. and Gt. to Ped.

The *maestoso* chords of the opening theme (two pages) should be played on the Gt. (The Octave can be omitted if desired.) After the long chord at the bottom of the second page, put off the Gt. Diapason and Octave. Play the L. H. fragment of the opening theme on the Gt. During this fragment, put off the Ped. Diapason, Gt. to Ped. and Sw. to Gt. During the following descending notes in the Ped. (Bourdon and Gedeckt), which can all be played by the L. foot (*rit.*), close the swell and add Voix Céleste. Then follows the second theme (*quasi Andante*), which should be played on the Sw. At the top of the fourth page, before the five eighth-notes in the Ped., put on the Gt. to Ped. Play the next six measures on the Gt. (Melodia, Dulciana, and Flute 4 ft.). The following phrase in E-minor should be played on the Sw., opening the swell wide for the *forte* and closing it for the *Dim*. At the last measure at the bottom of the fourth page, put off the Voix Céleste, add the Gt. Diapason, and play the three notes of the first theme on the Gt., the staccato chords on the Sw. (partly open). This effect is repeated five times (transposed). For the fifth time (B, F-sharp, B) put off the Diapason and gradually close the swell. In the last two measures of the third brace of the fifth page, the repeated thirds of the L. H. should be played on the Gt. The broken octaves of the R. H. should alternate between the Gt. and Sw. At the top of page 6, for the return of the second theme (key of B), put off the Gt. Flute 4 ft. and play both hands on the Gt. for six measures. For the next six measures (a transposition and variation of the second theme, in the key of G), push Sw. Piston No. 2, and play both hands on the Sw. The lower brace consists of repetitions of the first three notes of the first theme (L. H.). Add the Oboe (Piston No. 3), and play these three notes on the Sw., with the contrasted, staccato chords (R. H.) on the Gt. Melodia (Piston No. 1). For the last measure of this page the Tremolo is indicated. Push Sw. Piston No. 1, add the Tremolo, and play both hands on the Sw. At the rest (R. H. and Ped.), push Gt. Piston No. 2 and turn the leaf. At the

---

* This registration is intended specifically for the organ whose specification is given on page 158.

top of the seventh page, play both hands on the Gt., for six measures. After the first eighth-note of the next measure, push Gt. Piston No. 1 and play six measures on the Gt. At the bottom of the page, play both hands on the Sw. with Piston No. 2. In the last measure of the upper brace of the eighth page, we have the introductory notes of the first theme in the Ped. The Gt. to Ped. and Sw. to Ped. should be added for these notes. The fragments of the second theme (manuals), which accompany this fragment of the first theme, should alternate between the Gt. and Sw. During the sustained chords of the last repetition, push Gt. Piston No. 2, to add the Diapason, and play the following return of the second theme on the Gt. (both hands) for fifteen measures. (The Piston also gives the required Ped. combination.) At the rest, in the next to the last measure of the second brace on the ninth page, push Sw. Piston No. 3, Gt. Piston No. 1, and put off Gt. to Ped. Play the following four measures both hands on the Sw. For the following eight measures play the R. H. solo on the Gt. Melodia. The sustained chords of the last measure of the page and the first two measures at the top of the last page should be played on the Gt. In the third measure continue the L. H. on the Gt., and play the R. H. on the Sw., open for the Mf and closed for the P. At the second measure of the second brace, play both hands on the Gt. During the rests, in the last measure of the brace, push Sw. Piston No. 1, and prepare Gt. Flute 4 ft. only. For four measures of the third brace, play the L. H. on the Sw. and the R. H. on the Gt. an octave lower. Play the last three measures of the brace with both hands on the Gt. an octave lower. Play all of the lower brace on the Sw. Add the Gt. to Ped. (reversible) for the fragment of the first theme in the Ped. Play the last chord on the Æoline (Gt. to Ped. off).

A. Chauvet, * Andantino in D-Flat

There are four or five American editions of this composition, all but one of which indicate the first 35 measures to be played on one manual, the melody being given sufficient prominence by means of the phrasing which is indicated.

Prepare: Gt. Melodia; Sw. Gedeckt, Violina, and Tremolo; Ped. Bourdon. Play the first 35 measures with both hands on the Sw. For the second theme, change the Sw. combination to Oboe, Gedeckt, and Flute 4 ft. Play the solo (R. H.) on the Sw. and the accompaniment on the Gt. (Dulciana). When the key returns to D-flat, change the Sw. combination to Vox Humana (or Voix Céleste) and Flute 4 ft. Play both hands on the Sw. In the last four measures, during the rests in the L. H., reduce the combination to Æoline (ad lib.).

Numerous modifications of the registration are possible; e. g., the first section can be played on the Bourdon, Violina, and Tremolo, playing an octave higher; or Gedeckt and Flute 4 ft.; or Bourdon and Gedeckt playing an octave higher; or Voix Céleste alone; or Æoline and 4 ft.

* This registration is intended specifically for the organ whose specification is given on page 158.

Coupler with the swell open. The middle section can be played with both hands on the Gt. (Melodia), or the R. H. on the Gt. and the L. H. on the Sw., with Gedeckt and Flute 4 ft. Similar variations of the combination for the last section are possible, according to the voicing of the individual organ.

SAMUEL ROUSSEAU, * ELEVATION

Prepare: Gt. Melodia; Sw. Voix Céleste (or Salicional) and Flute 4 ft.; Ped. Bourdon. Play the first eight measures both hands on the Sw. Add Gedeckt and play R. H. on the Sw. and L. H. on the Gt. for 12 measures. Play the following measure (*rall*) both hands on the Gt. Add the Vox Humana and play eight measures with R. H. on the Sw. and L. H. on the Gt. At the top of the third page, play both hands on the Gt. In the second measure, play the L. H. imitation on the Sw. Third measure, both hands on the Gt. Fourth measure, L. H. imitation on the Sw. Fifth measure, R. H. on the Gt. and L. H. on the Sw., continuing for four measures. This is followed by a return of the first theme. At the rest, preceding the theme, prepare: Sw. Vox Humana alone and Gt. Flute 4 ft. alone. Play both hands on the Sw. for two measures. Play the L. H. solo on the Gt. an octave lower. As the solo is transferred to the R. H., play it on the Gt. an octave lower, with the L. H. on the Sw. For the last two measures use the Æoline only.

THÉODORE SALOMÉ, * GRAND CHOEUR IN G

Prepare: Sw. 8 and 4 ft. with Oboe (Piston No. 3); Gt. to Octave (Piston No. 2 with Octave added); Ped. Diapason, Bourdon, and Gedeckt (obtained by Gt. Piston No. 2); Sw. to Gt., Gt. and Sw. to Ped.; Grand Cresc. open full. Play 34 measures on the Gt. (FF). Close the Grand Cresc. and play four measures on the Sw. Continue with both hands on the Gt. During the sustained note (D) in the Ped. gradually open the Grand Cresc. until the return of the first theme. Use the Sfz to the end.

ROLAND DIGGLE, * AT SUNSET

The registration indicated by the composer is for three-manual organs. A few minor changes are necessary for this organ. Prepare: Gt. Dulciana; Sw. Oboe, Voix Céleste and Flute 4 ft.; Ped. Bourdon. Play the first theme (as far as the double bar) with the R. H. on the Sw. and the L. H. on the Gt. For the repeat, add the Sw. to Sw. 16 ft. Coupler, as indicated. For the second theme on the second page, for which the Gamba is indicated, put off the 16 ft. Coupler, add Melodia, open the swell, and play the L. H. on the Sw. and the R. H. on the Gt. At the rest in the measure preceding the double bar, where the key changes back to D-flat, put off the Oboe and add the Vox Humana. At the rest in the following measure, put off the Melodia. After these changes, the

* This registration is intended specifically for the organ whose specification is given on page 158.

R. H. theme can be played on the Sw. (Vox Humana, Voix Céleste, and Flute 4 ft.) and the L. H. accompaniment on the Gt. (Dulciana). For the last eleven measures, put off the Voix Céleste and Flute 4 ft. in the Sw. and prepare the Gt. Flute 4 ft. only. Play the L. H. melody on the Gt. an octave lower, and the R. H. on the Sw.

JACQUES LEMMENS, * FINALE IN D

The only printed indications for the registration in the original copies are: " FF " for the first and last sections and " Sw. P " for the Hymn in the middle section. More variety is obtained by playing the first section F instead of FF.

Prepare: Sw. 8 and 4 ft. with Oboe (Piston No. 3), (open); Gt. to Octave (Piston No. 2 with Octave added); Ped. Diapason, Bourdon and Gedeckt; Sw. to Gt., Sw. and Gt. to Ped.

Play three and a half pages on the Gt. For the last three eighth-notes, in the second measure before the double bar, push Gt. Piston No. 1. On the second eighth-note of the next measure, play on the Sw., *ritard molto*, and close the swell. Push Sw. Piston No. 2 on the last count of the measure. For the Hymn add the Vox Humana. If there is no Vox Humana or the stop is out of order, put off the Gedeckt and Violina and add the Oboe and Tremolo. Two measures before the second double bar, push Sw. Piston No. 4, put off the Vox Humana and Tremolo, and open the swell. At the chord after the double bar, open the Grand Cresc. full, and play the ascending scale on the Gt. Use the Sfz for the last three measures.

OSCAR WAGNER, * SONATA IN E-MINOR

There are only manual indications in the printed copies. Prepare: Gt. to Octave; Sw. 8 and 4 ft. with Oboe (open); Ped. Full; Sw. to Gt., Sw. and Gt. to Ped.

Play the first page on the Gt. After the chord, in the fourth measure at the top of page 3, play both hands on the Sw. Gradually close the swell, and put off the Gt. to Ped. At any convenient point in the first three measures of the second brace, push Sw. Piston No. 3, which puts off the heavy Ped. stops without changing the Sw. combination. During the rests (L. H.) at the end of this brace, add all the Ped. stops and put on the Gt. to Ped. Gradually open the swell. At the third measure of the third brace, play both hands on the Gt. At the top of page 4, after the first two pages have been repeated, play both hands on the Sw. (after the chord). Gradually close the swell. At a convenient point after the double bar, push Sw. Piston No. 3, which puts off the heavy Ped. stops, and put off the Gt. to Ped. In the fifth measure of the second brace, add all the Ped. stops (Piston No. 2), the Gt. to Ped., and open the swell. At the first measure of the third brace, play both hands on the Gt. At the third measure at the top of page 5, open the Grand Cresc. full.

---

* This registration is intended specifically for the organ whose specification is given on page 158.

Larghetto. Prepare: Gt. Melodia and Flute d'Amour; Sw. **Gedeckt,** Salicional, Flute 4 ft. and Violina; Ped. Bourdon, Sw. to Ped.

Play the R. H. solo on the Gt. and the L. H. accompaniment on the Sw. At the last eighth-note of the fourth measure of the second brace play both hands on the Sw. At the last eighth-note, in the fourth measure of the third brace, open the swell and add the Sw. to Gt. (L. H.). In the next measure (key of A), play the last three chords with both hands on the Gt. Add the Gt. to Ped. At the rest in the sixth measure at the bottom of the page, add Sw. Oboe and Diapason (Piston No. 3). At the second measure at the top of page 7, push Gt. Piston No. 2. At the rest in the next measure push Gt. Piston No. 1. In the fourth measure, change to the Sw. on the G-natural. Put off the Gt. to Ped. and gradually close the Sw. In the last measure of the upper brace, push Sw. Piston No. 2 and put off the Sw. to Gt. At *Tempo Primo,* play the R. H. on the Gt. and the L. H. on the Sw. At the rest, in the next to the last measure of the second brace, push Sw. Piston No. 3 and play both hands on the Sw. At the second count of the fifth measure of the third brace, push Sw. Piston No. 2 and play R. H. on the Gt. and L. H. on the Sw. After the first eighth-note, in the second measure at the bottom of the page, play both hands on the Sw. For the last two chords, use Sw. Salicional and Flute 4 ft.

Allegro Molto. Prepare: Gt. to Open Diapason; Sw. Full (open); Ped. Bourdon and Gedeckt; Sw. to Gt. and Sw. to Ped., Grand Crescendo Full.

Play the first seven measures on the Gt. After the first chord in the eighth measure, play both hands on the Sw., close the Grand Cresc. and gradually close the swell. In the ninth measure, play the solo (R. H.) on the Gt. and the L. H. on the Sw. At the top of page 9, open the Grand Cresc. full and play both hands on the Gt. In the first measure of the third brace, close the Grand Cresc. on the second count, and play the 16th-notes on the Sw. In the next measure, play the R. H. solo on the Gt. and the L. H. on the Sw. At the first measure of the second brace on page 10, push Gt. Piston No. 2, and play both hands on the Gt. Put on the Gt. to Ped. (foot) while playing. In the next brace, gradually open the swell. At *Presto* open the Grand Cresc. full. Use Sfz for the last three measures.

S. B. WHITNEY, * PROCESSIONAL MARCH

On this organ, the registration indicated by the composer can be carried out in the following manner. Prepare: Gt. Diapason, Melodia, and Flute d'Amour (Piston No. 2); Sw. 8 and 4 ft. with Oboe (Piston No. 3); Ped. Diapason, Bourdon, and Gedeckt; Sw. to Gt. and Gt. to Ped.

After playing the first two measures on the Gt., push Sw. Piston No. 4 and Gt. Piston No. 2. (It is necessary to push Gt. Piston No. 2, in order to bring on the Ped. Diapason which is put off by the Sw.

---

* This registration is intended specifically for the organ whose specification is given on page 158.

Piston No. 4.)   Gradually open the swell.   On the third count of the
last measure of the upper brace, add the Gt. Octave.   Open the Grand
Cresc. full where "FF" is indicated.   After the third count in the first
measure of page 5, close the Grand Cresc.   At the rest (L. H.) in the
third measure, push Sw. Piston No. 4 (this does not change the Sw.
combination but puts off the heavy Ped. stops) and put off the Gt. to
Ped.   Gradually close the swell.   Before playing the next section (key
of B-flat) put off the Sw. to Gt. and the Gt. Octave; push Sw. Piston
No. 1 and add Sw. Bourdon, Flute 4 ft. and Flautino, to give the
indicated combination.   The Gedeckt is not called for but is generally
necessary.   In the third measure at the bottom of the page, add the Gt.
to Ped.   At the top of page 6, open the Grand Cresc. full.   In the second
measure at the bottom of the page, close the Grand Cresc. and put off the
Gt. to Ped.   In the last measure of the second brace of page 7, put on
the Gt. to Ped.   Gradually open the Grand Cresc. to full.   At the rest
before the double bar, at the bottom of the page, close the Grand Cresc.
and push Sw. Piston No. 4.   The Gt. to Ped. should remain on for the
figure in the first measure, but should be put off in the following measure.
At the top of page 8, put on the Gt. to Ped. for the second measure.
Put it off in the third measure.   It should be put on again in the first
measure of the second brace, and off again in the second measure.   Just
before the last count of the third measure of the third brace, push Sw.
Piston No. 1 and add Flute 4 ft. and Flautino.   In the first measure of
the second brace of page 9, put on the Gt. to Ped. and gradually open
the Grand Cresc.   At the double bar, close the Grand Cresc., put on the
Sw. to Gt., and push Sw. Piston No. 3.   In the last measure of the
brace, push Sw. Piston No. 4 and Gt. Piston No. 2.   Gradually open the
Grand Cresc. to full for the FF.   Use the Sfz for the last eight
measures.

ALFRED HOLLINS, * SPRING SONG

Prepare: Gt. Melodia and Flute 4 ft.; Sw. Gedeckt, Salicional and
Oboe; Ped. Bourdon and Gedeckt; Sw. to Gt., Gt. and Sw. to Ped.
     The only suggestion necessary for the first two pages is, to use the
Grand Cresc. to bring on the Gt. Diapason, which is indicated in the
upper brace of page 3, and close it near the end of the middle brace.   At
the rest at the end of this page, put off the Oboe and the Gt. to Ped. and
add the Voix Céleste.   While playing the first two measures at the top
of page 4, put off the Flute d'Amour in the Gt. and the Sw. to Gt.   For
the middle brace, put off the Voix Céleste and add the Vox Humana.
Play the R. H. obligato on the Gt. Melodia (already prepared).   At the
rest in the first measure of the lower brace, put off the Vox Humana and
add the Voix Céleste.   At the third measure at the top of page 5, put
off the Voix Céleste and add the Vox Humana.   In the last measure of
the page, while holding the chord as indicated, with one hand on the two
manuals (the thumb holding the one note on the Gt.), draw the Sw.

* This registration is intended specifically for the organ whose specification is
given on page 158.

to Gt. At the following rest, add Flute d'Amour in the Gt., Oboe and Flute 4 ft. in the Sw., and Gt. to Ped.; put off the Vox Humana and Gedeckt. Play both hands on the Gt. For the Cresc. to F on both the sixth and the seventh pages, use the Grand Cresc. to the Diapason. During the hold, in the first measure of the middle brace of the last page, put off the Gt. to Ped. and Oboe. At the rest put off the Melodia and Sw. to Gt. and add the Tremolo. This prepares the combinations as follows: Sw. Salicional, Flute 4 ft. and Tremolo, Gt. Flute d'Amour, and Ped. Bourdon. The Oboe can be used as indicated (*ad lib.*). The R. H. part can be played on the Gt. an octave lower to give the effect of an 8 ft. stop, or it can be played as indicated, when it will sound an octave higher. No other change of stops is necessary, unless the Oboe is used, in which case it must be put off later as indicated.

CHAPTER XIX

REGISTRATION ON A MODERN THREE-MANUAL ORGAN
(with non-movable combinations)

SPECIFICATION OF A THREE-MANUAL ORGAN
40 Speaking Stops, 14 Adjustable Combination Pistons (Non-movable)

GREAT ORGAN

1. Diapason   16 ft.
2. First Diapason   8 "
3. Second Diapason   8 "
4. Doppel Floete   8 "
5. Gamba   8 "
6. Harmonic Flute   4 "
7. Octave   4 "
8. Twelfth   2 ⅔ "
9. Fifteenth   2 "
10. Mixture   III Rks.
11. Trumpet   8 ft.

SWELL ORGAN

12. Bourdon (treble and bass)   16 ft.
13. Diapason   8 "
14. Gedeckt   8 "
15. Viol d'Orchestre   8 "
16. Voix Céleste   8 "
17. Salicional   8 "
18. Æoline   8 "
19. Flauto Traverso   4 "
20. Violina   4 "
21. Flautino   2 "
22. Dolce Cornet   III Rks.
23. Cornopean   8 ft.
24. Oboe   8 "
25. Vox Humana   8 "

CHOIR ORGAN

26. Dulciana   16 ft.
27. Geigen Principal   8 "
28. Melodia   8 "
29. Dulciana   8 "
30. Flute d'Amour   4 "
31. Fugara   4 "
32. Piccolo   2 "
33. Clarinet   8 "

PEDAL ORGAN
(augmented)

34. Diapason   16 ft.
35. Violone   16 "
36. Bourdon   16 "
37. Flute   8 "
38. Cello   8 "
39. Gedeckt   8 "
40. Quint   10⅔ "

COUPLERS

Gt. to Ped.	Sw. to Sw. 16 ft.
Sw. to Ped.	Sw. to Sw. 4 "
Ch. to Ped.	Sw. to Gt. 16 "
Sw. to Gt.	Sw. to Gt. 4 "
Ch. to Gt.	Ch. to Gt. 16 "
Sw. to Ch.	Ch. to Ch. 4 "

ADJUSTABLE COMBINATION PISTONS
(set as follows)

Gt. No. 1. Stops Nos. 4, 5, 6, 36
Gt. No. 2.   "   "   2, 3, 4, 5, 6, 34, 36, 39
Gt. No. 3.   "   "   1-7, 34, 35, 36, 38, 39
Gt. No. 4. Full Gt. and Full Ped.
Gt. No. 0. Release
Sw. No. 1. Stops Nos. 14, 17
Sw. No. 2.   "   "   13, 14, 17, 19, 20, 36, 39
Sw. No. 3.   "   "   13, 14, 15, 17, 19, 20, 24, 36, 39
Sw. No. 4.   "   "   14, 15, 17-20, 23, 24, 36, 39
Sw. No. 5. Full Sw. and Nos. 35, 36, 39
Sw. No. 0. Release
Ch. No. 1. Stops Nos. 28, 29, 30, 36
Ch. No. 2.   "   "   27-31, 36, 39
Ch. No. 3. Full Ch. and Nos. 36, 39
Ch. No. 0. Release
Ped. No. 1. Stops Nos. 36, 39
Ped. No. 2. Full Ped.
Ped. No. 0. Release
No. 00. General Release

PEDAL MOVEMENTS	NOTES
Sforzando (Full Organ with all Couplers)	The Combination Pistons remain " set " as above for most of this Chapter.
Grand Crescendo with Unison Couplers	The Pedals for the Sfz and Tremolos notch down when " on."
Gt. to Ped. (reversible)	The Combination Pistons do not move the draw-stops.
Swell Tremolo	
Choir Tremolo	Indicators show which Pistons are " on."
Crescendo Pedal for Swell	This Specification with " Movable Combination Pistons " is treated in the next chapter.
Crescendo Pedal for Choir	

In presenting this particular specification for illustration, I have attempted to select a representative specification of a medium-sized three-manual organ. Many modern electric organs have been constructed with practically this specification, slight variations of the specification being immaterial. This organ has 40 speaking stops. An organ with 45 speaking stops frequently has, in addition, a Contra Fagotto 16 ft. in the Sw., a 32 ft. Bourdon and a 16 ft. Trombone in the Ped., and possibly a Third Diapason and a Gemshorn 8 ft. in the Gt. In the specification of an organ with only 35 speaking stops the following stops are frequently omitted: Mixture in the Gt., Viol d'Orchestre and Vox Humana in the Sw., Fugara in the Ch., and Quint in the Ped. Occasionally, the Dolce Cornet instead of the Vox Humana is omitted.

Before proceeding to suggest the registration for various compositions on this specific organ, I wish to call attention to some of the variations of the specification in other organs of about the size of this organ. In organs which have a Rohr Floete 8 ft. in place of the Gedeckt, or a Rohr Floete 4 ft. in place of the Flauto Traverso 4 ft. in the Sw., those stops must be substituted in the indicated registration. Some of the combinations will be less pleasing with those substitutions but no other course is open to the organist. If the organ contains a Lieblich Bourdon 16 ft. instead of a Bourdon in the Sw., its substitution in the registration will be perfectly satisfactory.

Many organs of about this size contain only two 8 ft. string-tone stops in the Sw., Salicional and Voix Céleste. In these organs the Voix Céleste is somewhat of a compromise. The best Voix Célestes consist of two ranks of keen and pungent, though not loud, string-tone pipes, called " Viol " or " Viol d'Orchestre." Such a Viol d'Orchestre is too strong and stringy to serve as the only 8 ft. string-tone stop in the Sw. It does not balance well with the Gedeckt and is too pronounced in tone-quality to serve as a soft 8 ft. stop between the Æoline and the Gedeckt. Therefore, a less pungent Salicional is also included in the above specification for this purpose. If the Voix Céleste consists of two ranks of ordinary Salicional pipes (in the absence of a Viol d'Orchestre) it is less effective, though it must be used the same as the stronger string-tone Voix Céleste.

Some Sw. organs do not contain a soft 4 ft. string-tone stop (Violina). This is unfortunate, as many delicate combinations cannot be obtained if such a stop is absent. A strong 4 ft. string-tone stop named " Violin " or " Salicet " is occasionally found. It is not as useful as the softer string-tone stop.

In the Gt. a Gross Floete (or Gross Flute) is frequently found instead of a Doppel Floete. These two stops can be used interchangeably, though the tone of the Doppel Floete is generally more refined in character.

In the various Ch. organs we find different forms of a 4 ft. Flute (Flute d'Amour, Flauto Traverso or Harmonic Flute, Rohr Floete, and Wald Floete). In the registration it is necessary to use whichever 4 ft. Flute is found in the Ch., even if some of the combinations or effects are less pleasing than expected. The 8 ft. Flute-tone stop in the Ch. also varies in name — Hohl Floete, Melodia, or Concert Flute. The tonal difference between these stops is not always pronounced and they can be used interchangeably in the suggested registration.

Since an effective combination of stops depends largely on the relative power of the individual stops, I will state that I am presuming that the stops of each manual of this organ are well regulated in power with relation to each other: i. e., in the Sw. I am presuming that the Æoline is extremely soft, that the Salicional and Gedeckt are of about the same power, that the Viol d'Orchestre has a strong, pungent, string tone, and that the Voix Céleste is of the same quality; that the Flauto Traverso is softer than the Gedeckt and that the Violina is softer than the Salicional; that the Bourdon is softer than the Gedeckt and that the Flautino is softer than the Flauto Traverso; that the Vox Humana is a little softer than the Gedeckt and that the Oboe is a little louder than the Gedeckt; that the Diapason and Cornopean are the loudest stops in the Sw. Unfortunately, in quite a number of organs the 4 ft. stops so overpower the 8 ft. stops that many desirable combinations are of little avail.

I am also presuming that the same balance of power prevails in the stops of the other manuals.

With an organ of the size and specification of this organ, the Grand Crescendo is used many times for FF passages, as it brings on Full Organ (without the 16 and 4 ft. couplers) with one quick motion of the foot and releases the Full Organ with a reverse motion. For example: if the organist wishes to use Full Gt., Sw., and Ped., with the Sw. to Gt. and Gt. to Ped. Couplers, the Grand Crescendo gives the desired combination of stops. (The Ch. stops which are included in the Grand Crescendo have practically no influence on the FF combination.) If the Sfz pedal is used instead of the Grand Crescendo pedal the 16 and 4 ft. couplers (especially the latter) are frequently not desirable.

It should be noted in this specification that no Ped. couplers are included in the combinations which have been adjusted on the combination pistons. When these couplers are included many annoying complications arise which are easily avoided by omitting them in the combinations. It is an easy matter to control the Ped. couplers by hand, except the Gt. to Ped. Coupler, which can be controlled either by hand or by the foot (Gt. to Ped. reversible). In some large organs there are reversible pedals to control the Sw. to Gt. and Sw. to Ped. couplers, similar to the Gt. to Ped. reversible.

A List of Twenty Organ Compositions
For which the Registration is Suggested for the Three-Manual Organ
Whose Specification is given on page 169

J. S. Bach	Toccata and Fugue in D-minor
Arthur Foote	Pastorale in B-flat
H. Davan Wetton	Andantino
Alex. Guilmant	Sonata in D-minor (No. 1)
Césare Galeotti	Offertoire
Gustav Merkel	Pastorale in G, Op. 103
George E. Whiting	Melody in B-flat
Edmond Lemaigre	Marche Solennelle
Théodore Salomé	Cantilène
Samuel Rousseau	Entrée Nuptiale
Will C. Macfarlane	Romanza
Henry M. Dunham	Sonata in G-minor
W. Wolstenholme	Serenata
Ralph Kinder	Festival March
John Hyatt Brewer	A Spring-Time Sketch
Georges MacMaster	Pastorale in D-flat
Horatio Parker	Vision in D
Adolph Kroeger	Marche Pittoresque
W. J. Stewart	Festival March
R. Huntington Woodman	Epithalamium

J. S. Bach, * Toccata and Fugue in D-Minor

With an organ in which the stops are not moved by the combination pistons, the registration can easily be arranged in sequence, which simplifies the registration movements as the composition progresses: e. g., prepare: Ch. 1, Sw. 5, Gt. 3, Sw. to Gt., Sw. and Gt. to Ped., Grand Crescendo open full. Both swells open. The first part of the Toccata can thus be played on Full Organ without octave couplers. Some performers change the registration of this Toccata every two or three measures. As frequently stated, tastes in registration differ. I do not consider that a rest in a composition is a signal to change the registration. It seems to me that the dignity of this Toccata and Fugue is best preserved when only a few changes of manuals are made. This is only my opinion and I am well aware that some organists do not agree with me on the subject.

Begin the Toccata on the Gt. At measure 12 (16th-notes alternating between the hands) play both hands on the Sw. Gradually close the swell in the last three or four counts of this phrase. In measure 16 return to the Gt. Just before beginning the Fugue close the Grand Crescendo and the Sw. swell pedal. This leaves Gt. to Octave with Full Sw. coupled and appropriate Ped. stops, as prepared at the outset.

Begin the Fugue on the Gt. In the two measures preceding the entrance of the theme in the pedal part, the swell should be gradually

* This registration is intended specifically for the organ whose specification is given on page 169.

opened. At measure 30, third count (with the descending scale passage), play on the Sw. and gradually close the swell. At measure 41, with the fugal theme in the R. H., suddenly open the swell. Gradually close it again three measures later, with the descending scale passage. At measure 54 gradually open the swell. At measure 56 (ascending scale of D-minor in the L. H.) play on the Gt. At the last measure of the Fugue proper, just before the hold on the chord of B-flat, *ritard* and open the Grand Crescendo full on the chord. Close it again and play the passage in the 32nd-notes on the Ch. The last seven of these 32nd-notes, beginning with F-sharp, should be played on the Gt. Open the Grand Crescendo full at the same time. After the second hold (chord of C) close the Grand Crescendo and play on the Ch. In the last measure of this passage in 32nd-notes *ritard*, open the Grand Crescendo full, and play the last three notes (G, A, B-natural) on the Gt. The following *Vivace* passage should be played on the Sfz.

ARTHUR FOOTE, * PASTORALE IN B-FLAT

The original edition of this Pastorale contained no indications for the registration except manual changes (I, II, III) and the Vox Humana for the last phrase. A later edition contains definite registration indications which are possible on the organ which we are considering in this chapter, as follows:

Prepare: Gt. Doppel Floete; Sw. Gedeckt and Violina; Ch. Clarinet, Melodia and Dulciana; Ped. Bourdon and Sw. to Ped.

The solo (R. H.) should be played on the Ch. and the accompaniment (L. H.) on the Sw. The object of including the Dulciana in the Ch. combination is to avoid the necessity of drawing that stop when the Ch. combination is reduced to the Dulciana, at the bottom of the third page. It is practically unnoticeable in the first combination. For the accompaniment combination (L. H.) one can use Gedeckt and Flauto Traverso or Gedeckt and Violina according to taste. For the repetition of the first sixteen measures the solo should be played on the Gt. for contrast. After the second ending at the double bar, it is a good plan to return to the Ch. (R. H.) for the solo. Four measures later the theme is in the key of G-flat and a good contrast is obtained by playing these 8 measures of the solo on the Gt. At the last count of the second measure, at the top of the second page, one should return to the Ch. for the solo, thus ending this section consistently as it began. For convenience put off the Clarinet at the end of this solo.

The second theme in the L. H. (second page, second brace, second measure) ought to be quite prominent. A keen-toned Gamba will answer, but it seems to me that the Sw. Cornopean (with one or two stops to " fill in ") gives a more desirable tone-quality for this theme. Ordinarily, adding the Cornopean and Salicional to the two stops used in the preceding section makes a good combination for this solo. If the tone of the Cornopean is thin, coarse, and unsatisfactory, the Oboe and Diapason can

* This registration is intended specifically for the organ whose specification is given on page 169.

also be added. However, the distinctive tone-quality of a good Cornopean
when played in the octave around middle C, which is somewhat like the
tone of the G string of a violin in the same octave, is modified and sometimes destroyed if too many stops are added. The portamento chords
in the R. H. sound best as a contrast to the solo if played on a Flute-
tone stop. The Doppel Floete, if it is not too loud, is effective. The
Melodia in the Ch. can also be used, though the tone is less distinctive.
Sometimes the Flute d'Amour in the Ch., if one plays an octave lower,
is satisfactory. The staccato Pedal notes require the addition of an 8 ft.
stop (Gedeckt) to the Bourdon.

On the third page, second brace, the last four measures are of a slightly
different character. The L. H. part sounds well if played on the Doppel
Floete. The R. H. part can also be played on the Gt. or on the Ch.
Melodia. At the beginning of the third brace we have a return of the
Cornopean solo (L. H.) with a Flute obligato (R. H.). The latter
sounds well if played on the Doppel Floete. In the last measure of this
page the R. H. part is a connecting link between the Flute obligato and
the L. H. accompanying chords of the next page. If this measure is
played on the Ch. (Melodia and Dulciana) the Sw. combination (Oboe,
Salicional and Flute 4 ft.) for the return of the first theme (R. H.) can
be prepared and the 8 ft. Ped. stop put off with the L. H. Just before
commencing this theme the chord on the Ch. can be taken with the L. H.,
and the Melodia put off, leaving the Dulciana for the following accompaniment. Numerous other solo combinations can be selected according
to the taste of the organist.

At the seventh measure of the third brace (last page), where the Vox
Humana is indicated, there are two methods of making the change.
First, a short break can be made while one puts off the stops and draws
the Vox Humana. Second, without any break in the last sustained B-flat,
the Vox Humana can be added and the Oboe, Salicional and Flute 4 ft.
quickly put off. The second method is nearer the composer's indication.
If the organ contains a Vox Humana in an Echo organ, or if the Vox
Humana is in the Ch., it can be prepared and played exactly as indicated
by the composer. For a very soft ending one can add the Æoline and
put off the other stops between the last two chords in the L. H. part.

H. DAVAN WETTON, * ANDANTINO IN D-FLAT

This short offertory piece has an effective registration outlined in the
printed copy. It is only necessary to suggest an easy method of obtaining the effects indicated by the composer, as a few of the stops named
are not in the organ under consideration. The composer's indications
are as follows:

Prepare: Sw. Voix Céleste: Gt. with Open Diapason: Ch. Gedeckt 8 ft.:
Ped. Bourdon, Sw. to Gt. and Ch. to Ped.

In the organ which we are considering in this chapter there is no
Gedeckt in the Ch. The Melodia can be substituted for the Gedeckt on

---

* This registration is intended specifically for the organ whose specification is
given on page 169.

general principles as both are Flute-tone stops, but the tone-quality of the Melodia is quite different from that of the Gedeckt, and generally is too loud for these opening measures. With the Ch. swell-box closed the tone is obviously softer but the tone-color remains the same. One can use the Flute d'Amour 4 ft., playing an octave lower, as the tone-color is practically the same as that of the Gedeckt.

With the stops thus prepared one can play the first sixteen measures of introduction alternating between the Sw. and the Ch. as printed. Then follows the first theme — a solo for the Vox Humana with accompaniment for the Dulciana in the Ch. The composer has left to the taste of the performer the selection of stops, if any, to be combined with the Vox Humana. As the solo and accompaniment are repeated (without any change) at the end of the composition, it seems advisable to modify the combinations for the solo to gain variety. I suggest the Vox Humana, Voix Céleste and Gedeckt for this solo the first time, and Vox Humana with Bourdon 16 ft. or with 16 ft. Coupler for the second time. The Ch. Dulciana must be drawn in place of the Flute d'Amour, and its power for the accompaniment must be regulated by the Ch. swell-box.

The middle section of this composition consists of four measures of harmony on a Mf Diapason combination followed by alternating measures between the Sw. and Ch. The composer has indicated Gt. Diapason with the Oboe coupled and manual indications (without naming any stops) for the Sw. and Ch. I suggest using the Second Diapason, Doppel Floete and Gamba, which can be drawn at the outset. Before playing the middle section the player should put off the Vox Humana and add Sw. Piston No. 3 and Gt. to Ped. These changes can easily be made in a fraction of a second. At the end of four measures, which should be played on the Gt., the Melodia can be added in the Ch. The next eight measures, alternating between the Sw. and the Ch., require no change of stops. The following four measures on the Gt. end the middle section. Then follows an exact repetition of the first section.

To carry out the composer's indication, push Sw. 0, put off the Sw. Gedeckt, and exchange the Flute d'Amour for the Dulciana and Melodia in the Ch. At any time during the next sixteen measures put off the Gt. to Ped. by means of the reversible pedal. At the end of the sixteen measures exchange the Dulciana for the Flute d'Amour in the Ch. and prepare Sw. Vox Humana with Bourdon 16 ft. or with 16 ft. Coupler. The lower brace is a short Coda descending in pitch to a low chord which necessitates putting off the Bourdon or the 16 ft. Coupler. This Coda can be played on the Vox Humana without any change, but I suggest the following: Play four measures on the Vox Humana (R. H.), the next two measures on the Salicional and Æoline, and the last three measures on the Æoline alone, beginning with the swell-box open and gradually closing it.

This composition is susceptible of a great variety of registration according to the contents of the individual organ, and can even be effectively registered without either Vox Humana or Voix Céleste. For example: the sixteen-measure introduction can be registered in two different ways: (1) The chords of the first two measures can be played on the Ch. (or Gt.) Dulciana. The solo of the next two measures can be played on the Oboe with the accompaniment on the Dulciana. Similar alternations of manuals for each pair of measures through the introduction. (2) The chords of the first two measures can be played on the Sw. Gedeckt, the solo of the next two measures on the Ch. Clarinet or Melodia or Gt. Doppel Floete, continuing in like manner through the introduction. The next sixteen measures can be varied as follows: (1) The solo on the Gt. Doppel Floete with Ch. to Gt. 16 ft. Coupler and Ch. Clarinet. The accompaniment on the Sw. Gedeckt and Violina or Flute 4 ft. (2) The solo on the Sw. Oboe and Gedeckt with the accompaniment on the Ch. (or Gt.) Dulciana.

For the middle section any Mf combination of a chorus character can be used for the first and last four measures. The measures alternating between the Sw. and the Ch. can be played: (1) On the Ch. (or Gt.) Melodia and Sw. Gedeckt and Violina; (2) on the Sw. Salicional and Flute 4 ft. and Ch. Dulciana; (3) on the Ch. Melodia and Flute d'Amour and Sw. Salicional and Flute 4 ft.; (4) by playing all the measures on the Sw. using the Gedeckt, Salicional and Flute 4 ft., putting the Gedeckt off and on again for the alternating measures.

For the repetition of the first section the registration can be chosen from the optional registration given above or the solo can be played on the Salicional, and Flute 4 ft., 16 ft. Coupler and Tremolo, the 16 ft. Coupler being put off for the Coda.

ALEX. GUILMANT, * SONATA IN D-MINOR (No. 1)

I. INTRODUCTION AND ALLEGRO

Only somewhat meagre indications for the registration of this composition appear in the printed copies. It will be noticed that the Introduction and first three pages are indicated " FF," that the " modulating passage " with diminuendo leads to the second theme, and that the second theme consists of several eight-measure phrases alternating between the Sw. and the Ch. Naturally these phrases should be registered in contrast. With these observations in mind I suggest the following preparation:

Prepare: Gt. Doppel Floete; Sw. Oboe, Voix Céleste, and Flute 4 ft.; Ch. Melodia, Dulciana and Flute 4 ft.; Ped. Bourdon and Gedeckt; Sw. to Gt., Ch. to Ped., Sfz, Grand Crescendo and both swells open.

(I again call attention to the specification of the organ which we are considering in this chapter. The piston combinations are supposed to be of the non-movable type having no effect on the draw-stops.)

The object of using both the Grand Crescendo and the Sfz is to have the benefit of the 16 and 4 ft. Couplers in the Introduction, which are included only in the Sfz, and later to be able to make a gradual diminuendo by means of the Grand Crescendo pedal, after putting off the Sfz.

In the middle of the Introduction there are three measures to be played on the Sw. For these three measures it is a good plan to put off the Sfz, as the 16 and 4 ft. couplers of the Sw. are objectionable in these measures, and put it on again afterward. At the top of page five, when the diminuendo begins, one should first put off the Sfz (unless it has been put off at the beginning of the Allegro movement) and gradually close the Grand Crescendo, taking care not to close it more than three-fourths during the first two braces of the page. At the last measure of the second brace one should play on the Sw. As the Gt. to Ped., which is included in the Grand Crescendo, goes off in due time it requires no attention here. During the first two measures of the third brace, which should be somewhat ritarded, the swell should be closed and the Grand Crescendo closed entirely. This leaves the prepared combination (Oboe, Voix Céleste and Flute 4 ft.) for the second theme, which begins at the third measure. In the second measure of the third brace, the repetition of this phrase of the second theme should be played on the Ch. as indicated. The Ch. swell should be regulated as desired during the preceding eight measures.

The upper brace of page 6 is another phrase of the second theme to be played on the Sw. For the sake of variety add the Gedeckt for this phrase. The second brace is a transposition of the first brace and should be played on the Ch. The ascending scale in the first measure of the third brace (played on the Sw.) leads to a return of the first phrase of the second theme. On one of the half-notes (E-flat or D) put off the Gedeckt and use the same combination for this phrase that was used when the theme was first played.

The lower brace consists of the "ending of the exposition." This can be played on the Sw. and Ch. as indicated; or the registration can be slightly modified, by adding the Gedeckt and putting off the Oboe and Voix Céleste on the G of the second measure, and putting off the Flute 4 ft. in the Ch. before playing on the Ch. During the six measures which are played on the Ch. the Gt. and Sw. should be prepared for the next page. (The repetition of the "exposition" is generally omitted.) Add Sw. 4, Gt. 3 and Gt. to Ped. Gt. 3 must be added *after* Sw. 4 as the last piston which is pushed controls the Ped. combination. If Sw. 4 is pushed *after* Gt. 3, only the Ped. combination of Sw. 4 remains "on," and this is too soft for Gt. 3. At the rest at the top of page 7 add the Ch. Flute 4 ft.

From the preceding preparation the "development" (page 7) begins on Gt. to Octave (with appropriate Ped. stops) with Sw. 8 and 4 ft., Oboe and Cornopean coupled. This combination seems to me to be more pleasing for the "development" than Full Gt. and Sw., which are indicated in the printed copy. After ten measures of polyphonic treatment of a *motif* of the first theme, the first phrase of the second theme can be played on the Sw. reeds — a good contrast to its first presentation. After another ten measures of polyphonic treatment of the same *motif* of the first theme, four measures of the second theme in another key can be played on the Ch. with a *ritard*. During these four measures push 00, put off Gt. to Ped., and add Sw. Tremolo. This prepares the combinations for pages 8 and 9. The melody with arpeggio accompaniment at the top of page 8 can then be played on the Sw. with Gedeckt, Flute

4 ft. and Tremolo. The phrase of the first theme which appears in the pedal part in the second and fourth braces can be emphasized by adding the Gt. to Ped., the Doppel Floete being the only stop left on the Gt. (see first preparation).

Page 9 can be registered as indicated with the combinations already prepared, but I suggest playing the L. H. melody (second theme) in the second brace on the Gt. instead of on the Ch. In the last measure of this page, during the hold over the rest, quick preparation should be made for the following page: viz., put off the Tremolo during the last chord, and add Sw. Oboe, and Voix Céleste, Sw. 5 and Gt. 3 during the rest. While playing the first three measures of page 10, open the swell and add Gt. to Ped. At the first chord of page 11, which is the climax of this section, being "the second theme in the major," add Sfz. During any one of the rests of the upper brace push 00, thus releasing all piston combinations. At the first measure of the second brace, just before playing the last note of the measure on the Sw., put off the Sfz. This leaves the Sw. combination (Oboe, Gedeckt, Voix Céleste and Flute 4 ft.) which was prepared by the draw-stops at the end of page 9. During this brace the swell should be gradually closed and the Gt. to Ped. put off. The next phrase of the second theme should be played on the Ch., which is all prepared (Melodia and Flute 4 ft.). At the top of page 12 the ascending scale can be treated the same as on page 6, by putting off the Gedeckt on one of the half-notes (E-flat or D).

In the third brace the combination should be changed for the measures marked "Andante" and "Adagio." I suggest Gedeckt and Flauto Traverso for the Andante (putting off the Ped. Gedeckt if necessary) and the Ch. Dulciana for the Adagio. While playing the Adagio open the swell-box of the Sw. Just before starting the Ped. theme (last measure of the third brace) put on the Sfz. Obviously, many variations of this suggested registration are possible and effective according to personal taste.

II. PASTORALE

The preparatory registration for this Pastorale printed in the Schirmer edition of this sonata (barring its antiquated stop-names) can be followed on this organ or can be slightly modified.

Prepare: Gt. Doppel Floete, Gamba, and Flute 4 ft.: Sw. Oboe, Voix Céleste and Flute 4 ft.: Ch. Melodia and Clarinet: Ped. Bourdon and Gedeckt: Sw. to Gt.

The manual indications should be followed. On the second page, last measure of the third brace, add Sw. Piston No. 2 on the third count of the measure, to give a little more body to the combination which is used to accompany the L. H. theme on the Gt. It is unnecessary to put off the Clarinet in the Ch. in the last measure of the page (as printed), because the Ch. is not used again until the lower brace of the fourth page, when the Clarinet is again required.

In the third measure, second brace of the third page, follow the indicated registration. (Put off Sw. to Gt. and Oboe and add Vox

Humana and Gedeckt. Also push Sw. piston 0.) Before playing the
choral on the Vox Humana (with or without Gedeckt and Voix Céleste),
the Gt. to Ped., and possibly the Ped. Gedeckt, should be put off. This can
be done during the rests. While playing this choral (L. H.) the Gt. must
be prepared with Doppel Floete only. During the rests in the L. H.
part at the end of the fourth page, the Sw., Gt., and Ped. should be
prepared as at first. I suggest that the Gedeckt be included in the Sw.
combination. At the third measure at the top of the sixth page, the
Clarinet should be put off with the L. H. on the first count and the
Oboe with the R. H. during the rests.

In the third measure of the third brace of the last page, the Vox
Humana in the Sw. is again required. I suggest that it be used alone
this time. The Flute obligato will be softer if played on the Ch. Flute
d'Amour an octave lower than on the Gt. Flute. In the last two measures
the L. H. theme will be too loud if played on the Gt. To make a softer
ending I suggest the Ch. Dulciana with the swell-box open for the L. H.
theme and the Sw. Æoline with swell-box open for the R. H. chord. If
the Ped. Bourdon is too loud one can use the Sw. Bourdon Bass with
Sw. to Ped.

III. FINALE

Prepare: Gt. First and Second Diapasons, Doppel Floete, and Flute
4 ft.; Ch. Piccolo and Piston No. 2; Sw. Piston No. 5; Sw. to Gt.; Grand
Cresc. and both swells open.

The first two and a half pages can be played without change of manual.
In the middle of the third page, where the Sw. is indicated, close the
Grand Cresc. during the rests in the Ped. part. This puts off the heavy
Ped. stops and the Gt. to Ped. The Sw. and Ch. combinations were
prepared at the outset. At any point in the fourth brace of the fourth
page, open the Grand Cresc. full and put on the Gt. to Ped. (As the
Full Sw. is " on " by Piston No. 5, the Grand Cresc. does not affect the
combination being used while it is being opened.)

At the last measure of the fifth page (rests for both hands and feet),
close the Grand Cresc., push Sw. 3, Ped. 2, and put off the Ch. Piccolo.
At the top of the sixth page, play on the Ch., instead of on the Gt. (Ch.
Piston No. 2 being on). The Ped. figure will be prominent, as Ped. 2
and the Gt. to Ped. are on. During the rests in the Ped. part of the
lower brace, put off the Gt. to Ped., push Ped. Piston No. 1, and close
the swell of the Sw. At the top of the seventh page, play on the Sw.
(instead of on the Ch.). In the second brace the third and fourth measures should be played with the L. H. while the Ch. Piccolo is added
with the R. H. Near the end of the brace play the L. H. on the Gt. as
indicated, and in the third brace play the R. H. on the Gt. as indicated.
The third and fourth measures of the fourth brace should be slightly
ritarded while Sw. Piston No. 5 is pushed (it is generally within easy
reach of the R. H.). The following page and a half can be played on
the Sw., Ch., and Gt., as indicated. During the upper brace of the
ninth page, the swell should be opened gradually and the Grand Cresc.

opened full for the return of the first theme. The *Andante maestoso* movement of the last pages can be played on the Sfz.

While this registration which I have suggested for this particular organ is definite, it is not arbitrary, as numerous effective variations can be made according to the taste of the performer. When the performer has no personal idea of how to register this composition, this registration will be found effective. If he has decided personal ideas for the registration no outside suggestions will prove acceptable.

CÉSARE GALEOTTI, * OFFERTOIRE, OP. 100

Prepare: Gt. Doppel Floete and Gamba; Sw. Vox Humana; Ch. Clarinet and Dulciana; Ped. Bourdon.

The first four measures of slow, slurred chords are indicated for the Vox Humana. The last chord should be held slightly longer than its value. In the break between this chord and the next theme, the Vox Humana should be put off and the Gedeckt and Flute 4 ft. put on. The R. H. solo can be played on the Ch. and the L. H. accompaniment on the Sw. Only those who have a large hand can reach the E and F-sharp (L. H.) in the last measure of the second brace. The E can be omitted.

At the top of the second page, add the Voix Céleste. Play two measures (both hands) on the Gt., and the following two measures on the Sw. Put off the Clarinet at the rest. After the hold in the first measure of the third brace, put off the Voix Céleste, add the Tremolo, and play both hands on the Sw. At the return of the theme (second measure at the top of the third page), add the Oboe, and play the R. H. on the Sw. and the L. H. on the Ch. At the last measure of the second brace, the return of the introductory chords should be played on the Voix Céleste as indicated. For the next five measures the solo can be played on the Voix Céleste and Vox Humana, with the accompaniment on the Ch. Dulciana, or both hands can be played on the Vox Humana alone. The last chord is effective on the Gedeckt and Tremolo.

GUSTAV MERKEL, * PASTORALE IN G, OP. 103

Prepare: Gt. Doppel Floete: Sw. Oboe, Salicional and Flute 4 ft.: Ch. Melodia and Flute 4 ft.: Ped. Bourdon and Sw. to Ped.

Play the first brace on the Sw. In the first measure of the second brace, just before the chord on the fourth count, add Gedeckt. In the lower brace, first measure, last note (G) of the R. H. part, play on the Ch. as a solo. At the last chord of the second measure, put off the Ch. Flute 4 ft. and Sw. to Ped., and play both hands on the Ch. In the last measure of the page, beginning with the last chord of the measure, play both hands on the Sw. In the third measure of the second page, play the L. H. solo on the Gt. Second brace, first measure, play the last chord in the L. H. on the Sw. Add the Ch. Flute 4 ft. and play the R. H. solo on the Ch. In the first measure of the third brace, play all of the

* This registration is intended specifically for the organ whose specification is given on page 169.

upper staff on the Ch. until the last note which should be played on the Sw. In the last measure of the third brace, play the L. H. imitation on the Gt. At the last part of the second count of this measure, play the R. H. on the Gt. Put on the Gt. to Ped. for the imitation in the Pedal part. In the lower brace play the L. H. on the Sw. Put off the Gt. to Ped. after the first note, and play the sixteenth-notes of the R. H. on the Ch.

During the rest in the L. H. in the last measure of the page, push Gt. piston No. 1. Before the last chord of the measure, push Sw. piston No. 3, and play the R. H. on the Sw. At the top of page 3 play the L. H. on the Gt. until the last chord of the second brace, when both hands should be played on the Gt. In the first measure of the third brace, the last chord should be played on the Ch. In the lower brace add Sw. to Gt., and play the R. H. on the Sw. At the last count of the second measure, play the L. H. on the Gt. Add the Gt. to Ped., and, in the last measure, play both hands on the Gt. In the first measure at the top of page 4, push Gt. 2 before the first count, Sw. 5 on the third count, and Gt. 3 before the last B-flat. In the second measure open the swell and the Grand Crescendo. Have the latter full at the climax at the beginning of the second brace. In the first measure of page 5, at the last count, play both hands on the Sw. At the bracket at the end of the second count, in the second measure, play both hands on the Gt.

In the second measure of the second brace, while holding the chord, push Gt. 0, Sw. 2 and put off Gt. to Ped. After releasing the chord close the Grand Crescendo, put off the Oboe and play both hands on the Sw. Gradually close the swell. In the first two measures of the third brace, there are three separate chords which can be played with the L. H. During one of these chords put off the Ch. Melodia, which leaves the Flute d'Amour alone. During another of these chords put off the Salicional and Flute in the Sw., and add the Gedeckt. At the third count of the second measure, push Sw. Piston No. 1. At the *A tempo*, when the key changes to G-major, push Sw. 0 and add the Vox Humana. During the next two measures put off (with the L. H.) the Sw. to Gt. and the Sw. to Ped. In the second measure of the lower brace, play the L. H. broken octaves on the Ch. In the last measure of the page, play both hands on the Sw. At the rests in the R. H. turn the leaf, add Sw. Flute 4 ft. and put off the Gedeckt. At the top of page 6, play the R. H. solo on the Ch. In the first measure of the second brace, continue the upper part as a solo and play the balance of the chords on the Sw. At the last eighth-note of this measure, play the R. H. on the Sw. and the L. H. on the Ch. an octave lower.

In the first measure of the third brace, play the last chord of the L. H. on the Sw. Play the sixteenth-notes (R. H.) of the last measure on the Ch. At the last note of the first measure of the lower brace, add the Gedeckt, and play the R. H. on the Sw. In the last measure of the page, play both hands on the Sw. In the first measure of the last page, play the sixteenth-notes of the R. H. on the Ch. and the chords on the Sw. The last two sixteenth-notes of both hands (in this first measure) should be played on the Sw. In the second measure the first and third counts should be played on the Sw. The second and fourth counts (which include the Ped. notes) should be played on the Gt.

In the first measure of the second brace, play both hands on the Sw. with the Vox Humana alone. In the third measure of the third brace, after the first chord, put off the Vox Humana and push Sw. piston No. 1. During the rest in the R. H., add the Gedeckt and Æoline. In the first measure of the lower brace, play the R. H. on the Ch. and the L. H. on the Sw. In the second measure, after the first chord, push Sw. 0 and play R. H. on the Ch. and L. H. on the Sw. At the third count in the R. H. part, put off the Gedeckt, open the swell and play both hands on the Sw. (Æoline only). Gradually close the swell to the end.

George E. Whiting, * Melody in B-Flat

The registration for this composition is indicated in the printed copies, with the exception of three or four points where the necessary registration is either omitted or is ambiguous. The registration which is suggested below is planned to fully carry out the apparent intention of the composer.

Prepare: Gt. Gamba: Sw. Gedeckt and Violina: Ch. Melodia and Clarinet: Ped. Bourdon and Gedeckt: Sw. to Gt. (no Ped. Coupler).

Follow the manual indications of the first page. At the last measure of the page, put off the Clarinet and draw the Cornopean as indicated. On the second page, at the last count of the second measure of the second brace, the indication is " PP." Put off the Cornopean and play R. H. on the Sw. and L. H. on the Gt. At the rest in the fourth measure of the lower brace, add Gt. to Ped. and push Gt. Piston No. 1. At the top of the third page push Gt. No. 2, which adds the Diapason as indicated. At the fourth measure, last count, open the Grand Crescendo about two-thirds. This generally gives Full Sw. and Gt. to the Octave. At some convenient point in the second brace, the thumb of the L. H. can push Gt. piston No. 1 for future use. At the climax in the third brace open the Grand Crescendo full. In the fourth measure the Grand Crescendo can be gradually closed. Keep both hands on the Gt., instead of the L. H. on the Sw. as indicated.

In the first measure of the lower brace put off the Gt. to Ped. Play the R. H. on the Ch. Add the Cornopean and Voix Céleste and play the L. H. on the Sw. At the last chord of the page put off the Cornopean, and play the R. H. on the Sw. At the top of the last page push Gt. 0, and play L. H. on the Gt. In the third measure of the second brace, add the Oboe, and play both hands on the Sw. The manual indications can be followed to the end. Use the Voix Céleste alone for the last three measures.

Edmond Lemaigre, * Marche Solennelle

The original edition (Leduc) contains no registration indications of any value. I suggest the following:

* This registration is intended specifically for the organ whose specification is given on page 169.

Prepare: Sw. Oboe, Voix Céleste, Flute 4 ft. and Piston No. 3: Ch. Melodia and Piston No. 2: Gt. Doppel Floete and Piston No. 2: Ped. Bourdon; Sw. to Gt., Gt. to Ped. Ch. swell open. Sw. swell closed. (Gt. Piston No. 2 should be pushed after the other Pistons to leave the desired Ped. combination on.)

Play the first brace on the Gt. At the beginning of the second brace, push Gt. 3. At the rest in the last measure at the top of the second page, put off the Gt. to Ped. (by the foot) and push Gt. 1 to throw off the heavy Ped. stops. Play on the Ch. At the second count of the fourth measure in the lower brace, push Gt. 3 and add the Gt. to Ped. (foot).

For the trio at the double bar in the third page, push 00, put off Gt. to Ped. and Sw. to Gt. and draw the Sw. Tremolo. The 00 releases all the combination Pistons, leaving the draw-stops which were prepared at the outset: viz., Gt. Doppel Floete, Sw. Oboe, Voix Céleste and Flute 4 ft., Ch. Melodia and Ped. Bourdon. After making these changes the R. H. should be played on the Sw. and the L. H. on the Ch. At the double bar in the middle of page 4, add Ch. Flute d'Amour. Play the L. H. chords on the Ch. and the obligato on the Gt. In the fourth measure of the lower brace, the eighth-notes should be played on the Ch. While ritarding these notes put off the Flute d'Amour. The next phrase should be played as at first. This section (between the double bars) can be repeated or not according to the taste of the performer.

At the rest in the last measure of the upper brace of the fifth page, push Sw. 3 and add Sw. to Ped. and Sw. to Gt. At the rest in the fourth measure of the second brace, push Ch. 2 and play both hands on the Ch. Also push Gt. 2 while playing these two last measures. In the last measure of this brace, draw Gt. to Ped. by hand, for the eighth-note figure in the pedal part. Play both hands on the Gt. in the following measure. At the rest in the second measure of the third brace, push Gt. 3. At the last measure of the upper brace of the sixth page, open the Grand Crescendo full. At any one of the rests in the pedal part of this page, put off the Gt. to Ped. (with the foot), as it is also included in the Grand Crescendo. At the rest in the third measure of the lower brace, close the Grand Crescendo, push Sw. 5, and play both hands on the Sw. At the first measure of the third brace of the seventh page, push Gt. 3 (to put on its Ped. combination, which was put off by Sw. 5) and draw Gt. to Ped. At the fourth measure of the lower brace open the Grand Crescendo full. At the last count of the last measure of the second brace of the last page, play both hands on the Sw. Return to the Gt. in the next brace, using the Sfz.

THÉODORE SALOMÉ, * CANTILÈNE

Prepare: Gt. Doppel Floete: Sw. Oboe, Gedeckt and Flute 4 ft. (closed): Ch. Melodia and Dulciana (closed): Ped. Bourdon and Gedeckt,

Play the L. H. chords on the Ch. and the R. H. solo on the Sw. At

* This registration is intended specifically for the organ whose specification is given on page 169.

the twenty-second measure, where the theme is in E-minor, add Sw. to Sw. 16 ft. After the double bar, where the key changes to A-major, play the two measures of the L. H. on the Ch. and prepare (R. H.) Sw. Gedeckt, Violina, Sw. to Sw. 4 ft. (or Flautino) and Tremolo. Play the R. H. on the Sw. and the L. H. solo on the Gt. At the end of the middle section, where the L. H. has a sustained chord and the R. H. has a full measure rest, play the L. H. on the Ch. Dulciana (swell partially open), which can be prepared by the R. H. during the rests. While sustaining the L. H. prepare the Sw. Vox Humana, Flute 4 ft. and Sw. to Sw. 16 ft. Put off the Ped. Gedeckt. Play the R. H. solo on the Sw. At the end of this solo, the ascending scale, partly in the L. H. and partly in the R. H., should be played on the Ch. While playing the last part of this scale (R. H.) put off the Sw. to Sw. 16 ft. Play the solo (L. H.) on the Sw. Continue the sixteenth-note run on the Sw. Play the last three measures on the Æoline.

SAMUEL ROUSSEAU, * ENTRÉE NUPTIALE

Prepare: Sw. Piston No. 3 (swell partially open) : Ch. Melodia, Flute d'Amour and Piston No. 2 (swell open) : Gt. Trumpet and Piston No. 2: Ped. Bourdon and Gedeckt; Sw. to Gt.

Play the first eight measures on the Gt. and the next four measures on the Sw. Put off the Trumpet at the end of the page. In the upper brace of the second page, play the R. H. on the Sw. and the L. H. (beginning with the 16th-note run) on the Gt. (or Ch.) for two measures, and afterward on the Sw. In the second brace, at the return of the first theme, add the Trumpet, Gt. to Ped. and play both hands on the Gt. Put off the Trumpet at the end of the page. At the top of page 3 push Sw. 5 (Full Sw.), close the swell and play both hands on the Sw. At the beginning of the third brace, play both hands on the Gt. During the last two measures of the page, open the Grand Crescendo (full on the last count).

At the double bar, in the second brace of the fourth page, while holding the chord of E-flat, close the Sw. swell, push 00, put off the Gt. to Ped. (with the foot), and draw the Tremolo. On releasing the chord, close the Grand Crescendo and push Sw. 4, which gives 8 and 4 ft. with Oboe and Cornopean. Play the R. H. solo on the Sw. and the L. H. accompaniment on the Ch. (swell partially open if necessary). At the last measure of the page, push Gt. 2 and add the Gt. to Ped. (foot). Play two measures with both hands on the Gt., two measures on the Sw., two measures on the Gt., two measures on the Sw., and two measures on the Gt., to the hold. During the rest push Gt. 0 and put off the Gt. to Ped. Play the solo and accompaniment as before. At the last measure of the page, during the hold, put off the Tremolo. Before playing the last count of the page, turn the leaf, push Ch. 2, Sw. 5, Gt. 2, and draw the Trumpet and Gt. to Ped. (foot). Play

* This registration is intended specifically for the organ whose specification is given on page 169.

both hands on the Gt. At the fourth measure of the second brace, put off the Trumpet and Gt. to Ped. Play the R. H. solo on the Gt. and the L. H. accompaniment on the Ch. At the first measure of the lower brace open the Grand Crescendo full and play on the Gt. At the last measure of the upper brace of page 7, close the Grand Crescendo, draw Sw. to Sw. 16 and 4 ft. Couplers, and play on the Sw. (swell closed). At the lower brace push Gt. 3, play on the Gt. and gradually open the swell. At the last count of the second measure, in the second brace of the last page, put on the Sfz and play on the Gt.

WILL C. MACFARLANE,* ROMANZA

Prepare: Gt. Gamba and Har. Flute 4 ft.: Sw. Gedeckt, Salicional and Oboe (swell closed): Ch. Melodia (swell partially closed): Ped. Bourdon.

For the student, I will state that the composer's indication, " Ch. (or Gt.)," signifies that on three-manual organs the Ch. is intended, but on two-manual organs one must play on the Gt.

No suggestions are necessary for the first page. At the A tempo on page 3 the Tremolo can be added (ad lib.). If it is added it must be put off at the end of the page. All the composer's indications must be followed in the next two pages. At the return of the original key (A) at the bottom of page 5, the composer has indicated L. H. " Gt. with Gamba." As the Gamba in different organs varies considerably I call attention to three combinations with the Gamba which are possible for this theme. I have suggested Gamba and Har. Flute 4 ft. If the Flute is too loud it will be objectionable. If the Gamba is very loud it may be necessary to omit it and use Doppel Floete and Flute 4 ft. If it is not too loud it can be used alone. If the Gamba is too soft and slow in speech the Doppel Floete and Gamba may prove more satisfactory. It is frequently necessary to use a firmer combination in the Sw. than the one mentioned above. In that event I suggest the addition of the Viol d'Orchestre with or without the Flauto Traverso. If these stops are added they should be put off on the last page where " slower " is indicated. For the Adagio put off the Oboe and add the Tremolo. Sometimes the last six measures are more effective when played on the Gedeckt and Tremolo. They can also be played on the Salicional alone.

HENRY M. DUNHAM, * SONATA IN G-MINOR

The composer's registration is minutely indicated in the printed copies and is a good model for students to study. The only suggestions which I wish to make are along the line of what I consider the best method of obtaining the indicated registration on this particular organ.

---

* This registration is intended specifically for the organ whose specification is given on page 169.

I. Allegro Moderato

The composer's indications at the outset are: " Full Gt., Sw. and Ped., Ch. 8 and 4 ft." By using the Grand Crescendo open full we obtain all the above. At the same time we can have the combinations required on the third page prepared by means of the draw-stops. Therefore, I suggest the following: —

Prepare: Sw. 8 and 4 ft. without reeds and Piston No. 5 (swell open): Ch. Diapason, Melodia and Flute d'Amour: Gt. Second Diapason, Doppel Floete, Gamba, Har. Flute and Piston No. 3 (pushed last): Ped. Bourdon and Gedeckt (Gt. 3, if pushed last, gives the heavy Ped. stops required part of the time): Sw. to Gt., Gt. and Sw. to Ped.: Grand Crescendo open full.

By analyzing the above, the student will observe that the Full Organ is on by means of the Grand Crescendo. When that is closed, Gt. to Oct. is on by means of Gt. 3, Full Sw. by means of Sw. 5, and the heavy Ped. stops also by means of Gt. 3. Later, when Gt. 3 is released, there will be left four stops which were drawn by the draw-stops at the outset. Likewise, when Sw. 5 is released there will be left the 8 and 4 ft. stops without reeds which were drawn at the outset. It will thus be seen that we have prepared three sets of combinations on the Gt., Sw. and Ped. at the outset. This is not possible if the combination pistons are of the movable type.

The first two pages are indicated " Full Gt. and Sw." At the last count of page 3, close the Grand Crescendo. We can then play on F Gt. and Full Sw. for two braces. At the last count of the second brace, on page 4, push Sw. 3, which gives 8 and 4 ft. with Oboe (Mf as indicated). At the *Adagio* in the fourth brace, push Sw. 2. After the hold at the bottom of the page, push Sw. 5 and Gt. 3. At the *Tempo 1mo*, in the second brace of page 5, push Gt. 2 and Sw. 4. The latter gives 8 and 4 ft. reeds as required. While playing on the Ch., in the fourth brace, push Sw. 5 for Full Sw., which is required. In the fourth measure, before playing on the Gt., push Gt. 3. In the third measure of the lower brace, push Sw. 2. In the following measure push Sw. 5.

For the *sostenuto* passage in the upper brace of page 6, push Gt. 2. In the next two braces, gradually open the Grand Crescendo and use it full at the return of the first theme. At any point in the next sixteen measures, where there are rests in either hand, push Sw. 0 and put off Gt. to Ped. (The Grand Crescendo holds Full Organ and all couplers on.) On page 7, where the key changes to the major, close the Grand Crescendo. The desired combinations in the Sw. and Ped. for this passage were prepared at the outset, and have not been disturbed. At the *A tempo* in the second brace of page 8, push Gt. 2. At the *Tempo 1mo* on page 9, open the Grand Crescendo full. At the *Largemente* on page 10 use Sfz.

II. Adagio

Prepare the stops as indicated except the Ped. Violone 16 ft., which in this organ is too loud to be used with the Sw. Salicional. I suggest the Bourdon as a substitute. Follow the manual indications without exception. At the fourth measure at the top of page 11 push Sw. 1 to " add St. Diap." (Gedeckt). At the second measure of the second brace push Sw. 2 to " add Op. Diap." At the second measure of the third brace push Sw. 1 for " Op. Diap. off." At the third measure " add Oboe " by the draw-stop. In the next measure to " add Op. Diap." push Sw. 3, which includes Oboe and Op. Diap. At the second measure of the fourth brace push Gt. 2, which puts on the Ped. Diapason as well as the Gt. stops, though the latter were drawn at the outset. At the first measure at the bottom of page 11, push Gt. 3. In the middle brace of page 12, gradually open the Grand Crescendo (somewhat difficult but possible). At the indication " FFF " have the Grand Crescendo open full. At the rest (L. H.) in the last measure of the page add Ch. Piccolo. At the beginning of the second measure of page 13, push Gt. 1. In the second brace close the Grand Crescendo and put off Gt. to Ped.

At the third measure of the fourth brace, push Gt. 2 and put on the Gt. to Ped. At the rests, in the third measure at the bottom of the page, put off the Diapason (draw-stop) of the Gt. (Piston No. 2 is still on and thus holds this stop on). During the *ritard* at the bottom of the page push Gt. 1. Before playing the last octave on the Sw. push Sw. 2 and put off the Oboe. Put off the Gt. to Ped. at the top of page 14. While holding the octave B-flat on the Sw. prepare Ch. and Gt. as indicated. Before playing the next measure push Sw. 1 and draw the Oboe. The last five measures are indicated for the Salicional (both hands). A softer effect is possible (*ad lib.*) by using the Æoline and Sw. to Sw. 4 ft. with the swell open.

III. ALLEGRO MOLTO

Prepare: Sw. 8 and 4 ft. (draw-stops) and Piston No. 3: Gt. Piston No. 3: Ch. 8 and 4 ft.: Ped. Bourdon and Gedeckt: Sw. to Gt., Sw. and Gt. to Ped.: Grand Crescendo full.

The above preparation gives all that is indicated at the outset and prepares for several combinations which are required later. Play on the Gt. At the double bar in the middle of page 16, close the Grand Crescendo. At the *A tempo* at the top of page 17, push Gt. 2. During the rests in the Ped. part, put off the Gt. to Ped. (foot). At the fifth measure of the second brace, put on the Gt. to Ped. At the third measure at the top of page 18, put off the Gt. to Ped. and push Sw. 2. At the hold in the middle of the page, for " Sw. Reeds " push Sw. 4. Also push Gt. 2 to add the Ped. Diapason, which is needed in the next phrase. At the top of page 19 open the Grand Crescendo full and at " FFF " put on the Sfz. While holding the last chord at the bottom of the page, close the Grand Crescendo (if the Sfz is on) and push 00. Before playing at the top of page 20 put off the Sfz and prepare the Sw. as indicated. As there is no Quintadena in this organ substitute the 4 ft. Flute. (Note: The Flute is not a legitimate substitute for the Quintadena, but the combination, Salicional and Flute 4 ft. is a fairly good substitute for " Salicional and Quintadena," which is indicated). For the *Tempo 1mo* open the Grand Crescendo full. Use the Sfz (*ad lib.*) at the end.

The foregoing suggestions must be considered as supplementary to the indicated registration, as they are intended only as suggestions to facilitate the carrying out of the composer's indications.

W. Wolstenholme, * Serenata in A

The composer has indicated only a bare outline of the registration. I suggest the following: —

Prepare: Gt. Doppel Floete: Sw. Oboe, Flute 4 ft., Tremolo and Sw. to Sw. 16 ft. (swell closed): Ch. Dulciana (swell open): Ped. Bourdon.

The first page is indicated R. H. Sw., L. H. Ch. In the fifth measure of the second brace of page 3 it is necessary to add Melodia in the Ch., as the R. H. thirds are indicated for the Gt. Doppel Floete. The Dulciana is not loud enough to balance these thirds. The Melodia can easily be added with the L. H. at the rest. In some organs the Melodia and Dulciana in the Ch. with the swell closed is a satisfactory combination for the accompaniment (L. H.) on the first page. In that case the player need only to open the swell when the R. H. thirds require more power in the L. H., and close it again for the softer accompaniment of the R. H. solo. If the Melodia is too loud to be used at the beginning it can be added as suggested above. In the third brace the solo on the Sw. is indicated " Mf." If the swell is opened about half-way the combination generally balances the L. H. accompaniment on the Ch. On page 4 the Ch. swell can be regulated to balance the combinations of the Sw. and Gt. In the third brace of page 5 both hands should be played on the Gt. In the lower brace both hands should be played on the Ch. During the *ritard* in the last measure of the page, and the single note (L. H.) in the first measure at the top of page 6, prepare: Sw. Vox Humana, Flute 4 ft., and Sw. to Sw. 16 ft.; Gt. Harmonic Flute, and put off the Ch. Melodia. Play the return of the first theme, R. H. Sw., L. H. Ch. The power of the Ch. Dulciana must be regulated by means of the Ch. swell. In the fourth brace the phrase indicated for the Gt. must be played an octave lower, as the Har. Flute is a 4 ft. stop. This Flute is generally softer than the Doppel Floete and of a different quality. This gives a pleasing variety of tone. For the last ten measures of the composition put off the Sw. to Sw. 16 ft., the Flute 4 ft., and play both hands on the Sw. (Vox Humana). Instead of using the Gt. to Ped. (indicated) use Ped. Piston No. 1.

Ralph Kinder, * Festival March

The composer's indications are limited mostly to manual changes, leaving the selections of the stops to the player. I suggest the following: —

Prepare: Sw. Full (Piston No. 5), (swell closed) ; Ch. 8 and 4 ft.

---

* This registration is intended specifically for the organ whose specification is given on page 169.

(Piston No. 2), (swell open): Gt. to Octave (Piston No. 3): Ped. Bourdon and Gedeckt: Sw. to Gt., Sw. and Gt. to Ped.

After the four measures of introduction on the Gt., open the Grand Crescendo full for the FF. At the double bar at the top of page 3, close the Grand Crescendo, push Sw. 5, and put off Gt. to Ped., and play on the Sw. Follow the manual indications, opening and closing the swell, until the last measure of the page, when the Gt. to Ped. should be added. At the double bar in the second brace of page 4, open the Grand Crescendo full. While holding the last chord of the page (R. H.), push Sw. 3, and Gt. 2. After this chord close the Grand Crescendo, and play on the Gt. and Sw. as indicated. For the return to the Gt. push Gt. 1, Sw. 2, and put off the Gt. to Ped. While holding the last chord before the double bar, prepare Ch. Clarinet, Melodia and Flute d'Amour. Play Ch. and Sw. as indicated, using the Ch. swell for expression in the solo. For the repeat of this thirteen-measure solo on the Ch. one can either put off the Clarinet or add the Piccolo for variety. After the double bar push Sw. 3, and play both hands on the Sw. Add Gt. to Ped. and play four measures on the Gt. At the end of the page put off Gt. to Ped., push Sw. 2, and prepare Ch. as at first (on preceding page). After the double bar push Sw. 5 and Gt. 2. Gradually open the swell and the Grand Crescendo. Use the Sfz for the last five measures.

JOHN HYATT BREWER, * SPRING-TIME SKETCH

The composer's indicated registration requires a few suggestions for the student.

Prepare: Sw. Bourdon, 16 ft., Salicional, Flute 4 ft., Dolce Cornet, and Tremolo (swell closed), or Bourdon, Gedeckt, Flute 4 ft., Flautino and Tremolo: Gt. Doppel Floete: Ch. Melodia and Dulciana (swell open): Ped. Bourdon and Gedeckt: Ch. to Ped. (*ad lib.*).

There is no manual indication for the first phrase, but obviously the Sw. is intended. The other manual indication on the first page is obvious. In the first measure of the second brace on page 3, the indication is " Ch. (or Sw.)," meaning that either manual can be used according to the taste of the performer. In the third brace, for " Ch. add 4 ft." add Flute d'Amour. For the last two measures of the page, the indication is " Sw. or Gt." Frequently, the Gt. combination is too loud for these measures; hence, the Sw. should be used. At the top of page 4 is the optional indication " Sw. or Ch." Playing on the Ch. at this point gives variety, but the Sw. is generally more pleasing.

In the two measures previous to the *Più mosso*, while playing on the Sw. (with or without the optional notes), add the Gamba in the Gt. and the Sw. to Gt. Just before beginning the *Più mosso*, put off the Sw. Bourdon, Dolce Cornet and Tremolo, and push Sw. Piston No. 3. In the upper brace of page 5 is the indication, "(Clar. Ch. on)." This added stop is for the phrase in the middle brace which is indicated, " Sw. or Ch." Unless the Clarinet is a soft one it will be better to omit it. In the two

* This registration is intended specifically for the organ whose specification is given on page 169.

measures preceding the *Tempo 1mo*, on page 6, while playing on the Sw. with the R. H., prepare the Gt. Doppel Floete and Har. Flute, put off the Clarinet (if it is on). On the last note before the double bar, add Sw. Bourdon, Gedeckt, Dolce Cornet (or Flautino) and Tremolo, and push Sw. 0. At the bottom of the page, where the indication is " on Mf Gt.," open the Grand Crescendo about one-third. In the middle brace of the last page, open the Grand Crescendo to include the Gt. Second Diapason. In the lower brace, close the Grand Crescendo, and, while holding the last two chords on the Gt., put off the Sw. Bourdon and Dolce Cornet (or Flautino). Play the last three measures both hands on the Sw. Gedeckt only.

Georges MacMaster, * Pastorale in D-Flat

The printed registration requires considerable modification for American organs.

Prepare: Gt. Doppel Floete: Sw. Æoline and 16 ft. Coupler (swell open) : Ch. Melodia (swell open) : Sw. to Ped. (no Ped. stop).

Play the first four measures on the Sw. Close the swell, put off the 16 ft. Coupler and draw the Voix Céleste. Continue on the Sw. At the double bar on the second page, put off the Voix Céleste, push Sw. 1 and add Ped. Bourdon. Play R. H. on the Ch. and L. H. on the Gt. In the first measure of the second brace, play L. H. on the Sw. At the fourth measure play both hands on the Sw. In the last measure of the brace, play R. H. on the Gt. In the next measure put off the Ped. Bourdon. In the second measure of the third brace, play both hands on the Sw. In the fourth measure play the R. H. on the Ch. and the L. H. on the Gt. The chord in the Ped. requires only the Sw. to Ped., which is on.

At the last count of the first measure of the lower brace, play the R. H. on the Sw. In the fourth measure play both hands on the Sw. Gedeckt only. At the top of the third page play both hands on the Sw. Voix Céleste as at first. The two Pedal figures of eighth-notes in the second and third braces can be made sufficiently prominent by putting on the Gt. to Ped. (foot). Put it off again in the following measure. The A-flat of the right foot can be delayed an eighth-count for that purpose. At the top of the fourth page play the R. H. on the Ch. for the first three measures, and on the Sw. for the last three measures. At the change of key to A put off the Sw. to Ped. and add Ped. Bourdon. While holding the two Ped. notes prepare Sw. Oboe and Flute 4 ft., and add Ch. Clarinet (swell closed). Play the R. H. on the Sw. and the L. H. on the Ch. In the middle section of this theme play all the measures *which have harmony in the L. H.* on the Sw. (both hands). In the other measures, play the L. H. melody on the Ch. At the beginning of the third brace of the fifth page, add Sw. Tremolo as indicated. If desired the Ch. Tremolo can also be added. In the second measure of the lower brace play both hands on the Sw. In the lower brace of the sixth page, play the first two measures on the Ch., the second two measures on the Gt. and the last four measures on the Ch. (an octave lower) with the Flute d'Amour only. While holding the last notes, put off the Ped. Bourdon, add Sw. to Ped. and prepare Sw. Salicional, Flute 4 ft. and Tremolo. At the top of the last page play both hands on the Sw. The printed indications for this page (" Gt. with Sw. coupled," and " add Gamba ") are hardly in keeping with the foregoing registration. In the third brace, play the R. H. solo on the Ch. an octave lower. In the lower brace, play the R. H. solo on the Sw. *loco.* For the *Lento* use Salicional only. For the last two chords use the Æoline.

HORATIO PARKER, * VISION IN D-FLAT

The registration in the printed copies requires a few suggestions for the student.

Prepare: Gt. Doppel Floete and Har. Flute: Sw. Salicional and Flute 4 ft. (swell closed): Ch. Melodia (swell open): Ped. Bourdon and Gedeckt: Sw. to Gt.

Follow the manual indications. At the first measure of the second brace, push Sw. 1. (The Salicional and Flute 4 ft., or the Salicional alone as indicated, sounds somewhat thin for this phrase.) At the first measure of the lower brace, push Sw. 0, thus returning to the first combination. At the next to the last measure of the page, add Gt. to Ped. and play both hands on the Gt. or the L. H. part can be played on the Ch. During the rests in the first measure of the second brace of the second page, push Gt. 1 (which adds the Gamba). At the corresponding measure of the lower brace, push Gt. 0 and continue both hands on the Gt. At the top of page 3, play both hands on the Sw. At the fifth measure add Oboe and play L. H. on the Gt. If the Ped. notes are too loud with the Gt. to Ped. on, it can be put off with the foot. In the second measure of the second brace of the third page, put off the Gt. to Ped. and play both hands on the Ch. At the second measure of the lower brace, push Sw. 3, put on the Gt. to Ped. and play R. H. on the Gt. and L. H. on the Sw. During one of the rests in the upper brace of the last page, put off the Oboe (draw-stop) as the Piston still holds it in. At the last measure of the upper brace push Sw. 0 and put off the Gt. to Ped. This reduces to the combinations drawn at the outset. Use the Æoline for the last three measures.

E. R. KROEGER, * MARCHE PITTORESQUE

Prepare: Gt. Doppel Floete: Sw. 8 and 4 ft. with Oboe: Ch. Piccolo (swell open): Ped. Bourdon and Gedeckt: Ch. to Gt. Grand Crescendo open full.

The first page and a half are indicated FF. In the first measure of the third brace of page 3 gradually close the Grand Crescendo. At the third measure, with the Grand Crescendo closed, we have the combina-

---

* This registration is intended specifically for the organ whose specification is given on page 169.

tions indicated. Play the R. H. on the Gt. and the L. H. on the Sw.
(For the Gt. combination, Doppel Floete and 2 ft., we have prepared the
Doppel Floete, Ch. Piccolo and Ch. to Gt. as the Fifteenth of the Gt. is
frequently too harsh for such an effect.) The power of the Ch. Piccolo
can be regulated by the Ch. swell. At the beginning of the second
brace on page 4, open the Grand Crescendo full. At the double bar at
the top of page 5, close the Grand Crescendo, put off the Ch. to Gt., and
add Ch. Melodia and Clarinet. These changes prepare the organ for
this page as indicated: viz., Sw. 8 and 4 ft. with Oboe, Ch. Melodia,
Clarinet and Piccolo, Ped. Bourdon and Gedeckt. Follow the manual
indications. Before playing the return of the first theme, at the top of
page 6, put off the Clarinet, add Ch. to Gt. and open the Grand Crescendo
full. In the first two measures of the lower brace of page 7, close the
Grand Crescendo gradually, which leaves the combinations indicated in
the third measure. At the lower brace of page 8, open the Grand
Crescendo full. The Sfz can be used for the last eight measures.

H. J. STEWART, * FESTIVAL MARCH

Prepare (as indicated by the composer): Sw. 8 and 4 ft. stops and
Piston No. 5 (Full Sw.), (swell closed): Ch. Clarinet, Melodia and Flute
4 ft. (swell open): Gt. Doppel Floete and Piston No. 4: Ped. Bourdon
and Gedeckt, Sw. to Gt.

On this organ, as the Pistons do not move the draw-stops, we can
prepare, at the outset, the combinations desired in the middle section,
in addition to the Piston combinations required at the beginning. By
pushing Gt. 4 last the heavy Pedal stops required for the first Ped. figures
will be on. After the first four measures, push Gt. 1 and put on the Sw.
to Ped. In the second measure of the lower brace of the first page,
open the Grand Crescendo full. At the rest in the L. H. part at the top
of page 3, push Sw. 4. At the rest in the third measure of the third
brace, close the Grand Crescendo one-half. With the swell open, the
reeds of Piston No. 4 will stand out prominently. At the rest in the
last measure of the page, put off the Gt. to Ped. and play on the Sw.
In the last measure of the upper brace, push Gt. 2. Follow all the
manual indications of page 4. The Gt. Trumpet, which is indicated in
the third brace, can be drawn during the rest two measures previous.
In the last measure of the page, open the Grand Crescendo full.

At the end of page 5 push 00 and put off the Gt. Trumpet and Gt. to
Ped. This will leave the draw-stops, which were prepared at the outset,
all ready for the middle section. Play Ch. and Sw., as indicated, on page
6. At the second measure of the lower brace, play the R. H. solo on the
Gt. (Doppel Floete) for variety. Return to the Gt. at the last count
of the second brace on page 7. At the rest at the end of page 7, open the
Grand Crescendo full. At the rest in the first measure of page 9 close
the Grand Crescendo about one-half and push Sw. 4. Follow the manual
indications of this page. Draw the Gt. Trumpet during the rest in the

---

* This registration is intended specifically for the organ whose specification is
given on page 169.

last measure. At the FF on page 10 open the Grand Crescendo full.
Use the Sfz for the last six measures.

R. HUNTINGTON WOODMAN, * EPITHALAMIUM

In order to carry out the registration indicated by the composer, it is
advisable to readjust some of the Piston combinations. This will enable
the player to follow the indications without awkward breaks, at the
points where there are no rests. As the Piston combinations in this
organ are all " adjustable," it is a simple matter to adjust the required
combinations. Therefore, for this composition I suggest the following
preparation: —
Adjust Sw. Piston No. 2 to bring on Voix Céleste, Flute 4 ft. and Ped.
Bourdon.
Adjust Sw. 3 to bring on Voix Céleste, Flute 4 ft., Violina, Flautino
and Ped. Bourdon.
Adjust Ch. 1 to bring on Clarinet, Flute 4 ft. and Ped. Bourdon.
(The composer calls for a Quintadena. As there is no Quintadena in
this organ I have substituted the Clarinet.)
Adjust Ch. 2 to bring on Melodia, Clarinet, Flute 4 ft. and Ped.
Bourdon.
After adjusting the above combinations push Ch. 1, Sw. 5 and Gt. 3.
Draw Gt. Gamba and Gt. to Ped.
Play the first three braces on the Gt. Open the Grand Crescendo
full for the next brace (FF). Close the Grand Crescendo for the three
braces indicated F, and open it full for the next two braces (FF).
While holding the last chord on page 4, put off the Gt. to Ped. and push
Gt. 0. After the chord, push Sw. 1. Play the R. H. on the Sw. and
the L. H. on the Ch. for five measures. Add the Oboe and play the L. H.
on the Gt. for six measures. In the next measure the changes indicated:
viz., " II add 2 ft. or Fugara, and III add 8 ft." can be obtained by
pushing Sw. 3 and Ch. 2, these Pistons having been adjusted for these
combinations at the outset. Play Sw. and Ch. as indicated. At the
bottom of the page, the indication is a little ambiguous. The R. H. part
is indicated, " Couple II." As " II " is the Sw. and the R. H. is already
on the Sw., I suggest the opening of the Grand Crescendo about one-half,
which will bring on Full Sw. and the desired Ped. stops. Gradually open
the swell. In the first measure at the top of page 6, open the Grand
Crescendo two-thirds and play both hands on the Gt. At the return of
the first theme (*Tempo 1°*), open the Grand Crescendo full. At the
bottom of the page, close the Grand Crescendo about one-third. On the
last page, open the Grand Crescendo full and put on the Sfz for the
FFF.

* This registration is intended specifically for the organ whose specification is
given on page 169.

CHAPTER XX

REGISTRATION ON A MODERN THREE-MANUAL ORGAN
(with movable combinations)

IN the preceding chapter the specific organ, for which the registration of the various compositions is intended, contains combination pistons of the *non-movable* type. In this chapter the suggested registration for the various compositions is intended for an organ which has the same specification as that in the preceding chapter, with the exception that the combination pistons are of the *movable* type.

In registering compositions on organs which have combination pistons of the movable type, quite a different plan must be followed from that used in registering compositions on organs which have combination pistons of the non-movable type. The difference is a difference of method more than a difference of design; although the selection of stops must, occasionally, be modified to avoid the complication which sometimes arises when one is using combination pistons of the movable type.

With combination pistons of the non-movable type the combination of stops which is " set " on a piston is *added* to the combination of stops which is already drawn or is *subtracted* when that particular piston is released. This enables the player to return to the combination of stops which is first drawn, or to change to any desired combination of stops which he may prepare while he is playing on the combination of the added piston, with the one condition that the prepared combination must be selected from the stops which are in the set combination of the piston.

If the combination piston is of the movable type the combination which is " set " on the piston is arbitrary. When the piston knob is pressed any draw-stops that are not included in the combination of that piston, which happen to be out, are put in, and the stops of the set combination are brought out. The player cannot prepare any other combination of stops while he is playing on the combination of the piston under consideration. It is necessary to use some other piston for any change of stops which cannot be conveniently made by means of the draw-stops. The relative merits of the two systems (movable and non-movable) have caused much arguments among organists. Each system has strong supporters.

A LIST OF TWENTY ORGAN COMPOSITIONS
For which the Registration is suggested for the Three-Manual Organ
Whose Specification is similar to that given on page 169
With the exception that the Piston Combinations
are of the Movable Type

J. S. Bach	Fantasia and Fugue in G-minor
Felix Borowski	Prayer in F.
Théodore Dubois	In Paradisum
Joseph Callaerts	Prayer in D-flat
Gottfried N. Federlein	Serenade
Alfred Hollins	Grand Choeur in G-minor
J. S. Bach	Choral Prelude, " Wir danken dir "
J. S. Bach	Choral Prelude, " Der Tag, der ist so freudenreich "
Clifford Demarest	Cantilena
Felix Mendelssohn	Sonata in F-minor (No. 1)
Alöys Claussmann	Pastorale in A
Henry M. Dunham	Andante in A-flat
Alex. Guilmant	Marche Religieuse
Arthur Foote	Nocturne
H. A. Wheeldon	Canzona
Dudley Buck	Nöel
John A. West	Melody in A-flat
Gabriel Pierné	Cantilène in E-flat
Frederick N. Shackley	At Eventide
Alex. Guilmant	First Offertory on Christmas Hymns

J. S. BACH, * FANTASIA AND FUGUE IN G-MINOR

Prepare (in this order) : Sw. 5, Gt. 3, Ped. 2, Sw. to Gt., Sw. and Gt. to Ped., Grand Crescendo full, Swell partly open.

Play the first eight measures on the Gt. (Full organ with unison couplers being on by means of the Grand Crescendo). On the first count of the ninth measure, close the swell, and on the second count, close the Grand Crescendo. This leaves Gt. to Octave, Full Sw. and Full Ped. for the next phrase. At the second count (rest) of the fourteenth measure, open the Grand Crescendo full. At the second count (G in the Ped.) of the twenty-fifth measure, close the Grand Crescendo. In the thirty-first measure, begin a gradual crescendo. This can be obtained by opening the swell gradually during the playing of the last three or four notes of each of the descending scales (in the Ped. part), which can be played by the left foot. At the second count of the 44th measure, open the Grand Crescendo full for the last six measures.

Personal tastes differ greatly in registering the Fugue. Some players use F Gt. and Full Sw. from the beginning to the last two chords, which they play on the Full Organ. I suggest the following registration, with the idea of giving prominence to the various entrances of the theme, and a gradual progressiveness to the climax of the Fugue.

---

* This registration is intended specifically for the organ whose specification is given on page 169 with movable combinations substituted for the immovable combinations.

Prepare: Full Sw. (Piston No. 5), F Gt. (Piston No. 3), Full **Ped.** (Piston No. 2), Sw. to Gt., Sw. and Gt. to Ped.

Begin the Fugue on the Sw. (closed). After the ninth measure, gradually open the swell. Have it wide open when the theme enters in the Ped. part. This theme stands out prominently (by means of the Gt. to Ped.). At the seventeenth measure, last count, play both hands on the Gt. At the 37th measure, play the R. H. on the Sw., beginning with the second eighth-note. This causes the theme in the L. H. to stand out. At the 39th measure, play the last three sixteenth-notes of the L. H. part on the Sw. and continue both hands on the Sw. The swell should be gradually closed until the 46th measure when it should be entirely closed. In the next four measures gradually open the swell. At the 50th measure play the last sixteenth-note of the L. H. on the Gt., which gives prominence to the theme. At the 53rd measure play the last eighth-note of the L. H. on the Sw. The theme in the Ped. part thus stands out prominently. At the 57th measure play the last three eighth-notes of the L. H. on the Gt. and follow with the R. H. in the next measure. At the 63rd measure, with the entrance of the theme in the R. H. part (last half of the second count), open the Grand Crescendo full. The left foot can easily play G, A, F-sharp and D, which permits the right foot to open the Grand Crescendo. At the 80th measure close the Grand Crescendo on the second count. At the 93rd measure the descending scale in the L. H. should be played on the Sw. and the R. H. should play the other notes. The last note of the measure in the R. H. should be played on the Sw. At the 100th measure play the last sixteenth-note of the L. H. part on the Gt. to give prominence to the theme. The R. H. should remain on the Sw. At the 103rd measure return to the Sw. with the L. H. on the F-natural. At any point in the next few measures open the Grand Crescendo full. It does not affect the Sw., which is already full. At the 110th measure the entrance of the theme in the Ped. stands out prominently. Play both hands on the Gt. on the last eighth-note of the measure.

FELIX BOROWSKI, * PRAYER IN F

The registration of the composer, which is indicated in the printed copies, requires only a few changes to adapt it to the organ which is under consideration in this chapter.

Prepare: Gt. Doppel Floete and Gamba: Sw. Oboe, Salicional and Gedeckt (closed): Ch. Melodia (closed): Ped. Bourdon, Gt. and Ch. to Ped.

The introduction is indicated to be played on the Gt. If the combination is too loud for the taste of the player it can be played on the Ch., with the Ch. swell open. At the entrance of the solo theme in the lower brace, " add Oboe " is indicated. I have suggested drawing the Oboe at the outset, as the Sw. is not used until this measure. The Gt. to Ped. should

---

* This registration is intended specifically for the organ whose specification is given on page 169 with movable combinations substituted for the immovable combinations.

be put off before beginning this solo. On page 4 put off the Gamba at the end of the upper brace, and play the manuals as indicated in the second brace. The first two measures of the third brace, indicated both hands on the Gt., will be improved by opening the Grand Crescendo a little to bring on the Sw. to Gt. (without the awkward break which would be necessary to draw the coupler by hand). In the third measure of this brace, where both hands are indicated for the Sw., the Grand Crescendo should be closed again.

At the top of page 5, second count of the first measure, push Gt. 1, Sw. 3, and play both hands on the Gt. Add Gt. to Ped. before the Ped. notes come in. In the third measure, during the eighth-rest (R. H.), while the L. H. is holding the A, push Gt. Piston No. 2. At the first measure of the second brace, add Sw. 5, and draw the Ped. Diapason, which is put off by the Sw. Piston. Gradually open the swell and *accellerando* to the F of the last two measures of the page, when Gt. Piston No. 3 should be pushed.

On page 6, third measure, open the Grand Crescendo full for the climax. At the bottom of the page close the Grand Crescendo and open it again for the FF chord. At the long rest at the end of the page, close the Grand Crescendo, close the Sw. swell, push Sw. 1 (which will put in most of the stops of the Sw. and the Ped. Diapason) and prepare Sw. Vox Humana and Flauto Traverso. While playing the first measure of page 7 on the Sw., put off all the couplers. At the second measure of the second brace, the solo on the Ch. (R. H.) should be regulated in power by the Ch. swell pedal. At the third measure the two whole notes (R. H.) should be played on the Ch. The melody (L. H.) can be made prominent by opening the Sw. swell-box. In the last measure of this brace, the chords of the upper staff should be played on the Ch. and the two parts of the middle staff (L. H.) should remain on the Sw. The first measure of the lower brace should be played as indicated — both hands on the Sw. In the second measure, on the second eighth-note of the L. H. part, push Sw. 1, which changes the combination to Gedeckt and Salicional. The Æoline should be added while playing. In the next to the last measure put off the Salicional on the first rest and the Gedeckt on the last rest, which leaves the Æoline for the ending.

THÉODORE DUBOIS, * IN PARADISUM

The original edition calls for a very soft 8 ft. Flute (Gt.) for the R. H. arpeggio accompaniment, and a Vox Humana for the L. H. melody. The middle section is registered for Ch. " Bourdon et Gambe." This registration, which is effective on French organs, is not always practical on American organs. It requires several changes on the organ which is being considered in this chapter. I suggest the following registration, which gives variety, and yet carries out the main idea of the composer's registration.

---

* This registration is intended specifically for the organ whose specification is given on page 169 with movable combinations substituted for the immovable combinations.

Prepare: Sw. Oboe, Salicional, Voix Céleste, Flute 4 ft. and Tremolo (closed) : Ch. Melodia (closed) : Ped. Bourdon.

Play the R. H. part on the Ch. and the L. H. melody on the Sw. For the trio (*un peu animé*) put off the Oboe and play both hands on the Sw. The two-measure arpeggio phrases of the R. H. should be played on the Ch. with the Ch. swell closed. Between the phrases of the last four measures, previous to the return of the first theme, change the Ch. from the Melodia to the Flute d'Amour. Just before beginning the returned theme in the L. H. part, add the Vox Humana. Play the R. H. arpeggios on the Ch. an octave lower than they are printed, as a 4 ft. stop is on. If the Ch. organ contains an 8 ft. Gedeckt it can be substituted for the Flute d'Amour, in which case it will not be necessary to play an octave lower. The Ch. swell must be opened partially to make the Flute d'Amour (or the Gedeckt) balance the L. H. melody. If preferable this R. H. part can be played on the Melodia as at first.

Obviously, many variations of this registration are possible. If the Ch. Melodia is soft enough (with the swell closed), the L. H. melody can be played on the Sw. Vox Humana with or without a Gedeckt or Flute 4 ft. This L. H. melody is also effective played an octave lower than it is printed (equivalent to using a 16 ft. stop), using the Cornopean, Oboe, Voix Céleste, Flute 4 ft. and Tremolo, in which event the Ch. swell must be partially open. Occasionally, the Harmonic Flute 4 ft. in the Gt. (if it is not too loud), when played an octave lower than the music is printed, sounds well for this R. H. part. The trio in the middle of the composition sounds well on any one of several combinations: viz., Sw. Viol d'Orchestre and Flute 4 ft., Voix Céleste alone, Vox Humana and Bourdon (played 8va), Bourdon and Violina (played 8va). The Tremolo should be used with all these combinations. Whichever combination is selected should be somewhat of a contrast to the combinations used for the first and last sections of the composition.

Joseph Callaerts, * Prayer in D-Flat

The registration which I suggest is an adaptation for American organs of the printed registration which is for French organs.

Prepare: Gt. Doppel Floete, Sw. Vox Humana and Gedeckt, Ch. Melodia and Flute d'Amour (partly open), Ped. Bourdon and Sw. to Gt.

Play the first eight measures on the Sw. Use the swell pedal to produce the changes of power indicated. In the next four measures play the R. H. solo on the Gt. and the L. H. on the Sw. Play one measure with both hands on the Gt. (swell half open) ; one measure with both hands on the Sw.; one measure with both hands on the Gt.; one measure with both hands on the Sw. *Ritard* and close the swell. Add the Sw. Flute 4 ft. and continue the theme (two measures) on the Sw. Change both hands to the Gt., open the swell, and for the Mf chords open the Grand

---

* This registration is intended specifically for the organ whose specification is given on page 169 with movable combinations substituted for the immovable combinations.

Crescendo about one quarter. Close the Grand Crescendo and end the section on the Sw.

For the middle section (key of G-flat) put off the Vox Humana, add the Oboe and play both hands on the Ch. for nine measures. Change both hands to the Sw. with the swell partly open (Mf) for four measures. Close the swell for two measures. In the following six measures, which are a return of the theme of this middle section, play both hands on the Gt. and open the swell wide. Play the last three measures on the Sw. and close the swell. For the return of the first theme (key of D-flat), play both hands on the Sw. Vox Humana and Gedeckt for four measures. Play both hands on the Gt. (with swell wide open) for four and a half measures. Play the ending with both hands on the Sw., *molto ritard* and *diminuendo*.

GOTTFRIED H. FEDERLEIN, * SERENADE IN B-FLAT

The composer's registration is carefully indicated and can be followed explicitly on this organ, with the exception of the indications for the Ped. Couplers. The latter indications are somewhat confusing to students though they are perfectly clear to experienced organists. The first indication, " Ped. to Ch. off — on Sw.," means Ch. to Ped. off, Sw. to Ped. on. The next indication, " Off Sw. to Ch.," might be interpreted as Sw. to Ch. off. As it is placed just over the Ped. staff, it is intended to indicate Sw. to Ped. off, Ch. to Ped. on. In the next to the last measure the indication, " Ped. off Ch. on Sw." means Ch. to Ped. off, Sw. to Ped. on.

ALFRED HOLLINS, * GRAND CHOEUR IN G-MINOR

Prepare: Gt. Doppel Floete: Sw. Piston No. 3 (8 and 4 ft. with Oboe) with swell open: Ch. Melodia and Flute d'Amour: Ped. Bourdon: Grand Crescendo full.

The Grand Crescendo supplies the FF and F combinations as well as the couplers for the first three pages, and the stops that are drawn at the outset give the desired combinations for the first part of the middle section. The first two pages, indicated " FF," should be played on the Gt. with the Grand Crescendo open full. For the eight measures indicated " F Gt.," close the Grand Crescendo about one-third, which reduces to " Gt. to Octave with Full Sw." At the return of the theme (" FF ") open the Grand Crescendo full. For the two measures of sustained chords, preceding the Trio, close the Grand Crescendo, play on the Sw., and gradually close the swell. Put off the Sw. Diapason and play the first sixteen measures of the Trio on the Ch. (partly open) as indicated. Only a few hands are large enough to reach the tenths (R. H.) in the first and fifth measures of the Trio. Those who cannot reach these tenths can play the sustained B-flat in the base with the Ped. 8-va, for eight measures. This permits the organist to play the two middle parts with the L. H. and avoids the tenths in the R. H. part.

---

* This registration is intended specifically for the organ whose specification is given on page 169 with movable combinations substituted for the immovable combinations.

After adding the Clarinet (for future use), play the next sixteen measures as indicated — the R. H. on the Gt. and the L. H. on the Sw. At the top of page 6 add Sw. Diapason, by hand or by Piston No. 3. Play the R. H. on the Sw. and the L. H. on the Ch. for eight measures. Play the R. H. on the Gt. and the L. H. on the Sw. for four measures; then play both hands on the Sw. On page 7, third measure, play the R. H. on the Gt. and the L. H. on the Sw. Eight measures later play both hands on the Sw. After the hold at the bottom of the page push Sw. Piston No. 1 and add the Voix Céleste. The repetition of the last half of the Trio can well be omitted.

At the top of page 8 push Sw. Piston No. 3 and add Sw. to Ped. At the last measure of the upper brace, push Gt. Piston No. 2 and put on (with the foot) Gt. to Ped. In the middle brace is indicated, " Gt. full and couple Tuba to the Pedals." As there is no Tuba in this organ and " Gt. full " would be abrupt and awkward, I suggest the omission of the indication. In the third or fourth measure of the lower brace push Gt. Piston No. 3. At the top of page 9 open the Grand Crescendo full. At the last measure of the page close the Grand Crescendo about one-third. In the middle of page 10 (FF), open the Grand Crescendo full. During the rests in the Pedal part, in the first measure of the middle brace of page 11, put off the Gt. to Ped. At the rest in the R. H. part, before the hold over D, in the middle of this brace, close the Grand Crescendo, and draw the Sw. Tremolo. While holding this note (D) push Gt. 1, put off the Sw. to Ped., close the Ch. swell and play as indicated — the R. H. solo on the Sw. and the L. H. on the Ch. At the top of the last page put on the Sfz.

J. S. Bach, * Choral Prelude, " Wir danken dir, Herr Jesu Christ "

Prepare: Sw. Cornopean, Oboe, Voix Céleste, Gedeckt (closed): Ch. Melodia and Dulciana (closed): Ped. Bourdon and Ch. to Ped. If the Cornopean is loud and coarse it should be omitted.

Play the R. H. solo on the Sw., the L. H. accompaniment on the Ch. Use the swell pedals for expression.

J. S. Bach, * Choral Prelude, " Der Tag, der ist so freudenreich "

Prepare: Sw. Vox Humana, Voix Céleste and Flute 4 ft.: Ch. Dulciana: Ped. Bourdon and Ch. to Ped.

Play the solo on the Sw. and the accompaniment on the Ch.

Clifford Demarest, * Cantilena

The composer's registration in the printed copies can be followed closely on this organ. On the second page, where " Sw. Vox Humana " is indicated for the R. H. solo, it may be advisable to add either the Gedeckt

---

* This registration is intended specifically for the organ whose specification is given on page 169 with movable combinations substituted for the immovable combinations.

or Flute 4 ft. At the bottom of the page is the indication, " Add Sw. Sub-Octave." The player can add the Sw. to Sw. 16 ft. Coupler or the Sw. Bourdon 16 ft. according to taste. On the last page is the same indication. If either of the above stops is used it must be put off for the lower brace of the last page.

FELIX MENDELSSOHN-BARTHOLDY, * SONATA IN F-MINOR, No. 1

1. ALLEGRO MODERATO

Prepare: Sw. 8 and 4 ft. (Piston No. 2) : Ch. Melodia and Flute 4 ft.: Gt. to Octave (Piston No. 3) : Ped. with Open Diapason (Gt. Piston No. 3, if pushed last, gives the desired Ped. combination) : Sw. to Gt., Sw. to Ch. and Gt. to Ped.: Grand Crescendo full.

The first section, to the entrance of the Choral (half notes), is indicated " FF " and should be played on the Gt. The Choral — " *Was mein Gott will* " — can be played on the Ch. as prepared at the outset (the Sw. to Ch. Coupler can be omitted *ad lib.*). The Grand Crescendo should be closed on the second eighth-note of the measure in which the Choral begins. This gives a slight diminuendo and puts off all the undesired stops of the Sw. and Ch. Alternating with the various lines of the Choral are imitative phrases of the first theme. These phrases are indicated " FF," but it seems to me that a *forte* combination on the Gt. sounds better than a *fortissimo* combination. Gt. Piston No. 3, which was prepared at the outset, is suitable. Each line of the Choral should be played on the Ch. and the alternating phrases of the first theme should be played on the Gt. Near the end of this movement, in the measure preceding the hold, the Grand Crescendo should be gradually opened to full organ, which should be used as a climax on the chord with the hold. Immediately after this chord, the Grand Crescendo should be closed and the four measures of the Choral should be played on the Ch. The last four measures of the movement are the closing measures of the Choral for which the Grand Crescendo can be opened full, or these measures can be played on the Gt. with the 8 ft. stops only, according to taste.

II. ADAGIO

Prepare: Gt. Gamba, Sw. Gedeckt, Ch. Dulciana, Ped. Bourdon, Ch. to Ped.

Play the first eight measures on the Ch., the second eight measures on ·the Sw. Beginning with the last eighth-count of the sixteenth measure, play on the Gt. for four measures. With the last eighth-count of the 20th measure, play both hands on the Sw. At the last eighth-count of the 24th measure, play on the Gt. At the 27th measure, add Ch. Melodia and play on the Ch. At the 29th measure, add Voix Céleste and Flute 4 ft., and play on the Sw. In the 32nd measure, play the first two counts

* This registration is intended specifically for the organ whose specification is given on page 169 with movable combinations substituted for the immovable combinations.

with the R. H. alone. On the second count add the Oboe and continue both hands on the Sw. On the last count of the 36th measure, play both hands on the Ch. In the 40th measure play with the L. H. alone and put off the Melodia on the last count. In the next measure play the R. H. solo on the Sw. and the L. H. on the Ch. At the 49th measure play the L. H. on the Gt. In the 52nd measure play both hands on the Sw. In the first part of the 54th measure, while playing with the L. H. alone, add the Ch. Melodia. Play the last count of this measure with the R. H. and, in the next measure, play the L. H. on the Ch. At the last count of the next measure, play on the Gt. At the last count of the next measure, play on the Sw. At the last count of the next measure, put off the Oboe. On the second count of the 64th measure, put off the Flute 4 ft. In the 69th measure play the L. H. theme on the Ch. At the 73rd measure put off the Voix Céleste (leaving the Gedeckt alone). While playing this measure put off the Melodia (leaving the Dulciana alone). Play the L. H. part in the next measure on the Ch. Thus to the end.

III. ANDANTE RÉCIT.

This movement consists principally of short phrases of a *recitative* character, alternating with two measures of sustained chords. In the early editions of this sonata, presumably with the composer's personal indications, the *recitative* phrases are indicated " PP " and the sustained chords " FF." If these indications are followed literally — with a PP combination for the *recitative* phrases and Full Organ for the chords, an exaggerated contrast, which is rarely pleasing, is the result. It seems to me that a better effect is obtained by playing the chords on the Gt. to Octave, and the *recitative* phrases on a soft combination including the Oboe. Beginning with the second of the *recitative* phrases, each phrase is of an imitative character between the parts for the two hands. This suggests a separate manual for each hand, but in the last measure of each phrase the imitative character disappears. If the two hands play on different manuals a third hand seems necessary in order to finish the phrase and to play the first of the following chords on a third manual. Tastes differ with regard to the registration of this movement. Some players give prominence to the imitations, and compromise at the end of each phrase. Others play both hands on the same manual, as indicated in the early editions. With the latter plan the imitations are distinctly audible and no compromise is necessary at the end of the phrases. I suggest the latter plan, though either can be followed with the combinations given below.

Prepare: Sw. Oboe, Voix Céleste, and Flute 4 ft. (closed) : Ch. Clarinet and Melodia (swell partly open) : Gt. to Octave (Piston No. 3) : Ped. 16 and 8 ft. (prepared by Gt. piston) : Sw. to Gt. and Gt. to Ped.

Play the first three measures of the *recitative* on the Sw. and the chords on the Gt. The second phrase (measure 6) I prefer to play with both hands on the Sw. Those who prefer can play the R. H. on the Sw. and the L. H. on the Ch., which necessitates playing the last two notes on the same manual (Sw.). The third phrase (measure 12) should be treated similarly to the second. In the fourth phrase (measure 17) the parts for the two hands cross in the first measure. This is, of course, avoided if separate manuals are used for the two hands; but the phrase can easily be played on one manual, and it seems to me that the last measure of the phrase (measure 21) is more satisfactory when the whole phrase is played on one manual. The same point is noticeable in the first measure of the fifth phrase (measure 24). During the measure of F chords (measure 28), add the Full Sw. (Piston No. 5) with the swell closed. Immediately afterward, push Gt. 3 to restore the Ped. stops which are put off by the Sw. Piston. Play the following three measures on the Sw. The effect of the arpeggio, with all the notes tied, building up a volume of suppressed tone, is pleasing. Play the next four measures (beginning with measure 31) in the same manner. While playing the following two chords on the Gt. (F) with the R. H. push Sw. 3 and Gt. 3 (to restore the Ped. stops). Play the sustained chord of the third and fourth counts on the Sw. with the L. H., and the two notes (E-flat and A-flat) of the *recitative* theme on the Ch. Play the next two measures (38 and 39) in the same manner. In measure 40 play the chord of the upper staff on the Sw. with the L. H. In the following measure play the two notes (G and C) of the *recitative* theme on the Sw. with the R. H. Transfer the L. H. chord to the R. H., in order to play the imitation in the bass clef with the L. H. on the Ch. In measure 44 the F of the upper staff must be omitted in order to play the chord on the Gt. (F) with the R. H. (This note is inaudible if played.) The last seven measures of this movement, which lead to the last movement, sound well when played on the Sw. Salicional or Voix Céleste.

IV. ALLEGRO ASSAI VIVACE

This movement is indicated, and is usually played, " FF " without any change of registration. It is only necessary to open the Grand Crescendo full.

ALOŸS CLAUSSMANN, * PASTORALE IN A

In the printed copies the composer's registration (in French) with the English translation is quite specific and can be followed quite closely on the organ which we are now considering. A few minor details, relative to the best method of obtaining the combinations indicated by the composer, are helpful to the student. The printed preparation is here given with suggestions (in parentheses) for the best method of obtaining the combinations.

Prepare: Sw. 8 and 4 ft. with swell open (Piston No. 3): Ch. 8 and 4 ft. with swell open (Piston No. 2): Gt. 8 and 4 ft. (Piston No. 2): Ped. 16 and 8 ft. (Gt. Piston No. 2 gives this combination): Sw. and Ch. to Gt., Gt. to Ped.

---

* This registration is intended specifically for the organ whose specification is given on page 169 with movable combinations substituted for the immovable combinations.

No suggestions are necessary until the top of the third page, where
" Sw. and Ch. to Gt. off " is indicated. This change of couplers should
be made during the rest (L. H.) in the preceding measure. Gt. to Ped.
and Ped. Op. Diapason should also be put off at this point. The Ped.
stop can be put off easily by pushing Sw. Piston No. 3, which does not
change the Sw. combination. In the second measure, to " reduce Ch.
to 8 ft." it is necessary to put off the Flute 4 ft. and Fugara with the
hand. In the last measure of the second brace, while holding the E in
the L. H., the combinations indicated can be prepared by the R. H. in
this order: Put off Ch. Diapason and all Sw. stops except Oboe and Flute
4 ft. Add Sw. Tremolo and prepare Gt. Doppel Floete and Har. Flute 4.
The Ped. combination — Bourdon and Gedeckt — which is preferable to
" Bourdon and Flute," has been previously prepared by Sw. Piston
No. 3.

In the next five braces the indicated variations in power for the Sw.
manual should be obtained solely by means of the swell pedal. At the
top of page 4 the L. H. staccato phrase is more effective if played on the
Gt. instead of on the Ch. In the second brace the absence of definite
manual indications is liable to confuse students. In the upper brace
the indication is, R. H. on the Sw. and L. H. on the Ch. This indication
holds good through the next two braces. My suggestion of a change for
the L. H. to the Gt. in the upper brace should not apply to the other two
braces. At the second measure at the bottom of this (fourth) page, the
Tremolo should be put off. The R. H. Flute solo is indicated " Gt." The
L. H. naturally must continue on the Ch. On page 3 we prepared Gt.
Doppel Floete and Flute 4 ft. This combination is effective at this
point or, if the player prefers, the Doppel Floete alone can be prepared
on page 3. At the last measure of the second brace on the fifth page,
the L. H. can play on the Ch. as indicated, and the R. H. remain on the
Gt. This L. H. phrase, which consists of a sustained melody (upper
notes) and short chords, is more effective and characteristic if played
on the Sw. with Piston No. 4 (reeds). This piston can be pushed during
any of the rests in the L. H. part in the previous measures. At the
top of page 6 both hands can play on the Ch. as indicated, or the R. H.
solo can be made more prominent if played on the Sw. (reeds as suggested
above). The indication " add Ch. to Gt." may well be omitted. At the
bottom of the page there is a return of the theme and the combinations
of the third page. If Sw. Piston No. 4 has been used (as suggested
above) it is necessary, during the rests in the R. H. (two measures), to
prepare the Sw. as before (Oboe and Flute 4 ft.).

In the last measure at the top of page 7, there is no manual indication.
This is surely an omission. If the R. H. is played on the Sw. and the
L. H. on the Ch. as previously, the effect is far from satisfactory. Both
hands should be played on one manual, either the Gt. or Ch. according
to taste. At the whole measure rest (hands) in the second brace of
page 7, the desired combination for the next section can be prepared.
Either of the indicated combinations in the Sw. can be used or one can
substitute Vox Humana and Gedeckt, which is very effective for this
section. The manual indications for this and the following page should

be followed irrespective of which combination the player has selected for the Sw. At the last note at the top of the 8th page, it is a good plan to push Sw. 2 in order to give a change of tone-color for the next two braces, irrespective of which combination in the Sw. has been selected for the previous phrase. At the bottom of the page " Add Sw. to Gt." is indicated, but it is unnecessary and may be omitted. During the rest (R. H.) in the third brace of the 9th page, prepare Sw. as indicated (Oboe and Tremolo). If the Oboe is poor and uneven in tone it can be improved by adding the Gedeckt or Flute 4 ft. On the last page, if both hands are played on the Sw. as indicated (without the Tremolo), a good suggestion of the pastoral bagpipe is sometimes produced. In the last four measures the L. H. should be played on the Ch. Dulciana instead of on the Gt.

Henry M. Dunham, * Andante in A-Flat

The composer's indications for the registration, in the printed copies, can be followed closely on this organ for two pages. At the first measure of the middle brace on page 5, to obtain the effect which is indicated by the composer, push Gt. 2 just before playing the ascending scale (L. H.) on the Gt. Add the Gt. to Ped. at the second measure. In the middle of the brace open the Grand Crescendo full. At the last measure of the page push Gt. Piston No. 1 (for future use). At the end of the first measure of the middle brace of page 6, close the Grand Crescendo and put off the Gt. to Ped. In the second measure at the top of the last page, prepare, Sw. Vox Humana and Gedeckt, Ch. Dulciana only, Gt. Doppel Floete, and put off Sw. to Gt. and Gt. to Ped. The Ch. to Ped. indicated can be used, or not, according to taste. Play the last two chords on the Æoline.

Alexandre Guilmant, * Marche Religieuse

The printed registration of this composition is in the old style and is somewhat confusing to the student.

Prepare: Gt. Doppel Floete and Flute Har.: Sw. Piston No. 2 (closed): Ch. Piston No. 2 with Clarinet (open): Ped. Bourdon and Gedeckt: Sw. to Gt. and Sw. to Ped.

Play the first eight measures on the Sw. Add the Oboe (Piston No. 3) at the rest in the ninth measure, and gradually open the swell. Play the last three notes (L. H.) of the last measure of the third brace on the Gt. Add the Gt. to Ped. and, in the following measure, play both hands on the Gt. At the rest in the fourth measure of the lower brace, add the Gamba by means of Piston No. 1. At the sixth measure at the top of the second page, push Gt. 2. At the fourth count of the fourth measure, push Gt. 1. In the following measure change to the Sw. on the second count, put off the Gt. to Ped., and gradually close the swell.

---

* This registration is intended specifically for the organ whose specification is given on page 169 with movable combinations substituted for the immovable combinations.

In the second measure of the second brace, put off the Oboe by means of Piston No. 2.

Before beginning the *Più mosso* movement, push Sw. 4 and Gt. 3, and add Gt. to Ped. The change of manuals indicated in the last two measures of the fourth page, does not appear in the original edition. It seems to weaken the progression and is unnecessary. At the last rest at the bottom of this page, push Gt. 2. This leaves the organ prepared as follows: Gt. to Open Diapason, Sw. 8 and 4 ft. with reeds, Ch. 8 and 4 ft. with Clarinet, Ped. Diapason, Bourdon and Gedeckt. At the first measure of the third brace of page 6, push Sw. 5 and Gt. 2. The latter is necessary in order to restore the Ped. Diapason, which is put off by Sw. 5. Gradually open the swell. At the last measure of the page push Gt. 3. At the second measure of the last page open the Grand Crescendo full. The Sfz can be used at this point if the 4 ft. couplers do not stand out so prominently as to be objectionable, in which case it can be reserved for the last five measures.

ARTHUR FOOTE, * NOCTURNE IN B-MINOR

In the first edition of this Nocturne there were no stop indications; only indications for the manuals. In a later edition combinations of stops have been indicated, which can be followed closely on the organ which is under consideration in this chapter. For the benefit of those who happen to have a copy of the first edition, the stop combinations are here given.

Prepare: Gt. Doppel Floete: Sw. Oboe, Voix Céleste and Flute 4 ft. (closed): Ch. Dulciana (partly open): Ped. Bourdon. The printed indication, " Ped. 16 ft. coupled to Swell," is an error. The coupler should be omitted.

On the first page play the manuals as indicated. During the rest in the L. H. part, in the third measure of the second brace on the second page, before playing both hands on the Sw., put off the Oboe. At the last note of the second measure of the third brace, add the St. Diapason (Gedeckt) or add the Vox Humana. In the next phrase, if the Doppel Floete in the Gt. is too loud for the L. H. part, play the part an octave lower on the Gt. Flute Har. 4 ft. or on the Ch. Flute d'Amour 4 ft. This phrase can also be played on the Ch. Melodia with the Ch. swell closed, if the stop is not too loud. In the third measure of the upper brace of the third page, the hands change places, and in the same measure of the second brace, the hands change back again. The R. H. part on the Gt. must be played an octave lower, if in the preceding phrase the L. H. part is played an octave lower.

In the third measure of the third brace, the indication in the later edition is, " Ch. or Echo Vox Humana." This change is possible only on four-manual organs. There is insufficient time at this point to change

---

* This registration is intended specifically for the organ whose specification is given on page 169 with movable combinations substituted for the immovable combinations.

the stops. It seems better to play the phrase on the Ch. as the manual is prepared — an octave lower if only a 4 ft. stop is on. In the first measure of the lower brace, the quarter-rest and *ritard* enable the organist to prepare the combinations for the following return of the first theme. Prepare Sw. Voix Céleste, Vox Humana and Bourdon, and Ch. Dulciana. Play the R. H. solo on the Sw. and the L. H. accompaniment on the Ch. At the double bar on the last page put off the Voix Céleste and Bourdon. Play both hands on the Sw. Play the last chord on the Sw. Æoline.

H. A. WHEELDON, * CANZONA

Prepare: Gt. Doppel Floete, Sw. Voix Céleste (closed), Ch. Melodia and Dulciana (closed), and Ped. Bourdon.

Play the first two braces as indicated. At the lower brace, add the Oboe and Flute 4 ft. in the Sw. Play the L. H. solo on the Sw. and the R. H. on the Ch. If the Ch. Melodia is too loud, even with the swell closed, open the Sw. swell to make the solo louder. At the top of page 4 the composer has indicated R. H. on the Ch. with Flute 4 ft. added and the L. H. on the Gt. This page is also effective with the R. H. played on the Sw. and the L. H. on the Gt. The Open Diapason of the Ped. is indicated for the two lower braces. This stop is generally too heavy for this passage. I suggest the addition of the Gedeckt, by means of Ped. Piston No. 1. At the top of page 5 return to the first combinations. At the top of page 6 change the Sw. combination to Salicional, Gedeckt and Flute 4 ft. and play the R. H. on the Sw. and the L. H. on the Gt. At the top of page 7 add the Oboe, and play the R. H. on the Gt. and the L. H. on the Sw. At the rest at the end of the page, before turning the leaf, put off all the Sw. stops except the Oboe. Play the first measure at the top of the next page with both hands on the Sw. In the second measure play the outside notes on the Sw. and the two inside notes (thumbs) on the Gt. In the measure before the double bar, while playing the A's on the Ch. (closed), prepare the Sw. Vox Humana, Voix Céleste and Flute 4 ft. Play the R. H. on the Ch. and the L. H. on the Sw. Frequently, the Ch. Melodia (already prepared) is too loud for this passage, and the Flute 4 ft. (as indicated) is too high in pitch. In such a case one can use the Dulciana alone with the Ch. swell open, or one can play an octave lower on the Flute d'Amour. In the second brace of page 9 it is occasionally satisfactory to play the R. H. on the Ch. Melodia and Flute 4 ft and the L. H. on the Gt. as indicated. If not, play the R. H. on the Sw. and the L. H. on the Ch. Melodia and Dulciana (open). In the second brace of page 10 return to the former combinations. For the last six measures play the R. H. on the Sw. Voix Céleste (or Salicional and Flute 4 ft.) and the L. H. on the Ch. Dulciana.

* This registration is intended specifically for the organ whose specification is given on page 169 with movable combinations substituted for the immovable combinations.

DUDLEY BUCK, * NÖEL

Prepare: Gt. Doppel Floete: Sw. Bourdon 16 ft., Voix Céleste and Violina: Ch. Melodia and Dulciana: Ped. Bourdon and Gedeckt: Sw. to Gt. and Ch. to Ped.

Play the first eight measures on the Sw. Add the Gedeckt at the ninth measure. Add the Oboe and Open Diapason in the tenth measure. Push Sw. Piston No. 5 at the 13th measure and gradually open the swell to the 16th measure. Push Sw. Piston No. 1 and play the L. H. on the Ch. While playing, prepare Sw. Salicional and Flute 4 ft. with Tremolo. At the double bar play both hands on the Sw. for four measures. For the next four measures, play the L. H. on the Ch. Continue with both hands on the Sw. Put off the Tremolo for the last two measures before the change of key to the key of C. Before playing the last note (Gt.) of the measure before the double bar, push Sw. 3 and Gt. 2. Play one measure on the Gt. and one measure on the Sw. Open the Grand Crescendo full and play two measures on the Gt. and four measures on the Sw. Gradually close the Grand Crescendo while playing on the Sw. Push Gt. 1 and play two measures on the Gt. Push Sw. 1 and play two measures on the Sw. For the *Andante non troppo* push Sw. 4 and draw the Tremolo. Play the R. H. on the Sw. and the L. H. on the Ch. Two measures before the *Allegro Vivace* put off the Tremolo. One measure before the double bar, open the Grand Crescendo full and play on the Gt. for nine measures. Play four measures on the Sw. Close the Grand Crescendo about one-third, and play on the Gt. for four measures. Open the Grand Crescendo full and continue on the Gt. six measures. Play one measure on the Sw., close the Grand Crescendo and play one measure and a half on the Ch. (L. H.), during which prepare the Sw. Gedeckt, Flute 4 ft. and Tremolo. As the key changes to the key of A, play both hands on the Sw. (*poco lento*). For the *Allegro* put off the Tremolo and push Sw. 4 (reeds). Play four measures (R. H.) on the Sw. While playing push Gt. 3. For the *Poco maestoso* open the Grand Crescendo full, and play on the Gt., for twelve measures. Play on the Sw. for four measures and on the Gt. for seven measures. At the " *lunga Pausa* " close the Grand Crescendo and prepare Sw. Vox Humana and Ped. Bourdon without any couplers for the last six measures.

JOHN A. WEST, * MELODY IN A-FLAT

While the registration of the first page which is indicated in the printed copies (solo on the Gt. or Ch. and accompaniment on the Sw.) is possible on a few organs, it is ineffective on many organs and perhaps impossible on some organs. In view of this fact, I venture to suggest a different registration, with the idea that the student can choose the one best suited to his organ. As the solo melody is the most important part of the composition, it seems to me advisable to play it mostly on the Sw., which is

---

* This registration is intended specifically for the organ whose specification is given on page 169 with movable combinations substituted for the immovable combinations.

the most flexible manual with regard to combinations and expression. I am conscious of the fact that in a few organs no suitable combination can be obtained for the accompaniment on the Gt. or Ch. This may necessitate the following of the printed registration; thus sacrificing some of the flexibility and expression of the melody for the sake of a desirable combination for the accompaniment. When the Ch. stops are in a swell-box, it is generally a simple matter to obtain a suitable combination on the Ch. for this accompaniment.

Prepare: Gt. Doppel Floete: Sw. Oboe, Gedeckt, Salicional, Flute 4 ft. and Tremolo: Ch. Melodia and Dulciana (closed): Ped. Bourdon and Sw. to Gt.

Play the melody of the first page on the Sw. and the accompaniment on the Ch. On some organs the Melodia, even with the swell closed, is too loud for this accompaniment. On such organs I suggest the use of a louder combination on the Sw. for the solo. If this is impractical the accompaniment can be played on the Ch. Dulciana, or an octave lower on the Ch. Flute d'Amour or Gt. Flute Har. On page 4 play the solo on the Gt. with the accompaniment on the Ch. This addition of the Doppel Floete to the solo combination (by means of the Sw. to Gt.) gives a pleasing variety to the solo. On page 5, second measure, the melody should return to the Sw. as at first.

In the last measure at the bottom of page 5, while the L. H. note is held, there is sufficient opportunity to make any desired changes of stops. As the last two pages are mostly a repetition of the first two pages, it seems advisable, when possible, to change the registration. For this reason I suggest the following: put off the Melodia (which leaves the Dulciana) and turn the leaf while holding the note (L. H.) on the Sw. As this note is released, the Sw. combination can be changed to Oboe, Salicional, and Flute 4 ft. with Tremolo. (A Vox Humana or a Voix Céleste in place of the Oboe, or added to the Oboe, is frequently attractive.) These combinations can be continued to the last measure but one, when the Sw. combination should be reduced to the Æoline, during the rests (R. H.), for the ending on the Sw.

GABRIEL PIERNÉ, * CANTILÈNE IN E-FLAT

Prepare: Sw. Bourdon 16 ft., Oboe, and Voix Céleste (closed): Ch. Dulciana (partly open): Ped. Bourdon.

Play the R. H. solo on the Sw. and the accompaniment on the Ch. In the 20th measure shorten the B-flat (R. H.) sufficiently to be able to put off the Sw. Bourdon. In the 24th measure play both hands on the Sw. In the 27th measure play the solo on the Sw. and the chord on the Ch. The low B-flat of the L. H. chord is duplicated in the Ped. and can be omitted to enable the L. H. to reach the rest of the chord. During the last three eighth-notes of the measure (*molto rit.*) add the Vox Humana and Flute 4 ft. and put off the Oboe. During the rest (R. H.) in the 41st

---

* This registration is intended specifically for the organ whose specification is given on page 169 with movable combinations substituted for the immovable combinations.

measure, add the Oboe. During the rest (R. H.) in the 45th measure, put off the Oboe. At the end of the 47th measure put off the Vox Humana and play R. H. on the Sw. and L. H. on the Ch. Play the last five measures with both hands on the Sw. Æoline and Sw. to Sw. 4 ft. Coupler. The coupler can be put off (*ad lib.*) for the last two chords.

FREDERICK N. SHACKLEY, * AT EVENTIDE

The composer's registration in the printed copies can be followed closely on this organ. The following optional registration is planned to give more nerve, vitality, and emotion to the principal solo theme than is possible when that theme is played on the Gt.

Prepare: Gt. Doppel Floete, Gamba and Flute 4 ft.: Sw. Cornopean, Oboe, Voix Céleste and Flute 4 ft. (closed): Ch. Melodia and Dulciana (closed): Ped. Bourdon and Gedeckt, Sw. to Gt.

Play the four measures of introduction on the Ch. Open the Ch. swell for the third measure and close it in the fourth measure. Add the Sw. Tremolo and play the R. H. solo on the Sw. and the accompaniment on the Ch. The expressive character of the solo should be controlled by means of the Sw. swell, and the proper balance between the solo and the accompaniment preserved by means of the Ch. swell. At the hold (R. H.) in the last measure of the page, add Sw. to Sw. 16 ft. Coupler (or Sw. Bourdon 16 ft.). Open the Ch. swell to balance the increased volume of the solo combination. At the end of the second brace on page 3, put off the Sw. to Sw. 16 ft. Coupler (or Sw. Bourdon), draw Gt. to Ped. and play on the Gt. Near the end of the second measure in the third brace, put off the Cornopean and play both hands on the Sw. Near the end of the brace, push Gt. 2 and play on the Gt. In the last measure of the page, the printed indication for the first chord, " Sw.," obviously is a misprint. The chord should be played on the Gt. At the top of page 4, push Sw. 5. For the short Ped. notes either add Ped. Flute 8 ft. or let the Gt. to Ped. remain on, according to taste. At the sixth measure of the brace, open the swell half-way. At the third measure of the second brace, push Gt. 3 and play on the Gt. If the Gt. to Ped. is not on it should be put on. Near the end of the brace open the Grand Crescendo gradually. Use the Sfz for the first three measures of the third brace. Near the end of the last chord of these three measures, release the right foot in order to close the Grand Crescendo and put off the Gt. to Ped. During the "*lunga*" rest put off the Sfz, push Gt. 1 and Sw. 3, and close the Sw. swell about two-thirds. Follow the manual indications until the last measure of the page. In this measure put off Sw. Gedeckt and Diapason, add Vox Humana and Cornopean, and play the two notes of the solo (R. H.) on the Sw. In the last measure of the second brace of page 5 add Sw. to Sw. 16 ft. (or Bourdon 16 ft.).

At the top of page 6 (*Più mosso*) put off the Sw. to Sw. 16 ft. Coupler (or Bourdon) and select a complete change of tone-color for the next

---

* This registration is intended specifically for the organ whose specification is given on page 169 with movable combinations substituted for the immovable combinations.

section, either Gedeckt and Flute 4 ft. or Gedeckt and Violina. Play both hands on the Sw. In the second brace play the fourth measure on the Gt. Gamba alone, and follow the other manual indications until the lower brace. While playing the lower brace on the Sw. with Gedeckt and Salicional (Piston No. 1), prepare Ch. Dulciana (open), and Ped. Bourdon only. At the rest at the end of the page, prepare Sw. Vox Humana, Voix Céleste, Flute 4 ft. and Tremolo. On the last page play the R. H. solo on the Sw. and the L. H. on the Ch. At the hold (R. H.) in the second brace, add Sw. to Sw. 16 ft. Coupler (or Bourdon 16 ft.). In the second measure of the lower brace, put off the Sw. to Sw. 16 ft. Coupler (or Bourdon) and the Voix Céleste. Play the second measure on the Sw. (closed), the third measure on the Ch. (partly closed) and the fourth measure Ch. (closed) and Sw. with Vox Humana only. Play the last two measures on the Sw. Æoline.

ALEXANDRE GUILMANT, * FIRST OFFERTOIRE ON CHRISTMAS HYMNS

The printed registration in the original edition and translation in the American reprint can be followed to a certain extent on this organ; but numerous details which are omitted will be of assistance to the student.

Prepare: Sw. 8 and 4 ft. with Oboe (Piston No. 3): Gt. to Octave (Piston No. 3): Ch. Melodia and Clarinet: Ped. Op. Diapason, Violone, Bourdon, Cello, and Gedeckt (Gt. Piston No. 3 brings on this combination of Ped. stops): Sw. and Gt. to Ped.

The first page and a half should be played on the Gt. On the last half of the fourth measure of the middle brace of the second page, push Gt. Piston No. 1. Two measures later play both hands on the Sw., and put off the Gt. to Ped. Gradually close the swell. While holding the last chord before the double bar, push Sw. Piston No. 2 and put off the Gt. Doppel Floete. Before beginning the Hymn put off the Sw. Diapason. Follow the printed manual indications except in the upper brace of the third page, where the melody in the L. H. is indicated to be played on the Sw. or Ch. Bassoon. As this organ does not contain that stop, the melody can be played on the Ch. (Melodia and Clarinet), which was used for the first presentation of the hymn, or it can be played on the Gt. Gamba and Flute 4 ft., which was prepared on the previous page. At the second eighth-note, in the first measure of the fourth brace of this page, push Gt. Piston No. 3 and add the Gt. to Ped. Play on the Gt. At the rest in the third measure, push Sw. Piston No. 3. As this Piston throws off the heavy Ped. stops, it is necessary to push Gt. Piston No. 3 to bring them on again, when returning to the Gt. in the fifth measure. In the second measure at the top of the fourth page, during the rest in the R. H. part, put off the Clarinet and add the Flute d'Amour. This can be done by means of the Ch. piston No. 1; but that piston also throws off the heavy Ped. stops which are being used at the time; hence, it is advisable to put the stops off by the hand instead of by the piston.

* This registration is intended specifically for the organ whose specification is given on page 169 with movable combinations substituted for the immovable combinations.

At the double bar the long sustained chord can be held with the R. H. alone by omitting the lowest note (F), which is supplied by the Ped. This enables the player to prepare the next Sw. combination with the L. H.: viz., Vox Humana, Gedeckt and Flute 4 ft. At the rest, before the hymn (Adeste Fidelis), push Gt. Piston No. 1 and Ped. Piston No. 1, put off all Couplers and put off the Gt. Gamba. Follow the manual indications. In alternating the figures of the L. H. between the Gt. and Ch. it may be necessary to use a different combination in the Gt. from that suggested. The printed indication is " Doppel Floete and Gamba." The Gamba seems objectionable to me. I prefer Doppel Floete and Flute 4 ft. unless the latter stop is too loud, when it must be omitted. In the last measure of the upper brace of the last page, the printed indication is for both hands on the Gt. I venture to suggest Sw. for both hands as preferable. In the first measure of the fourth brace, I also suggest that the player put off the Vox Humana and continue on the Sw. instead of on the Ch. as printed. For the last two measures of the brace, the Ped. Bourdon and Gedeckt are necessary for the theme in the Ped. If the Gedeckt is not already on it should be put on. At the last measure of the fourth brace, prepare the Ch. for the R. H. phrase. Some organists prefer the Melodia and some prefer the Flute d'Amour. Either can be used.

CHAPTER XXI

REGISTRATION ON FOUR-MANUAL ORGANS
(*with non-movable combinations*)

MANY of the fundamental principles of registration, which have been mentioned in the preceding chapters, in connection with small and medium-sized organs, are of equal force with four-manual organs. In addition, there are many details of registration which must be more or less magnified when a composition is played on a four-manual organ.

As the large organs are generally located in large churches or halls, many soft and delicate effects of registration, which are distinctly audible and distinguishable in small auditoriums, are frequently of no avail in the large organs in large auditoriums. Therefore, it is, oftentimes, necessary to enlarge many of the combinations, in order to meet the conditions of the increased size of the auditoriums. Furthermore, one must consider the lack of approximate silence which generally prevails in large churches and halls, and also, the lack of intimacy, so to speak, between the source of the sound and the auditors. The last-named condition is frequently the cause of much of the proverbial lack of emotion, expression, and rhythm, with which organ music is often maligned.

With four-manual organs, there is such a great variety of methods in registering any composition, according to the personal taste of the performer, that it is impossible to indicate, even in several chapters, all the available combinations or the methods of obtaining the combinations. Nearly every organist who has occasion to play on a four-manual organ has long since passed the student period, and has developed his own individuality in registration. Generally, he needs no suggestions from another; and frequently, he considers such suggestions an intrusion if not a reflection. However, a work of this character would be far from complete without some suggestions for registration on large organs.

The following suggestions are offered, to give the student an idea of registration on organs which are larger than the ordinary two and three-manual organs — to indicate how the principles of registration, which have been sketched in the foregoing chapters, are broadened and further developed as the organs increase in size.

A few remarks relative to the voicing of the pipes of some of the stops in a large organ are here necessary. Theoretically, the pipes of many of the individual stops of a large organ ought to be voiced with relation to the size of the auditorium. This theoretical principle is generally carried out in the voicing of the pipes of the powerful stops. In most large organs, such stops as the Diapasons, Gross Flute, Gamba, Trumpet, and Trombone, are made of large scale and are voiced to produce a

strong tone, as should be the case. In some large organs the power and
volume of tone which is produced by the pipes of the individual stops
of medium power is, likewise, in keeping with the size of the auditorium;
and the necessary relative power of the stops which are most used in
combinations has been preserved. On the other hand, we occasionally
find a four-manual organ in which the relative power of many of the
stops is out of balance — so to speak — and many beautiful effects are
impossible, or are extremely difficult to obtain, on such an organ.

In some large churches or halls, the size of the auditorium and the
distance between the origin of the sound and the ears of the auditors,
cause such a diminution of the audible effect of certain combinations
that it is necessary to add stops to the specific combinations, in order
to produce the required effect. Under such conditions, an Oboe and Flute
4 ft. in the Sw. for a solo, with a Dulciana in the Ch. for the accompaniment, may happen to be inadequate for the desired effect. In this event,
it is advisable to add a Cornopean and possibly a Voix Céleste in the Sw.,
and a Melodia or a Viol d'Amour in the Ch. Ordinarily, the addition of
these stops materially changes the tone-color of the combinations; never-
theless, the musical effect to the auditor in the large auditorium, when
these stops are added, is nearer the desired effect than if they were
omitted.

Again, a Stopped Diapason (Gedeckt) and a Violina with the Tremolo
is effective for a certain passage, when it is played on a medium-sized
organ in a medium-sized auditorium. This same combination on a
large four-manual organ in a large church is frequently most ineffective.
If one adds a Salicional and a Flute 4 ft. the effect of the combination
is much improved. By adding the Salicional the eight-foot tone of the
combination is made a little firmer, and by adding the Flute the four-
foot tone of the combination is brightened. The effect of the whole
combination (St. Diapason, Salicional, Flute 4 ft. and Violina) in the
large auditorium is soft and buoyant, as desired, and yet it is not too
strong for the particular passage, as would be the case on the smaller
organ in the smaller auditorium.

The foregoing remarks relative to the voicing of some of the stops
in large organs, which are, to a certain extent, critical, are inserted solely
for the purpose of explaining to the student the reasons for certain
necessary changes of registration when compositions are played in large
auditoriums.

There is another phase of the subject which is very interesting and
more than compensates for the necessity of changing the combinations in
the large auditoriums. The increased distance between the pipes and
the auditors in large churches and halls, to which reference is made
above, together with the increased reverberation and a slight echo (if
these be not too great), exert an influence on the tone of many combinations which is oftentimes very pleasing and must not be underestimated.
Many combinations of stops produce a more pleasing effect in the large
auditoriums than in the small auditoriums, *provided the relative power
of the individual stops is such that the proper balance of tone-color is
preserved in the combination.* A loud four-foot stop combined with a

soft eight-foot stop which sounds unsatisfactory in a small auditorium does not sound any better in a large auditorium. Distance fails to " lend enchantment " to any combination which is inherently objectionable.

SPECIFICATION OF A FOUR-MANUAL ORGAN
77 Speaking Stops, 28 Couplers, 14 Pedal Movements,
34 Adjustable Combination Pistons (non-movable)

GREAT ORGAN, FOURTEEN STOPS

1. Double Diapason	16 ft.	8. Gamba	8 ft.
2. First Diapason	8 ft.	9. Harmonic Flute	4 ft.
3. Second Diapason	8 ft.	10. Octave	4 ft.
4. Third Diapason	8 ft.	11. Twelfth	2⅔ ft.
5. Gross Flute	8 ft.	12. Fifteenth	2 ft.
6. Doppel Floete	8 ft.	13. Mixture	IV Rks.
7. Gemshorn	8 ft.	14. Trumpet	8 ft.

SWELL ORGAN, EIGHTEEN STOPS

15. Bourdon(treble and bass)	16 ft.	24. Octave	4 ft.
16. Diapason Phonon	8 ft.	25. Flauto Traverso	4 ft.
17. Spitz Floete	8 ft.	26. Violina	4 ft.
18. Viol d'Orchestre	8 ft.	27. Flautino	2 ft.
19. Voix Céleste	8 ft.	28. Dolce Cornet	III Rks.
20. Hohl Floete	8 ft.	29. Contra Fagotto	16 ft.
21. Gedeckt	8 ft.	30. Cornopean	8 ft.
22. Salicional	8 ft.	31. Oboe	8 ft.
23. Æoline	8 ft.	32. Vox Humana	8 ft.
		Tremolo	

CHOIR ORGAN, FOURTEEN STOPS

33. Dulciana	16 ft.	41. Quintadena	8 ft.
34. Diapason	8 ft.	42. Flute d'Amour	4 ft.
35. Melodia	8 ft.	43. Fugara	4 ft.
36. Gedeckt	8 ft.	44. Piccolo	2 ft.
37. Flute Céleste	8 ft.	45. Clarinet	8 ft.
38. Viol d'Amour	8 ft.	46. Physharmonica	8 ft.
39. Dulciana	8 ft.	Tremolo	
40. Unda Maris	8 ft.		

SOLO ORGAN, EIGHT STOPS (on a high pressure)

47. Stentorphone	8 ft.	51. Flute Ouverte	4 ft.
48. Philomela	8 ft.	52. Tuba Mirabilis	8 ft.
49. Gross Gamba	8 ft.	53. Orchestral Oboe	8 ft.
50. Gamba Céleste	8 ft.	54. Chimes	
		Tremolo	

ECHO ORGAN, SEVEN STOPS

55. Echo Bourdon	16 ft.	59. Wald Floete	4 ft.
56. Lieblich Gedeckt	8 ft.	60. Vox Humana	8 ft.
57. Muted Viol	8 ft.	61. Harp	
58. Viol Céleste	8 ft.	Tremolo	

PEDAL ORGAN, FOURTEEN STOPS AND TWO BORROWED STOPS

62. Double Diapason	32 ft.	70. Dulciana		16 ft.
63. Contra Bourdon	32 ft.	71. Octave		8 ft.
64. First Diapason (wood)	16 ft.	72. Gedeckt		8 ft.
65. Second Diapason (metal)	16 ft.	73. Cello		8 ft.
66. Violone	16 ft.	74. Quint		10⅔ ft.
67. Bourdon	16 ft.	75. Contra Trombone		32 ft.
68. Lieblich Bourdon (from		76. Trombone		16 ft.
Sw.)	16 ft.	77. Trombe		8 ft.
69. Echo Bourdon (from				
Echo)	16 ft.			

COUPLERS, THIRTY-ONE

Swell to Great		Great to Pedal	Solo on Echo off (or
Swell to Great	16 ft.	Choir to Great	Echo on Solo off)
Swell to Great	4 ft.	Choir to Great	16 ft. Echo to Great
Swell to Swell	16 ft.	Choir to Choir	4 ft. Echo to Swell
Swell to Swell	4 ft.	Choir to Pedal	Echo to Choir
Swell to Choir		Solo to Great	Echo to Pedal
Swell to Choir	4 ft.	Solo to Swell	Echo to Echo 16 ft.
Swell to Pedal		Solo to Choir	Echo to Echo 4 ft.
Swell to Pedal	4 ft.	Solo to Pedal	Chimes to Pedal
Great to Swell		Solo to Solo	16 ft. Chimes to Great
Great to Solo		Solo to Solo	4 ft.

ADJUSTABLE COMBINATION PISTONS, THIRTY-FOUR
(non-movable)

Six and Release for Great and Pedal

Eight and Release for Swell and Pedal

Three and Release for Solo and Pedal

Four and Release for Choir and Pedal

Three and Release for Echo and Pedal

Five and Release for Pedal

Five and Release for Whole Organ

General Release

PEDAL MOVEMENTS AND COMBINATION PEDALS, THIRTEEN
(Fixed combinations)

Sforzando — Full Organ with all Couplers

FF Great and Pedal

F   Great and Pedal

FF Swell and Pedal

F   Swell and Pedal

F   Pedal

P   Pedal

Great to Pedal (Reversible)

Grand Crescendo (Full Organ without Tuba and Octave Couplers)

General Release for all Pedals

Crescendo Pedal for Swell

Crescendo Pedal for Choir

Crescendo Pedal for Solo and Echo

In this organ the Combination Pedals are presumed to be non-adjustable and are presumed to bring on the following combinations: —

FF Gt. Full Gt. with all Ped. stops except the reeds (Nos. 75-77).

F Gt. Gt. to Octave (stops Nos. 1-10) with Ped. stops Nos. 64-67, 72 and 73.

FF Sw. Full Sw. with Ped. stops Nos. 66, 67, 70 and 72.
F Sw. 8 and 4 ft. with Oboe (stops Nos. 16-18, 21-26 and 31) with
               Ped. stops Nos. 67 and 72.
F Ped. Full Ped.
P Ped. Bourdon and Gedeckt (Nos. 67 and 72).

The Combination Pistons are adjustable for any conceivable combination of stops. For our present purpose they should be adjusted as follows: —

Gt. No. 1. Stops Nos. 6 and 9 with Ped. Bourdon (67).
Gt. No. 2. Stops Nos. 5-9 with Ped. stops Nos. 67 and 72.
Gt. No. 3. Stops Nos. 3-9, with Ped. stops Nos. 66, 67, 72 and 73.
Gt. No. 4. Stops Nos. 1-7, and 9, with Ped. stops Nos. 63-67, 72
              and 73.
Gt. No. 5. Stops Nos. 3-6, 9 and 14, with Ped. stops Nos. 66, 67,
              72 and 73.
Gt. No. 6. Full to Fifteenth (stops Nos. 1-12) with Ped. stops Nos.
              63-67, 70-73.
Sw. No. 1. Gedeckt and Salicional (stops Nos. 21 and 22).
Sw. No. 2. Gedeckt, Salicional, Flute 4 ft. and Violina (stops Nos. 21,
              22, 25 and 26), with Ped. stop No. 67.
Sw. No. 3. 8 and 4 ft. stops without reeds (stops Nos. 16-18, 20-22, 25
              and 26), with Ped. stops Nos. 67 and 72.
Sw. No. 4. Special combination to be adjusted when desired.
Sw. No. 5. Full to 2 ft. without reeds (stops Nos. 15-18, 20-27), with
              Ped. stops Nos. 66, 67, 70 and 72.
Sw. No. 6. Reeds (stops Nos. 30 and 31), and stops Nos. 18, 20-23, 25
              and 26, with Ped. stops Nos. 66, 67, 70 and 72.
Sw. No. 7. Full without Contra Fagotto and Mixture (stops Nos. 15-
              18, 20-27, 30 and 31), with Ped. stops Nos. 66, 67, 70
              and 72.
Sw. No. 8. Full Sw. and Sw. to Sw. 16 and 4 ft. Couplers, with Ped.
              stops Nos. 66, 67, 70, 72 and 73.
Ch. No. 1. Stops Nos. 35 and 42.
Ch. No. 2. Stops Nos. 35, 36, 39, 42 with Ped. stop No. 67.
Ch. No. 3. Stops Nos. 34-36, 38, 39, 42 and 43, with Ped. stops Nos.
              67 and 72.
Ch. No. 4. Stops Nos. 33-36, 38-44, with Ped. stops Nos. 66, 67, 70 and 72.
So. No. 1. Stops Nos. 48 and 51.
So. No. 2. Stops Nos. 47-49, 51 and 52.
So. No. 3. Stops Nos. 47-49, 51 and 52 with So. to So. 16 and 4 ft.
              and Gt. to So. Couplers.
Echo No. 1. Stops Nos. 57 and 58 with Ped. Echo Bourdon (69).
Echo No. 2. Stops Nos. 56 and 60, with Ped. Echo Bourdon (69).
Echo No. 3. Stops Nos. 59 and 60, with Ped. Echo Bourdon (69).
Ped. No. 1. Stops Nos. 66, 67 and 70.
Ped. No. 2. Stops Nos. 64, 67, 70 and 72.
Ped. No. 3. Stops Nos. 64-67, 70 and 72.

Ped. No. 4.   Stops Nos. 63-67, 70 and 72.
Ped. No. 5.   Full without reeds (stops Nos. 62-74).
Whole Organ No. 1.   Diapasons and Flutes; stops Nos. 1-6, 9, 15-17, 20, 21, 25, 35, 36, 42, 47, 48, 51, 62-67, 70-73 with Couplers, So., Gt., Sw., and Ch. to Ped.; So., Sw., and Ch. to Gt.; Sw. and Ch. to Gt. 16 ft.
Whole Organ No. 2.   The combinations of " F Gt.," and " F Ped." (see above) with Sw. to Gt., Sw. and Gt. to Ped.
Whole Organ No. 3.   The combinations of " F Gt.," " FF Sw.," " F So." and " F Ped." with Sw. to Gt., So. to Gt., Sw. to Gt. 16 and 4 ft., Gt., So. and Sw. to Ped.
Whole Organ No. 4.   To be adjusted for any special composition.
Whole Organ No. 5.   To be adjusted for any special composition.

SEVEN ORGAN COMPOSITIONS FOR WHICH REGISTRATION IS SUGGESTED FOR THE ABOVE FOUR-MANUAL ORGAN

Homer N. Bartlett	Toccata in E
F. de la Tombelle	Marche Pontificale
M. E. Bossi	Scherzo in G-minor
Josef Rheinberger	Vision in D-flat
Louis Thiele	Concert Satz in E-flat minor
W. T. Best	Pastorale in G.
Alfred Hollins	Concert Rondo

HOMER N. BARTLETT, * TOCCATA IN E

Prepare: Gt. F Combination Pedal (to Octave); Sw. Draw Voix Céleste and Gedeckt, and put on FF Sw. (Full Sw.) Combination Pedal; Ch. Draw Melodia and Gedeckt, and Piston No. 2 (swell open); So. Stentorphone, Philomela, Gross Gamba and Flute Ouverte 4 ft. (swell slightly open); Echo, Vox Humana and Lieblich Gedeckt; Ped. Bourdon; Sw. to Gt. and Gt. to Ped.

As the combination movements of this organ do not move the drawstops, the small combinations of stops on the Sw., Ch. and Ped., which are required in the middle section of the composition, can be prepared at the outset. When the combination movements are released, the drawstops remain as prepared.

Play the first two pages with the organ as prepared. Beginning with the Sw. swell closed, the crescendi and diminuendi can be made by means of the swell pedal. On page 4, the changes which are indicated require no change of stops, except to put off the Gt. to Ped. On some organs it is unnecessary to put off the Gt. to Ped. at this point, as the next three Ped. notes are with chords (L. H.) on the Gt. In the third brace, draw the Gt. to Ped. again (if it has been previously put off). At the top of page 5, put off the Gt. to Ped. The short Ped. notes generally sound all right with the Ped. combination which is included in the F Gt. Combination Pedal. If these Ped. stops are too loud, one can put off

* This registration is intended specifically for the organ whose specification is given on page 215.

the F Gt. Combination Pedal, thus leaving only the Ped. stops which are included in the FF Sw. Combination Pedal. If the F Gt. Pedal is put off, it must be put on again at the second measure of the third brace (page 5). At the bottom of page 6, where the Full Organ is indicated, open the Grand Crescendo full.

On page 7, the single half-note chords, which are indicated for the Sw., are effective if played on the Solo (as prepared). For the last three measures of page 7 (" Sw. or Ch."), push General Release, Ped. Release, and Ch. Piston No. 1. While playing the three measures on the Ch., put off the Gt. to Ped. (foot). At the top of page 8, push Whole Organ Piston No. 1. At the return of the first theme (last measure of the upper brace), push Whole Organ Piston No. 2, which gives F Gt. and Full Sw. At the first measure of the third brace on page 9, open the Grand Crescendo full. No other changes except the use of the swell pedal are necessary until the Trio is reached.

While holding the chord before the double bar, push the General Release and the Ped. Release. This releases all the combination movements except the Grand Crescendo. The draw-stops which were prepared at the outset give the necessary combinations for the following phrases; viz., Sw. Voix Céleste and Gedeckt; Echo, Vox Humana and Lieblich Gedeckt; Ch. Melodia and Gedeckt; Ped. Bourdon. Before playing the Trio, close the Grand Crescendo. While playing the first eight measures of the Trio on the Sw., the Gt. to Ped. can be put off by the foot. The second eight measures of the Trio can be played on the Echo. The third eight measures (indicated " Mf ") can be played on the Sw. (partly open). The fourth eight measures (indicated " Vox Humana PPP ") can be played on the Echo, after putting off the Gedeckt (ad lib.). This antiphonal effect between the Sw. Voix Céleste and the Echo Vox Humana is generally pleasing. If it is not to the taste of the performer, the whole thirty-two measures can be played on the Sw., varying the combination for each period of eight measures.

At the top of page 12, the two measures reminiscent of the first theme should be played on the Sw., after putting on the F Sw. Combination Pedal (8 and 4 ft. with Oboe). The next eight measures of the Trio theme should be played on the Echo. The next two measures, reminiscent of the first theme, are indicated for a solo stop (R. H.). This phrase is effective if the R. H. is played on the Ch. and the L. H. on the Sw. It may be necessary to put off the F Sw. Pedal and put on Sw. Piston No. 2. Another eight measures of the Trio theme on the Echo are followed by four measures (Lento) modulating for the return of the first theme. These four measures can be played on the Ch. (as indicated). Just before beginning the Tempo 1, push Whole Organ Piston No. 1. This gives the Diapasons and Flutes of the Gt., Sw., Ch. and Ped., with the necessary couplers. Four measures later, at the return of the original key (E), push Whole Organ Piston No. 3, which gives a good combination for the next two pages. At the bottom of page 14 (indicated " FF "), open the Grand Crescendo full. For the last two braces (" Finale "), use the Sfz.

It is obvious that an endless number of variations of this registration are possible on such an organ. To attempt to indicate many of these would be confusing to the student, therefore I will only call attention to a variation in the *method* of registering a composition on such an organ. Some organists, when about to play a composition on an organ of this character, adjust nearly every important change of stops on the combination pistons. This is certainly convenient *after the pistons have been adjusted*, but if this method is followed for every composition of a program, the delay between the compositions, while the organist is adjusting the several pistons, becomes annoying to the audience after two or three such delays. If all the pistons are adjusted to useful combinations before beginning a program, most of the registration of the whole program can be easily done without further adjustment. If, however, some special changes of stops are too complicated to be made easily, within the time allowed by the rests in the composition, those changes can be adjusted on pistons before beginning the composition.

In considering the registration suggested above, it must be remembered that in this organ all combination movements are supposed to be of the non-movable type, having no effect on the draw-stops. Several changes in the method of obtaining the smaller combinations of the Trio would be necessary if the combination movements were of the movable type.

F. DE LA TOMBELLE, * MARCHE PONTIFICALE

Prepare: Gt. Second Diapason, Gross Flute and F Gt. Combination Pedal; Sw. Oboe, Voix Céleste and Gedeckt, with Piston No. 6; Ch. Piston No. 2; So. Philomela, and Flute Ouverte 4 ft.; Ped. Violone, Dulciana, Bourdon and Gedeckt; Sw. to Gt., Gt. and Ch. to Ped.

Play the first sixteen measures on the Gt. (F), or, if the performer prefers, the Grand Crescendo full can be used, as the printed indication is " FF." The subsidiary theme of twelve measures which follows should be played on the Sw. reeds as prepared. For the return of the first theme (twelve measures), use Grand Cresc. open full. For the second subsidiary theme (D-minor), close the Grand Cresc., put off the F Gt., the Gt. to Ped., and play on the Ch. (as indicated). After twelve measures of this theme, add Gt. to Ped., and play on the Gt. For the long crescendo to FF, use the Grand Cresc. (gradually) to full for the return of the first theme (FF).

For the middle section (" *Cantando* "), put off all the combination movements by means of the 00 and the Pedal Release. The Sw. combination prepared at the outset is effective for the R. H. part of this section. The L. H. part, which is rhythmic rather than melodic, ought to stand out quite prominently. If this is played on the So., it is generally effective. If, however, the So. combination is unsatisfactory, one can play this L. H. part on the Gt. as prepared at the outset. After sixteen measures of this theme, the L. H. part becomes harmonic, and should be played on the same manual as the R. H. After four measures,

* This registration is intended specifically for the organ whose specification is given on page 215.

the repetition of the theme should be played on the Ch. as indicated. The rhythmic figure in the Ped. should be prominent. For this purpose, choose one of the following three additions; viz., Ped. Octave, So. to Ped., or Gt. to Ped. After eight measures of this theme, add FF Sw. After four more measures, add the Gt. to Ped. (if it is not already on), and play on the Gt. After four measures, add Whole Organ Piston No. 1. After four measures, add Whole Organ Piston No. 2, and gradually open the Sw. swell and the Grand Cresc. At the return of the first theme (FF), have the Grand Cresc. open full. For the last five measures, use the Sfz.

For a variation of this registration, the middle section can be played on the Sw. with the So. to Sw. and So. Gamba added to the combination mentioned at the outset, in which case the rhythmic figure in the L. H. must be played on the Gt.

M. E. Bossi, * Scherzo in G-Minor

Prepare: Gt. Gross Flute, Doppel Floete and Flute 4 ft.; Sw. Oboe, Voix Céleste, and FF Sw. Combination Pedal; Ch. Melodia, Gedeckt and Flute d'Amour; So. Philomela; Ped. Bourdon and Gedeckt; No couplers.

Play the first page on the Sw. (closed). In the last measure of the upper brace of the second page, and in the three succeeding measures, play the L. H. broken octaves on the Gt., and the rest of the notes on the Sw. Before the last two sixteenth-notes in the third measure of the middle brace, open the Grand Cresc. a little less than one-half (which generally includes one or two of the Diapasons, etc.), and play on the Gt. Also add the Gt. to Ped. At the top of page 3, open the Grand Cresc. a little more (to include Full Sw. and Gt. Octave). At the measure indicated " FF," open the Grand Cresc. full, and play five measures. At the rests previous to the return of the first theme, close the Grand Crescendo. Play on the Sw. (closed), as at first. In the next to the last measure in the upper brace of page 4, and in the three succeeding measures in the middle brace, the single B-flats in the L. H. part are indicated for the Gt. They are like horn notes, and are generally effective when played on the three stops which were prepared on the Gt. If this combination is not loud enough, the Third Diapason should be included at the outset.

For the second theme, beginning in the last measure of the middle brace (page 4), release all combinations by means of the Pedal Release and the General Release, add the Vox Humana in the Sw., and play both hands on the Sw. (Oboe, Voix Céleste and Vox Humana). The staccato broken octaves in the R. H. should be played on the So. This alternation of the R. H. part between the Sw. and the So. should continue until the third measure of the middle brace of page 5, when Whole Organ Piston No. 1 should be pressed. Play both hands on the Gt. for four measures. Add Whole Organ Piston No. 2, and continue on the Gt. Gradually open the Sw. swell until the fifth measure of the middle

---

* This registration is intended specifically for the organ whose specification is given on page 215.

brace of page 6. At this point, open the Grand Crescendo full. At the
last count of the first measure of the middle brace of page 7, close the
Grand Crescendo. At the last count of the third measure of this brace,
push Whole Organ Piston No. 1. One measure later, push the General
Release. Continue both hands on the Gt. until the second measure of
the lower brace (*dim. sempre*). Play the R. H. on the Ch., and,
during the rests (L. H.), put off the Sw. Vox Humana and add the
Cornopean. The three sustained notes in the L. H. are effective when
played on this combination in the Sw., the R. H. remaining on the Ch.
If the Gt. to Ped. is on, it should be put off before the following Ped.
note. During the rests, while the B-flat is sustained in the Ped., push
Sw. 3. Play both hands on the Sw. for two measures. Put off the
Cornopean, Oboe and Voix Céleste. Continue on the Sw. and push suc-
cessively Sw. Nos. 2 and 1.

At the rests, before the return of the first theme (*Tempo 1°*), put on
FF Sw. Play both hands on the Sw. (closed). At the top of page 9,
the L. H. part can be played on the Gt. (*ad lib.*), with the R. H. on the
Sw. (if the original combination on the Gt. has been changed, it should
be returned during previous rests). At the last measure of the upper
brace of page 9, and in the five succeeding measures, the broken octaves
in the L. H. should be played on the Gt. and all the other notes on the
Sw. At the last two notes of the middle brace, push Whole Organ Piston
No. 1, and play both hands on the Gt. Gradually open the Grand Crescendo to full at the FF (middle brace of page 10). For the last measure
of the middle brace, close the Grand Crescendo. Play the first two
measures of the lower brace on the Ch. (with a *ritard*). During these
two measures, push General Release and Pedal Release, and prepare Sw.
Oboe, Vox Humana and Voix Céleste. For the next two braces of the
second theme, play, as previously, all on the Sw., except the broken
octaves in the R. H., which should be played on the So. At the fourth
measure of the middle brace of page 11, a gradual but somewhat rapid
crescendo to Full Organ begins. To obtain this crescendo, open the
Grand Crescendo about one-third, play the R. H. on the Gt., and the
L. H. on the Sw., for two measures. As the staccato notes in the R. H.
cease, play both hands on the Gt. and gradually open the Grand Crescendo to full for the FF. The last four measures (*Maestoso*) can be
played with the Sfz.

JOSEF RHEINBERGER, * VISION IN D-FLAT

Prepare: Gt. No stops; Sw. Gedeckt, Salicional, Flute 4 ft. and
Violina; Ech. Lieblich Gedeckt and Vox Humana; Ped. Ech. Bourdon;
Sw. to Gt. and Ech. to Ped.

The first ten measures of this composition are indicated "PP," the
next four measures "FF," the next eight "PP," and the following
measures "FF." It seems to me that this contrast between *pianissimo*
and *fortissimo* is not pleasing. I have always preferred a *forte* com-

---

* This registration is intended specifically for the organ whose specification is
given on page 215.

bination of Diapasons and Flutes instead of the *fortissimo* which is indicated.

I suggest that one play the first ten measures on the Echo. By adding Whole Organ Piston No. 1, during the rest (Ped.) of the tenth measure, a good Diapason and Flute combination on the Gt., Sw. and Ped. is obtained for the following four measures. If the So. Stentorphone is too loud for this combination, the So. to Gt. Coupler can be taken off of the combination, at the outset, by means of the combination adjuster. (Note: If the couplers cannot be adjusted on the combination pistons, as is the case in some organs, the Gt. to Ped. should be drawn at the outset, and left on all through the composition. As no stops on the Gt. are drawn, this coupler does not cause any inconvenience during the PP phrases, which are played on the Echo.)

At the rest (L. H.) in the fourteenth measure, push 00 and play on the Ech. For measure 23, push Whole Organ Piston No. 1. During the next eight measures, the Grand Cresc. can be slowly opened about one-third, and closed again, which will give a slight crescendo and diminuendo. At any one of the L. H. rests in this phrase, draw the Ech. Wald Floete. At the rest (L. H.) in measure 38, push 00, and play on the Ech. At measure 43, push Whole Organ Piston No. 1, and play on the Gt. At the second count of measure 46, push 00, and play on the Ech. At measure 49, put off the Ech. Wald Floete. At the rest (L. H.) in measure 51, push Sw. 3, and play on the Sw. At the last count of the following measure, push Sw. 0, and play on the Ech. On the A-natural in measure 55, add the Unda Maris. During the rests (R. H.) in measure 59, put off the Vox Humana. At the rest in measure 64, put off the Lieblich Gedeckt, thus leaving the Unda Maris alone. For the last two measures use the Muted Viol.

The above registration is planned for antiphonal effects between the Ech. Vox Humana and the Diapasons and Flutes of the main organ. A somewhat similar effect, though not antiphonal, can be secured by drawing at the outset the Sw. Vox Humana and Gedeckt, Ped. Bourdon, and Sw. to Ped., and adjusting on one of the Gt. pistons the Diapasons and Flutes of the Gt. and Ped., without any Sw. stops or the Sw. to Gt. Coupler. All the phrases indicated above for the Ech. can then be played on the Sw., and the Gt. can be used as indicated.

Louis Thiele, * Concert Satz in E-Flat Minor

Prepare: Gt. Piston No. 4; Sw. Piston No. 7 (closed); So. Full except reeds; Ped. Piston No. 4; Sw. and So. to Gt., Sw. and Gt. to Ped.

Play the first page with both hands on the Gt. At the rests in the last measure of the upper brace of page 4, add FF Sw. In the second brace play the fourth, fifth and sixth measures on the Sw. Return to the Gt. in the last measure of the brace, the L. H. on the first count, and the R. H. on the second count. At the next to the last measure on

---

* This registration is intended specifically for the organ whose specification is given on page 215.

page 5, add F Gt. In the sixth measure of the upper brace on page 6, open the Sw. swell. Open the Grand Crescendo full at the last measure. At the rests in the next to the last measure of the second brace, close the Grand Crescendo. At the fifth measure of the lower brace on page 8, open the Grand Crescendo full. At the rests in the fourth measure of the upper brace of page 9, close the Grand Crescendo. In the second brace, play the three measures on the Sw. as indicated. Return to the Gt. at the fourth measure. In the lower brace of page 10, where the key changes to E-flat major, add Whole Organ Piston No. 3. On page 11, at the fifth measure (*piu animato*), open the Grand Crescendo three-quarters. At the fourth measure of the third brace, open the Grand Crescendo full. Put on the Sfz at the A-flat in the Ped. of the next to the last measure of the composition. On some organs the Sfz can be used for the last nine measures, but the Tuba is occasionally too loud for the triple trill.

As this composition is planned for massive effects, there is little or no opportunity to use combinations of distinctive color. The use of the larger combinations and Full Organ can be varied but a little.

W. T. BEST, * PASTORALE IN G

Prepare: Gt. Gross Flute, Doppel Floete and Flute 4 ft.; Sw. Oboe and Flute 4 ft. Adjust Sw. Piston No. 4 as follows: Bourdon, Gedeckt, Flute 4 ft., Flautino and Tremolo; Ch. Viol d'Amour and Dulciana (open); Ped. Bourdon and Gedeckt; Sw. to Gt. and Gt. to Ped.

Play the first eight measures with both hands on the Sw. Put off the Oboe, and play both hands on the Gt. for twelve measures. Add the Voix Céleste, and play both hands on the Sw. for eight measures. Play the next two measures on the Ch. Put off the Voix Céleste, add Sw. 2, and play both hands on the Sw. for eight measures (second page). Play the next seven measures (to the double bar) on the Gt. Push Whole Organ Piston No. 2, and play both hands on the Gt. until the three measures rest at the bottom of the third page. During this rest push the General Release, put off the Gross Flute and Flute 4 ft. in the Gt., and open the Grand Crescendo full. Play three measures on the Gt. Close the Grand Crescendo, and push Sw. Piston No. 4. Play five measures on the Sw. Push the Sw. Release, add the Voix Céleste, and play two measures on the Sw. Play two measures on the Ch. Open the Grand Crescendo full, and play three measures on the Gt. At the rests, close the Grand Crescendo, put off the Voix Céleste, and push Sw. Piston No. 4. Play five measures on the Sw. At the last note on the fourth page (indicated " Ch. Voix Céleste "), push Sw. Release, add Voix Céleste, and play two measures on the Sw. Play two measures on the Ch., two measures on the Gt., and two measures on the Ch. Play six measures on the Sw., and one measure on the Ch. Play one measure on the Sw. with the Oboe alone, and two measures on the Sw. with Gedeckt and Tremolo. While holding this sustained chord, prepare Gt. Gross Flute, Doppel Floete and Flute 4 ft., as at first.

At the return of the first theme (*A Tempo*), use Sw. Oboe and Flute (as at first) for eight measures. Play the next fourteen measures on the Gt. At the rest in the last measure of the middle brace, on the sixth page, push Sw. 2 and continue on the Gt. for four measures. Play four measures on the Sw. The first six measures of the last page should be played on the Gt. Push Sw. Release during the rests in the L. H. Play the L. H. figure of the next three measures on the Sw. (Oboe and Flute 4 ft.). Put off the Gt. to Ped. and Ped. Gedeckt. Continue the L. H. melody on the Sw., and play the R. H. on the Ch. If the Viol d'Amour is too loud with the swell closed, use only the Dulciana with the swell partly open. As an eight-foot stop is indicated for the next few Ped. notes, play them 8va on the Bourdon, which gives the same effect. At the sixth measure from the end, play both hands on the Sw. with Salicional only. The last two staccato chords are indicated for the Oboe. This stop can be added, or the chords can be played on the Salicional, according to taste. The last two Ped. notes are indicated "16 ft." The Bourdon (*loco*) is satisfactory.

ALFRED HOLLINS, * CONCERT RONDO

Prepare: Gt. Gross Flute and Piston No. 1; Sw. Piston No. 3 and F Sw. Comb. Pedal (open); Ch. Melodia, Gedeckt, Flute 4 ft. and Clarinet (open); So. Philomela, Orchestral Oboe and Flute Ouverte 4 ft.; Ped. First Diapason, Bourdon and Gedeckt; Sw. to Gt. and Sw. to Ped.; Grand Crescendo open full.

Play the first eight measures on the Gt. Close the Grand Crescendo, and play nine measures on the Sw. For the first theme (second page), the solo is indicated " Ch. Flutes and Clarinet," which was prepared at the outset. For the L. H. accompaniment on the Sw., 8 and 4 ft. without Oboe (Sw. 3 after F Sw. Pedal has been put off) is generally satisfactory. If the Clarinet combination of the Ch. is somewhat loud, even with the Ch. swell closed, the F Sw. Pedal can be left on, thus adding the Oboe to the other combination. The staccato Ped. notes on this page are sometimes a problem. The Ped. First Diapason (wood) is frequently too ponderous, even if the notes are played very staccato, and the Second Diapason (metal) is out of the question. Sometimes the Ped. Octave (frequently called " Flute ") can be used with the Bourdon and Gedeckt for these notes. Occasionally the Gt. to Ped., with the Doppel Floete drawn on the Gt., added to the Bourdon and Gedeckt, is a satisfactory combination.

At the rest in the L. H., in the second measure at the bottom of page 2, push Gt. Piston No. 3, play the L. H. chord on the Gt., and put on the Gt. to Ped. (foot). In the next measure, the R. H. should also play on the Gt. At the rest in the last measure of the third brace of page 3, push Gt. Piston No. 1, and add Sw. Cornopean. The following six

---

* This registration is intended specifically for the organ whose specification is given on page 215.

manual changes, which are indicated " III " and " I " (Sw. and Ch.), can be followed, after the Clarinet has been put off. There is a little more decided character in the Flutes (8 and 4 ft.) on the Gt. than in the corresponding stops on the Ch., hence I suggest the substitution of Gt. for Ch. (after the Sw. to Gt. Coupler has been put off) for these six changes. The Ped. First Diapason (or the Gt. to Ped., if it is on) must be put off before the short Ped. notes are played. At the fifth measure of the second brace of page 4, with the R. H. on the Sw., the L. H. can draw the Clarinet (if it has been put off). The next eight measures of the L. H. are indicated for the Ch. A little variety is obtained by playing this L. H. passage on the So. as prepared at the outset. At the rest in the second measure at the bottom of page 4, push Gt. 3, add FF Sw. (pedal), and Sw. to Gt. Play the L. H. on the Gt. and the R. H. on the Sw. for the following four measures. Play four measures on the Sw. At the end of the upper brace of page 5, add F Gt. (pedal) and Gt. to Ped. Play the balance of the page with both hands on the Gt. At the rest at the end of the page, the Pedal Release throws off both combination pedals at once, leaving on Gt. Piston No. 3 for the next page. Play both hands on the Gt. At the third measure of the third brace on page 6, push Gt. Piston No. 2, and add Sw. Oboe (if it is not already on). Play both hands on the Sw. Put off the Gt. to Ped. (foot) during the rests in the Ped. part. At the rest in the second measure at the bottom of the page, push Gt. 3, draw Gt. to Ped. (foot), and play both hands on the Gt. for six measures. Play two measures on the Sw. and two measures on the Gt. Push Sw. Piston No. 3, put off the Gt. to Ped., and play two measures on the Sw. to the holds.

The next passage is a return of the first theme. This can be played as at first, or, for the sake of a little variety, one can add the So. to Ch. coupler, the Ped. First Diapason, and open the Sw. swell. These additions make the solo and accompaniment a little stronger than at first. Play the R. H. solo on the Ch. and the L. H. accompaniment on the Sw. In the last measure at the top of page 8, add F Gt. (pedal) and the Gt. to Ped. At the beginning of the second brace, play both hands on the Gt. as far as the double bar at the top of page 9.

Before playing the following middle section (in E-flat), release all combinations by the Pedal Release and the General Release (00); put off Sw. to Gt., Sw. and Gt. to Ped. and Ped. First Diapason; and draw Sw. Vox Humana, Voix Céleste, and Oboe. Play both hands on the Sw. (closed). At the rest at the end of page 9, prepare Gt. Doppel Floete only. On page 10, play the R. H. obligato on the Gt. and the L. H. chords on the Sw. The Flauto Traverso 4 ft. can be added to the Sw. combination if desired. For the last two measures of the page, add Sw. Piston No. 2, and play both hands on the Sw. as indicated. For the diminuendo at the top of page 11, put off the Oboe and Vox Humana during the rest (L. H.). At the rests during the *ritard*, in the first measure of the second brace, draw Sw. to Gt. and Sw. to Ped. Before playing the second measure, push Gt. 3, and put on FF Sw. (pedal). Play the R. H. on the Gt. and the L. H. on the Sw. In the third brace, draw the Gt. to Ped., and play both hands on the Gt. At the last measure of the brace (*sempre Cresc.*), add F Gt. (pedal). In the third brace of page 12, gradually open the Sw. swell. In the lower brace gradually open the Grand Crescendo to full on the last chord. While holding this chord, release F Gt. pedal, put off Gt. to Ped., and close the Sw. swell. After the chord, close the Grand Crescendo, put on So. Piston No. 3 and Gt. to So. Coupler. At the top of page 13, play the R. H. on the Gt. (Piston No. 3 being on) and the L. H. on the Sw. (FF Sw.). At the fourth measure of the second brace, push Whole Organ Piston No. 2 and play both hands on the Gt. Gradually open all the swells. At the top of page 14, put on FF Gt. (pedal), and play R. H. on the Gt. and L. H. on the So. In the middle brace (second measure), play both hands on the Gt. In the lower brace and at the top of the last page, alternate between the So. ("IV") and the Gt. ("II"), as indicated. At the third measure of the middle brace (last page), put on the Sfz.

In playing a composition of the character of this Rondo on various four-manual organs, even if each organ has about the same specification as the organ which we are now considering, quite a number of modifications of the indicated registration are often necessary, in order to obtain the intended effects. As I have stated several times in previous chapters, these modifications are due partly to the voicing of the different organs, and partly to the effect on the tone of the organs which is caused by a difference of location. For example, the combination which I have suggested for the R. H. solo, on the second page of this composition (Ch. Melodia, Gedeckt, Flute 4 ft. and Clarinet, with the Ch. swell open), varies in power on different organs. On one organ it may be necessary to have the Ch. swell open wide. On another organ it may be necessary to have the swell nearly closed. In addition, the necessary power for the L. H. accompaniment cannot always be obtained by the combination suggested (Sw. 8 and 4 ft. without reeds). If the Oboe is added and the swell opened slightly, the balance of power between the solo and accompaniment may be satisfactory on one organ, while on another organ it is necessary to omit the Oboe and have the swell closed entirely. The composer has indicated the Sw. to Ch. coupler in addition to the stops in the Ch. for the solo. This coupler strengthens the combination of the solo and insures a balance of power between the combinations of the solo and the accompaniment, but it modifies the tone-quality of the solo combination, and reduces the contrast between the solo and the accompaniment combinations.

Later in the composition, I have suggested the addition of the So. to Ch. coupler, which adds the Philomela, Orchestral Oboe and Flute 4 ft. (prepared at the outset). On some organs these stops are too loud to be added to the Ch. combination, even if the So. swell is closed. Either the Philomela or the Flute 4 ft. can be omitted. Various other modifications of the registration may be necessary, but from the above suggestions the student can get an idea of how the modifications are effected to meet the conditions.

CHAPTER XXII

REGISTRATION ON FOUR-MANUAL ORGANS
(with movable combinations)

THE organ whose specification was given on page 215 had combination pistons and pedals of the non-movable type. If an organ with exactly the same list of stops and couplers has combination pistons of the movable type, quite a different method of procedure is necessary in order to obtain the specified effects in the registration of various organ compositions. To illustrate this difference of procedure, we will consider an organ with the following specifications:—

SPECIFICATION OF A FOUR-MANUAL ORGAN, NO. 2

All the speaking stops and couplers to be the same as those given in the preceding specification (page 215).

ADJUSTABLE COMBINATION PISTONS, THIRTY-FOUR
(movable)

Six for Great and Pedal
Eight for Swell and Pedal
Four for Choir and Pedal
Three for the Solo with Neutral Pedal

Three for Echo and Pedal
Five for Pedal alone
Five for the Whole Organ

(Note: No releases are necessary when the combination pistons are of the movable type.)

PEDAL MOVEMENTS, SIX

Sfz Pedal (Full Organ with all Couplers)
Grand Crescendo (Full Organ without
    Tuba and Octave Couplers)
Great to Pedal (reversible)
Crescendo Pedal for the Swell
Crescendo Pedal for the Choir
Crescendo Pedal for the Solo and Echo

As there are no combination pedals on this organ, and the combination pistons are of the movable type, it is advisable to adjust the combinations of the pistons on a different plan from that of the preceding organ, as follows:—

Gt.   No. 1.   Stops Nos. 6 and 9 with Ped. Bourdon (No. 67).
Gt.   No. 2.   Stops Nos. 5-9 with Ped. stops Nos. 67 and 72.

Gt.	No. 3.	Stops Nos. 3-9 with Ped. stops Nos. 66, 67, 72 and 73.

Gt. No. 3. Stops Nos. 3-9 with Ped. stops Nos. 66, 67, 72 and 73.

Gt. No. 4. (F Gt.) Gt. to Octave (stops Nos. 1-10) with Ped. stops Nos. 64-67, 70, 72 and 73.

Gt. No. 5. Full to Fifteenth (stops Nos. 1-12) with Ped. stops Nos. 64-67, 70, 72 and 73.

Gt. No. 6. (FF Gt.) Full Gt. with all Ped. stops except the reeds (Nos. 75-77).

Sw. No. 1. Gedeckt and Salicional (stops Nos. 21 and 22).

Sw. No. 2. Gedeckt, Salicional, Flute 4 ft. and Violina (stops Nos. 21, 22, 25 and 26) with Ped. stop No. 67.

Sw. No. 3. Stops Nos. 16, 17, 20-23, 25 and 26, with Ped. stops Nos. 67 and 72.

Sw. No. 4. (F Sw.) 8 and 4 ft. with Oboe (stops Nos. 16-18, 20-26) with Ped. stops Nos. 67 and 72.

Sw. No. 5. Special combination to be adjusted when desired.

Sw. No. 6. Reeds (stops Nos. 30 and 31) and stops Nos. 18, 20-22, 25 and 26, with Ped. stops Nos. 66, 67, 70 and 72.

Sw. No. 7. (FF Sw.) Full Sw. with Ped. stops Nos. 66-68, 70 and 72.

Sw. No. 8. Full Sw. and Sw. to Sw. 16 and 4 ft. Couplers with Ped. stops Nos. 66-68, 70 and 72.

Ch. No. 1. Stops Nos. 35 and 38, with Ped. stop No. 67.

Ch. No. 2. Stops Nos. 35, 36 and 42 with Ped. stop No. 67.

Ch. No. 3. Stops Nos. 34-36, 38, 39 and 42 with Ped. stops Nos. 67 and 72.

Ch. No. 4. Stops Nos. 33-36, 38, 39, 42-44 with Ped. stops Nos. 66-68 and 72.

So. No. 1. Stops Nos. 48 and 51.

So. No. 2. Stops Nos. 47-49 and 51.

So. No. 3. Stops Nos. 47-49, 51 and 52.

Echo No. 1. Stops Nos. 56 and 57 with Ped. Echo Bourdon (No. 69).

Echo No. 2. Stops Nos. 58 and 59 with Ped. Echo Bourdon (No. 69).

Echo No. 3. Stops Nos. 56 and 60 with Ped. Echo Bourdon (No. 69).

Ped. No. 1. Bourdon and Gedeckt (Nos. 67 and 72).

Ped. No. 2. Stops Nos. 66, 67, 70 and 72.

Ped. No. 3. Stops Nos. 64-67, 70 and 72.

Ped. No. 4. Full without reeds (stops Nos. 62-68, 70-73).

Ped. No. 5. Full Ped. (stops Nos. 62-67, 70-77).

Whole Organ No. 1. All Diapasons and Flutes (stops Nos. 1-6, 9, 15-17, 21, 22, 25, 34-36, 42, 47, 48, 51, 62-67, 70-72); Couplers, So., Gt., Sw., and Ch. to Ped.; So., Sw., and Ch. to Gt.; Sw., and Ch. to Gt. 16 ft.

Whole Organ No. 2. Gt. to Octave, Full Sw., Ped. stops Nos. 63-68, 70, and 72; Couplers, Sw. to Gt., Sw. and Gt. to Ped.

Whole Organ No. 3. Gt. to Octave, Full Sw., So. stops Nos. 47-49, 51, Ped. stops Nos. 63-68, 70-73; Couplers, Sw. and So. to Gt., Sw. to Gt. 16 and 4 ft., Gt., Sw., and So. to Ped.

Whole Organ No. 4.　To be adjusted for any special combination as
　　　　　　　　　　desired.
Whole Organ No. 5.　To be adjusted for any special combination as
　　　　　　　　　　desired.

SIX ORGAN COMPOSITIONS

For which registration is suggested for the above four-manual organ

L. Boëllmann	Suite Gothique
F. de la Tombelle	Pastorale in E
César Franck	Finale in B-Flat
Edwin H. Lemare	Romance in D-Flat
Tertius Noble	Solemn Prelude
Ch. M. Widor	Fifth Organ Symphony

L. BOËLLMANN, * SUITE GOTHIQUE

I. INTRODUCTION

Prepare: Sw. Piston No. 2 (swell partly open); Gt. Piston No. 3;
Ech. Viol Céleste, Wald Floete, Tremolo and Ech. to Ech. 16 ft.; Ped.
Second Diapason, Violone, Bourdon and Gedeckt; Sw. to Gt. and Gt. to
Ped.; Grand Crescendo open full.

After playing the first eight measures on the Gt., close the Grand
Crescendo and play eight measures on the Ech. If this effect, which
on some organs sounds like a large organ heard at a great distance,
is not to the taste of the performer, he can play the phrase on the Sw.
as prepared. In this Introduction, open the Grand Crescendo for each
FF phrase and close it for each P phrase. Play the last four measures
(*rall*) of the Introduction on the Sw., gradually closing the swell.

II. MENUET

Push Sw. Piston No. 4 and Gt. Piston No. 3. (Note: It is necessary
to push Gt. Piston No. 3 to restore the desired Ped. stops which are put
off by Sw. Piston No. 4.) Follow the manual indications (Sw. and Gt.).
At the bottom of page 5 (*A Tempo*) push Gt. 4. In the third measure
at the top of page 6 (" Sw. PP "), push Sw. 3. In the second brace,
before playing on the Gt., it is necessary to push Gt. 4 to restore the
Ped. stops which are put off by Sw. 3. In the first measure at the top
of page 7, push Sw. 2. In the fifth measure, before playing on the Gt.,
it is necessary to push Gt. 4 again. At the second measure of the
second brace, push Sw. 4. At the sixth measure, push Gt. 4 again. At
the third measure of the third brace, open the Grand Crescendo full,
but continue on the Sw. Gradually open the swell in the upper brace
of page 8. In the fifth measure play both hands on the Gt. to the
end.

---

* This registration is intended specifically for the organ whose specification is
given on page 228.

III. Prière à Notre Dame

Prepare: Sw. Voix Céleste and Gedeckt; Ch. Melodia and Viol d'Amour; Ech. Vox Humana and Lieblich Gedeckt; Ped. Bourdon and Sw. to Ped.

Play the first sixteen measures on the Sw. All the gradations of power which are indicated should be obtained solely by means of the swell pedal. At the double bar (*Animato*), add the Ch. to Ped. and play on the Ch. At the last count of the third brace on page 11, play the L. H. on the Sw., and continue the R. H. on the Ch. At the last measure of the upper brace of page 12 (*1° Tempo*), put off the Sw. and Ch. to Ped., the Ped. Bourdon, and draw the Echo Bourdon on the Ped. These changes can be made while playing the last three counts with the L. H. alone. Play both hands on the Ech. At one of the rests in the second brace, prepare Sw. Gedeckt only. At the last measure of the brace, play the R. H. on the Sw. (partly open) and the L. H. on the Ech. In the third measure, at the note G in the R. H., play both hands on the Ech. In the last two measures, play the L. H. on the Sw. (closed). If the use of the Ech. is not to the taste of the performer, the Vox Humana and Gedeckt of the Sw. can be substituted.

IV. Toccata

Prepare: Ch. Piston No. 3; Sw. Piston No. 7; Gt. Piston No. 3 (pushed last); Ped. as prepared by the Gt. Piston; Sw. to Gt., Ch. and Sw. to Ped. (The Sw. to Ch. and Ch. to Gt. Couplers are indicated in the printed copies. These can be drawn at the outset if desired.)

Follow all the manual indications. Put on the Gt. to Ped. (foot) while the Ped. is silent on page 15, and put it off again at the rest in the second measure of the second brace on page 16. Put on the Gt. to Ped. (foot) at any point during the upper two braces of page 18. At the top of page 19, gradually open the swells, and push Gt. 4 on the D-flat in the third measure. At the last measure of this page, open the Grand Crescendo full. For the last two measures use the Sfz.

F. de la Tombelle, * Pastorale in E

Prepare: Gt. Gross Flute, Doppel Floete and Flute 4 ft.; Sw. Oboe Voix Céleste, Flute 4 ft. and Tremolo (closed); Ch. Gedeckt (closed); So. Philomela (open); Ped. Bourdon and Gedeckt; No Couplers. Adjust Whole Organ Piston No. 4 as follows: Gt. Gross Flute, Doppel Floete and Flute 4 ft.; Sw. Cornopean, Oboe, Salicional, Gedeckt and Flute 4 ft.; Ch. Melodia, Gedeckt, Flute 4 ft. and Clarinet; So. Philomela; Ped. Bourdon and Gedeckt.

Play the first four measures on the Ch. (If there is no Gedeckt in the Ch., practically the same effect can be secured by playing an octave lower on the Flute d'Amour.) At the fifth measure, put off the Ch.

* This registration is intended specifically for the organ whose specification is given on page 228.

Gedeckt and draw the Viol d'Amour. Play the solo (R. H.) on the Sw. and the accompaniment on the Ch. If the Viol d'Amour, with the Ch. swell closed, is too loud and stringy, use the Dulciana with the Ch. swell partly open. At the last count of the 28th measure, push Ch. 3, and play both hands on the Ch. for five measures. Push Gt. 2, draw the Gt. to Ped., and play four measures on the Gt. Push Gt. 3, and continue on the Gt. At the rest in measure 46, push Gt. 2, and continue on the Gt. At measure 50, push Gt. 1, and continue on the Gt. At the rest in measure 52, put off the Gt. to Ped., push Ch. 1, and play both hands on the Ch. While prolonging the last note in the L. H. in measure 56, add Ped. Gedeckt (which was put off by Ch. 1), put off the Ch. Melodia, and play on the Sw. and Ch. as at first. At the end of the first section, play the long notes (G-sharp and E) in the L. H. on the So. While sustaining the second note, close the So. swell, and push Whole Organ Piston No. 4, which was adjusted at the outset especially for the following middle section.

Play all the staccato notes and chords on the Sw., and the two sustained notes (E) on the So. for twelve measures. Continue the L. H. staccato chords on the Sw., and play the R. H. solo on the Ch. for six measures. Play the next R. H. solo on the Gt. for three measures, and return to the Ch. for three measures. At this point (twenty-fifth measure after the change of key to A-minor), push Gt. 2, and play the R. H. on the Sw. and the L. H. on the Gt. for three measures. Play three measures with both hands on the Sw.; three measures with the L. H. on the Gt. and the R. H. on the Sw.; and three measures with both hands on the Sw. Push Gt. 1 and Ped. 1. Play the R. H. on the Gt. and the L. H. on the Sw. for six measures. Play four solo notes (R. H.) on the Ch.; two short chords on the Sw.; four solo notes (R. H.) on the Ch.; and two short chords on the Sw. Continue both hands on the Sw. for four measures. Play four solo notes (L. H.) on the Ch.; two staccato chords (R. H.) on the Sw.; four solo notes (L. H.) on the Ch.; and two staccato chords (R. H.) on the Sw. While playing the following seven solo notes (L. H.) on the Ch., push Gt. 2. At the 1° *tempo* play the R. H. on the Sw. and the L. H. on the Gt. for six measures; the R. H. solo on the Ch. and the L. H. chords on the Sw. for three measures; and both hands on the Sw. for three measures. The following four solo notes (R. H.) are effective when played on the So. (Philomela) with the swell closed. Play the two staccato thirds on the Sw., and the six solo notes (R. H.) on the So. Push Ch. 1, and play both hands on the Ch., with the swell open for one measure and closed for two measures, to the hold over the note A. Play the next two measures (*molto rit.*) on the Ch. Gedeckt as at first. While sustaining the A-sharp (R. H.), prepare Sw. Vox Humana, Voix Céleste, Flute 4 ft., Sw. to Sw. 16 ft. Coupler, and Ped. Bourdon and Gedeckt. Before resuming, prepare Ch. Dulciana (or Unda Maris) alone, with the Ch. swell partly open. Play the R. H. solo on the Sw. and the accompaniment on the Ch. At the rest (R. H.), fifteen measures before the end, put off the Sw. to Sw. 16 ft. Coupler. Play the last two chords on the Sw. Æoline and Ped. Lieblich Bourdon.

CÉSAR FRANCK, * FINALE IN B-FLAT

Prepare: Sw. Piston No. 7 (open); Ch. Piston No. 2 with Clarinet (open); Gt. Piston No. 4 (pushed last); Ped. prepared by Gt. Piston No. 4; Sw. to Gt., Sw. and Gt. to Ped.

After the long Ped. solo, play both hands on the Sw. (with *dim.*) for five measures. The R. H. solo in the next seven measures can be played on the Ch., or both hands can be played on the Sw. At the top of page 4, play both hands on the Sw. Gradually open the swell to the Ped. solo. After the Ped. solo, play both hands on the Sw. (with *dim.*) for five measures. Play the R. H. solo on the Ch. for three measures. Continue both hands on the Sw. At the top of page 6, play both hands on the Gt. At the third measure at the top of page 8, push Gt. 3 and Sw. 4. In the next measure, push Gt. 2. At the third measure at the top of page 9, push Ch. 2, and play both hands on the Ch. Put off the Gt. to Ped. while playing. After eight measures played on the Ch., play both hands on the Sw. (closed). At the top of page 11, play the R. H. on the Ch. and the L. H. on the Sw. At the rest in the second measure of the lower brace, push Ch. 3 and Gt. 3. Continue both hands on the Sw. At the bottom of page 12, play the L. H. on the Gt. and the R. H. on the Ch. (open). At the end of the upper brace of page 13, close the Ch. swell part way. In the lower brace, open the Ch. swell, and play the R. H. on the Gt. in the third measure. In the last measure, push Whole Organ Piston No. 2. Play the last chord of the page (R. H.) on the Ch. In the upper brace of page 14, play the second measure with both hands on the Gt. At the bottom of page 17, while holding the long B-flat (Ped.) push Whole Organ Piston No. 3. In the last measure of page 19, open the Grand Crescendo full. For the last four chords the Sfz can be used (*ad lib.*).

EDWIN H. LEMARE, * ROMANCE IN D-FLAT

Prepare: Gt. Harmonic Flute 4 ft.; Sw. Voix Céleste and Flute 4 ft. (closed); Ch. Melodia, Gedeckt, and Viol d'Amour (open); So. Flute Ouverte 4 ft. and Tremolo (closed); Ped. Bourdon, Gedeckt and First Diapason (?); Sw. to Gt.

The Ped. combination for the staccato Ped. notes is a problem on many organs. The Ped. Diapason (wood) is frequently too ponderous for these notes. Sometimes the Bourdon, Gedeckt and Octave (or Flute) is a better combination. If the Ped. combination is heavy, the notes must be played extremely staccato. Play the first page with both hands on the Sw. At the top of the second page, add Sw. Bourdon, and play the L. H. on the Gt. At the bottom of the page, push Sw. 3 (which changes the combination to 8 and 4 ft. without reed or Voix Céleste), and substitute the Doppel Floete for the Har. Flute in the Gt. (The Sw. Piston puts off the heavy Ped. stops.) The L. H. imitations should be played on the Ch., the other measures (L. H.) on the Sw. At the

* This registration is intended specifically for the organ whose specification is given on page 228.

end of the third brace of page 3, add the Vox Humana as indicated, and put on the Gt. to Ped. to give prominence to the Ped. imitation. At the end of the middle brace of page 4, put off the Gt. to Ped. At the rest in the last measure of the page, push Sw. 2. At the *Tempo Primo* on page 5, add the Voix Céleste and Vox Humana in the Sw. Play the R. H. on the Sw. and the L. H. on the So. For the double Ped. at the bottom of the page, add the Gt. to Ped. (*ad lib.*). In the last half of the third measure at the top of page 6, put off the Gt. to Ped. Just before playing the first measure of the middle brace, add Ped. First Diapason. Play the R. H. on the Sw. and the L. H. either on the Gt. or the So. an octave lower. Before playing the last two notes of the page, push Ped. Piston No. 1 (which puts off the Ped. Diapason), and put off the Voix Céleste, Salicional and Violina in the Sw. (leaving Vox Humana, Gedeckt, and Flute 4 ft.). (Note: For this passage, Whole Organ Piston No. 4 can be adjusted, at the outset, to give Sw. Vox Humana, Gedeckt and Flute 4 ft., Gt. Flute 4 ft., and Ped. Bourdon; in which event the L. H. imitation can be played on the Gt.) For the " Flute 4 ft." imitation (L. H.) at the top of the last page, play on the So. (closed). In the middle brace, add Ped. Contra Bourdon 32 ft. Sometimes the Double Diapason 32 ft. is effective here. For the last two measures, use the Æoline and Ped. Lieblich Bourdon.

T. TERTIUS NOBLE, * SOLEMN PRELUDE

Prepare: Gt. Gamba and Flute 4 ft.; Sw. Voix Céleste (closed); Ch. Viol d'Amour; So. Flute Ouverte 4 ft. (closed); Ped. Bourdon 16 ft. and Contra Bourdon 32 ft.; Sw. to Ch. and Sw. to Gt. For special use in the last page, adjust Whole Organ Piston No. 5 as follows: Gt. Doppel Floete; Sw. Voix Céleste; Ch. Melodia and Flute 4 ft.; So. Orchestral Oboe; Ped. Contra Bourdon 32 ft. and Bourdon 16 ft.

Play the first four measures on the Ch. (with Sw. to Ch. as prepared). Play the next four measures with the R. H. on the Sw. and the L. H. on the So. (an octave lower, as the stop is a 4 ft. stop). If the Philomela is somewhat soft (with the swell closed), it can be used (*loco*) in place of the Flute Ouverte 4 ft. The next eight measures should be played on the same manuals as the first eight measures. With the entrance of the Ped. in the third brace, push So. Piston No. 2, and draw Gt. to So. Coupler. Play the L. H. on the Ch. and the R. H. on the Sw. Four measures later (*A Tempo*), play both hands on the Ch. Before playing the second measure at the top of page 3, push Ped. Piston No. 1 (to put off the Contra Bourdon and add the Gedeckt). Play both hands on the Gt. Gradually open the swells of the Sw. and So., and open the Grand Crescendo about three-fourths. Be careful not to open it far enough to bring on the So. to Gt. Coupler.

In the first measure of the second brace, push Gt. 6. In the second measure, play the L. H. on the So. and the R. H. on the Gt. At the last measure of the third brace, push Gt. 4, and play both hands on the

Gt. During any one of the rests in the L. H., push Sw. 3, and add Ch. Clarinet and Flute 4 ft. for future use. For the first measure at the top of page 4, open the Grand Crescendo full. Close it again in the second measure. Push Gt. 1 at the end of the third measure. Play the fourth measure with the R. H. on the Sw. and the L. H. on the Ch. (The Gt. to Ped. has not been drawn at any time, as it has been controlled satisfactorily by the Grand Crescendo.) In the second measure of the second brace, play both hands on the Sw. While playing the third measure with the R. H. alone, prepare (L. H.) So. Philomela with So. to So. 16 and 4 ft. Couplers, and add Ped. Contra Bourdon 32 ft. In the third brace play four measures on the So. as indicated. This effect is not always satisfactory, in which case omit the couplers. In one of these measures put off the Sw. to Gt. and Sw. to Ch. At the *A Tempo*, push Whole Organ Piston No. 5, which was especially prepared for this passage at the outset. Play both hands on the Sw. for four measures; then the R. H. on the Sw. and the L. H. on the Ch. In the third measure at the top of the last page, play the L. H. on the Sw. and the R. H. on the So. The imitations indicated for the Oboe and Flute can be obtained by alternating between the So. and the Gt., as the desired stops were brought on by Whole Organ Piston No. 5 (adjusted at the outset). At the second measure of the second brace, play the R. H. on the Ch. and the L. H. on the Gt. These two manuals were also prepared by the Whole Organ Piston. At the beginning of the lower brace, put off the Ch. Flute d'Amour, and play the R. H. on the Ch. and the L. H. on the Sw. At the last count of the second measure, reverse the hands (the R. H. on the Sw. and the L. H. on the Ch.). Between the octaves (B-flat) of the L. H., put off the Sw. Flute 4 ft. and Ped. Gedeckt. Play the last measure with both hands on the Sw.

Сн. M. Widor, * Symphony No. 5

I. Allegro Vivace

Adjust Sw. Piston No. 5 for the following special combination: Bourdon, Hohl Floete, Gedeckt, Sw. to Sw. 4 ft. and Ped. Bourdon and Gedeckt.

Prepare: Gt. No stops at the outset; Sw. Full (Piston No. 7), (open); Ch. Piston No. 3; Ped. (prepared by Sw. Piston No. 7); Sw. to Gt. and Sw. to Ped.

Play the first sixteen measures (as indicated) on the Sw., the next eight measures on the Ch., and the following eight measures (to the double bar) on the Sw. Push Gt. 3 and draw Gt. to Ped. After four measures played on the Gt., put off the Gt. to Ped., and play on the Sw. until the second double bar. Repeat the eight measures in the same manner. After the repeat, push Sw. 4, which reduces to 8 and 4 ft. with Oboe. Play both hands on the Sw. until the last count of the second brace on page 5; then play the L. H. on the Ch. and the R. H. on the Sw. for three measures. Play the following two measures with both hands on the Sw., and three measures with the L. H. on the Ch. and the R. H. on the Sw. Continue with both hands on the Sw. until one measure before the double bar at the top of page 6. In this measure, play the L. H. on the Ch., and push Sw. 7. Continue with both hands on the Sw. until the last count of the second measure of the third brace (page 6). Push Gt. 3, draw Gt. to Ped., and play both hands on the Gt. At the *A tempo* at the bottom of the page, play the L. H. on the Gt. and the R. H. on the Sw. At the *A tempo* in the second brace of page 7, put off the Gt. to Ped., push Sw. 7, and play both hands on the Sw. At the last count of the second measure of the fourth brace, play both hands on the Gt. Before playing at the top of page 8, push Sw. 5, which was adjusted, at the outset, for a special combination of 16, 8, and 4 ft. Flute-tone, for this passage. Play the L. H. on the Ch. and the R. H. on the Sw. At the last count of the last measure of the third brace, play the R. H. on the Ch. and the L. H. on the Sw. At the last count of the first measure of the lower brace, play the L. H. on the Ch. and the R. H. on the Sw. Continue in this manner until the double bar in the middle of page 10. Push Whole Organ Piston No. 1, which gives a combination of Diapasons and Flutes, and play on the Gt. After the hold in the third measure of the third brace of page 11, push Sw. 5, and play both hands on the Sw. For the one measure of Ped. solo, push Ped. 3. For the next five measures (indicated " Sw. Reeds "), push Sw. 6. Before playing the last Ped. note of the page, push Ped. 3. After the Ped. notes in the first measure at the top of page 12, push Gt. 3, and play the L. H. on the Gt. and the R. H. on the Sw. Draw the Gt. to Ped., and play both hands on the Gt. in the second brace. The last chord (R. H.) of the brace should be played on the Sw., and the L. H. part of the third brace should be played on the Gt., similar to the first brace. The fourth brace should be played similar to the second brace, and the fifth brace similar to the third brace. At the top of page 13, play both hands on the Gt. At the second measure of the fourth brace, push Sw. 7 and Gt. 3 (the latter to restore the heavy Ped. stops which are put off by Sw. 7). Gradually open the swell, and, in the first measure of the second brace of page 14, open the Grand Crescendo full. After the chord in the last measure of the third brace, close the Grand Crescendo. At the last count of the upper brace on page 15, push Sw. 4 and Gt. 3 (the latter to restore the heavy Ped. stops which are put off by Sw. 4). At the last count of the second measure of the third brace, push Gt. 2. At the last count of the fourth brace, put off the Gt. to Ped., and play both hands on the Sw. At the last count of the first measure at the top of page 16, push Gt. 3, draw Gt. to Ped. (foot), and play on the Gt. Gradually open the Grand Crescendo to full at the double bar in the second brace.

II. ALLEGRO CANTABILE

Prepare: Gt. Gross Flute; Sw. Oboe, Cornopean, Voix Céleste, Gedeckt and Flute 4 ft. (closed) ; Ch. Melodia and Flute 4 ft. (closed) ; So. Philomela (closed) ; Ped. Bourdon and Gedeckt; Ch. to Ped. (*ad lib.*).

Play the first brace (L. H.) on the So. While holding the last note (C), change to the Ch. Play the R. H. solo on the Sw. At the last note of the middle brace of page 19, play both hands on the Gt. (The L. H. is indicated for the Ch., but more variety can be obtained by playing this part on the Gt.) Play the last note of the page (R. H.) on the Sw., and at the top of page 20, play the L. H. on the Ch. The counter-melody for the R. H. thumb on this page must, of course, be played on the Gt. In the middle of the last measure of the third brace, play both hands on the Gt. as indicated. At the double bar in the upper brace of page 21, play the counter-melody with the thumb of the R. H. on the Gt. If the player has a hand of sufficient size, the second and third fingers of the R. H. can also be used in playing this counter-melody. In the second measure of the third brace, play both hands on the Gt. as indicated. In the latter half of the measure before the double bar, at the top of page 22, play the two staves of the L. H. part on the Ch., and the R. H. solo on the Sw. On page 23, the R. H. melody should alternate between the Gt. and Sw. (" G " and " R ") as indicated. The L. H. accompaniment can be played alternately between the Gt. and Ch., as indicated, or all on the Ch. To give due prominence to the Ped. figure in the lower brace, draw the Gt. to Ped. (ad lib.). Put off the Gt. to Ped., and play the last four measures with both hands on the Ch.

In the middle section (page 24), the L. H. sustained chords can be played on the Sw. Voix Céleste or Vox Humana (or both), with the R. H. obligato on a soft 4 ft. Flute (Flute d'Amour); or the L. H. chords can be played on the Ech. Vox Humana and Gedeckt, with the R. H. obligato on the Sw. Flauto Traverso. In either case, the Ped. Bourdon must be used alone. In the lower brace (page 24), the melodic phrases in the Ped. part must be sufficiently prominent. The Gt. to Ped. (put on by the foot) adds the Doppel Floete to the Ped. Bourdon and generally answers. Another plan is to draw the Ped. Gedeckt with the R. H. in the third measure of the third brace. The last note of the previous phrase (R. H.) can be shortened sufficiently for this purpose. At the double bar on page 25, the repeat can be omitted (ad lib.). In the first measure at the bottom of the page (second ending), shorten the R. H. note, push Sw. 4 and Gt. 1, draw Gt. to Ped. and Sw. to Gt. Play both hands on the Gt. The two measures in the first and second braces of page 26 which are indicated " PP " should be played on the Sw. (closed). It is not necessary to put off the Gt. to Ped. In the first half of any measure, push (L. H.) Ch. 3. At the third measure of the third brace, play the R. H. chord on the Sw. and the L. H. figure on the Ch.

In the sixth measure, play both hands on the Gt. In the third measure of the fourth brace, play the R. H. chord on the Sw., the L. H. figure on the Ch., and put off the Gt. to Ped. In the sixth measure, play both hands on the Sw. Put off the Sw. to Gt. (L. H.). In the third measure of the lower brace, play the R. H. chord on the Sw., and the L. H. melody on the Gt. While playing this L. H. melody (twelve measures), push Ch. 1, Ped. 1, and prepare Sw. Oboe, Voix Céleste, Vox Humana, Flute 4 ft. and Sw. to Sw. 16 ft. Coupler. In the next

to the last measure of the upper brace of page 27, play on the Ch. with
molto rit., and prepare Gt. Doppel Floete only. Also arrange the swell
pedals of the Sw. and Ch. to produce a proper balance of power
between the following solo and accompaniment. Play the R. H. solo on
the Sw. In the last measure of the page, play the R. H. on the Gt. and
open the Sw. swell one-third (for future use). At the top of page 28,
play the L. H. on the Gt. (the printed indication for this L. H. is Ch.).
At the end of the third measure in the second brace, play the R. H. on
the Sw. In the following measure, play the L. H. on the Ch. The
counter-melody for the R. H. thumb in the next two braces should be
played on the Gt., as at first. In the latter half of the fourth measure,
in the upper brace of page 29, play both hands on the Gt. In the first
measure of the third brace, play the L. H. on the Ch. and the R. H. on
the Sw. The counter-melody in this and the next brace should be played
as previously. In the last measure of the page, play the R. H. on the Gt.,
and at the top of the following page, play the L. H. on the Gt. In the
first measure of the third brace (page 30), play the L. H. on the Ch.,
close the Sw. swell, and play the R. H. solo on the Sw. In the last three
braces of the last page, the R. H. solo phrases are indicated to alternate
between the Gt. ("G") and Sw. ("R"). The So. Philomela can be
substituted for the Gt. (*ad lib.*). In the lower brace the melodic figure
in the Ped. part is generally of sufficient prominence when played on
the Bourdon and Gedeckt (which are already on). If more prominence
is necessary, the Gt. to Ped. can be put on by the foot. The last five
measures can be played on the Ch. as indicated, with the Melodia alone,
or the last three measures can be played on the Sw. Gedeckt.

III. ANDANTINO QUASI ALLEGRETTO

Prepare: Sw. Piston No. 4 (open) ; Ch. Piston No. 3 (open) ; Gt. Piston
No. 3 (pushed last) ; Ped. (Piston No. 3 on the Gt. provides a suitable
Ped. combination) ; Sw. to Gt., Gt. and Ch. to Ped.
At the end of the Ped. solo, put off the Gt. to Ped., and play on the
Ch. for ten measures. Put on the Gt. to Ped., and play on the Gt. until
the last measure of the second brace on page 33. Put off the Gt. to Ped.,
and push Ch. 3 (to put off the heavy Ped. stops of the Gt. 3). Play the
R. H. on the Gt. and the L. H. on the Sw. for four measures. Play
both hands on the Sw. for ten measures, and the L. H. on the Ch. for
six measures. In the last measure of the page, push Sw. 6 (reeds), and
play both hands on the Sw. (closed). (The Ch. to Ped. with the Ch.
and Ped. stops already on generally produce sufficient power for the
staccato Ped. notes.) In the second measure at the bottom of the page,
push Gt. 3, put on the Gt. to Ped., and play both hands on the Gt. In
the second measure at the top of page 35, gradually open the Grand
Crescendo to full in the fourth measure. During any one of the rests
in the L. H. part, push Gt. 2 and Sw. 6. In the first three measures of
the middle brace, gradually close the Grand Crescendo, and put off
the Gt. to Ped. In the fourth brace, play both hands on the Sw. In the
third measure of the middle brace of page 36, push Gt. 3, draw Gt. to

Ped., and play on the Gt. In the third measure of the fourth brace, gradually open the Grand Crescendo to full (FF). Push Gt. 2 during any one of the L. H. rests. Close the Grand Crescendo and put off the Gt. to Ped. at the top of page 37. In the fourth measure, play the L. H. on the Gt. and the R. H. on the Sw. At the last measure of the second brace, play the L. H. on the Ch.

At the *Tempo 1°* in the fourth brace, play both hands on the Sw. In the third measure at the top of page 38, play the L. H. on the Ch. At the last count of this brace, push Sw. 4, add Gt. to Ped. and play both hands on the Gt. At the last count of the page, push Gt. 1, and put off the Gt. to Ped. At the top of page 39, continue the R. H. on the Gt. and play the L. H. on the Sw. Play the last two measures of this brace with both hands on the Sw. In the second brace, play the L. H. on the Ch. and the R. H. on the Sw. In the middle brace, play both hands on the Sw. During the rest in the fifth measure of this brace, push Ch. 2. In the last measure, and in the following brace, play both hands on the Ch. Play the last two measures on the Sw. Use Sw. 2 for one measure and Sw. 1 for the last measure.

IV. Adagio

Prepare: Gt. Harmonic Flute 4 ft.; Sw. Voix Céleste; Ped. No stops; Gt. to Ped.

Play both hands on the Sw. The Ped. part is indicated for a 4 ft. Flute solo stop. If the Flute in the Gt. is not loud enough, one can use the Ch. Flute d'Amour (swell open) and Ch. to Ped. in addition to the Gt. Flute; or one can use the So. Flute Ouverte 4 ft. (open) with to So. to Ped. All the dynamics of this movement are intended to be controlled by the Sw. swell pedal. If the individual Voix Céleste is ineffective, the Gedeckt, Flute 4 ft. or Vox Humana can be added. At the beginning of the fourth brace of page 41, draw the Sw. to Ped. Put it off in the middle of the next to the last measure of the lower brace. Use the Æoline for the last three chords.

V. Toccata

Prepare: Sw. Piston No. 7 (open); Ch. Piston No. 3 (open); Gt. Piston No. 4 (pushed last); Ped. Suitable stops are brought on by Gt. 4; Sw. to Gt. and Sw. to Ch., Gt. and Sw. to Ped., Grand Crescendo open full.

Play the first three pages on the Gt. (" FFF "). At the last measure of the upper brace of page 45, close the Grand Crescendo and continue on the Gt. At the second measure of the second brace on page 46, play on the Ch. (the Sw. is coupled). Gradually close the Ch. and Sw. swells. At the double bar play on the Sw. At the top of page 48, gradually open the Sw. swell and open the Grand Crescendo full. (As Full Sw. is on, opening the Grand Crescendo does not affect the Sw.) At the double bar, play both hands on the Gt. The indication for four braces of the last page is R. H. on the Gt. and the L. H. on the Ch.

with the Sw. coupled. Frequently the L. H. part, if played on the Ch., is much too soft. There are two other methods of playing these braces; viz., Draw the Sw. to Sw. 4 ft. and 16 ft. Couplers during a convenient rest, and play the L. H. on the Sw. The Sw. Couplers generally do not act through the Sw. to Gt., hence the Sw. is much strengthened without any addition to the Gt. The second method for these four braces is to play both hands on the Gt., with the hands crossed. Occasionally, the latter method is the only possible way to preserve the relative power between the two parts. For the last three measures, use the Sfz (*ad lib.*).

INDEX AND GLOSSARY

INDEX AND GLOSSARY

A

C

Gt. }
Great } The principal manual with the wind-chest and pipes which belong
Great Organ } to it.
Great Mixture IV Rks 16
Gross Floete (Ger.). }
Gross Flute } 43
Grosse Flûte (Fr.). }
Gross Gamba. A powerful Gamba.
Grooved. An old-fashioned method of connecting part of one stop for an omitted part of another stop.
Ground Tone. Fundamental tone.
Gt. to Oct. All the 8 and 4 ft. flue stops of the Gt., frequently including a soft 16 ft. stop.
Gt. to Op. Diapason. Includes all the 8 ft. flue stops of the Gt.
Gt. to Fifteenth. All the stops of the Gt. except the Reeds and Mixtures.
Gt. to Ped. }
Gt. to Pedal } The Coupler that couples the Gt. to the Ped.
Guilmant, Felix Alexandre, Registration of:
    Elevation in A-flat..151, 155
    First Offertoire on Christmas Hymns................................. 211
    Marche Religieuse 205
    Sonata in D-minor, No. 1... 176

H

Half-stopped Pipes. Stopped pipes with a hole through the stopper.
Half Stops. In old organs certain stops contained pipes for only half of their compass.
Harmonia Ætheria. A soft three-rank Mixture sounding the 10th, 12th, and 15th.
Harmonic Clarion 4 ft. A Clarion with pipes of double length (in the treble) which are caused to sound the octave.
Harmonic Flute 44
Harmonic Pipes 17
Harmonics (Overtones, Upper Partials).............................. 22
Harmonic Series 22
Harmonic Stops 20
Harmonic Tuba. A Tuba with pipes of double length (in the treble) sounding the octave.
Harp (Celesta)...15, 58
Hautbois }
Hautboy } Oboe.
H. M. }
H. W. }
Hptm. }
Hptw. } (Ger.). Great Organ................................. 104
Hauptmanual }
Hauptwerk }
Helper. A stop which is planned or is used to assist the speech of another stop.
Hohl Floete }
Hole Flute } 41
Hollins, Alfred, Registration of:
    Concert Rondo.. 225
    Grand Choeur in G-minor.. 199
    Spring Song.. 167
Hopkins, John, Registration of "O Saviour of the World"................. 126
Horn 19
Huit (Fr.). Eight.

I

Id. (Fr.). Ditto.
Immovable Combinations (Non-Movable Combinations)..................... 77
Incomplete Stops. Stops of which the pipes of the lower or upper octave are omitted.
Indicating the Registration.. 104
Influence (Acoustical) of the Overtones..........................24-27, 29, 34
Influence of the Overtones Illustrated............................... 27-30
Interference (Sympathy) of Vibrations, the Effect of...................... 34
Inverted, Conical, Metal Pipes.. 49
Inverted Lip. See Melodia.

J

Jeu (Fr.). Stop.
Jeu au Clochette (Fr.). A 1 ft. stop.
Jeu Douce }
Jeux Doux } (Fr.). Soft stops.
Jeu Expressif (Fr.). Stops whose pipes are enclosed in a swell-box.

PAGE

Jeux d'Anches (Fr.). Reed stops.
Jeux de Detail (Fr.). Solo stops.
Jeux de Fonds (Fr.). Foundation stops.
Jouez une octave plus haut (Fr.). Play an octave higher.

K

Keraulophon 38
Kinder, Ralph, Registration of Festival March............................ 188
Klarinette (obsolete). Clarinet.
Kleine Erzahler 55
Kontra (Ger.). Contra.
Koppel (Ger.). Couple.
Kroeger, Ernest R., Registration of Marche Pittoresque.................... 191

L

Laisser (Fr.). To leave on.
Languid. The horizontal division of a pipe between the upper and lower lips.
Larigot. A Mutation stop which sounds a 19th above the normal pitch.
Leathered Lip. See Diapason Phonon.
Lemaigre, Edmond, Registration of Marche Solennelle.................... 182
Lemare, Edwin H., Registration of Andantino in D-flat.................150, 154
Lemmens, Jacques, Registration of Finale in D.......................... 165
L'Expr. (Fr.). Swell manual..
Lieblich. Delicate tone.
Lieblich Bourdon (Ech. or Ped.)...................................... 42
Lieblich Gedeckt 41
List of 11 Anthems for which Registration is Suggested.................119, 134
  Joseph Barnby,   "O how amiable ".................... 124
  John Hopkins,   "Lift up your heads ".............. 125
  John Goss,   "O Saviour of the world".......... 126
  Berthold Tours,   "O come let us sing unto the Lord "...... 127
  John E. West,   "The woods and every sweet-smelling tree " 128
  Rev. H. H. Woodward,   "The radiant morn hath passed away ".... 129
  Horatio W. Parker,   "In heavenly love abiding "........... 130
  Dudley Buck,   "Sing Alleluia forth ".............. 131
  Arthur Foote,   "Still, still with thee "........... 132
  John Hyatt Brewer,   "O, Lamb of God ".................. 133
  George W. Chadwick,   "Peace and light ".................. 134
List of Combination Movements 76
List of Combinations of 16, 8, 4, and 2 ft. pitch with the aid of the 16 ft.
  Couplers 71
List of Couplers in a Modern Four-Manual Organ...................... 66
List of 63 Effective Solo Combinations with the aid of the 16 ft. Couplers...... 72
List of 9 Compositions which require Chimes.......................... 58
List of 90 Organ Compositions for which registration is suggested for
  various specific organs.
  One-manual Organ, 6 speaking stops. First specification.............. 140
    Henri Deshayes,   Andante Religioso.................. 141
    Walter Porter,   Three Short Andantes, No. 1.......... 141
    Walter Porter,   Three Short Andantes, No. 2.......... 141
    Walter Porter,   Three Short Andantes, No. 3.......... 141
    Théodore Salomé   Gothic March...................... 142
    J. Frank Frysinger, Berceuse 142
  One-manual Organ, 6 speaking stops. Second specification.............. 143
    Henri Deshayes,   Communion in A.................... 144
    Walter Porter,   Allegretto Grazioso................ 144
    Gustav Merkel,   Prelude in B-flat.................. 144
    Gustav Merkel,   Prelude in G...................... 144
    E. Silas,   March in B-flat................... 145
  One-manual Organ, 7 speaking stops. Third specification.............. 145
    William Faulkes,   Finale in E-flat.................. 145
    Henry M. Dunham,   Meditation in E-flat.............. 146
    F. R. Rickman,   Andante Grazioso.................. 146
  Medium-sized two-manual Organ, 15 speaking stops.................... 147
    Uso Seifert,   Fantasia in C-minor............... 148
    William Faulkes,   Postlude in A.................... 148
    César Franck,   Andantino in G-minor.............. 148
    Edwin H. Lemare,   Andantino in D-flat............... 150
    Arthur Foote,   Festival March.................... 151
    Alexandre Guilmant, Elevation in A-flat............... 151
    Georges MacMaster,   Grand Choeur in D................. 152
  Very small two-manual Organ, 7 speaking stops...................... 153
    (The same 7 compositions as above)........................154, 155
  Very small two-manual Organ, 7 speaking stops, with duplexed Swell Organ 156
    Berthold Tours,   Allegretto Grazioso............... 157
    William Faulkes,   Grand Choeur in A................ 157
    S. Tudor Strang,   Cantique d'Amour................. 157
    Johannes Pache,   Prayer in A-flat................. 158

M

Add Salicional

Gamba off

Sw.   Sw.   Sw.   Sw.

Pointers used to denote the exact part of a measure on which the indication should be effected.

PAGE

W

Wind Pressure. The pressure of the wind which is forced into the pipes varies with different stops, with different departments, of the organ, and with different organ builders for the same stops. This pressure varies from 2½ inches in a few old organs to 50 inches for the most powerful Tubas.

Z

Zart Flute. A slender scale 4 ft. Flute.
Zauber Floete. A full-toned stopped Flute which sounds the second overtone—the twelfth.
Zylophone. One of the Traps in theatre organs.

LIST OF
ADVANCE SUBSCRIBERS

LIST OF ADVANCE SUBSCRIBERS

ADAMS, BERTIS H., Worcester, Mass.
ADAMS, MRS. CROSBY, Montreat, N. C.
ADAMS, FRANK STEWART, A. A. G. O., New York City.
ALLEN, ROBERT, A. A. G. O., New Bedford, Mass.
AMBROSE, PAUL, Trenton, N. J.
ANDREW, MRS. ALICE S. G., West Medford, Mass.
ANDREWS, J. WARREN, A. G. O., New York City.
ARNOLD, LELAND A., Brookline, Mass.
ARTIQUES, A. L., San Francisco, Cal.
ASHTON, JOSEPH N., Phillips Academy, Andover, Mass.
ASPINWALL, JOHN, Newburgh, N. Y.
AUDSLEY, GEORGE A., LL.D., F. R. I. B. A., Architect, New York City.
AUSTIN, H. R., Boston, Mass.
AUSTIN ORGAN CO., Organ Builders, Hartford, Conn.
BACON, ALLAN, Parsons College, Fairfield, Iowa.
BACON, MISS KATHERINE H., Orange, Mass.
BANGERT, MRS. LOUIS J., Buffalo, N. Y.
BARNARD, MISS GRACE H., Boston, Mass.
BARRINGTON, JOHN W., A. A. G. O., Worcester, Mass.
BARROWS, DONALD S., Rochester, N.Y.
BARTHOLOMEW, EDA E., Atlanta, Ga.
BECKER, LUCIEN E., F. A. G. O., Portland, Ore.
BENJAMIN, MISS HARRIET F., Rochester, Minn.
BENNETT, MRS. MABEL WINSLOW, Boston, Mass.
BERLIN, HARRY D., Reading, Pa.
BIDWELL, MARSHALL S., Boston, Mass.
BIRD, MISS ETHEL F., Edgewood, R. I.
BIRGE, EDWARD B., Indianapolis, Ind.
BLANDING, GORDON, Belvedere, Cal.
BOLLINGER, MRS. WILLIAM, Memphis, Tenn.
BOPPERT, MRS. MARGARET E., St. Louis, Mo.
BOYD, CHARLES N., Pittsburgh, Pa.
BRACKETT, LYMAN W., Boston, Mass.
BRASE, HAYBARD, Lindsborg, Kans.
BROCK, MRS. BLANCHE T., Dorchester, Mass.
BROWN, MISS FLORENCE M. C., Chicago, Ill.
BROWN, HAROLD W., Athol, Mass.
BROWN, ROBERT H., Kansas State College, Manhattan, Kans.
BROWN, WILLIAM H., Torrington, Ct.
BUCKINGHAM, JOHN D., A. G. O., Quincy, Mass.
BUDDEN, CHARLES L., Arlington, Mass.
BURN, REV. JOHN HENRY, D. D., Whatfield Rectory, England.
BURTON, HALBURT G., Cambridge, Mass.
CAMP, HARRY UPSON, Reading, Mass.
CAMPBELL, L. H., Los Angeles, Cal.
CARL, WILLIAM C., Mus. Doc., A. G. O., Guilmant Organ School, New York City.
CASAVANT, J. C., Organ Builder, St. Hyacinthe, Quebec, two copies.

CHADWICK, CHARLES F., Organ Builder, Springfield, Mass.
CHANDLER, MILTON A., Roslindale, Mass.
CHAPIN, MISS MARION LOUISE, Boston, Mass.
CHAPMAN, GEORGE II., Chicago, Ill., nine copies.
CHARLTON, MELVILLE, A. A. G. O., Brooklyn, N. Y.
CHECK, MRS. T. E., Durham, N. C.
CLEMSON, WALTER J., M. A., A. G. O., Taunton, Mass.
COLSON, WILLIAM B., A. G. O., Cleveland, O.
COMEY, JAMES, D. D., Boston, Mass.
CONOVER, MRS. E. M., Knoxville, Tenn.
COOK, LEROY J., Winthrop, Mass.
COREY, N. J., A. G. O., Detroit, Mich.
COVINGTON, MISS DORA B., Boston, Mass.
CRANE, HARRY L., Groton School, Groton, Mass.
CRANE, JESSE G., Indianapolis, Ind.
CROWELL, MRS. MAYTIE CASE, So. Manchester, Conn.
CULLIS, WILL F., Oil City, Pa.
CUTLER, FRANK C., Worcester, Mass.
DALY, MISS AGNES GRACE, Boston, Mass.
DAVIDSON, MRS. GEORGE G., Watertown, Mass.
DAVIS, MISS BLANCHE NATHALIE, Providence, R. I.
DEAL, MISS ALICE R., Chicago, Ill.
DEAN, FLOYD BIGLOW, N. E. Conservatory, Boston, Mass.
DELANO, BENJAMIN A., Winthrop, Mass.
DEMAREST, CLIFFORD, F. A. G. O., Warden of American Guild of Organists, New York City.
DENISON CONSERVATORY OF MUSIC, Granville, O.
DEXTER, THEODORE E., Central Falls, R. I.
DICK, HAROLD, Webster City, Iowa.
DICKINSON, MISS ETHEL LOOMIS, Hartford, Conn.
DIECKMANN, C. W., F. A. G. O., Agnes Scott College, Decatur, Ga.
DIEHM, MISS EMMA C., Waukesha, Wis.
DREISKE, H. O., Chicago, Ill.
DUNHAM, HENRY M., A. G. O., New England Conservatory of Music, Boston, Mass.
DURFEE, MISS GRACE P., Marion, O.
DUSTIN, JOSEPH K., F. A. G. O., Gloucester, Mass.
DYER, MISS RUTH ELIZABETH, Mount Holyoke College, South Hadley, Mass.
EDDY, CLARENCE, A. G. O., Chicago Musical College, Chicago, Ill.
EICKHOFF, MISS EMMA C., Spring Valley, N. Y.
ENSIGN, MISS GERTRUDE A., Newton, Mass.
ESTEY ORGAN CO., Organ Builders, Boston, Mass.
EYER, FRANK L., Limestone College, Gaffrey, S. C.

FALK, DR. LOUIS, A. G. O., Chicago, Ill.
FARMER, W. W., Worcester, Mass.
FAVROT, MISS LOUISE, New Orleans, La.
FEATHERSTON, MISS LILLIAN, San Francisco, Cal.
FEIL, HANS C., Kansas City, Mo.
FISHER, GEORGE E., Rochester, N. Y.
FISHER, MISS MARY CHAPPELL, A. G. O., Niagara Falls, N. Y.
FLAHERTY, CHARLES A., Boston, Mass.
FLEISSNER, OTTO, California School for the Blind, San Francisco, Cal.
FOBES, WILLIAM H., St. Paul, Minn.
FOSTER, AUGUSTUS C., Boston, Mass.
FOSTER, MRS. GERTRUDE MARCH, Worcester, Mass.
FOWLER, ELISHA, Organ Builder, Boston, Mass., two copies.
FOWLER, JAMES H., Fremont, Nebr.
FRAMPTON, JOHN ROSS, Iowa State Teachers College, Cedar Falls, Iowa.
FRANCIS, J. HENRY, Charleston, W. Va.
FRANK, WILLIAM F., Boston, Mass.
GALE, MISS ELLA LEONA, A. A. G. O., Lowell, Mass.
GALLOWAY, CHARLES, St. Louis, Mo.
GASKINS, MISS GENEVIEVE BAUM, Oregon State School of Music, Carvallis, Ore.
GATES, L. D., Miami, Fla.
GEER, E. HAROLD, A. M., Mus. Bac., F. A. G. O., Vassar College, Poughkeepsie, N. Y.
GEHRKEN, WARREN H., Brooklyn, N. Y.
GERNET, HERBERT, Allentown, Pa.
GLEASON, HAROLD, Rochester, N. Y.
GOODRICH, WALLACE, New England Conservatory of Music, Boston, Mass.
GOTTFRIED & CO., A., Pipe Organ Supplies, Erie, Pa.
GRANT, GEORGE W., Lebanon, Pa.
GRANT, MRS. IRENE OSBORNE, Somerville, Mass.
GREELEY, CHARLES G., Boston, Mass.
HALL, MISS HELEN W., North Pembroke, Mass.
HALL, J. R., Cleveland, Ohio.
HALL ORGAN CO., Organ Builders, West Haven, Conn.
HALLETT, P. SHAUL, F. A. G. O., A. R. C. O., Pasadena, Cal.
HAMMOND, WILLIAM C., A. G. O., Mt. Holyoke College and Holyoke, Mass.
HARDING, E. H., Washington, D. C.
HART, CLARENCE D., W. Somerville, Mass.
HART, MISS DELLA L., Lynn, Mass.
HARVARD MUSICAL ASSOCIATION, Boston, Mass.
HASCALL, WILBUR, Boston, Mass.
HAZELL, WILLIAM ALBERT, Perth, Ontario, Can.
HEATH, LESTER J., Chicago, Ill.
HEDDEN, WARREN R., Mus. Bac., F. A. G. O., New York City.
HEINZELMAN, GEORGE W., Houston, Tex.
HEMENWAY, MRS. MYRA POND, Needham, Mass.
HERING, J. NORRIS, A. A. G. O., Baltimore, Md.
HIBBARD, MISS RUTH, Hollins College, Hollins, Va.
HILL, JAMES W., Haverhill, Mass., two copies.

HINNERS ORGAN CO., Organ Builders, Pekin, Ill.
HINZE, J. OTTO, Chicago, Ill.
HIRSCHLER, DANIEL A., Mus. Bac., A. A. G. O., College of Emporia, Emporia, Kans.
HOOK & HASTINGS CO., Organ Builders, Kendal Green, Mass.
HOPKINS, EDWIN M., Lawrence, Kans.
HOWE, MISS JEANETTE HART, A. A. G. O., Natick, Mass.
HUMPHREY, HOMER C., New England Conservatory of Music, Boston, Mass.
HUNT, HAMLIN, A. A. G. O., Minneapolis, Minn.
HURD, HERBERT A., Fryeburg, Me.
HYSLOP, MRS. KATHERINE, Lebanon, Mo.
IBBOTSON, ERNEST M., Hartford, Conn.
IRWIN, CHARLES D., Brookline, Mass.
JENKINS, WILLIAM M., St. Louis, Mo.
JOHNSON, DAVID WARREN, Chicago, Ill.
JONES, WENDELL M., Chicago, Ill. .
LANKART, MISS MAY D., Chicago, Ill.
LEACH, ERNEST DAWSON, A. C. M., Memphis, Tenn.
LEARNED, CHARLES, Watertown, N. Y.
LEHMAN, JAMES, Philadelphia, Pa.
LEWIS, F. PERCYVAL, F. A. G. O., Winchester, Mass.
LIST, MISS LOLO, Massillon, O.
LOCKE, WARREN A., A. G. O., Cambridge, Mass.
LORD, J. E. W., Mus. Doc., Meridian, Miss.
LOUD, GEORGE R., Newton Highlands, Mass.
LOUD, JOHN HERMANN, F. A. G. O., Boston, Mass.
LYNES, TWINING, Groton School, Groton, Mass.
MacARTHUR, MRS. R. F., Tulsa, Okla.
MACDOUGALL, H. C., Mus. Doc., A. G. O., A. R. C. O., Wellesley College, Wellesley, Mass.
MALTBY, MRS. IVAN, F. A. G. O., A. R. C. O., Richmond, Va.
MARDEN, MRS. BELLE CONANT, Orange, Mass.
MARTIN, A. PERRY, Organ Builder, Newtonville, Mass.
MARYOTT, HAROLD B., Chicago Musical College, Chicago, Ill.
MATHER, JUDSON WALDO, Seattle, Wash.
MAYER, FREDERICK C., Woodville Normal and Academy, Woodville, O.
MAYO, ARTHUR D., Washington, D. C.
MAYO, WALTER L., Richmond, Va.
McCARRELL, FRANK A., Harrisburg, Pa.
McCLARY, FRANK W., Utica, N. Y.
McDOWELL, J. B. FRANCIS, Columbus, O.
McELROY, WALTER F., Carthage, Mo.
McHOSE, CLARENCE N., Lancaster, Pa.
McSWEENY, FRANCIS E., Berkshire Music School, Pittsfield, Mass.
MESSMER, MISS IDA, St. Louis, Mo.
MEWS, ARTHUR, C. M. G., St. John's, Newfoundland.
MILLER, C. LOUIS, Organ Builder, Baltimore, Md.
MILLER, DAYTON C., Case School, Cleveland, O.
MILLER, MISS GERTRUDE, Rochester, N. Y.

MILES, FRANK T., Spokane University, Spokane, Wash.
MOLLER ORGAN WORKS, M. P., Organ Builders, Hagerstown, Md.
MOORE, MISS FANNIE, Newton, Mass.
MOORE, FREDERIC G., Andover, Mass.
MOREY, C. E., Organ Builder, Utica, N. Y.
MOURÉ, F. A., University of Toronto, Toronto, Can.
NAGEL, RAY C., Norwich, N. Y.
NEW YORK PUBLIC LIBRARY, Reference Dept., New York City.
NEWMAN, ARTHUR T., Bristol, R. I.
OBERLIN COLLEGE LIBRARY, Oberlin, O.
ODELL & CO., J. H. & C. S., Organ Builders, New York City.
OHIO WESLEYAN MUSIC DEPT., Delaware, O.
PALMER, MISS MARTHA M., Franklin, Ind.
PARKERTON, MISS MILDRED M., Nahant, Mass.
PARTRIDGE, MISS MILDRED M., Boston, Mass.
PAUL, WILLIAM FORREST, F. A. G. O., Philadelphia, Pa.
PEARSALL, JOHN V., Arlington, N. J.
PEARSON, HENRY WARD, Illinois Woman's College, Jacksonville, Ill.
PHELPS, MISS ROSE, Hackensack, N. J.
PIERCE, MRS. JOSEPHINE SMITH, Beverly, Mass.
PIERCE ORGAN PIPE CO., SAMUEL, Reading, Mass.
PIERCE, WILLIAM M., Philadelphia, Pa.
PITTS PIPE ORGAN CO., Organ Builders, Omaha, Neb.
POLLEN, J. SHELTON, Boston, Mass.
POOLE, HARRY, Methuen, Mass.
PORTER, F. ADDISON, New England Conservatory of Music, Boston, Mass.
POWER, RICHARD A., Charlestown, Mass.
PRATT, WALDO S., Hartford, Conn.
REED, EARLE W., Organ Builder, West Boylston, Mass.
REHLING, MRS. LOUISE CUTLER, Roslindale, Mass.
REINIGER, LOUIS D. P., Dorchester, Mass.
REUL, MISS CLARA LOUISE, Mendota, Ill.
REYNOLDS, MRS. ALICE J. T., Belmont, Mass.
REYNOLDS, ALLAN D., Framingham, Mass.
REYNOLDS, MISS MARTHA B., Portland, Ore.
RHODE, ALOYSIUS, St. Louis, Mo.
RICE, MISS ALICE L., Holliston, Mass.
RICHARDS, SENATOR EMERSON, Atlantic City, N. J.
RIENSTRA, ALBERT R., Whitinsville, Mass.
ROBERTS, MISS RUTH O., Saco, Me.
ROBINSON, WILLIAM APPLEBYE, A. A. G. O., Cornwall, N. Y.
ROGERS, MARK D., Los Angeles, Cal.
ROLFE, DR. WILLIAM A., Boston, Mass.
SALTER, SUMNER, A. G. O., Williams College, Williamstown, Mass.
SAWYER, J. W., Clinton, Mass.
SCHAEFER, MISS HELEN J., A. A. G. O., Flemington, N. J.
SCHATZ, GEORGE J., Brooklyn, N. Y.
SCHORR, C. A., Dayton, O.

SCHWIND, MRS. EUGENIA HATCH, Wollaston, Mass.
SENCINDWER, MISS BLANCHE M., Catonsville, Md.
SHAW, HARRIS S., A. A. G. O., Boston, Mass.
SHERRARD, ROBERT A., Johnstown, Pa.
SHIELDS, T. EDGAR, Bethlehem, Pa.
SHUEY, W. H., Oak Park, Ill.
SIMMS, J. H., A. A. G. O., Omaha, Neb.
SIMPSON, MISS KATHLEEN G., Watertown, N. Y.
SIRCOM, E. RUPERT, Boston, Mass.
SKAIFE, ROBERT E., Spencer, Mass.
SKEELE, W. F., University of Southern California, Los Angeles, Cal.
SKILTON, C. S., B. A., F. A. G. O., Lawrence, Kans.
SKINNER ORGAN CO., ERNEST M., Organ Builders, Boston, Mass.
SMALL, MRS. ALFA L., A. A. G. O., Providence, R. I.
SMITH, C. FORMAN, Newark, N. J.
SMITH, C. WENHAM, Newark, N. J.
SMITH, EDGAR J., Newton Highlands, Mass.
SMITH, HARLAND W. D., Lockport, N. Y.
SMITH, SUTHERLAND DWIGHT, Pittsburgh, Pa.
SPENCER, CHARLES, J. P., Grande Prairie, Alberta, Organ Builder.
SPRINGMEYER, THEODORE W., New York City.
STANSFIELD, WILLIAM, Mus. Bac., F. R. C. O., F. A. G. O., Washington, D. C.
STEVENS, MOSES T., North Andover, Mass.
STEWART, MISS A. MAUDE, Elizabeth, N. J.
STIVEN, FREDERIC B., A. A. G. O., Oberlin Conservatory of Music, Oberlin, O.
STONE, A. H., Sanford, Fla.
STONE, HARVEY E., Syracuse, N. Y.
STRANCH, MRS. BEULAH MEDLAR, A. A. G. O., Pottsville, Pa.
STUCKE, P. T., Mus. Bac., Portland, Ore.
SWAN, WILLIAM L., Oyster Bay, N. Y.
SWINNEN, FIRMIN, New York City.
SWITZER, MRS. GRACE, Dallas, Tex.
TALBOT, MISS A. M., Boston, Mass.
THOMAS, AUSTIN D., Twin Falls, Ida.
THOMPSON, VAN DENMAN, De Pauw University, Greencastle, Ind.
TILTON, FREDERICK W., Hartford, Conn.
TINDALL, GLENN M., Shelbyville, Ind.
TITCOMB, MISS RUTH E., Amesbury, Mass.
TRAYNOR, MISS WINIFRED M., Omaha, Neb.
TREADWELL, MISS IDA LOUISE, W. Roxbury, Mass.
TROLAND, EDWIN, Malden, Mass.
TWADDELL, W. P., Baltimore, Md.
UNIVERSITY OF ILLINOIS LIBRARY, Urbana, Ill.
UPTON, IRVING H., Roxbury, Mass.
VANTINE, LEWIS A., Milwaukee, Wis.
VASSAR COLLEGE LIBRARY, Poughkeepsie, N. Y.
WADE, MISS BELLE S., Memphis, Tenn.
WADE, HENRY T., A. A. G. O., Lake Erie College, Painesville. O.
WANGERIN-WEICKHARDT CO., Organ Builders, Milwaukee, Wis.
WARE, GENE, Providence, R. I.

WARNER, FRANK H., New York City.
WEISSMANN, MRS. F. W., Cincinnati, Ohio.
WELLESLEY COLLEGE DEPARTMENT OF MUSIC, Wellesley, Mass.
WESTLUND, MISS SIGNE H., Summit, N. J.
WHELPLEY, B. L., Boston, Mass.
WHITNEY, S. C., Darien, Conn.
WHYTOCK, MRS. ANTOINETTE HALL, Providence. R. I.
WILD, HARRISON M., A. G. O., Chicago, Ill.

WILDE, EDWIN E., F. A. G. O., Brown University, Providence, R. I.
WISMAR, WALTER, St. Louis, Mo.
WOOD, CARL PAIGE, A. M., F. A. G. O., University of Washington, Seattle, Wash.
WOOD, HARRISON E., Yonkers, N. Y.
WOOD, WILLIAM E., Arlington, Mass.
WOODMAN, R. HUNTINGTON, F. A. G. O., Brooklyn, N. Y.
WRY, HENRY E., Boston, Mass.
YERRINGTON, HERBERT L., A. A. G. O., Norwich, Conn.